'A valuable book which should be read by every M.P. and town and country planner.' *Tatler and Bystander*

'Physical decay, rather than politics, is Mr Cormack's main theme. Again and again he hammers home with a wealth of detail and an accumulation of love, the consequences of neglect, rapacity and greed, not just for what is beautiful merely, but for the whole structure of the environment.' *Spectator*

'This book is the expression of one man's love for things of real value in Britain today. It is not in any provocative sense a political work. Mr Cormack is a Member of Parliament and, I have no doubt, belongs to some political party, but the book could be written by any sensitive lover of the countryside, of buildings and articles of beauty.' The Lord Goodman, C.H.

Patrick Cormack was born in Lincolnshire in 1939, and is now M.P. for South West Staffordshire. He is the founder secretary of the All Party Committee for the Heritage. He is also the author of *The Palace of Westminster* and is currently writing a book about ducal houses to be published by Quartet.

HERITAGE IN DANGER

Patrick Cormack

QUARTET BOOKS
LONDON MELBOURNE NEW YORK

Published by Quartet Books Limited 1978
A member of the Namara Group
27 Goodge Street, London W1P 1FD

First published by New English Library Limited, London, 1976

Copyright © 1976, 1978 by Patrick Cormack
Foreword copyright © 1978 by Roy Strong

ISBN 0 7043 3186 1

Typesetting by Bedford Typesetters Ltd.

Printed in Great Britain by litho at The Anchor Press Ltd
and bound by Wm Brendon & Son Ltd
both of Tiptree, Essex

Contents

Acknowledgements   7
Foreword by Roy Strong   10
Introduction   13

1   Background to Protection   17
2   The Countryside We Take for Granted   27
3   The Country House and the Great Estate   49
4   The Country House under Siege   59
5   Urban Dignity and Decay   81
6   Country Town and Village   101
7   Our Greatest Legacy   117
8   Artists and Craftsmen – the Rescue of the Past   135
9   Treasures on Earth – Private Patrons and
    Public Collections   149
10 A Wider Heritage   165
11 Some Solutions – the Preservation of the Heritage   181

A Gazetteer of the Heritage County by County   201
A Select List of Conservation and Amenity Societies   416
Bibliography   423
Index   426

To Charles and Richard in the hope that they learn to enjoy their heritage and play their part in preserving it, and in memory of my father, who taught me to see.

Acknowledgements

It is always gratifying for an author when his work goes into a second or paperback edition but I must confess that my feelings on the appearance of *Heritage in Danger* in paperback are a trifle mixed. I am glad to know that the book was found sufficiently interesting to merit a second appearance, but sorry that the need for a work of warning such as this is even greater than it was when the book first appeared.

I have sought to bring this volume up to date and have changed some of the examples that were given in the first edition, but the message remains essentially the same: that each and every part of our indivisible national heritage stands in danger. As before I have sought to deal with everything that is roughly encompassed by the term 'national heritage', although I have not dealt in any detail with the threats to our flora and fauna which are so often consequent upon the other menaces that threaten our countryside and the structure of our landscape.

I would like to extend my most grateful thanks to all those who have helped me during the preparation and writing of the book and during its subsequent revision. A special word of thanks must go to those who gave me the opportunity to visit their houses and study their accounts and, in particular, to the Earl of March, the Marquess of Tavistock, Commander Michael Watson of Rockingham Castle, John Chichester-Constable of Burton Constable, the Earl of Bradford of Weston Park, Peter Giffard of Chillington Hall and to the

7

Earl of Rosebery and all those with whom I worked during and after the Mentmore episode, especially Peter Mimpriss, Mrs Jennifer Jenkins, Chairman of the Historic Buildings Council, Marcus Linell of Sotheby's and the Earl of Perth, whose strenuous efforts in the fund-raising field almost brought off the rescue of the century.

I have learned much from my friends and colleagues on the Grants Committee of the Historic Churches Preservation Trust and I would like to express my thanks to the past Chairman of the Grants Committee, the Very Reverend Seriol Evans, the Secretary, Hugh Llewellyn Jones, Raymond Richards, foremost authority on the churches of his native Cheshire, Canon Ian Dunlop of Salisbury Cathedral, Lady Harrod, whose work in Norfolk is a shining example to us all, Henry Thorold, working so valiantly in Lincolnshire, and to Marcus Binney and Peter Burman, who did so much to draw attention to the plight of religious buildings in that remarkable exhibition 'Change and Decay – the Future of Our Churches' held at the Victoria and Albert Museum in the summer of 1977.

To Hugh Leggatt around whose luncheon table the Heritage in Danger Committee and this book were conceived; to Lord Cottesloe, that most distinguished servant of the arts and Chairman of Heritage in Danger; and to Andrew Faulds, my fellow Vice-Chairman, I owe thanks for help and support in what I have sought to do.

I am particularly grateful too to Lord Goodman who found time in his incredibly busy life of public service to write the foreword of the first edition and to Roy Strong who has performed the same service for me in respect of this one.

I would like to reiterate the thanks I expressed at the time of the first edition to my research assistants, James O'Shea, Jock Black and Ian Stanley. Ian Stanley in particular worked very hard on the expanded Gazetteer which accompanies this edition.

Every married author has reason to be grateful to his wife and I am no exception. Mine typed the original tapes of this book and the corrections for this edition, ably assisted in this task by Heather Cameron and by those of the St Stephen's Secretarial Agency in the House of Commons.

To everyone I have named, and to all who have written to me and talked to my research assistants, I express my grateful thanks. If any mistakes remain they are mine alone, but I hope that they do not mar the work unduly or invalidate the message it seeks to convey.

Patrick Cormack
Enville, Staffordshire
1978

Foreword

More than ever before British people are aware of their heritage. Nothing could be a more natural sign of the times than that we hear more about it in the seventies than we did in either the fifties or the sixties. The reason is a very simple one. It is in times of danger, either from without or from within, that we become deeply conscious of our heritage. The glories of our royal palaces and great houses, the splendours of our cathedrals and larger churches, the modest charm of the village church, the old manor house and rectory, the sweep of downland or the rugged moors, the fragrance of an English garden or the heady exhilaration of cliffs and coastline – these are just some of the assaults on the senses which we categorize as our heritage. And within this word there mingle varied and passionate streams of ancient pride and patriotism, of a heroism in times past, of a nostalgia too for what we think of as a happier world which we have lost. In the 1940s we felt all this deeply because of the danger from without. In the 1970s we sense it because of the dangers from within. We are all aware of problems and troubles, of changes within the structure of society, of the dissolution of old values and standards. For the lucky few this may be exhilarating, even exciting, but for the majority it is confusing, threatening and dispiriting. The heritage represents some form of security, a point of reference, a refuge perhaps, something visible and tangible which, within a topsy and turvy world, seems stable and unchanged. Our environmental heritage, which is the subject of this book, is therefore a deeply stabilizing and unifying element within our society.

And yet how few people, even in an age of universal education, really know about it let alone actively care. For many it has come as a discovery rather late in life. This is the result, I believe, of two factors. Up until the last twenty years or so British art was very little appreciated, most of all by her own people. The arts of Britain were regarded as derivative and provincial within a European context. It is to art historians (and, to our shame, American collectors) that we in fact owe the rediscovery of our own contribution to the European tradition. In the second place, travel in the post-war period meant getting abroad, often for the very first time, with the lure of the Costa Brava or the Costa del Sol and the age of the package sunshine holiday of the fifties and sixties, until a poor exchange rate and appalling inflation has led to a forced rediscovery of our own country. And this in itself has been encouraged by the influx of tourists to Britain from both Europe and the New World. These visitors now actually come to Britain for our art, something totally inconceivable twenty years ago when all such roads led either to Rome or Paris.

And yet in spite of all this widespread ignorance persists. Television cultural spectaculars and a vast explosion in art books has certainly broken new boundaries but not enough of them. A feeling for the fabric of our visual heritage has no recognized place in our educational system. As the social structure of this country evolves and changes, the burden of caring and paying for our heritage can no longer be borne by the few, in former ages the aristocracy or the so-called middle classes. In an atmosphere which demands increasing equality there is the coda of an increasing equality of responsibility. Art and heritage can no longer be subjects which have no place in the curriculum. The widespread love, understanding and making of music, for instance, since 1945 was made possible not only through the radio and the record player but by means of the school orchestra. Heritage should form an integral part of the educational experience of every child. And this has yet to happen. Within this lies the future, for example, of our fast vanishing and decaying country houses, obsolete as vehicles for living, and of our cathedrals and parish churches, sustained by the ever diminishing few who still believe.

In this way the individual who cares has a great role still to play. Nothing should replace the will and idiosyncracy of the

11

individual in the arts. To own a work of art is a natural expression of a genuine love of beauty which is otherwise inexpressible. How strange that there should exist a minority who really think that to own a work of art, be it old or new, is somehow a crime against the community. To own an old work is to care for the heritage of the past. To purchase a new is to give an artist encouragement and a living, both laudable practices. What we need is not a diminution of private collections but an expansion of them. At root everyone who has a house, flat or room to furnish is a patron. Every piece of furniture, fabric or ceramic is an expression of an individual's taste and feeling for the beauty of his immediate surroundings, a response to form, function, design and colour. We are all collectors and to invite anyone into one's home is to show them our 'collection'.

This concern with things present brings to the forefront what may be the crucial issue of the 1980s, the reconciliation of heritage with contemporary creativity. Up until now the public seems to be continuously confronted by two warring factions, the conservationists, a motley crew of preservation societies, antiquarians, historians, environmentalists and collectors, and the dreaded planners, the architects and the contemporary artist and craftsman. I find this polarization disturbing as there seems so little sign of interplay between the two. There desperately needs to be because the latter, however bad we may often think their work, are contributing to what in the future we will hopefully regard as our heritage. The story of the history of art is a continuously unfolding one. It is not a saga suddenly cut off at something called Modern Art. All new art goes back in order to go forward and this surely is the clue. The enjoyment and preservation of our heritage must not only be a negative narcissistic indulgence but a positive forward looking one. So that we must be seen not only to guard and treasure it for the sake of the past but for what it can give to the creators of the future.

Roy Strong, 1978

Introduction

Soon after I entered Parliament at the 1970 General Election my wife and I sought a brief rest in Herefordshire, loveliest of counties. One day we visited Abbey Dore in the Golden Valley and looking round that glorious church I suddenly became acutely aware that my children might never have the same privilege. Miles from anywhere, enormously costly to maintain, one marvelled at how the dedicated efforts of the few had ensured its preservation to date, and I came away determined to try to do something to ensure the survival of the thousands of medieval churches which adorn our countryside and give dignity to our towns. It seemed to me then, as now, that they could only be saved for posterity if the nation recognized the importance of making funds available for their repair. That visit was the background to an attempt to get an Historic Churches Bill through Parliament, a Bill which would have made aid available from public funds to assist in the preservation of religious buildings still in use but utterly beyond the capacity of their often tiny congregations to sustain. The Bill foundered but a scheme has now been prepared along the lines that many of us advocated at that time.

Abbey Dore was a catalyst and an inspiration, and during the past seven years I have become ever more conscious that almost every part of our national heritage – landscape, buildings, great collections – is at risk. To the natural and inevitable dangers facing anything old and lovely, but often frail, have been added the menaces of twentieth-century civilization, the urge to change,

13

to modernize, to redevelop. And on top of this is an increasing tendency by Government to impose ever more onerous burdens of taxation upon those on whom the final responsibility for safeguarding the heritage often rests.

When the Labour Government in the summer of 1974 published its Green Paper on the Wealth Tax it became apparent that the heritage, though recognized as being worthy of extra consideration, was not to be exempt from extra fiscal impositions. Many were alarmed and stirred into action and I was one of those involved in setting up a Committee called Heritage in Danger, whose aim and object was to point out the danger that a Wealth Tax would impose on the national heritage.

When I am asked to define our heritage I do not think in dictionary terms, but instead reflect on certain sights and sounds. I think of a morning mist on the Tweed at Dryburgh where the magic of Turner and the romance of Scott both come fleetingly to life; of a celebration of the Eucharist in a quiet Norfolk church with the medieval glass filtering the colours, and the early noise of the harvesting coming through the open door; or of standing at any time before the Wilton Diptych. Each scene recalls aspects of an indivisible heritage and is part of the fabric and expression of our civilization.

Never has there been a wider appreciation of this true quality of life, never a more general determination to preserve and enhance it – and never has each and every aspect of our heritage stood in greater danger. The pressures and the rush of modern life have heightened man's individual awareness of the need for spiritual and cultural enrichment. Yet, at the same time, they have made him collectively responsible for endangering the quiet and beauty of our rural surroundings, of what remains of our urban dignity, and of many great and humble buildings which express as vividly as the words of playwright, poet or philosopher the spirit of a nation.

It is doubtful if there is any country in the world that has more varied rural beauties or more buildings upon which, as Hazlett said, 'the eye may dote and the heart take its fill'. We can lament what acts of deliberate destruction, casual indifference, or the ordinary ravages of fire and time have removed, and we can feel shame at the havoc that has been wrought in the name of improvement and redevelopment even during an era of increased awareness and appreciation. The fact remains, however, that Britain still has an incalculably rich heritage.

The devastation of mining and quarrying, the urban sprawl spawned to house a growing and consuming population, the march of the pylon bringing electricity to the Highlands, the swathe cut by the motorway, all these have reduced the countryside, but not destroyed it. Our landscape remains as varied and as wonderful as any in Europe, from the rugged grandeur of the far north through the romance and drama of the borders, and the bare austerity of the high Yorkshire Moors to the dry golden brecks of East Anglia. The traveller in this island still has, like Johnson, many places he can visit and wonder at, the artist many scenes he can copy and admire. And, although unthinking and haphazard development has suffocated many rural communities in layers of undistinguished suburbia, there are as many authentic villages in England alone as almost anywhere in Western Europe. The Cotswolds, for instance, still house many rural communities and within half an hour's drive of a number of our sprawling cities there are oases of village life. One does not have to go far from Manchester or Birmingham, from Glasgow or Leeds – or even from London itself – to light upon a village scene that many of the more pessimistic doom watchers would claim had disappeared for ever.

Towns, like villages, have often been spoilt. One cannot think of the 'redevelopment' of Worcester or Gloucester without shivers of disgust, dismay and shame running down one's spine. Yet, our urban treasures are by no means all destroyed. The story of Bath is a sad one but we can rejoice that much has been saved, that the developers have been curbed, and their lorries at last restricted in their journeyings. And there are still places like Cirencester and Tewkesbury, Ludlow and Louth, Rye and Berwick, where the developer has been kept at bay, or where civic pride has been mobilized in time to civilize his schemes. Many of our old towns, too, have cathedrals or great churches as their crowning glories and, in spite of the ever increasing difficulties of maintenance and repair, most of them remain in remarkably good order, lovingly cared for, regularly visited and appreciated, and collectively in a far better state than those of almost any other country.

It is perhaps in our country houses and churches that one comes closest to the spirit of England. Two remarkable exhibitions held at the Victoria and Albert Museum, 'The Destruction of the English Country House' in 1974, and 'Change and Decay – the Future of Our Churches' in 1977, showed with dramatic

15

effect just what we have lost and what still stands in peril. But both exhibitions ended on a note of hope, for there remains a wealth of country houses that are lived in and loved. And so it is with our churches and chapels. Although the wear and tear of time and inflation and often dwindling congregations make their preservation a matter of acute concern, there are still nearly 8000 medieval churches in this country, and almost all could be saved by a nation that had its priorities right.

And here we come to the nub: the question of priorities. The safeguarding of our finest buildings can be achieved at remarkably little cost, as can the preservation of our great public and private art collections. The dangers they face are either man-made or assisted by man's indifference. In the chapters that follow, I shall endeavour to spell out some of the dangers and to show how they can be overcome – if we have the will to overcome them.

By touching on all aspects of the visible heritage this book highlights some of the many dangers facing it, and seeks, by taking some brief examples, to 'point a moral and adorn a tale'. Many will be disappointed that gems they value and have striven to save get no more than a passing mention, if that. However, the moral is that our heritage is one and indivisible and that the acutest dangers are of our own creation and could be relatively easily solved by individual and by Government action or, indeed, inaction.

Inevitably, in a work of this nature, there is much reference to what has been lost, but I hope that the message conveyed is essentially one of optimism. It would be a tragedy if in bemoaning what has gone we wasted our time. The best tribute any of us can pay to departed glories is to fight to preserve those that remain.

Chapter One
Background to Protection

'Are the absurd relics of our barbarian predecessors, who found time hanging heavily on their hands, and set about piling up great barrows and rings of stones, to be preserved at the cost of infringement of property rights?'

Thus spoke Lord Francis Hervey in the House of Commons, during the Second Reading of Sir John Lubbock's National Monuments Preservation Bill, in 1875. The Bill, which had taken Lubbock two years to get to the floor of the House since he first attempted to introduce it, had a stormy passage. Another Tory Member, Cavendish Bentinck, 'did not pretend to be either an antiquary or a man of taste – he was particularly glad he was not a man of taste'. The official Government line was advanced by the Attorney-General, Sir John Holker, who objected to the introduction into the law of the land of a principle that could have disastrous consequences: namely, putting public interest above private rights. Why, he asked, should one stop at ancient remains? Why should one not also preserve medieval abbeys and castles, or impose restrictions on the owners of pictures, or statues of great national interest? If a circle of stones was worth preserving, could not the same be said for a row of beech trees?

Not surprisingly, Lubbock's Bill did not achieve a Second Reading. Nor did it when he sought to get it through the House in 1878 and 1879. It was a far-sighted though, in the light of subsequent developments, a modest enough measure, which sought to establish a National Monuments Commission,

17

and a schedule of monuments to be protected by the Commission. Its essential purpose was to provide time in which the nation or local authority might buy a threatened monument. And it was immediately inspired by the attempted sale for building land of part of the Avebury Stone Circle. It was appropriate, therefore, that, when he was finally elevated to the peerage, Lubbock should take Avebury as his title.

However, Lubbock was not the first to attempt some measure of architectural conservation. Although our present provisions, enshrined in the Town and County Planning Act of 1971–2, and the Country Amenities Act of 1974, logical successors of a whole series of measures, provide a protection for historic buildings and areas of outstanding beauty to an extent which would have been unthinkable even a decade ago, we must not forget our obligations to the pioneers.

One of the first of these was John Ruskin, who in 1854 proposed to the Society of Antiquaries that an association be formed to make and constantly revise a record of buildings of interest threatened by destruction *or restoration*. This latter point showed a nice awareness of the already too apparent effects of Victorian zeal. A year later the Society of Antiquaries did establish a Conservation Fund to finance the formation of a catalogue of existing monuments and buildings of interest. Thereafter there was something of a fallow period until Lubbock began his long, brave, and at first almost unaided attempts at legislation. Parliament's obduracy in the face of his pleadings did not, however, still the Conservation Movement. In 1877, alarmed at the specific danger posed by the threatened restoration of Tewkesbury Abbey, William Morris founded the Society for the Protection of Ancient Buildings, initially to advise on the correct restoration of such buildings: an echo of Ruskin's cry two decades previously.

Appropriately enough, it did fall to Lubbock to pilot the first piece of legislation through the Commons. In 1880 he had lost his seat, in spite of the defeat of the Conservative Government and the return of Gladstone. However, his absence from the House was a temporary one and, in 1881, he was returned as the Member for London University. Immediately he resumed his battle, moving on a Supply Day that 'it is desirable that the Government should take steps to provide for the protection of ancient monuments'. This unexciting and unprovocative proposition was accepted and Gladstone agreed that the Govern-

18

ment would consider any plan Lubbock cared to submit. Out came his carefully prepared Bill which, in 1882, was finally enacted as the Ancient Monuments Protection Act. It had an initial schedule of twenty-one monuments, which the nation could purchase or take into guardianship if they were threatened. Monuments, stone circles, including Stonehenge, and notable earthworks were those 'as to the value of which there was an agreement among all persons interested in the preservation of ancient monuments'. The Act provided no element of compulsion or any real power over an owner; it merely stated that the nation might, if the owner agreed, purchase an ancient monument and look after it; or might take it into guardianship. The owner remained owner, but lost his power to demolish or to remove in return for State aid in maintenance.

For all its lack of teeth – an element common to almost all subsequent preservation and conservation measures – the Act was a notable milestone in the progress of the Conservation Movement.

In 1895, another very significant development occurred with the founding of the National Trust. The increasing spread of railways over the countryside had disturbed many with a care for Britain's rural beauty, and the National Trust was born of this concern for the preservation of open spaces. The 'open space' which inspired Canon Rawnsley, one of its progenitors, was the Lake District, and it was a meeting between Rawnsley and Sir Robert Hunter, solicitor to the Post Office and lover of the Surrey Commons, with one of the most remarkable women in British social history, Octavia Hill, that led to the establishment of the Trust. Octavia Hill was a genius in what would today be called public relations, and had remarkable powers of persuasion. Thus, from small beginnings, the Trust soon acquired national attention and esteem. In the early days its efforts were directed solely to the acquisition of beautiful places which would be managed for the benefit of the nation. There was no initial desire or intention to acquire buildings, and it was many years before any important houses, or indeed any houses at all, were acquired, except as a by-product of its other endeavours. The Trust's position and importance were recognized in 1907, when Parliament gave it the right to hold land 'inalienably'. This meant that no one could acquire National Trust property without permission from Parliament, and it was by this legislative protection and recognition that the Trust was inspired to widen its horizons and ambitions, and to begin the purchase of neglected or threatened historic buildings. It is interesting to note that the powers conferred by Parliament upon the Trust pre-dated by some forty years the powers of compulsory purchase it conferred on local authorities.

Before this significant Parliamentary move, Lubbock's legislation had been significantly strengthened and extended by the Ancient Monuments Protection Act of 1900, which allowed county councils to proceed in the same limited way as the 1882 Act had allowed the State. The Act also established the principle of public access to scheduled ancient monuments. A natural consequence of this was the foundation in 1908 of the Royal Commission on Historical Monuments, which was charged to make and publish an inventory of ancient and historical monuments and constructions, and to specify which seemed most worthy of preservation. For all this laudable and notable advance, it was apparent to those who cared most deeply that the Acts of 1882 and 1900 were ineffective and insufficient in that they did not cover inhabited monuments and by 1912, when the Ancient Monuments (Consolidation and Amendment) Bill was presented to Parliament, a number of fine and notable buildings had already been destroyed, in spite of protective legislation.

One of the most significant contributions to the debate on the 1912 Bill was made by Lord Curzon. He lamented the attitude which his party (Conservatives) had taken in seeking to obstruct or vitiate earlier protective legislation: 'It is almost incredible if one looks back at the parliamentary history of the time [1882] to find how much opposition was excited by that mild, inoffensive measure . . . This is a country in which the idea of property has always been more sedulously cherished than in any other, but when you see that to get that Bill through Parliament it had to be denuded of its important features, and only after many years was it passed in an almost innocuous form into law, one feels almost ashamed of the reputation of one's countrymen.'

This time there was no concerted opposition, and the Act passed into law in 1913. New preservation powers were created by providing that the Commissioner for Works could make a preservation order in respect of a scheduled monument, although this order would fall unless it was confirmed by Parliament. It also established the right of pre-emptive purchase by

20

giving the Commissioner the chance of first refusal if the owner of such a monument decided to sell it.

The years between the wars saw further legislation. In 1931 there was another Ancient Monuments Act which extended control a little further by providing that preservation orders did not have to be confirmed by an Act of Parliament unless they were objected to. It also established the basic principle of protecting a whole area (thus anticipating the conservation area) by establishing 'preservation schemes', designed to protect the territory around a scheduled monument. A year later came the Town and Country Planning Act, which allowed local authorities to make a preservation order in respect of any building of special architectural or historic interest in their area, and abolished the requirement that a building of historic interest must be inhabited.

The most imaginative new development, however, came in 1944 when the Government began to anticipate the problems and the shape of post-war Britain. The Royal Commission on Historical Monuments had reported on only eight counties since its formation in 1908, and because there was thus no way of checking how many distinguished buildings had been destroyed by enemy action, the 1944 Town and Country Planning Act introduced the statutory listing of buildings of architectural and historic interest, whether inhabited or not, and for the first time gave Britain the prospect of a comprehensive list of such buildings. It was exactly ninety years since Ruskin had first advocated such a scheme.

Perhaps the most generally recognized achievement of the post-war Labour Government was the Town and Country Planning Act of 1947. It was indeed a landmark in the history of town-planning legislation, repealing as it did all previous Acts and laying the foundations of our present land-use system. As far as historic buildings were concerned, it incorporated the listing provisions of the 1944 Act and introduced a system of building preservation orders, which could be made either by local planning authorities or by the Minister of Housing and Local Government, when a building of architectural or historic interest was threatened. It therefore extended the principle, first established in respect of uninhabited ancient monuments in the 1913 Act, to cover the whole field of inhabited historic buildings.

The changing economic climate and the social ambitions of a Labour Government meant that an increasing number of

21

historic buildings were under threat just because of the straitened circumstances in which their owners found themselves. To his credit, Sir Stafford Cripps recognized this and set up a committee under Sir Ernest Gowers (see Chapter Three) to examine the problem. Its far-reaching report made important recommendations on financial assistance to owners through Government grants and tax relief. Many of its recommendations have lain neglected for over a quarter of a century but, in 1953, the new Conservative Government of Winston Churchill incorporated its main points in the Historic Buildings and Ancient Monuments Act. Thus, Historic Building Councils for England, Wales and Scotland were established, whose duty was to advise the Minister (of Works) on the making of grants and loans for the repair and upkeep of buildings of outstanding historic or architectural interest.

In 1962 the Macmillan Government produced another Town and Country Planning Act. A consolidation measure, it renewed the provisions of the 1947 Act regarding historic buildings, and it was accompanied in the same year by the Local Authorities (Historic Buildings) Act, piloted through Parliament by a private member, Mr Paul Channon, with Government blessing and support. This Act empowered local councils to make grants towards the upkeep of historic buildings. It was intended in particular to help those owners whose properties were not sufficiently outstanding to qualify them for a government grant from the Historic Buildings Council. Its deficiency was that it merely empowered; it did not oblige.

By the mid sixties it was increasingly obvious that not only individual buildings, but whole areas of historic towns, were at risk. So in 1966, following the determined and skilful advocacy of Duncan Sandys and the other founding fathers of the Civic Trust (established in 1957), the Preservation Policy Group was set up within the Ministry of Housing and Local Government in order to co-ordinate pilot studies of four historic towns – Bath, Chester, Chichester and York. The overall aim was to examine how conservation policies to ensure their survival, and that of other historic towns, could be most sensibly implemented. Individual town studies were published in 1968, and the Group published a list of general recommendations two years later. Many of these recommendations, which will be touched on later, were incorporated into the 1972 Town and Country Planning Act.

That this field was a particularly appropriate one for the activity of the public-spirited private member had been shown by Paul Channon, in 1962. And in 1967 Duncan Sandys, with all-party support, introduced the now famous Civic Amenities Act which, on the precedent of 1931, introduced unequivocally the concept of protection for whole areas of cities, towns or villages. Under the provisions of this Act local authorities were *required* to designate 'conservation areas', and were given a positive direction that they should 'from time to time determine which parts of their area are areas of special architectural or historical interest, the character or appearance of which it is desirable to preserve or enhance, and shall designate such areas as conservation areas'. The Secretary of State was also given power to direct authorities to take such action, and it was stipulated that applications for planning permission which could affect the character of such an area should be fully publicized. The Act also brought improvements in the control over listed buildings: six months' notice instead of two had to be given for proposals to alter or demolish such a building, and local authorities were given power to serve repairs notices on the owners of buildings urgently in need of repair and, if necessary, to carry out the repairs themselves. The Act also introduced further environmental improvements by requiring local authorities to plant and protect trees, to improve refuse facilities, and to remove abandoned cars from streets.

This far-reaching and very important measure was followed by other improvements in the law. The Town and Country Planning Act of 1968 devoted Part V to buildings of architectural and historic interest, introducing reforms in the protection of listed buildings, including higher fines for unauthorized demolition. Its measures were further consolidated by the Town and Country Planning (Amendment) Act 1968, which itself introduced two important new provisions affecting conservation areas. Local authorities were given power to control demolition of *unlisted* buildings in conservation areas, provisions further extended in the 1971 Town and Country Planning Act concerning listed buildings. This gave for the first time a positive protection to buildings which, although individually not of sufficient merit to be listed, contributed to the character of an area. Local planning authorities were also empowered to give a direction that specified buildings within a conservation area should be afforded special protection in the interests of the

23

character and appearance of the area.

The 1968 Act also made grants available for buildings within a conservation area, such grants to be administered through the Historic Buildings Council. These conservation grants were a major step forward in the battle for the improvement of the environment, especially in urban areas, in that they were available for unlisted buildings within a designated conservation area. Another improvement effected by these Acts was the provision which enabled a local planning authority to bring a building preservation notice into effect by attaching it to a building, rather than by trying to serve it on the owner. This measure was directly inspired by a case in Wheathampstead, where the St Albans' Council had been unable to serve a preservation order on the owners of a fine fifteenth-century farmhouse because they could not find their address. The house was subsequently demolished.

In 1974 another Private Member's Bill, introduced in the first Parliament by Sir John Rodgers and taken up in the second by Mr Michael Shersby, built upon the foundations of Duncan Sandys' Civic Amenities Act of 1967. This measure, enacted as the Town and Country Amenities Act, was described by its sponsors as 'Parliament's contribution to European Architectural Heritage Year'. It widened the scope of the previous Acts by yet further extending the powers of local authorities in dealing with conservation areas and historic buildings. The authorities were required to prepare, and make public, schemes for the preservation and enhancement of their conservation areas, thus taking a more positive attitude by inviting public interest and participation. The Secretary of State's powers to designate areas where local authorities were being particularly obdurate or unimaginative were further strengthened.

Another section of the Act gave increased control over advertising within conservation areas, and yet another required local planning authorities to give publicity to any proposal which affected the setting of a listed building. The basis of compensation in the case of compulsory purchase of a listed building was also altered. Compensation by the local authority now has to be assessed only on the value of the building, not as before on the value of the site, with the automatic assumption that listed building consent would have been granted for redevelopment. Another important aspect of this section of the Bill gave the Historic Buildings Council authority to make grants

24

towards the preservation of gardens of outstanding interest, whether or not associated with historic buildings.

Much has been said so far about the listing of buildings, and it is worth briefly describing the system. Under the 1947 Act the statutory list to be compiled by the Ministry's investigators consisted of three categories of building:

Grade 1. Buildings of outstanding interest too important to be destroyed.

Grade 2. Buildings of special interest which should be preserved as far as possible (a subsequent two-asterisk category was made within this grade to mark buildings of particular interest within it).

Grade 3. Buildings of interest which contribute to the general effect of an area.

The Grade 3 category was abolished in 1969, because it afforded no legal protection, and on its abolition some of the buildings within it were upgraded to Grade 2, and others were notified to their local authorities so that they could form an 'unofficial' supplementary list.

In choosing buildings for listing, special attention is paid to good examples of a particular architectural style, or piece of planning, or to good illustrations of social or economic history. Technical innovation, or an association with well-known people or events, are also taken into account, as are group value and examples of carefully planned and integrated layout. In practice, all buildings dating from before 1700 are listed automatically, as are most buildings erected between 1700 and 1840. Of those built between 1840 and 1914, only ones of definite character and quality are included, together with a number of selected buildings erected between 1914 and 1939.

The first listing programme ran from 1947 to 1968, and at that date there were in England and Wales 4351 Grade 1 Buildings, 111,300 Grade 2, and 136,752 Grade 3. With the abolition of Grade 3 and the reassessment of Grade 2, the total in England and Wales at December 1971 was 137,000. Another major listing programme is now under way, and should be completed by 1985. Some 25,000 buildings a year are being added to the list, and listing is now fully accepted as a continuing process which will increasingly reflect not only current needs but changing tastes and ideas. And thus we shall see a welcome increase in the number of Victorian, Edwardian and even more recent

25

buildings. It is estimated that the final list in 1985 will comprise approximately 250,000 buildings. As far as conservation areas are concerned, there are now almost 4000 in the United Kingdom, of which almost 10 per cent have been designated as 'outstanding'. New areas are constantly being designated.

All of this might seem to indicate a happy state of things, and no country with a history of legislation such as has been outlined need feel totally ashamed. Indeed, in many ways we have blazed the trail and set the example. But much is amiss, as will be demonstrated in the following chapters, and unless difficult new steps are taken, and unless the proper provisions which already exist on the statute book are taken correct advantage of, we stand to lose much of our heritage in the coming decade.

To end this chapter on a sober note, one can reflect on the number of listed buildings demolished since 1965. Official figures for all of the years are not available, but the estimated rate of demolition is approximately 500 a year, and in European Architectural Heritage Year alone the figure was nearly 400. As far as conservation areas are concerned, a decade after Duncan Sandys' Bill, some twenty local authorities in England and Wales had yet to designate a single area, and there was a disturbingly low return from many architecturally rich areas, such as Norfolk, Northumberland, Shropshire and Somerset.

We can claim a respectable legislative record. We can boast a burgeoning amenities movement. We should be proud of the valiant efforts of public-spirited and far-sighted individuals. But complacent we cannot, and must not, be, either about our buildings or about the countryside we can all too easily take for granted.

Chapter Two

The Countryside
We Take for Granted

The English landscape is at once the most obvious and enjoyed and also the most neglected aspect of our heritage: obvious and enjoyed because of the magnetic appeal of 'the countryside' to an urban population; neglected because that same population takes its presence and its permanence for granted. Hence, 'God made the country and man made the town' – and even an agnostic age instinctively accepts that the natural background and foil for man-made beauties, and escape from man-made ugliness, will always be there.

In a densely populated island such as ours this is a rash assumption. For one thing the pressures of commerce, industry and politics on finite resources of land and beauty are not easily withstood; for another the preservation of the land's natural beauty must be by conscious and deliberate action. That these factors have long been recognized is shown by the legislative sanctification of 'the green belt' and by the proliferation of local and national amenity societies dedicated to fighting insensitive planning decisions, and to achieving the balance between industrial and commercial needs and conservation. But from Dartmoor to the Cheviots the traditional landscape pattern, the beauty we all enjoy and take for granted, is at risk, and only new initiatives on the part of those who exercise a constant vigilance will save it. Though ruins will always have a powerful and romantic hold on our imagination and the presence of vanished villages beneath the furrows has inspired poets, land lost to twentieth-century developers is beauty lost for ever.

And land is being lost at a frightening rate.

Between 1945 and 1975 approximately 1 million acres were taken out of cultivation and although accurate statistics are hard to find (even the Ministry of Agriculture does not know how many acres of woodland have disappeared since the War) it seems only too clear that over 70,000[1] acres of agricultural land – English landscape – are built on or taken over each year. Motorways and their service areas alone accounted for 25,000 acres between 1960 and 1976. Motorways under construction in 1978 will take another 2000 acres or more. Twenty acres of land is required for a mile of motorway, a new electricity generation station requires 500 acres, an oil refinery 1000 acres or more, a North Sea gas terminal about 2000 acres. A thousand acres a year are buried under colliery spoil, and coal extraction affects some 6000 acres a year in South Wales alone, according to the Council for the Protection of Rural Wales. In Bedfordshire, clay production has now consumed almost 2500 acres and this total is increasing at the rate of 50 acres a year.

Of course, it is not just industry that requires land. In 1970, the National Playing Fields Association estimated that the number of people playing golf was increasing at the rate of 9 per cent a year. If taken literally, this expansion would mean we should be requiring four acres per hundred of the population just for golf courses by the turn of the century. Perhaps this gives some point to T. S. Eliot's remark that our only legacy would be 'the asphalt road and a thousand lost golf balls'.

One does not want to be unduly alarmist but anyone with two minutes to spare and a pocket calculator at his disposal can see that by the year 2000 another 1½ million acres will have been occupied and our farmlands shrunk by some 4 to 5 per cent. For green belt notwithstanding, there seems no coherent central plan to halt the urbanization rate of the countryside. As with most complex issues it is easier to indicate the problems than it is to propound acceptable solutions, but if food production is to be given the priority common sense dictates and if 'conservation', 'preservation', and the importance of the 'rural environment' and other clichés are to have any real significance there must be a slowing down in the process of urban encroachment.

1. According to a Parliamentary answer in July 1977, for the six-year period ending in June 1975, the latest for which information was available, the annual average net transfer out of agriculture in England and Wales alone amounted to a little over 76,000 acres, of which approximately 8500 acres was land taken over by the Forestry Commission.

In fact solutions do readily suggest themselves, and many have become more attractive in the wake of the energy crisis and attendant economic problems. For instance, though an industrialized country needs good speedy communications these do not necessarily have to be six-lane motorways. It is at least arguable that when those motorways at present under construction are completed there should be an absolute moratorium on motorway building for twenty years and the entire road building programme firmly concentrated on making our towns and villages more habitable. In this way not only would less land be taken up by road works, but there would be less desire to escape and build 'a place in the country' if fumes and noises were reduced within the towns. After all, towns are places for people to live in and they can only have a life and a civilizing influence if they house a living as well as a working and shopping community.

Towns and their problems are the subject of Chapters Five and Six but in the present context we can see that both town life and that of the countryside could be improved by a sensible policy of restoring good old houses, and by a more imaginative rehabilitation of derelict sites. It is surely the height of folly to house people at expensive distances from their work and in the process destroy land of great agricultural and scenic wealth when in and around our towns and cities are hundreds of thousands of sound, if dilapidated, houses and tens of thousands of acres of waste land. There were nearly 107,000 acres of waste land in England alone at the time of the last survey in 1974, of which nearly 82,000 were considered to justify treatment. At normal density, these could accommodate nearly a million homes – the land needed for overspill for almost a decade. And yet in the first two years after the survey, only a little over 900 acres of this derelict land was reclaimed. Of course some derelict land could never be built upon, but much could, and most of the rest could be transformed to acceptable park and recreation land, or even returned to farming. For though considerable reclamation has taken place, the amount of derelict land has remained frighteningly static for a decade or more. The inland waterway system, too, is almost totally neglected for commercial uses. Although only half its nineteenth-century length, many of the 2000 miles of our canal system could still be used to relieve congestion on the roads of Britain, even though it is unlikely that barge transport could ever assume the same significance here as on the Continent.[2] All these steps would help relieve the pressure on, and reduce the dangers to, the English landscape, but in themselves would not be enough to ensure its survival in anything remotely resembling its present form.

The problems, of course, are not new; they have been developing over the last 150 years. Whilst Britain changed from an agricultural into an industrial country, the population grew from a little over 10 million to over five times that number (1801 census 10.5 million; 1971 census 53.8 million). Early industrial changes brought commercial prosperity, but early industrialists showed scant regard for the countryside as they built their factories or encouraged the unchecked and destructive development of an urban sprawl around the agricultural hinterland of so many of our towns and cities.

One should not be over-critical about the lack of precautions because the problems of industrialization had never been faced before. But though commercial opportunities were often commendably exploited, expansion brought not only success but piles of waste, scars across the country, and factories erected with little or no thought to the effect they would have on the landscape. It was only relatively recently that stringent controls on all this development was imposed. And during the last half century we have seen a network of pylons criss-cross the countryside and have disfigured the domestic scene with the ubiquitous television aerial.

In the 1920s and 1930s the suburbs grew at a rapid rate, and as a consequence much fine countryside was eroded. In response to this, the idea of the green belt was born with its new stricter planning controls designed to arrest urban spread. But even today, the countryside is not safe in the face of demand and pressure from the huge corporation or from nationalized industry, which can suggest that the development advocated is essential for economic survival, and can then marshal armies of experts to cajole planning departments and impress inquiries. Sometimes the experts are beaten, as they were at the Dulas Valley Inquiry in 1970 when the Severn River Authority was forced into admitting that its estimates for extra water resources were grossly exaggerated. But local opinion is frequently brow-

2. This unexploited potential underlines the urgent necessity for a complete reappraisal of our whole transport system, and in particular of the rôle of the railways.

beaten and Ministers are often dazzled by the evidence of so-called infallible experts. As I write the battle to prevent building part of the M54 through one of the loveliest remaining parts of Staffordshire goes on, with the Midland Road Construction Unit insisting, although most of its estimates have been challenged, that the motorway will be essential, refusing to consider seriously new and telling evidence, and even embarking on expensive preparatory work in advance of the Minister's final decision.

In July 1977 perhaps the most significant battle yet between the exponents of industrial expansion and rural preservation was heralded with the long-expected announcement that the National Coal Board wished to apply for permission to mine extensively in the beautiful Vale of Belvoir. Local feeling was almost unanimous in its anger at the proposals, but the Chairman of the National Coal Board was adamant that the coal was necessary for the nation's industrial survival and that it must be mined as soon as possible.

The most remarkable victories over official decisions were those of Stanstead, Cublington and Maplin, over the siting of the proposed third London airport – but they became national campaigns. One of the tragedies is that beautiful local areas rarely incite national fervour, and it is difficult for local amenity societies or other bodies properly to challenge expert evidence. And expert evidence can be misleading. For instance in the 1960s, the figure that was frequently quoted for putting electricity transmission lines undergrou:.d was over £1 million per mile. What was not said was that this related only to major 1400 kV circuits.

And so the encroachments continue, questionable decisions are allowed to stand and countryside and farmland is lost – at the present rate, an area the size of Nottinghamshire goes every eight years. No one suggests that a proportion of this loss is not inevitable but it is vital to reduce the rate. Certain actions and policies are open to question, for instance the whole concept of the new town – and yet, in spite of Government recognition of this, Milton Keynes is going ahead and 22,000 acres of agricultural land will be built upon and an area at least twice as large as that adversely affected.

Even when particular bodies are conscious of their 'environmental duties', mistakes are made. The Central Electricity Generating Board, for example, is charged by Parliament 'to take into account any effect that their proposals might have on the natural beauty of the countryside or on flora or fauna, or natural creatures or buildings or objects of special interest'. Nevertheless they have built a nuclear power station in the Snowdonia National Park and, on a smaller scale, the Iron Bridge power station beside Buildwas Abbey, in the most beautiful stretch of the Severn Gorge. And it is not just the big decisions which are open to question. Much unnecessary damage is done by the widening of country lanes in the interests of convenience and tidiness. Quite often the only result is a spoilt area and more reckless driving.

The picture would, however, be much gloomier had it not been for the doughty campaigning of national and local amenity societies. Among the most vigorous in its efforts and successful in its achievements has been the Council for the Preservation of Rural England. Established in 1926 to combat such horrors as the ribbon development of the 1920s and 1930s, and to draw attention to the defacing of the countryside by long lines of hoardings on rural verges, the CPRE – the brainchild of Patrick Abercrombie – has many victories to its credit. Its agitation, more than anything else, led to the Town and Country Planning Acts of the 1940s which virtually controlled ribbon development; and its persistence was largely responsible for establishing the principle that the restoration of derelict industrial and mining sites should be regarded as normal procedure (although much remains to be done here). It was the CPRE, too, which fought a largely successful battle for Ullswater when Manchester Corporation wished to distort and destroy the whole beauty of the area with its plan for water extraction. The Council has also done much to prevent the proliferation of radio and television masts. At Fort William, for instance, it won the day when it called for one mast to cater for television and VHF, rather than two. There is still much to be done and it is significant that the Council decided to celebrate its Golden Jubilee in 1976 by launching an appeal for £500,000 to enable it to continue its vigilance and campaigning.

Certain parts of the landscape are recognized as being of such importance that special steps must be taken for their preservation. Thus, in 1949, the National Parks Commission was established, and as a result ten national parks were designated: the Lake District, Snowdonia, the Brecon Beacons, the Pembrokeshire coast, Exmoor, Dartmoor, the Peak District, the North Yorkshire Moors, the Yorkshire Dales, and Northumberland. The land and the parks generally remained privately owned, but agreements or orders to secure additional public access were made by local authorities. Steps were also taken to preserve and enhance the landscape's natural beauties by high standards of development and control and by such measures as extra tree planting and preservation, and the removal of manmade eyesores.

Under the Countryside Act of 1968, the Countryside Commission replaced the National Parks Commission and was charged with keeping under review all matters relating to the provision and improvement of facilities for the enjoyment of the countryside. Schedule 17 of the Local Government Act of 1972 stated that 'Every Town Planning Board, or National Park Committee established for a National Park shall (a) within three years of the First of April 1974 or of being established, whichever is the later, prepare and publish a plan to be known as a National Park Plan formulating their policy for the management of the park and the exercise of the functions exercisable by them (b) review at intervals of not more than five years the National Park Plan published under this paragraph making any amendments to it which they consider expedient and publish a report on their review and any such amendments.'

All but two of the national parks are administered by the local authorities in whose areas they fall and this has roused considerable criticism because it is often felt that unfortunate conflicts of interest could arise, and indeed some have arisen, over the parks' administration. Considerable controversy erupted in Exmoor, for instance, in the summer of 1977, when it was alleged that farmers, anxious to improve the yield of the moors, and actively encouraged by Government grants so to do, were gradually whittling away the open moorland. The conservationists' claim was that they were, as a consequence, turning a wild, free landscape into fenced and laundered grazing lands, and that they were being allowed to do so by a park committee composed largely of locally elected members. The argument not only highlighted the problem of administration, but also illustrated the difficulty of achieving a correct balance between the need for agriculture and the interests of conservationists in areas which are, in spite of their designation, still part of the agricultural, as well as the protected, landscape.

33

A beauty spot after contact with twentieth-century civilisation: Box Hill after a Bank Holiday *Dudley Styles, for the National Trust*

By common consent the most successful of the parks are those administered by park boards representing a number of authorities, amenity societies and other bodies. No one could seriously challenge the concept of the national parks for they are areas of great importance and great beauty. But by virtue of their very designation they attract enormous numbers of visitors, and balancing the needs of the residents, the demands of amenity and conservation groups and of the visitors, is not always an easy task. One wants to encourage recreation in the countryside and provide facility and opportunity for it, but there comes a point where the number of visitors, by their very presence, destroy the things they come to enjoy. In Snowdonia, for example, which has 210,000 visitors a year, paths and tracks are being worn away by walkers, who, according to the Council for the Preservation of Rural Wales, are 'making a molehill out of a mountain'. The same problems are found on the Pennine Way, where footpaths are being pounded to death, and there are even experiments being conducted on plastic footpaths in certain vulnerable areas. The problems faced by the national parks are faced in a similar measure by the thirty-four areas of outstanding natural beauty (see Appendix 1). These range from the Sussex

Downs to Cannock Chase, and include such large areas as the Cotswolds, and smaller ones like Dedham Vale. But their beauty, too, attracts visitors, and visitors create difficulties if they come in too great a number, as anyone knows who has visited Flatford Mill on a Bank Holiday Monday.

That people who live in constricted urban areas should have the opportunity for recreation in rural surroundings is beyond dispute. Residents of the Black Country, for instance, tend to look to Cannock Chase as one of their 'lungs'. But the balancing of agricultural needs, environmental preservation and the supply of recreational facilities is a difficult one to achieve. The Forestry Commission has attempted to achieve this balance and in some of its forests has set aside areas where people may picnic and walk, and has attempted to restrict them to places where they will not interfere with, or damage, the forestry. They have also established holiday villages and designated areas for camping and caravanning, which have become increasingly popular pursuits as mobility increases and inflation prices hotels beyond the reach of all but the more affluent families.

Conscious of the difficulties of reconciling recreation with preservation, the Sandford Committee, established in 1971, recommended the creation of 'heritage areas' which it defined as areas where 'the conservation of environmental qualities would be the supreme objective . . . taking precedence over all others'. These areas would contain no large car parks or public lavatories, no refuse bins or refreshments – they would all be sited in surrounding support areas. 'These conservation areas', the Report said, 'are to be kept for quiet and congruous public enjoyment, with access to them to be on foot, bicycle or horse. They should be conserved so as to be handed on unimpaired to future generations.' They were considered to be those rare areas which were especially vulnerable to encroachments and which must be given special consideration and protection if they were to survive. They were, in concept, not dissimilar from the nature reserves, the responsibility of the Nature Conservancy, which in 1974 covered almost 300,000 acres.

But national parks, areas of outstanding beauty, potential heritage areas, nature reserves, National Trust land, and reserves owned by such bodies as the Royal Society for the Protection of Birds, are not *the* landscape, *the* countryside, even though they represent vital and beautiful parts of it which deserve jealous guarding and special treatment. No, the greater part of our landscape is outside such areas of special protection. In Scotland, for instance, there are no national parks, and only 9 per cent of the coastline (of England and Wales) lies within the ten national parks. Indeed, our coastline, with its infinite variety and complexity, a special pride to an island race, is particularly vulnerable, in spite of the valiant efforts of the National Trust's Enterprise Neptune, a scheme devised to bring into Trust ownership some of the most beautiful and unspoilt coastal areas. By far the greater part of the countryside, therefore, is exposed to all the pressures of population growth, industrial exploitation and demand, and developers' dreams. Not that these are the only threats to the countryside.

In spite of all that has been written about the 'silent spring' and the menace of toxic wastes, in spite of the laudable legislative action that has followed public outcry and stimulated further public awareness, pollution remains a threat to the healthy growth of meadow and woodland, to the purity of the air and the life of the water. Industry's pollution of the air is inadequately controlled, and while great progress has been made in improving rivers and estuaries, there is much to be done before the work is complete. Our coastal landscape is threatened here, too. Stiffer penalties might have made oil pollution less likely, but penalties cannot prevent determined mischief or genuine accidents and damage done by oil from ship collisions. And our new position as an oil producing nation brings its own frightening pollution hazards: the ever present danger of 'blowouts' for instance, the first of which occurred in the summer of 1977.

But the pollution crises that reach the headlines, such as 'Danger from Radioactive Waste', 'Japanese to Send Atom Waste to UK', 'Cancer Warning on Chemicals', serious and potentially spectacular as they often are, do not perhaps pose the greatest threats to our countryside. It is more likely that they come from the industry which largely created, and still largely controls, the landscape pattern of England: farming. For in seeking to meet demands, and at the same time to cope with the problems created by fiscal and other pressures, farming has changed dramatically in the last three decades. The loss of good farmland has underlined the need for a more intensive cultivation of what remains, a need stimulated by a growing population and an ever greater demand to feed it, to make ourselves more self-sufficient as a nation. The increasing sophistication of farming

36

Traditional landscape: a scene on the Yorkshire Wolds near Huggate, looking east *A. F. Kersting*

techniques has produced a record of remarkable success in statistical terms. The average yield per acre of wheat in Great Britain was 17.3 cwts in 1885. By 1935 it had risen to only 18.6 cwts. By 1960, it was 28.5 cwts and by 1970, 33.3 cwts. This upward trend cannot be expected to continue in such a spectacular manner and, indeed, the very success that the figures represent must be viewed with some degree of concern, for it has been achieved by an intensification and alteration of farming methods which pose very real threats to the pattern of the English countryside as we know and love it.

Since the Agrarian Revolution and the enclosures of the late eighteenth century, farmers have known that unless waste and crop residues were returned to the land its fertility would deteriorate and yields would decline. Throughout the nineteenth century advanced farmers perfected the techniques of natural fertilizing: the ploughing in of the stubble in preparation for the next crop and the spreading of manure from cowsheds and cattle yards on the fields. However, by the middle of the last century, chemists were discovering that the organic substances used as manures and fertilizers contained a number of chemical elements in common, elements that were essential for plant nutrition, such as nitrogen, phosphorus and potassium. In their organic form nutrients are not immediately available to plants but must be processed by soil micro-organisms and random chemical reactions so that they are released slowly. Manufactured industrially, however, they can be delivered to the soil accurately and in a form that enters the water held in the soil to form a solution. This makes them available almost immediately and means that nutrients can be fed to the plant when its growth requires them, rather than to the soil.

This knowledge has been harnessed by a farming industry challenged to increase domestic food production. Between 1954 and 1973, the net output of the United Kingdom almost doubled, a rapid increase due to a transformation of British agriculture. Increased use of artificial fertilizers, partly to answer the challenge and partly to answer the problems brought about by the rising cost of labour, played a substantial part in this rise. Thus, the growing availability and use of chemicals, combined with the relative profitability of cereals, persuaded many farmers to abandon the practice of ley farming (the seeding of crop land back to grass every few years to rest and allow it to restore its natural structure and fertility). As a result soils in many areas have deteriorated and soil blows, seldom a problem before, have occurred more frequently in areas of East Anglia and the East Midlands.

By the mid sixties farmers had become concerned themselves by the adverse effects of new practices and the National Farmers' Union conducted a survey to discover the extent of the problem. A full inquiry by the Agricultural Advisory Council followed and, in their 1970 Report, they concluded that modern farming practices were indeed having a detrimental effect on soil structure in some regions. In addition, they claimed that continuous cropping had created serious problems in pest and disease control. In spite of this, pure organic farming has few devotees and very widespread use of artificial fertilizers continues. Most would agree that though artificial fertilizers have a future there is good reason to think that they have an 'addictive' effect, altering the ecology of soil population, depressing numbers of those species that make nutrients available in their own waste and decay products. Further, by ending the practice of returning fibrous organic matter to the soil it becomes more difficult for plant foods to reach the soil solution. These adverse effects are cumulative and farmers often find that as the years go by they are using ever increasing amounts of fertilizers to achieve the same yield.

If, therefore, the practice continues, and there is a further increase in the intensity of arable farming, there will almost certainly be further deterioration in soil structure and erosion, probably for only a very small increase in yield. If the process of soil deterioration is to be reversed there must be an increase in the acreage to be sown to grass and a re-integration of livestock and arable farming.

There may be a further restraint on increased fertilizer use. Whereas potash and phosphate fertilizer compounds are comparatively stable in the soil, this is not true of nitrogen. In an article in the *New Scientist* in 1972, Dr R. Scorer reported that the number of milligrams of nitrogen, in the form of nitrate, per litre of water at intakes on the Thames and Lea have, since 1972, approached, and in one case even exceeded, the 11.3 milligrams considered to be the safe limit. Above this concentration bottle-fed babies can develop methaemoglobaemia, a disorder affecting the oxygen-carrying capacity of the blood, and above a concentration of 20 milligrams the adult population could also be at risk.

To put it briefly, successive use of artificial fertilizers could well impose extra strains on the biology of farms and gardens which could have a damaging effect on our forests, rivers and waters, but above all on the general appearance of the countryside. Already there has been widespread loss of wildlife in the world through the destruction of habitats and the indiscriminate use of the more persistent pesticides.

But one must take a balanced view. We owe to our farmers the countryside that we enjoy. Its beauties are largely of their creation. For centuries they have looked upon themselves as trustees of the land replacing the resources extracted by their crops and acquiring, gradually, by trial and error, a philosophy of husbandry, largely inspired by their sense of stewardship. Today, farmers are no less responsible for what they have in trust, but the problems and pressures of producing food and earning a living in the twentieth century, and the fiscal inhibitions that a farmer faces, often make him, albeit reluctantly, put financial considerations first. Long-term dangers from fertilizers may be one result. More noticeably spectacular is the transformation in many parts of England of the traditional rural landscape of chequer-board fields and pastures enclosed by hedgerows.

The hedgerow has long been an indispensable and invaluable feature of the English country scene, a visual break and a shelter for plant, animal and insect life. The uprooting of hedgerows, and the creating of vast prairies in certain areas, has transformed the rural scene more than anything else since the enclosures of the eighteenth century, when most of our 500,000 miles of hedgerow were planted. It is estimated that 100,000 miles of these hedges have been removed in the last twenty years. In East Anglia, nearly half have gone, and the impact of their removal has aroused great criticism from a public often ignorant of farming needs, but deeply attached to the traditional landscape pattern. This attachment dates back well beyond the eighteenth century in many cases, for some of our hedges can be traced to Saxon times. Those who take an objective view appreciate the need for some hedgerow removal, but its scale is, enough to disturb even the most farming-conscious naturalist. For the hedgerows are not only valuable and beautiful in themselves. A survey in 1951 found that no less than a fifth of the nation's reserves of indigenous hard woods – oak, ash, elm, beech and sycamore – were hedgerow trees.

Aside from the devastation caused by Dutch Elm disease, every year these hedgerow trees become fewer and many of them will never be replaced because the modern hedge-cutting machine cannot distinguish between the unwanted elder sprays and the healthy young leaders of oak, ash or sycamore that might one day grow into fine trees. Indeed, the very machines themselves contribute to the death of the hedge by failing to remove dead grass heads, brambles and bracken that choke and eventually kill, by not allowing light and air to the rich part of animal life that it sustains. If it continues, this trend will lead to the virtual disappearance from the fields of the blackbird and thrush, the chaffinch and the other hedgerow-nesting birds. The hard fact is that because of our taxation system and changes or quirks in Government farming policy, it is often difficult for the farmer to obtain anything like a favourable return on his capital employed. So he saves money where he can and seeks to produce as much as he can. Thus hedges go down to save the bother and cost of maintaining them and to make larger units.

Between 1945 and 1970,[3] 4500 miles of hedgerow were removed each year. In that period, Norfolk lost half its hedges and Huntingdon 90 per cent. There are many dairy farmers who are re-organizing their holdings by removing hedges, the traditional stock-proof barriers, and creating instead large fields in which the paddocks are wired off.

Downland, too, is disappearing before the plough, often for the first time. Half the Winchester Chalk Downs have gone since the War and a quarter of Dorset's over the last fifteen years. Lowland heath, too, is disappearing. These changes not only alter and spoil the beauty of our countryside but they also destroy much of its life. As the cover disappears the balance of nature is upset and animals and birds and plants die. The scale of the damage was such that in 1962 the Countryside Commission set up a study to investigate how agricultural improvement could be carried out efficiently, but in such a way as to create new landscapes no less interesting than those destroyed in the process. The very terms of reference seemed to accept the inevitability of change. Some change *is* inevitable, and many of the more prosperous farmers have replaced hedgerows by clumps of trees for shelter where the fields meet, and those with an interest in conserving game and wildlife often insist on maintaining a few hedges in odd wild corners, even on the arable farm. But every yard of ground sacrificed in this way means a fractional loss in income and not every farmer is willing (or able to afford) to recognize that the future ecological health and balance of the landscape may depend on his making such a sacrifice.

It is not just the removal of hedgerows which has disturbed the appearance and balance of the countryside. Another casualty of the pressures of taxation and production demands is the traditional English meadow. As an article in the *Sunday Times* in July 1977 put it: 'Meadows once bright with ox-eye daisies now sway with monotonous maxi crops of Italian rye. In wildlife terms the loss is enormous. A good site can hold a hundred wild plant species or more.' And the plants, of course, harbour the insects and encourage the birds. Wildlife has been particularly affected, too, by the widespread use of pesticides.

3. For the last seven years there are no complete records available, but according to a Parliamentary answer in July 1977: 'Such information that is available . . . indicates that the decline in the rate of hedge removal is continuing.' Not a very reassuring or definite answer from the Minister!

For they are all poisonous to wildlife to a greater or lesser extent even when the manufacturers' instructions are followed carefully. And while an insecticide may eliminate a pest from a crop, it will also kill many other species which feed on the pest, so that when the pest does return, it can rapidly build up its numbers. This in turn can lead to the creation of new pests, such as the fruit tree red spider mite. At one time this mite, though common, was kept in check by its natural enemies, but so many of these have been killed off by the pesticides that now the mite has become a serious menace.

The use of pesticides to control weeds is also fast destroying aquatic plants and animals. There was a time when the many pools, lakes and meres and marshes and fens around the country supported distinctive plants and animals. The draining of farmland, the piping of water to fields, has meant that most of these natural habitats have gone, and as the few remaining ditches and ponds are now frequently being contaminated, yet another balance is upset. But it is not just the smaller ditches and ponds that are endangered. There have been increasingly alarming reports to the effect that the Norfolk Broads, one of the country's most beautiful and popular holiday areas, are at risk. They faced, said one, '. . . on a more modest scale, the kind of degradation that has occurred in the great lakes of America'.

The Norfolk Naturalist Trust has produced evidence that rich nutrients from washed-out fertilizers, and from sewage, are flowing into the Broads endangering all aquatic vegetation in eleven of the twenty-eight Broads studied. In another eleven the vegetation had been severely reduced. It is doubtful whether the prime responsibility for this disturbing state of affairs rests with the farmers for using too many artificial fertilizers, or with the holiday-makers for throwing refuse and pumping enormous quantities of sewage into the Broads. But, in spite of the new regulations for boats to carry chemical toilets, an increased use of organic fertilizers will be necessary if the Broads are to be saved.

In spite of frequent assertions to the contrary, advanced in some conservationists' lobbies, the farmer *is* concerned with the quality of his environment. The desire to maximize profits is rarely paramount and is balanced by a healthy concern for the countryside and its traditions. The ownership of land is still regarded as a trust, held for succeeding generations and for other members of society who regard the heritage in terms of recreation and amenity. However, today's farmer is under great financial pressure and new forms of taxation will increase this. The temptation is, therefore, to gain the greatest available profit in the short or medium term at the possible expense of the future. The owner-occupier, who for generations has demonstrated a sense of true responsibility, is in danger of being transformed by the actions of the State from the guardian of our agricultural heritage into a potential enemy.

It is easy for a farmer with a relatively modest holding to be a rich man on paper, but the return on the capital invested in farming is a very low one – often as low as 1 or 2 per cent. This is not a new situation, but the farmer now has to cope with the prospect of new capital taxes and the threat of a Wealth Tax. All this means that private ownership of land is not in possible danger: it is in peril. In the Budget of April 1976, the Chancellor of the Exchequer gave additional relief to farmers from Capital Transfer Tax, the tax which he had previously introduced to replace the old Estate Duty. The additional relief granted, though it will assist the working farmer with a holding of 1000 acres or less, will in no wise remove the threat to the larger estate – and it is mainly upon the productivity of flourishing large holdings that success in meeting targets for extra food production depends.

This explains why after the Budget there was still a mood of despondency in the ranks of landowners. James Douglas, the Secretary-General of the Country Land Owners Association, writing in *Country Life* on 15 April 1976, said: 'The Government is using capital taxation not to raise revenue but to carry out its social policies . . . when the consequence of investment is a direct increase in the liability for capital taxation – annually under Wealth Tax (postponed but not abandoned by the Chancellor) and once a generation under Capital Transfer Tax, with the break-up of the private landowning business the virtually certain conclusion – who will invest?' Douglas took a very gloomy view of what the future would hold without further mitigation of the tax burden faced by landowners. 'City institutions will buy some land but they have an overriding responsibility to their shareholders, policy holders or other investors, which it would be unethical for them to disregard. As companies with obligations to fulfil they can normally invest only in land which offers either capital appreciation or a good return . . . the National Trust for its part has declared that it cannot be used as a receptacle for land that has to be disposed of

43

and no one wants to buy. Only the State or its agents are left.'

At the end of the Parliamentary session in the summer of 1977, Mr Douglas felt able to breathe a small sigh of relief, commenting (again in *Country Life*) that, 'this is the first session since February 1974 that landowners have not been the target for unceasing attack'. He was able to welcome the fact that the Government had listened and altered course on Capital Transfer Tax since the White Paper of 1974. But his general prognosis remained the same and it is a fact that, even with the better terms offered in the 1976 Budget, private land, especially privately let land, bears a much heavier tax burden than land let by institutional landlords. The fiscal burdens of the landowner are daunting and he lives in a climate of uncertainty accentuated so long as introduction of a Wealth Tax remains the official policy of one of the major political parties. As James Douglas remarked, 'the efficiency of our agriculture and the beauty of our countryside stand testimony to the system of private ownership on which they flourish'. The danger is that the farmer will increasingly be obliged to look upon his farm as a purely economic unit to be exploited to the full during his particular ownership. Capital taxation, especially on the transfer of land, will inevitably reduce the interest of the farmer in his holding after his own retirement. And a Wealth Tax would inevitably increase pressure to earn as much money as possible in the minimum amount of time. The National Farmers' Union has calculated that Capital Transfer Tax and a Wealth Tax could together cost the industry over £200 million a year at 1974 prices – a sum which would account for more than a third of gross fixed capital in agriculture at that date. Financial pressures of this sort are bound to increase the damage on the rural landscape and environment. Farm buildings will be reduced in quality; there will be little incentive to use expensive, durable materials, like stone or slate.

All this is the more depressing when one considers that in Britain there is no general dislike of responsible private ownership: on the contrary most people *want* to own their own homes, and the old political slogan, 'a property-owning democracy', still has very real appeal. However, the imposition of new forms of capital taxation will inevitably result in the increase in the number of farms held on an institutional basis. And institutional landowners never have the same degree of human care, concern and control that the local farmer or landowner exercises and displays. If present trends continue the great private estate will rapidly become a thing of the past. This is certain to have a very damaging effect on the development of agriculture. Many of the great experiments of the past, the new techniques, have been conducted and perfected on the country estates. The landowner was more likely to have time, energy and resources for experimentation than an owner-occupier, whose total livelihood depended upon results, and whose resources of capital and land were often insufficient.

It is not just fiscal measures which have a depressive effect on agriculture. The effects of the Community Land Act of 1975 are potentially devastating, the central problem being one of land valuation. The development boom and the activities of the land speculators provoked widespread disquiet, and the Labour Government, elected in 1974, decided that they could both curb the speculators and advance the cause of Socialism by transferring power over land to the community. However, the Community Land Act does not give land to the community. It merely transfers power from the private owner to salaried planners and would eventually lead to the expropriation of development rights, a necessary step on the road to that public ownership of all land which remains the official policy of the Labour Party. In practice, the Community Land Act is discouraging even nationalized industries from selling their landed assets. Recently British Rail refused to negotiate the sale of a small patch of land in Staffordshire because they were apprehensive of its liability to Development Land Tax. The chances are that the Act will come to be recognized as cumbersome, almost to the point of unworkability, and a serious inhibition on those who would readily release land for necessary development. And it should not be forgotten that the sale of land at development prices did at least serve to put some badly needed capital into the industry. One thinks, for example, of Michael Watson, the owner of Rockingham Castle in Northamptonshire, selling land adjacent to Corby New Town and ploughing the money back into the development and sophistication of his estate for the benefit of farm-workers and of the local community.

With the Community Land Act on the statute books the danger is that, in areas threatened with development, land prices will slump and in safe areas will increase. The result would be that the ordinary farmer, whose farm was purchased at use value, would find the money received inadequate to meet the cost of a new farm of an equivalent quality in a 'safe' area. The landlord –

45

tenant relationship will also be disturbed by these latest moves, and by the Government's recently produced and well-motivated legislation to ensure the transfer of a tenancy from father to son. With the owner-occupying farmer being the only one to gain significantly from any concessions on Capital Transfer Tax, the temptation will always be to take a farm in hand when it becomes vacant, rather than to let it out again. Therefore, the landowner able to take a more detached and 'global' view of his holding will be obliged instead to concentrate almost exclusively on the actual business of farming. When one bears in mind how much the moulding of the landscape is owed to the great estate, one can hardly feel confident that the changes will benefit the future appearance of the countryside. Another Government-inspired change that will also have some effects on the balance of farming is the legislation designed to abolish the 'tied cottage'. Lurking behind all these measures, and the changes they are likely to effect, is the fear in the landlord's mind – and in the owner-occupier's, too – that land nationalization is next. This fear undermines such sense of stability and security as remains in agriculture, and the man who does not feel secure is unlikely to allow considerations for the landscape and the environment to loom large in his thinking.

The effects of this attitude of mind have already been noticed in forestry. It takes many years for a tree to mature, a long time to wait for any financial reward to accrue from its translation into timber. The unsympathetic treatment which private forestry has received from successive governments since the War has hardly given heart to those who wish to retain our English woodlands, so many of them planted 200 or more years ago, so many of them attached to our great estates. It is true that the Forestry Commission has begun to temper its policy of relying entirely on quick-growth softwoods and to plant a few hardwoods, at least on the fringes of its plantations. But the traditional contribution of English deciduous tree, copse and woodland to the landscape is certainly at risk, and it is doubtful whether the devastations of Dutch Elm disease, which by the beginning of the summer of 1977 had killed an estimated 9 million trees (roughly 30 per cent of the total original elm population), will ever be adequately compensated for, especially as uncertainty generated by fiscal threats has led to a substantial reduction in private planting. In 1976, for instance, there was a 40 per cent reduction and, in the same year, 2 million trees were

The gentle woodlands: autumn in the Buckinghamshire woods near
Turville *A. F. Kersting*

destroyed in nurseries. According to Lord Taylor, then Chairman of the Forestry Commission, in an article in *The Times*, this was because of the lack of confidence in the private sector. And it is not just the elms that are vulnerable to disease. In the summer of 1977 the English papers carried disturbing reports, not only of disease-afflicted cypresses in Italy but of sooty bark disease affecting increasing numbers of sycamores in the southern part of Britain, of beech bark disease on the chalk downlands. There is every reason in the future, therefore, not only to thank those who had the foresight and the imagination to create the landscape that we enjoy, but also to put pressure on Government to encourage those in a position to do so to plant for the beauty of the future.

Farming has always tended to be a traditional occupation and vocation. Those who have lived on the land, and loved the land, have wanted nothing more than for their sons to succeed them. This has applied to all levels and stages of farming. Unless current trends are reversed and Governments make a more determined effort to give back to farmers the sense that their efforts will be rewarded by a chance of continuing a tradition, the danger is that the philosophy of the quick return will inevitably dominate the agricultural deliberations where two or three farmers are gathered together. If this is the case, the alteration and deterioration of the landscape will inevitably continue. For personal commitment and loyalty would be more difficult to sustain, and all the efforts of statutory bodies, be they countryside commissions or nature conservancy interests, or an independent organization like the National Trust, would be able to do little more than ensure the preservation of pockets of traditional England – quaint museum-like reminders of what the countryside used to be.

Chapter Three

The Country House and the Great Estate

A nation's history is nowhere more arrestingly or poetically told than in its buildings. Most of our old towns, and far too many of our villages, have been disfigured, and the ever more protective and comprehensive legislation designed to preserve the best of the past has often come too late. Over the last few years there has been an increasing realization of what not only Britain, but Europe, has lost, and the determination to rescue what remains was most graphically underlined by the designation of 1975 as European Architectural Heritage Year. Much was achieved during that year to stimulate public awareness of dangers to the architectural heritage and some splendid rescue projects were launched. However, 1975 also brought sharply into focus – in the midst of public debate on Capital Transfer Tax and Wealth Tax – the problems facing one of our two most important groups of historic buildings: the country house.

These houses are a special public possession for it is in them and in our churches that we perhaps come closest to the soul and spirit of England. Germany has its castles, France its châteaux, Italy its villas and England its country houses. They are a unique and gentle blend of the craftsman's art and rural beauty, filled with the familiar acquisitions of generations: the collections of the dilettanti; the library of the local scholar-statesman; the domestic accumulations which themselves give a living commentary on men and manners through the centuries. Set in their spacious parklands and often containing priceless collections,

49

our country houses are part of the very fabric of our civilization.

Many of them, of course, have disappeared. One of the most spine-chilling experiences of recent years was to look into the Hall of Disaster in 'The Destruction of the English Country House' exhibition at the Victoria and Albert Museum in 1974, and to see, to the accompaniment of the appropriate 'noises off', the roll-call of the demolition men: 1000 houses, many of them outstanding, destroyed in the last hundred years – some 250 since the end of the Second World War. No one could suggest that every demolition was a national calamity, but equally no one could emerge from that exhibition without a sense of loss and a determination that the remaining treasures must be kept. And much does remain. There is no county without some houses in which it can take pride, but their survival depends upon their owners' ability to maintain them.

In spite of the valiant efforts of some local authorities alone or – as at Shugborough (Staffordshire) or Tatton (Cheshire) – in conjunction with the National Trust, the rescue potential of the ratepayers' representatives is of necessity strictly limited, as is that of Government. And it should be pointed out that the National Trust, one of the greatest of our national societies, cannot contemplate the cost of taking over more houses unless their owners are able adequately to endow them, and adequately in 1978 means a very large sum of money indeed. Thus, if the country house is not to become a rare and isolated architectural peculiarity, owners must be given every encouragement to remain servantless at the end of draughty corridors, guardians of much that is finest in our heritage.

These owners could more properly be called stewards or trustees. Their special position, and the importance of what they hold in trust for the nation, has been increasingly recognized since the end of the First World War, which marked the end of the great era of country-house living. As early as 1923 the National Trust was urging the Chancellor of the Exchequer to introduce legislation whereby the owners of historic buildings could receive tax concessions to enable them to meet the high cost of maintenance. In 1934 at the Annual Meeting of the National Trust, the Marquess of Lothian called on the Trust to extend its protecting arm in a definite and considered manner to the historic country houses of England. Characteristic of this country and unrivalled in any other, they were, he said, under sentence of death by taxation and Estate Duty.

Little was done, however, to assist their owners until the end of the Second World War, when many of the houses, having been requisitioned for national use during hostilities, stood in desperate need of repair. A realization that this unique English phenomenon was in danger of extinction led Sir Stafford Cripps to appoint the Gowers Committee. Its famous Report was published in 1950, and it signalled a new awareness of the importance of the country house to our heritage. As with most reports, many of the recommendations were ignored, but the Historic Buildings Council was set up and since 1953 grants have been made to the owners of country houses – grants which have often helped to save a house for the nation. One comes again to the phrase 'for the nation', because we are not discussing the distribution of public funds to wealthy individuals. It is for the nation that these houses must be saved. We will come to a detailed analysis of the problems facing owners in Chapter Four, but at the outset it is important to recognize that the country house is just that because it is surrounded by estate and parkland. That parkland, too, is of considerable importance to our national heritage. Indeed, it is arguable that much of what is best in our English countryside has remained unspoilt only because of the existence of the great country estate. For without the estates, there would be little parkland and few sweeping vistas. The works of the great landscape architects of the eighteenth century would be but a memory evoked in old views of 'gentlemen's seats'. The landowner with 2000 or 3000 acres or more is able to take a slightly more detached view than the ordinary farmer; is able to retain hedgerows and clumps of trees despite a possible reduction in short-term productivity or profitability.

This is something that is not readily grasped even by many of those who appreciate the architectural worth of the houses themselves. These well-meaning preservationists, primarily interested as they are in architectural history or works of art, tend to have little knowledge or experience of the realities of estate economy. What they do not recognize is that giving special legislative protection to the building is a hollow gesture, unless the land and estate surrounding it, and without which its owner could not maintain it, is similarly protected. There must be very careful provision, too, for inheritance, for the problems of the country house are not only fiscal, but physical. The owner has to do more and more physical work for himself, with the result that a large country house is no place for elderly people: hence the need to be able to hand on to the next generation – and the next generation will need just as much income, and probably more, than at present.

What becomes immediately apparent to anyone who starts to look into the question is that no one quite knows how many houses there are. Of course, we all know of the great ones – Chatsworth and Blenheim, Woburn and Longleat – but although they are of outstanding importance and must at all costs be preserved, they give a very unrepresentative picture of the country-house scene. To save them and to allow the hundreds of smaller houses, often unknown beyond their immediate locality, to fall into disrepair, or worse, would be to change and impoverish the English countryside. It would be similar to maintaining Canterbury, Lincoln and a dozen of our greatest cathedrals, but at the same time allowing the vast majority of our ancient parish churches to fall into disuse, decay and ruin. The tragedy is that such a thing could happen without the public being aware of it.

Awareness would certainly bring protest, for in 1976 15 million visits were made to historic houses in this country, 11 million of them to houses and grounds in private ownership. About 15 per cent of the visitors came from overseas – and Britain's tourist industry is now the single most important earner of foreign currency. But the vast majority, 85 per cent, were ordinary British people, most of them seeking escape from the grime of old industrial towns, or from the grim uniformity of the new. They came seeking to enjoy themselves in pleasant rural surroundings, to stimulate their imagination and their taste by looking at beautiful buildings and the lovely, interesting objects within them. In 1975, well over a million of these visitors petitioned Parliament to ensure that these houses could remain open.

In his report on the English country house, *Country Houses in Britain – Can They Survive?* (1974), John Cornforth suggested that there are probably 1500 country houses in the United Kingdom of which about 1000 could be considered notable and of historic and architectural importance. Of these about 430 were, in 1973, still in private hands and not regularly open to the public. About 152 were privately owned and open, and about 95 belonged to the National Trust or the National Trust for Scotland. Some 40 belong to the Department of the Environment and to local authorities and most of these are open to the public, and about 225 are adapted for various uses: schools, offices, trade union headquarters, flats and other private and public institutional purposes. These figures in themselves are slightly misleading for, of those 430 houses privately owned and not listed as being open, many are the focus of local activity, regularly accessible to local people. Many, too, are open to the public on numerous occasions during the year, often with the proceeds of the day going to some national or local charity. Furthermore, a number of new houses open their doors on a regular basis each year, and it is a condition of a major grant from the Historic Buildings Council that the public should have reasonable access to these properties.

Michael Watson, owner of Rockingham Castle in Northamptonshire, which dates back in parts to the time of William the Conqueror, sees his home as 'an active country house performing its rôle in every sense, rather than just a show piece'. Almost all the owners of country houses see their properties like this, and it is important if we are to put the issue in perspective to look at the rôle of the typical country house.

Rockingham is in many respects typical. The house has withstood the changes of fashion and the ravages of war, and now stands on its hill in Northamptonshire, a pleasing blend of medieval, Tudor and post Civil War architecture. It suffered considerably in that war and was altered fairly extensively inside in the nineteenth century. It is not a vast house, not in the same league as Chatsworth, Castle Howard, Blenheim or the other great ducal palaces, but to enter between its twin round towers, to walk through its hall or along its long gallery, or to survey the shires from its tower, is to absorb a vast panorama of English history. And its changes in structure and internal design reflect the changing tastes of generations of owners who have sought to make it more comfortable for themselves and their families. Its furnishings are fascinating but homely, its portraits and country pictures interesting, in some cases lovely, but in no case of outstanding national importance. Yet no one could argue that England would not be the poorer if the Reynolds or the Marshalls or the lovely Zoffany in the long gallery, or the intriguing portrait of Elizabeth I in the great hall, were lost to the nation. Every year 30,000 people or more enjoy its sense of timelessness and its tranquil domestic beauty and they can wander through the surrounding parkland. The parkland is important, not only to the house and its setting, but because this is the centre of an important agricultural holding, an estate that includes the village of Rockingham itself and over 4000 acres of agricultural land. The castle is very much the centre of a living community. If it were sold and its contents dispersed, the land bought by some pension fund or industrial organization – the most likely fate – and the houses in the village were sold off, the whole area would be considerably the poorer.

The owner of Rockingham does not live in any regal splendour. When he inherited the property in 1967 he faced a number of problems, not the least of which was an annual deficit of between £5000 and £10,000 on the running of the estate. But some £250,000 had been spent during the previous twenty years, some £85,000 on the maintenance of the castle alone. This money was mainly raised by the sale of land to the new town of Corby on the fringe of the present estate, and he has now been able to produce a small credit balance, though opening the castle to the public merely covers the cost of employing gardeners to keep the grounds in trim.

Rockingham seems a happy community in which villagers take considerable interest in their work and in their surroundings. The shooting on the estate is run on the basis of a co-operative with workers participating in both the sport and the maintenance, and they are able to shoot at specified times without restriction.

The attitude of the family to their visitors, most of whom are from the surrounding areas, is that each is a guest and should be treated as such. There is no desire here to commercialize. Indeed, if there were it would probably fail, for it is doubtful whether Rockingham could ever become a great national attraction. Northamptonshire, however, does not abound in museums or places where people can spend an enjoyable, inexpensive day in pleasant rural surroundings, and Rockingham serves a more than useful purpose for those who wish to spend their half-days or Sundays there during the six-month season when the house is open. Michael Watson and his wife, who run the place with the aid of a caretaker and three daily helps, see themselves as very much part of the continuing pattern of the Rockingham story. They have no desire for great riches and certainly will not achieve them, but they have a sense both of history and of stewardship and a genuine love of their area and its people.

So it is with many of the less famous country houses. They

54

stand, often at the end of tree-lined avenues, or on small promontories like Rockingham, up and down the land, centres of local feeling and patriotism and very often 'lungs' for nearby industrial towns. A glance through the list of those open to the public in 1978 reveals an astonishing spread of treasures for people to enjoy: architectural, artistic and rural. Each one is very much the centre of its own local community. Forgetting the large and the dominating, the loss of this random selection of relatively unknown houses which most people will never have seen would be seriously to impoverish the areas in which they lie and would create a local sense of deprivation.

Lincolnshire is a good example of a sparsely populated county with few nationally famous buildings except its supreme cathedral, no important national museum, and yet a number of interesting and some important houses. Houses like Marston Hall, near Grantham, home of the Thorolds since the fourteenth century, smaller than it once was but still a lovely blend of Tudor stone, with family portraits inside, a magnificent painted bedroom (brought from another family home) and a wonderful fireplace in what is left of the great hall, reduced by an earlier generation. Belton House, again near Grantham, certainly qualifies as a great house in its architectural splendour – it has been attributed to Christopher Wren – and the importance and beauty of its contents: magnificent Grinling Gibbons carvings, family portraits by Reynolds, and works by Titian, Rembrandt, and Canaletto, Van Dyck and Tintoretto. There is a remarkable seventeenth-century bed and some fine and rare silver, including the famous wine cistern presented to Speaker Cust. This exceptional house is well known by connoisseurs but only twenty thousand people visit it each year and its geographical location is such that the number is unlikely to increase beyond fifty thousand.

Yorkshire, too, is famous for its houses, but few will have heard of Bramham Park, near Wetherby. No one knows who the architect was, although both Gibbs and Archer (the most likely) have been suggested. It was built between 1668 and 1710 and is a fine example of a Queen Anne country mansion. It contains one of Kneller's portraits of Queen Anne presented to the first Lord Bingley, her Lord Chamberlain, whose descendants still live there.

Travelling from one end of the country to the other, one thinks of Braemore House, near Fordingbridge in Hampshire, built by William Doddington and completed in 1583. It is a typical Elizabethan country house with some fine Brussels tapestries and Queen Anne furniture. As with Rockingham, there are no outstanding national treasures, although it does contain one of the earliest seventeenth-century English carpets, and Sir Westrow Hulse, who lives there, has gone to great trouble creating a countryside museum for the exhibition of rural arts and agricultural machinery.

The visitor to Dorset can go to Smedmore, an early seventeenth-century house with a later façade, fine panelling and plasterwork, and examples of the Dutch minor masters. In Oxfordshire, there is Rousham House, a Royalist garrison in the Civil War, which was remodelled by William Kent in 1738. Kent redecorated it although the house does contain some seventeenth-century panelling and an original staircase. There are 150 paintings, mostly portraits, some good furniture and porcelain and a collection of miniatures by the great Samuel Cooper. Outside is an example of the first phase of English landscape gardens, remaining almost as Kent left it, one of the few gardens of that date to have escaped alteration.

These are just a few examples, but to select any is invidious. It is not suggested that they are more important than that considerable number of more famous houses like Burghley, Stratfield Saye, Holkham, Haddon (perhaps the most perfect house in all England) and Melbourne Hall in Derbyshire with its glorious gardens and exquisite furniture. Each is an integral part of the fabric of its own landscape and of the history of its corner of England.

Landscape is important to almost every one of these houses but, throughout this century, parks have been disappearing year by year in an unrecorded recession as towns have extended, mines been sunk, gravel worked and as farming has become more intensive. Every landscape park is obviously in some danger because of its age. Capability Brown began his work in about 1750, Repton died nearly a hundred and seventy years ago, and the great majority of the parks that have survived were in fact planted during the second half of the eighteenth century. Many are now past their prime because far too frequently succeeding generations have merely enjoyed what their ancestors planned for them without ensuring continuity by planting for themselves. Cirencester is the outstanding example of a park with a continual process of planting but, unfortunately, it is a rare example.

It is not that those who came after the innovators were particularly lax or negligent, but for the first hundred years or so no replanting was necessary and the price of hardwoods took away much of the incentive either to fell or to plant, while growing taxation discouraged landowners from looking ahead. Over the last generation attitudes have changed and a number of parks have been replanted, but it is an expensive process. Even the tree guards which have to be put around every sapling, especially in a deer park, cost upwards of £20 each. And, of course, apart from natural dangers of storm and tempest, such as the gales of January 1976, there is the twentieth-century problem of personal and corporate vandalism. Perhaps the most frightening examples of official corporate vandalism are the proposals for a by-pass and motorway through the superb Capability Brown parks at Petworth, Sussex, and at Chillington, Staffordshire, respectively. At Chillington, permission was given for the motorway almost immediately after the park had been declared a conservation area by the county council.

Landscapes are also at risk from taxation, for such exemptions from Capital Transfer Tax and Wealth Tax as may be granted to historic houses and their contents may not be extended to the parks themselves, even though they must stand or fall together. And landscapes are not graded like buildings according to their importance, or listed and protected. It is true that the Historic Buildings Council can now make grants towards the preservation of land attached to historic buildings, and under the 1974 Town and Country Amenities Act, grants can be given for the upkeep of 'deer garden or other land' which is of outstanding interest. But the funds are already stretched and it is unlikely that more than a handful of gardens can be helped.

As financial pressures mount it is hard to imagine how many owners will resist the temptation to amalgamate parkland with farms so as to make the land more productive and maximize profits. The plough and the tree-saw threaten, and we can only hope that some enlightened Government will allow owners to make a covenant not to alter the landscape and to allow some public access, and that in return they will be granted tax relief for maintenance and grant aid for repair and renewal.

It is a sobering thought that more houses are now under siege than at any time since the Civil War, though the weapons menacing them are fiscal rather than military.

Chapter Four

The Country House under Siege

The bleak prospect in 1978 for those who treasure our country houses and what they represent and embody is that there will be almost none in private hands by the turn of the century unless positive action is taken by the Government to help owners with maintenance. If it is thought desirable that they should survive, and if it is accepted that the cheapest way of ensuring their survival as interesting, lively, living-places is to allow their owners to carry on as stewards, then action on the part of the Government is needed. Perhaps we could follow the French example where owners of the more important houses are able to claim tax relief equal to 50 per cent of their expenditure on major repairs and the whole of their annual expenditure on maintenance. For in this country the burden is now a heavy one. As has been mentioned previously, to the weight of income and company taxation has been added the Capital Transfer Tax.

Country houses and works of art accessible to the public will be granted a degree of exemption from Capital Transfer Tax, but the fact remains that houses and contents cannot survive without the estates that sustain them. Only the land which the owner works himself as a farmer will benefit from the April 1976 additional Capital Transfer Tax concessions. This means that much of the estate will be taxed, or face crippling tax on transfer. And still in the wings lurks the threat of a Wealth Tax which would probably be levied along the same lines as Capital Transfer Tax – at the best. All this is not to mention the fact that repairs to historic buildings, far from qualifying for tax relief, *are liable* to Value Added Tax at 8 per cent.

'We have slaved for twenty years to rehabilitate this house, to make it an attraction to the public. We have lived in acute discomfort during that time and I am just not prepared to carry on if there is no chance whatsoever of my child inheriting.' Thus speaks the owner of an important, but not nationally famous, house in Yorkshire. And perhaps the problems facing owners can best be studied from specific examples.

Chillington Hall in Staffordshire stands on the same site as the home of the Giffards for the last eight hundred years. The present house dates in part from the early eighteenth century, but is largely the work of Sir John Soane and is one of his most notable houses. The Hall is the focal point of an agricultural and forestry estate of some 4000 acres. Without the estate the house could not continue as a private home. The present owner, Peter Giffard, who succeeded to the estate in 1972, pointed out in a memorandum to the Select Committee on the Wealth Tax that because of the size of the house and many of the rooms, and because of the architectural features, the cost of living in a house such as Chillington must always exceed the cost of living in any house of ordinary size. To keep it moderately warm he

The product of one civilisation threatened by the product of another: Capability Brown's magnificent pool at Chillington, Staffordshire, which may soon have a motorway within half a mile *Peter Giffard*

needs 5000 gallons of heating oil per year; in a small farmhouse where he lived before he inherited he used 700 gallons. In his former home it took three hours to clean the windows; at Chillington, it takes a hundred.

It follows that if owners like Peter Giffard are to continue to live in and be responsible for houses like Chillington they must, of necessity, have incomes sufficient to support them. Chillington has received a number of grants from the Historic Buildings Council towards the cost of restoration, but even with this help the cost of maintenance is a very heavy burden. In his memorandum Peter Giffard stated that all the income not required for payment of wages, interest and other outgoings has been spent on repairs and improvements to various buildings on the estate. The majority of the farms have had at least one new building, and the cottages and houses have been modernized at the rate of three or four a year over the last decade. These improvements have been financed out of private resources, but those are now exhausted and their source – the sale of some outlying parts of the estate – is exhausted likewise. Future improvements must be financed out of income or borrowing and there are no liquid resources from which to pay any annual capital tax.

Since Peter Giffard submitted his memorandum to the Wealth Tax Committee there have been welcome signs of recognition of the problems he outlined. In the 1976 Finance Act the Chancellor introduced a clause to give some relief from Capital Transfer Tax to maintenance funds for historic houses. However, the gesture, whilst establishing a useful precedent, proved to be a hollow one. Any owner wishing to take advantage of the scheme had to set up a special maintenance fund; the capital placed in the fund would be irretrievable, and any family falling on hard times would be unable to reclaim the residue. The fund could not be used for the maintenance of important chattels and any income from it would be liable for tax. The fund itself would come under the 'perpetuities rule' and would have to be wound up and given to charity after eighty years. The disadvantages of this scheme – a year later no one had sought to take advantage of it – were in turn recognized during the passage of the 1977 Finance Act, when a provision was introduced whereby tax on the income from maintenance funds was reduced to 50 per cent. Even so, the combination of the scheme's complexity and the existence of the perpetuities rule mean that few owners will be able to avail themselves of this latest concession. Indeed, unless relief is more far-reaching the problems will continue to be daunting, and as long as the threat of a Wealth Tax remains no owner can look to the future with any degree of certainty or confidence. More sensitive and flexible arrangements must be made if owners like Peter Giffard are to be encouraged to remain to struggle with their inheritance. For, as he demonstrated in his memorandum, one of the greatest problems facing most land-owners is that they often have little in the way of liquid assets. Therefore, unless their burdens are relieved, they will be left with little alternative but to forsake their homes and dispose of the contents. It would certainly be no adequate solution merely to exempt a building like Chillington and its contents from additional taxes, for house and estate must stand together and at the moment they stand at risk.

For the purpose of the rating valuation it is unlettable, as the valuer has to determine what rent it could command as a private dwelling-house on the open market. How many people could contemplate becoming the tenant of Chillington Hall? If, therefore, it is to survive there must be sufficient income from the remainder of the estate to discharge responsibilities for up-keep. The outcry would certainly be long and loud if this oasis, seven miles from Wolverhampton, and many more miles from the nearest similar collection in public hands, were to vanish.

There is a clear appreciation of this type of situation among those responsible for encouraging and promoting tourism. At the time of the Wealth Tax debates in the summer of 1975, the Director of the Heart of England Tourist Board wrote to the Chancellor: 'It is clear that by encouraging country house own-ers to retain and properly maintain their property, and to allow public access to it, a great deal more recreational resources, and a great many more works of art and fine craftsmanship would be available to the British people than in any other way. An empty shell is far less attractive than the ensemble of the building, its grounds and its contents, and often also the continued association of its historical owners.'

The latter point was well brought out in the Victoria and Albert's exhibition: 'The Destruction of the English Country House'. The original social and economic function of the country house, as the centre of rural life, activity and industry, may have largely ceased, but the exhibition stressed the beauty of the phenomenon as a whole – house, park, furnishings, community –

and how much would be lost if only the building survived, perhaps converted to some institutional use, or even retained as a lifeless museum. That such museums are often lifeless can be seen by anyone who visits Aston Hall in Birmingham. There the local authority has done its best to preserve and maintain an outstandingly fine Jacobean house, but almost all the original contents have gone and the life of the building with them. Drab rooms and sparse furnishings are a poor substitute, and uniformed attendants, however polite and helpful, seem very out of place in a domestic setting.

One cannot help but contrast Aston Hall with places like Weston Park on the Shropshire/Staffordshire border, some twenty miles away. To visit both of these historic houses in a day is a sobering experience. One leaves Aston Hall depressed at what has been lost, though grateful for what has been saved; one leaves Weston Park desperately anxious that what is there should remain. For Weston is not only a house but a home, containing beautiful furniture, one of the best collections of Van Dycks in private hands, fine porcelain, silver, tapestry – all perfectly maintained and in bright, spacious surroundings. In 1977, 170,000 people visited Weston. Almost all of them toured the house and to judge from their comments found the experience refreshing. If Weston closed, the Midlands would be much the poorer, even if every object of interest from the house were crammed into one museum or another.

The problems facing all owners are similar, but it is often mistakenly thought that the larger the house the securer the future. That this is not necessarily the case was very forcibly brought home by the Earl of March, owner of Goodwood House in Sussex, in an article in the *Daily Telegraph*, 3 October 1974.

The urgency of the present situation arises from a combination of rising costs and increasing taxation, existing and proposed. The really fundamental problem has always been with us, the sheer size of many of these houses whether or not families are still living in them, or whether they are in reality museums and used for some other purpose. The size and number of the rooms still requires a basic minimum amount of cleaning, heating and light for the place to be habitable and to prevent deterioration, and those wages, fuel and electricity bills have been rising faster than ever before over the last two years. Then there are the repairs and maintenance to the building which in an old house

The Earl of March sits in an empty room, demonstrating the devastating effect taxation could have at Goodwood *The Earl of March*

is regularly necessary . . . We are not simply trying to hang on to the house and its contents and live in it for our own benefit and enjoyment, we are endeavouring to share it with others and help them to gain as much pleasure and reward from doing so as we do . . . The number of staff we employ is entirely dictated by the size of the house, is mainly taken up with the maintenance of the house and the collection, rather than caring for personal needs . . . I never feel that I am the owner – only a steward for my lifetime, and not principally for the benefit of the family but for the whole community.

The Goodwood statistics are certainly formidable. The house has 9 major state rooms not occupied by the family, and 20 bedrooms, plus 26 rooms used as offices and 5 smaller reception rooms used by the family, and all this despite the fact that 30 rooms were demolished in 1969. The total cost of the house, excluding the direct cost of opening it to the public, is measured in tens of thousands of pounds a year, for which the gardens, electricity, heating and cleaning account for three-quarters of the total. At Goodwood, the broad distribution of assets is 50 per cent land and cottages, 45 per cent furniture and paintings and only 5 per cent Stock Exchange securities. Thus the gross return, before charging any costs on 95 per cent of the assets is very small – about 1½ per cent.

Lord March obviously feels a very special responsibility towards all those who live or work on the estate and there is a special written housing policy in which it is stated that, provided circumstances do not drastically change, the company will continue to offer a house for the rest of their lives to pensioners and their wives who have occupied company (estate) houses. In the house itself, every major work of art is available for public view and access to scholars is always granted, whatever the time of year. However, the struggle to maintain the collection is an uphill one and, since 1970, three pictures have been sold, 50 per cent of the proceeds going to the Treasury. But, in recent years, only one painting and that of historic rather than artistic value, has been added to the collection. To show the dramatic and devastating effect a wealth tax would have on the contents of the house, Lord March stripped a room bare in the summer of 1975 and asked his visitors whether they approved of the results. They did not.

In Yorkshire one can see the problem facing the owner of a house of middle rank by going to Burton Constable. Though not the most famous Yorkshire house, it is a great Elizabethan mansion and the contents, though not of Woburn or Chatsworth standard, are fine, too; there is much original Chippendale furniture. It had been virtually derelict for a generation and John Chichester Constable and his wife have struggled over the last fifteen years, with the aid of the Historic Buildings Council restoration grants, to make it an enjoyable place for people to visit from Hull and the surrounding countryside. That they do find it enjoyable is proved by the fact that 70,000 visitors come every year. But as with any vast house, there are constantly recurring problems of roof leakage, dry rot, and all the other accompanying ills that affect ancient buildings. The chances of the Chichester Constables being able to maintain the struggle during the next decade would be very remote if additional taxes were imposed. As another owner said: 'Even with the grant the cost of borrowing the 50 per cent that remains is almost impossible to find.'

One thing that emerges very clearly from studying the remarks of owners is how deeply they feel their sense of responsibility, but how pessimistic many of them are. As Michael Watson of Rockingham put it: 'By drawing on the moral responsibility that we feel for our inheritance, the Government has in us, the owners, the cheapest caretakers, but they must be in no doubt that if the pressures become too great many of us, particularly the younger ones, will not be prepared to sit it out.'

What also emerges very graphically in any study of the English country house is the way owners do struggle against adversity and in much discomfort to rescue what is in danger. Burton Constable furnishes an admirable example of this. Brympton D'Evercy in Devon another. There the contents of the house were sold to pay death duties and the house was then let to a school. The present owners managed to remove the school – which had not paid the rent – and they are turning the house back into a home.

> We, ourselves, decorated the seven state rooms open to the public and by furnishing the rooms with the few pictures that remained, along with a few purchases, we have managed to get the house back some of the way to what it looked like. But we have gone against all the advice of trustees and solicitors trying to keep the house in one piece. We know the place cannot be sold – the probate was put at £4000 – or let – the school could not find its rent for the last six years. The local authority already have one property in ruins and certainly would not like to be landed with another. We cannot pull the house down since it is scheduled Grade 1. I feel very strongly that unless we make the effort the house has no future. As it is we know we are running against the tides of time and will probably be the last generation to live here – but if we don't try no one else will.

What comes out time and time again in the words of those who own these houses is the fact that their visitors 'seem to enjoy seeing round a house that is well and truly lived in'; equally clear is the fact that so many owners cannot afford any living-in, or in some cases even daily, help. 'In the winter we cannot afford to heat the three rooms with the wonderful ceilings. The garden was lovely but now instead of a full-time gardener and a pensioner we just have a pensioner for four hours a day.'

Many owners have turned in despair to the National Trust, but often to no avail, as one rather desperately wrote:

> I tried to give the castle to the National Trust for Scotland but they said they would need an endowment of £80,000 which we could not provide, so now if we are taxed out of the house we have no option but to try and sell it, or take the roof off. We are

very pleased to show it to the public but no one could say it was a paying proposition as they cause a lot of wear and tear. I am not really complaining but if one is not allowed enough of an income to keep it up what good is it going to be to posterity? We come under the heading of unearned income but I feel we should get tax relief to heat and repair the house.

Another struggling owner writes: 'Every visitor without exception has been an ordinary town and country person and this is a point never taken by those who want to destroy our heritage. We have had fishermen, firemen, labourers, farmers and one man arrived last Sunday from the East End of London. He had cycled here (70 miles).' And from another letter: 'Nearly everybody comments on the completely different atmosphere of a house that is virtually a museum, and the general comment is that this one feels alive and much more interesting.'

The constantly repeated theme is one of public enjoyment and it is undeniable that museums, and particularly provincial museums with their scanty resources and almost complete lack of national financial support, are unprepared to take a flood of works of art when any such house closes. 'It is folly to attempt to foist a national responsibility on to local authorities' shoulders without preparation or calculation of the consequences,' wrote the Director of the Brighton Art Gallery and Museum in *The Times* in 1975, 'nor can I believe that my fellow curators would welcome acquisitions, however magnificent, that had been acquired at such a cost. English country houses and collections are entities far more coveted and of historical significance and it should be the national policy to preserve them as entities.'

Perhaps the greatest attribute of country houses is the opportunity they give to countless visitors to see and enjoy works of art amid pleasant surroundings, and this at a time when even national museums find it impossible to display many of the treasures that they already have. This makes it the more tragic that current tax laws act as a positive disincentive to owners to make the architectural heritage more widely accessible to the public. Only about twenty-five of the greater houses, such as Woburn and Longleat, are treated like other leisure industries and allowed to set the cost of maintenance against tax. Other houses open to the public are only allowed to set the actual cost of opening – guides, guide books, etc. – against income. Things are ordered differently in France where the more a

Leeds Castle in Kent, newly opened to the public *Country Life*

A great house saved: the east front of Erddig, one of the most recent acquisitions of the National Trust, remarkable for its contents, but in very poor structural condition when the Trust accepted it *National Trust*

building is open to the public, the more the cost of running it can be set against tax. In 1974, in the Province of Auvergne alone, more than sixty houses opened to the public for the first time. In Britain, in 1975, Architectural Heritage Year, eighty-five fewer historic gardens were opened than in the previous year. It is, nevertheless, encouraging to note that the last two years have seen the opening for the first time of a number of houses of great importance: Leeds Castle in Kent; Drumlanrig, Dumfriesshire; Plas Newydd, Anglesey; Houghton, Norfolk; Boughton in Northamptonshire; Chicheley, Buckinghamshire; Pencarrow, Cornwall; Erdigg, North Wales; Carlton Towers, Yorkshire; Mompesson House, Wiltshire; and Hatch Court, Somerset – to name just a few of the most magnificent.

But even the greatest show places have their difficulties. At Woburn, perhaps the most outstanding example of a great country house and popular attendant attractions, to which almost $\frac{3}{4}$ million people go each year, there are still problems. In a place that costs £400 a time to clean the windows, £2000 a year in material alone to maintain the wall around the park, £10,000 on heating, and where some 250 people are directly employed for most of the year, there is no overall profit shown.

Even the Game Park, the biggest single attraction, does not pay its way, although obviously it is of value in bringing visitors to the estate.

The picture, however, is not one of unrelieved gloom. The Historic Buildings Council has been responsible for channelling grants of some £4 million to historic houses over the last twenty years. But grants in themselves are not enough. Sometimes, as at Stonor Park, where £60,000 of public funds were spent on maintenance and repair, the struggle was still too great and the owner had to give up. There is no certainty that the house will survive.

The story of Stonor is a melancholy illustration of what can happen to a great country house when its owner is no longer able to face the battle to maintain it. Towards the end of 1975, Lord Camoys announced that he could no longer afford to live in Stonor or keep the house open to the public as had been his intention – an intention he had planned and worked towards for over twenty years. Instead the house was to be offered for sale and the contents dispersed separately.

Stonor Park is not a Knole or a Blickling, but its surroundings are glorious. Its landscape park, now a nature reserve, contains a herd of deer which was recorded here as long ago as the fourteenth century, and its history is as romantic as any in England. The house, with its elegant Georgian façade, bears witness to almost every period of domestic English architecture. Until Lord Camoys moved out it had been occupied by his family since the twelfth century and has one of the longest unbroken records set in the male line. Its particular importance, however, is as a Catholic shrine: the chapel at Stonor is one of only three in the country where Mass has never ceased to be celebrated. It has close links with Edmund Campion, the Jesuit martyr, and the most important recusant library in existence.

Its furnishings were not original, the vast majority of the contents having been auctioned in 1938. The tragedy, however, was that after that disastrous dispersal, the late Lord Camoys, who died in March 1976, decided to refurnish and restore the house after it had been derequisitioned at the end of the War. From 1955 he pursued his aim of making it into a house that would be interesting and attractive to visitors. He spent over £100,000, to which the Historic Buildings Council of England added a further £60,000 in grants, and it was during the restoration that much evidence of so many periods of English architec-

A great house threatened: Stonor Park, for nine centuries the home of the Stonor family, vacated by Lord Camoys in January 1976, its contents dispersed and its future unknown *Alex Starkey, for Country Life*

ture came to light. What had been casually assumed to be a Georgian house was seen to have traces of every period from Norman to Gothic behind its façade. While the restoration progressed, Lord Camoys collected as many suitable furnishings as he could, including a fine collection of eighteenth-century Gothic furniture.

In 1975, however, the family's financial situation was such that he had no alternative but to put Stonor, its park and its contents up for sale. Before doing so, he had offered them to the National Trust, but the Trust could not accept this proposition without a large endowment which circumstances made it quite impossible to supply. Lord Camoys then offered the house to the Government through the Land Fund, but the Government turned this down because it has been the policy of all Governments not to take on historic houses unless they are in immediate danger of collapse or decay, or there appears to be no alternative prospect of saving them. And so, in January 1976, the sale took place and the contents were dispersed.

One would have hoped that the story of Stonor would have acted as something of a warning to those in positions of public authority, a stimulus to provide a more flexible formula for safeguarding the national heritage. But it was not so. For even while the Stonor Park episode was coming to its dismal close another, and more spectacular and disastrous saga, was beginning, unknown even to most who had the greatest concern and responsibility for our heritage.

On 30 May 1974, the sixth Earl of Rosebery died and his son faced the prospect of enormous estate duties. The sixth Earl had been a very rich man but his son could not afford, for all that he had inherited, to maintain his father's two great homes at Dalmeny and at Mentmore. And so he decided that Mentmore and its collection would have to go. By September 1974 he had begun informal discussions with the Estate Duty Office on the procedure that should be followed if Mentmore were to be offered to the nation. Mentmore, one of that extraordinary group of Rothschild mansions built within easy reach of London during the latter half of the nineteenth century, was largely unknown, even to the connoisseur. It had been the creation of Baron Mayer de Rothschild, built to the design of the Crystal Palace architect Sir Joseph Paxton, and designed to house his fabulous collection, a collection especially rich in some of the very greatest masterpieces of eighteenth-century furniture. He is alleged to have remarked that he acquired these treasures because it was cheaper to buy French eighteenth-century furniture than to go to Maples!

However, in 1974, the new Earl of Rosebery appreciated their potential attraction and significance as national assets and, following his discussions with the Estate Duty Office, made his first official approach to the Department of the Environment about a settlement in February 1975. There was no immediate or ecstatic reaction to this proposition and it was a year later, after a visit by Dr Roy Strong (who was attracted by Mentmore's potential as a further outpost, like Osterley or Ham, of the Victoria and Albert Museum), before discussions had reached a stage where a formal offer of the house and its contents could be made. This amounted to a settlement of Lord Rosebery's outstanding tax liabilities, together with payment of some £2 million. In July 1976, Lord Rosebery, concerned by official silence, asked for a response to his offer by 30 September. Apart from a visit by the Historic Buildings Council, which immediately appreciated the importance of the offer and urged its acceptance, nothing happened. It was not until the beginning of November that Mentmore received a ministerial visitation

72

from the Baroness Birk, an Under-Secretary at the Department of the Environment. But still there was silence. On 16 December, the Rosebery executors explained that if no reply was received by 12 January 1977 their offer would have to be withdrawn and the house and contents offered for sale.

In spite of this, it was not until 20 January that the Secretary of State formally rejected Lord Rosebery's offer and an announcement to this effect was made. Throughout the two-and-a-half years since the sixth Earl's death no word, either of the offer or the possible dispersal of the collection, or even of its existence, had been made public. The Department of the Environment had wanted it that way, and had discouraged Lord Rosebery from approaching any museums or other bodies. He had accepted their advice, believing that a transfer to the nation was a mere formality. Apart from the involvement of its own Historic Buildings Council, and the visit of Dr Strong, nobody of authority had been officially consulted by the Department – neither the National Trust nor the National Arts Collection Fund, nor any of the other institutions or individuals who would have had sensible comments to make, and perhaps been in a position to stimulate private patronage, if they had been aware of what was going on. It was the withdrawal of a promise of private patronage, from some still mysterious source, on which the Department now blamed the collapse of negotiations and its inability to acquire this treasure house.

Once the official rejection was announced there was immediate interest and concern, anger and frustration, expressed from many quarters. The remarkable Save Committee produced an illustrated pamphlet in a matter of days, giving some idea of the scope and importance of the Mentmore collection. The newspaper correspondence columns printed the first of a whole series of letters. The Victorian Society seethed with indignation. And the Department itself designated Mentmore a Grade 1 listed building, one of only fifteen Victorian country houses to merit that designation. The Order Papers of Lords and Commons reflected Parliamentary concern and, under mounting pressure from all these quarters, the Government indicated that it would consider the whole matter afresh if Lord Rosebery were to make a new offer, and re-open negotiations.

On 12 February I met Lord Rosebery and we worked out a scheme whereby the Government would be able to pay a major portion of the new price of some £3 million – a price which took account of inflation and the fall in value of the pound since the first offer was made – over an extended period. Already official dithering had cost over £1 million! It was not until four weeks later, on 9 March, that the Government indicated that their maximum contribution would be £1 million from the National Land Fund[1] and the further £2 million would have to be found from private sources. Another month had been lost, for Lord Rosebery fixed his new deadline for 4 April after which date the catalogues of the sale, provisionally arranged for the second half of May, would be dispatched. Understandably, he was not prepared to cancel the sale without a firm indication that the deal would go through, and Sotheby's had already been some six months in the house cataloguing the contents.

There was no time to launch a public appeal, but strenuous efforts were made by Lord Perth and others to raise the sum. All the time public attention was focused on the drama, with letters and articles in the press, and reports on radio and television. By 4 April £1 million had been promised from various sources, including £500,000 and an offer to run the place (in return for a peppercorn lease) for fifty years by Trafalgar House, owners of Cunard and the Ritz (and, more recently, of the Beaverbrook Press). On that day I succeeded in asking an emergency question in the House of Commons and was able to indicate that Lord Rosebery would give yet another extension of his deadline if the Secretary of State would agree to explore the offers and hold further meetings. This he readily agreed to, but when we all sat round his table on 5 April – ministers, potential donors and others – it was quite obvious that the whole scheme was going to founder, mainly because of the total inflexibility of the Treasury. They were represented by a civil servant, rather than a Minister, at the meeting and he had the temerity to suggest to senior ministers that the Government's oft and publicly stated offer of £1 million would itself have to be the subject of detailed negotiations: negotiations that would guarantee to sabotage any quick rescue attempt.

It was made plain at the meeting that there would be no consideration of accepting a promised interest-free loan, or of granting Lord Rosebery an indemnity so that the sale could be cancelled while an appeal was launched. Government was apparently not even prepared to take the house and its contents and to sell just one or two items to raise any shortfall. And

1. For Land Fund, see page 187.

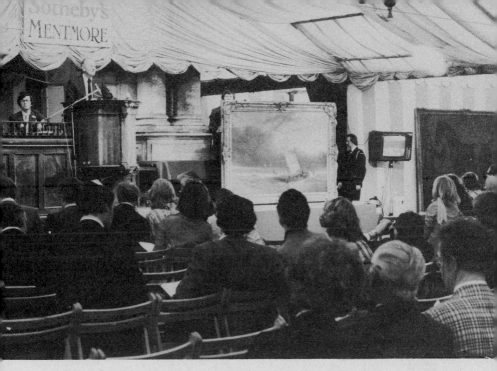

Under the hammer: the contents of a treasure house disappear *Sotheby's*

there certainly were many things that could have been sold to raise £1 million. I came away from that meeting deeply saddened, not just by the inflexibility displayed but by the total lack of imagination and vision that lay behind it.

And so, on 18 May, the sale began and it ended on 27 May after almost every record had been broken. Before the sale the Government did acquire four pieces of furniture of outstanding importance at a cost of almost £1 million, and the National Gallery was able to buy Drouais's famous portrait of the ageing Madame de Pompadour at an undisclosed sum, somewhere in the region of £300,000. This in itself represented something of a sacrifice by Lord Rosebery as the picture would have undoubtedly fetched three times as much at auction. As it was the sale raised well over £6 million, whilst the Government spent its million on acquiring a handful of objects. And when the marquees came down and the charter flights returned to Dallas and New York, and the treasures were taken away to grace the walls of American tycoons or Arab sheikhs, Mentmore stood empty and forlorn, a monument to the inadequacy of the official system which the State had erected to protect its heritage.

How much better it would have been if, having lost Stonor, the resources of the Land Fund could have been used to save Mentmore and its treasures, as they were used to save Hevingham, alas without its treasures. But neither State ownership nor a State rescue commended itself to a Government which repeatedly proclaimed itself determined never to acquiesce in the dispersal of the heritage. The truth is that vast Government departments are not geared to this sort of operation, and in the case of Mentmore the Government justified its decision on the grounds of public expenditure. But, as Lady Birk pointed out in the Lords, it will always be more economical for owners to be encouraged to remain in their own property than for Government to step in and rescue.

Local authorities, too, find their resources stretched. Tatton Park in Cheshire, which is in many ways a great success story, and is run by the Cheshire County Council in conjunction with the National Trust which owns the property, still costs the ratepayers of Cheshire £100,000 per year. How could a county like Yorkshire, still less a sparsely populated county like Norfolk, take on even half a dozen of its finest houses, if the owners departed?

One frequently hears the comment 'hand it over to the National Trust', but the Trust has repeatedly stressed, as it did to Lord Camoys, that it cannot afford to take on properties unless they are properly endowed. In 1975, in addition to Stonor, it had to turn down the offer of Arundel Castle, an important house by any standards, because the new Duke of Norfolk was unable to provide the necessary endowment. In almost every county there are similar stories of properties that the Trust has officially or unofficially been invited to take an interest in, but where the financial resources available for maintenance were insufficient for it to do so. No one could fail to marvel at the magnificent job done by the Trust and the superb and efficient and often homely way in which it runs the many properties that it now owns. The 'National Trust solution' is a good one if an owner has to go; but the key phrase here is 'if the owner has to go'. The National Trust has stated repeatedly, and especially during the last two years of financial debate, that the ideal solution is for the owner to be encouraged and, indeed, helped, to stay. Their pleas and entreaties in this regard have not fallen on deaf ears as far as the general public is concerned. This was evident from the remarkable response to the petition to Parliament organized by the Historic Houses Association during the summer of 1975,

76

which called on the Government to recognize the unique position of historic houses and the needs for special provision to be made for their survival. This petition, which was on show in most houses open to the public, was signed by 1,116,253 people, plus 200,000 from 57 overseas countries (9 from behind the Iron Curtain!). It was presented to Parliament by Mr Ted Graham, the Labour Member for Enfield/Edmonton, the first Chairman of the all-party Heritage Committee in Parliament. It was certainly the most public and probably the most successful enterprise undertaken by the Historic Houses Association.

The Association had its origins in 1966 in a committee of the British Travel Association, which in 1969 became a committee of the British Tourist Authority–the Historic Houses Committee. In those days it consisted of a small group of owners including the National Trust and the National Trust for Scotland, with an observer from the Department of the Environment. That it should have been instigated by national bodies responsible for tourism was an indication of how those entrusted with the development of this industry regarded our historic houses as one of our greatest tourist magnets.

In 1972, the Committee commissioned Mr John Cornforth to conduct an independent survey of the country houses of Britain and the problems facing their owners. This invaluable document, a mine of information for everyone interested in the country house problem, was published in October 1974 – entitled *Country Houses in Britain – Can They Survive?* By 1973, however, the Historic Houses Committee of the British Tourist Authority had been joined by a powerful new Historic Houses Association, with its own executive committee and executive secretary. It now represents over 400 owners of country houses most of which are regularly open to the public. In the spring of 1976, it launched an imaginative scheme for associate membership whereby members of the public could become 'Friends' and, in return for an annual subscription, be granted free admission to all but a handful of the houses in membership of the Association.

The Association campaigned vigorously during the debates on the Wealth Tax and Capital Transfer Tax and must indeed have been largely responsible for the detailed and unemotional arguments which led the Government to accept a number of its proposals during the passage of the Finance Act of 1975, whereby exemptions for transfer on death from the Capital Transfer Tax were granted for historic houses, their contents and surrounding land and other land of scientific or scenic interest. These exemptions were extended to lifetime gifts in the April 1976 Budget, but the criteria for determining eligibility were, according to the Chancellor, to be extremely strict.

Throughout, the Historic Houses Association has tried to make it plain that it has not been seeking preferential treatment for a selected group of people but for a selected group of properties, which not only form an integral part of our heritage but are a major source of attraction for native holiday-makers as well as tourists. Its contention, like the National Trust's, is that these houses are best and most cheaply maintained by their owners. But it has sought to demonstrate – and the Cornforth Report did this most effectively – that very few houses in private ownership make a profit from visits, and if they do, it is invariably used for restoration. The Association suggests that, with limited tax concessions, and those already granted are for this purpose too limited, more houses, particularly the smaller ones – which make up the majority – would be opened to the public and stand a much better chance of survival. Successive governments have in their halting way recognized this since Sir Stafford Cripps set up the Gowers Committee in 1950, but now the danger is that the shutters will go up in many of the finest houses during the course of the next decade as owners die, or decide that the game is not worth the candle. The Historic Houses Association has been able to show just how much more costly it would be for the nation if Government now reversed the trend of past policies and accentuated economic difficulties so that owners did give up their struggle. Even to keep a few of the more spectacular and idiosyncratic houses inevitably would be a continuing drain on public funds. Even Heveningham Hall, which the State bought through the Land Fund for £300,000, costs the tax payer £30,000 a year to maintain.

The Historic Houses Association made forceful representations to the Select Committee on the Wealth Tax and it was noticeable that the Committee in its Report took a very constructive approach to the problems facing the heritage, for instance, recommending that conditional exemption from Capital Transfer Tax and Wealth Tax should apply to maintenance funds on the same conditions as for the houses, subject to control and supervision. The Chancellor of the Exchequer made it plain that although he would not bring in a Wealth Tax during 1977 or 1978 it remained a firm item in Labour's programme, and would be introduced if that Party were returned to power again. The Association's campaign continues!

Everything therefore points to the fact that if the siege of the country house is to be lifted, Government must lift it. Some enterprising owners might find ways to stave off impending doom: some might persuade local authorities or other bodies to assist them; some might be able to afford to give their houses to the National Trust; some might be able to set up country house trusts. But the vast majority of houses, great and small, will close once and for all during the next twenty years, unless Government is prepared to give a generous measure of exemption from current fiscal burdens and to remove the threats of new ones. It is up to those in authority to decide whether the English country house is worth keeping or not. By the year 2000, the country house as we know it could either be a fond memory, or the majority of those still standing could be open and making as vigorous and as vital a contribution to the cultural and social life of the nation, and to the tourist economy, as they do today.

Chapter Five
Urban Dignity and Decay

Though there are still breathtaking exceptions, our larger towns and cities are something of a disappointment to the visitor. The city, which ought to be the highest expression of man's civilized moulding of his environment, is too often ugly, out of scale and out of sympathy with the requirements of civilized living and the demands of the cultured mind. This is not merely because of insensitive redevelopment since the Second World War. Thirty years ago, the first Lord Kennet, writing in *The Character of England* (1947), remarked that: 'The spirit of our towns is a dejected spirit . . . our countryside is a success . . . but our towns on the whole are a failure. They are not beautiful, and they are not convenient. They are not even cheap. Large sums have been wasted on them on ornament which does not beautify, and display which does not impress.'

Unfortunately, what was appropriate to an historical analysis in 1947 is even more true today. The years since the War have seen a distortion of scale and a disturbance of symmetry that has gone far to ruin such urban treasures as we had. Nowhere is this truer than in London itself. The London which replaced the city devastated by the Great Fire in 1666, enhanced and adorned by Georgian developers, was not long inviolate. So great was the havoc caused during the first confident decades of the Victorian era that the 'conservation movement' was born in the 1860s. Perhaps its first stirrings were seen in the unsuccessful attempts to save the Jacobean Northumberland House at the south-west corner of Trafalgar Square. By 1877, William Morris

81

had founded the Society for the Preservation of Ancient Buildings. This in itself was two years after the Society for Photographing Old London had been established because so many of the ancient buildings were being demolished, buildings such as the last of the sixteenth-century galleried coaching inns in the City.

The later years of the nineteenth century witnessed something of a battle between developers and conservationists, but although the developers triumphed the scale of their buildings was limited, largely by the London Building Act of 1888. This restricted the height of buildings to 80 feet, or the width of the street on which they stood, a restriction which played a crucial part in the development of London until it was removed in the 1950s. It meant, for instance, that although such glories as Nash's Regent Street, Norfolk House, Devonshire House, Grosvenor House, the eighteenth-century Grosvenor and Berkeley Squares, and the great Adelphi Terrace itself, were all replaced by impersonal and undistinguished slabs like those on Park Lane between the Dorchester and Grosvenor House, the scale of the new buildings was not so overpowering as to shadow totally such gems as remained.

During the War our enemies became the allies of those for whom age meant decay, and among the thousands of buildings destroyed was nearly a third of the City. There was thus a great excuse for those who advocated another and wider rebuilding programme. The first years after the War were years of controlled rebuilding of bombed buildings and government offices, although the meticulous and brilliant achievements of the Poles and Russians in rebuilding Warsaw and Leningrad were not emulated here. By 1954, when the building licences were removed, the bulldozers were able to encroach in force, and the last twenty years have seen a total transformation of the London scene and skyline. One has only to look at some of Canaletto's views, at nineteenth-century aquatints, or even at photographs taken up to the outbreak of the War, to realize that more has been done to alter the face of London in the last twenty years than in the previous two hundred. Although each change has brought new and more vigorous protest, the prospect is that the next ten or twenty years will see a greater transformation yet.

The conservation movement has come into its own, but for London it may well have come too late. If fifteen years ago it had been agreed to keep the centre of London low-scaled and to preserve the façades, as in Rome, Paris and Amsterdam, perhaps it would have been otherwise. As it is, while more and more battles have been successfully waged for the protection of particular buildings, the designation of conservation areas, the broad vista and the noble view have all too often been obliterated or deformed by unsightly or obtrusive new development. This transformation of the skyline has been perhaps the most unhappy feature of post-War redevelopment in London and, although the Greater London Council has made attempts to define and list views, more and more have been destroyed. And by the time the 600-foot National Westminster tower was 'topped out' in March 1977, there were well over 2000 buildings in the GLC area over 150 feet in height, and in the City alone there were fifty-five sites yet to be built on that had been deemed 'appropriate' for high buildings. However, a survey of some of the things that have happened in London might perhaps point some useful lessons for the future, and even reinforce the somewhat slender chances of success which the conservationists have in prospect.

One of the main factors in the destruction of much of London's architectural fabric has been the ease with which official bodies have been able to redevelop. For instance, in the squares of Bloomsbury, the London University bulldozers have plied remorselessly along the course laid down by Sir Leslie Martin, one of our foremost architects, in 1959. A catalogue of what has gone, and what is still threatened, makes gloomy reading, and any Rip Van Winkle returning to town after a twenty-year slumber would find himself adrift in a London he would hardly recognize! No longer could he even go into the stores that were the Mecca of so many shoppers as recently as the 1960s: no Maples, Marshall and Snellgrove, Gamages, nor Army and Navy; these and many more have either gone forever or been redeveloped.

Over thirty Victorian churches and some earlier ones, perhaps not distinguished in themselves, but local landmarks of great prominence, such as St Stephen's, Rosslyn Hill, or Holy Trinity in Bishop's Bridge Road, have been closed or demolished. The very stations where the visitor alights have, in some cases, altered beyond recognition, especially Euston. Covent Garden market has been taken across the river, and nearby there are nine separate schemes which will eventually result in the

83

removal of three-quarters of the existing buildings in Charing Cross Road, to be dominated by Town and Cities' massive tower block on the north-east corner of Cambridge Circus. These tower blocks – Warren Street, Centre Point and the grotesque one at the Elephant – dominate London and make one fear for posterity's regard for the twentieth century. They represent neither good working environments nor good planning decisions.

In 1973 Christopher Booker wrote that: 'It seems that the tide of conservationism has now broken through to become a major factor in shaping London's future.' Certainly things have been done to arrest the onward march of the developer. In Covent Garden extra buildings have been listed – a quadrupling of the old list of eighty-two, of which forty-eight were threatened with demolition. The scheme for Piccadilly Circus has been delayed, while the City of Westminster Council seeks a greater degree of public participation. And in general, it is harder to get schemes passed by more vigilant local authorities.

But the difficulties facing the conservationists were well illustrated in August 1975, during the saga of Tedworth Square. The Cadogan Estates sold large parts of the Square, and the nort-east side was due for demolition. The Kensington and Chelsea Planning Committee put the houses into the Royal Hospital conservation area and the GLC backed their plans. Unfortunately, the Council mislaid the GLC's reply and during the intervening altercations over what could and could not be done before specific committees had had their official meetings, the demolition men moved in and were only partially restrained by the concerted efforts of the residents.

Local authorities within the Greater London area have varying reputations.[1] Sometimes the same local authority is both guilty of enormity and also responsible for achievement. One would have thought that the bleak areas of Gospel Oak would have persuaded the Camden Borough Council to preserve its fine nineteenth-century streets wherever possible. Yet one finds its Housing Development Committee taking, and then, after being challenged, reaffirming, a decision to tear down a large part of Fitzroy Road in the Primrose Hill environmental area, in order to put up a new row of flats, a decision opposed by the local civic society and the local ward Labour Party. In spite of the latter's intervention, Camden Council still seems to stig-

1. The GLC itself does have a well-run Historical Buildings Division staffed by intelligent, sensitive people and with some outstanding schemes to its credit.

matize pressure groups as representing 'the middle class comfortably off'.

And yet the same Camden Council is responsible for the most sensitive restoration of Keats's house at Hampstead, on which it lavished £70,000 and took advantage of the fact that a decorator's order book of 1820 made it possible to choose not only wallpaper patterns that were in existence at the time, but also those that were popular in the sort of circle in which Keats and his friends moved. They collected period furniture and restored the library and altogether gave an excellent example of how a local authority can make significant achievements in conservation.

However, important as it is that individual houses, such as Keats's, should be preserved, it is the conservation of whole areas of perhaps individually undistinguished houses that so often is the key to safeguarding atmosphere and maintaining the warmth, unity and humanity of scale which has so often been destroyed in new developments. This is why it is comforting to know that the Grosvenor Estates have committed themselves to the preservation of 200 acres of Belgravia. One hopes that they will be able to withstand the pressure to redevelop, for the whole area is of interest and Eaton Square and Belgrave Square themselves contain perhaps the finest remaining examples of late Regency architecture in London.

Preservation and conservation not infrequently make good economic sense and one can only trust that the financial constraints of recent years will make councils think again before tearing down property that could easily be brought up to a high standard of comfort and convenience at much less cost than erecting an impersonal modern house or flat. An example of this is provided by Hackney Borough Council's decision in May 1975 to knock down fifty early Victorian houses in Shepherdess Walk, Hoxton. Over half of these were listed buildings, but the Council claimed that they were not worth rehabilitating and that they should be removed in order to extend the neighbouring park. Opponents of the scheme claimed that the houses could be renovated at a cost of about £10,000 each, whereas the park could be extended by taking over a derelict factory site. Bearing in mind the fact that the average cost of a two-bedroom council flat in Greater London is now (1978) over £30,000, one finds it difficult to justify this sort of decision from the guardian of the public purse.

Not all redevelopment is unnecessary or insensitive. The Victoria Street changes, providing as they have a new view of Westminster Cathedral, are a case in point. But this well-mannered exercise is, alas, not typical. Far too often scale is sacrificed for pseudo-grandeur and everything subjugated to the new. Nowhere is this truer than in the City itself. The square mile known as the City was, until the War, basically a medieval town with its courts and alleys following the pattern laid down centuries ago. It was a place of great contrasts ranging from churches to merchants' houses and Georgian livery stables. It survived changes of generations and parts of it even escaped the Great Fire of 1666. Parts of it, too, escaped the Blitz, when a third of the City was laid waste, but after the War, the authorities were determined that the City should not be rebuilt piecemeal and early post-War planning legislation facilitated comprehensive development, if necessary through compulsory purchase and drastic alteration of traffic routes and rights of way. No longer in the parts due for rebuilding was there the centuries-old discipline of permanent streets, frontages, public thoroughfares. All could be modified by local or national decree.

What could have been an opportunity, unfortunately came at a time when architects were at their least inspired. As a result, we had the total destruction of the scale of intimacy which had marked the old city. Tower blocks dominate the skyline even within yards of St Paul's itself. The trend has continued, though occasionally local pressure saves a particular landmark. A visit to the City is a depressing experience for anyone who possesses either a memory or a book of photographs of what was there before. And the process of change has also been a process of depopulation, for hardly anyone lives in the asphalt and concrete jungle of the square mile. That a place, which still prides itself – and quite rightly – on its maintenance of ceremonial tradition, could have encouraged one of the most wanton acts of architectural devastation in the history of man is one of the more curious paradoxes of the twentieth century, and shows that taste and discernment and wealth do not always go together. For the sadness is that hardly a building erected in the City since the War deserves more than a passing glance, nor is it likely that many will be regarded with affection by future generations. Perhaps recognition of this is in part responsible for the spectacular success of the St Paul's Cathedral appeal for £3 million for essential restoration work. At least we have the consolation of knowing that Wren's masterpiece is likely to remain, even if it is hemmed in by the grotesque buildings that cluster around. For it cannot be seen from many of the old familiar places and, indeed, can scarcely be discerned at all, until one comes upon it, noble, grand and glorious, submerged in the architectural débris of the twentieth century.

The urge to modernize, to improve, to redevelop, to change, is not a peculiarly twentieth-century one. Without it, no city would ever have progressed beyond the meanest dwellings and we owe to it many of the charms and much of the dignity for whose loss it is now responsible. The tragedy of the twentieth-century application of the urge lies in the dearth of inspired architects around at the time when so much money was available to indulge the whims and fancies of those who would improve and change. As we have seen, London has suffered incalculably as a result. And not just London: Newcastle, Birmingham, Manchester, Liverpool, Glasgow have suffered too. But with the exception of Newcastle, which until the reforming zeal of Mr T. Dan Smith (the council chief whose unfortunate involvement with Mr Poulson led to his fall from grace) was unleashed upon it was a charming Georgian city, gracious and well planned, most of the others do not evoke so many sadnesses.

Before looking in detail at some of the other black spots and some of the challenges that lie ahead, it would be as well to consider the dilemma which has faced so many local authorities since the War. These local authorities are important because, for better or for worse, Parliament has vested in English local government an almost total power over planning. True, the Secretary of State for the Environment has the opportunity to overturn planning decisions, but only if they are appealed against and the difficulties of co-ordinating strategy, and the frequent absence of local information, have very often acted as deterrents to would-be objectors. And even when an objection is lodged and an appeal heard, the expert evidence and official figures, on which decisions are said to have been based, give the local authority a considerable advantage and often lead to the Minister – who cannot know each local area – deciding in favour of local government.

But what is the nature of this dilemma? Local authorities need money to supply essential services, money depends upon the rateable value of their areas, and with the decline in population in city centres, the most valuable parts of their areas, they depend increasingly upon commercial ratepayers. Because old buildings are sometimes inconvenient and old streets sometimes over-congested, there is often a great temptation to pull down the one and widen the other. The revenue generated by development companies is an added attraction. So one finds that those in the local council chamber, frequently persuaded by self-styled experts on design and taste, are cajoled into thinking that they are serving posterity as well as the individual ratepayer, and voter, by allowing wholesale change to take place.

And so many of these changes took place before the individual objections of the articulate became the outraged protest of groups of civilized people. Nowhere is this truer than in Bath, where a perfect Georgian city, one of the supreme cities of Europe, was vandalized before the conscience of the nation was awakened to what was happening. Bath will provide an interesting study, but first, it might be as well to establish certain facts and factors in the changing urban scene.

As a result of the Parliamentary initiative of people like Lord Duncan-Sandys, the concept of the important (listed) building and the need to treat certain areas as 'conservation areas' has been firmly established in law and is increasingly recognized by planning authorities. There are now some 3000 conservation areas and something like £3 million is spent annually on grants and loans for their care. Within and outside them are 240,000 listed buildings which have statutory protection from arbitrary alteration and demolition. However, in spite of such welcome legislative developments and the growing awareness of what is in peril which has inspired so many able young people and which led, for instance, to the continent-wide European Architectural Heritage Year, the devastation and destruction are not at an end.

The foremost reason for this is financial. Although governments of both political persuasions have shown an increasing appreciation of the need for adequate and comprehensive conservation policies and have sought, as in Chester, Chichester, York and, above all, Bath, to work with local government, the amount of money made available centrally for conservation in general and the preservation of old buildings in particular, is very small indeed and in the context of gross national expenditure totally insignificant.

Substantial sums, however, are needed to cope with one of the central problems facing those who have responsibility for our towns' and cities' transport. Most of our urban centres were based on an elaborate railway system fed by horse-drawn vehicles and the basic form of most cities and towns, even villages, is unsuited to the general use of the motor car and the lorry. Either accommodating or excluding the car and the delivery vehicle does present problems. That they can be solved in a fairly novel and exciting way can be seen to some extent in York, where a whole area of the old city has been given over to pedestrians, a solution seen perhaps at its most spectacularly exciting in Copenhagen. But no one can pretend that the 'pedestrians only' idea is easy and even the 'park and ride' schemes as operated in Oxford present difficulties, not least that of consumer resistance.

London with its massive traffic flow and almost eternal congestion has this problem, as most others, in major degree. Some Londoners feel that London is a worse place to live in than ever before. As one of them said to me, 'The Planning Departments march across town and countryside building huge roads, spoiling communities and dumping people in the barren wilderness on the outskirts, miles from their own jobs and friends.' Some of the greatest controversies in the capital in recent years have concerned the three ringways. These motorways, consisting of two inner ringways (1 and 2) and an outer orbital route, were approved in principle by the Conservative Government in February 1973, but the Labour Party on the GLC was pledged to revise this decision. It did so, with considerable sighs of relief in many political quarters, soon after it was elected in April 1973. The 'Homes before Roads' campaign had won a signal victory. Ringway 3, renamed the Outer Orbital Route, remained a firm proposal for some time, but it was deleted from the Greater London Development Plan when the Minister approved that Document in 1976.

Many local authority officials see themselves being used as whipping boys and resent it. They point the accusing finger at Government and say it is all very well to be encouraged to go in for conservation and improvement of the environment, but where is the money coming from? Their cry is not entirely unreasonable, for although the Treasury has provided help from time to time, for example during Operation Eyesore in 1972, its generosity has been intermittent to say the least. Operation Eyesore was a Government-financed plan to clean up the débris of industrialization and had some spectacular successes: in Manchester and Newcastle, old Victorian buildings positively gleamed, though in Newcastle, admiration of what has been achieved is overshadowed by recollection of what was pulled down before. In Glasgow, there has been a special Government grant of £5 million for environmental improvement. But Glasgow is a city of problems and has suffered considerably from the property developers' tendency to move in and build, and then happily leave office blocks empty because rates are not due and losses can be offset against other investments. In Glasgow, for instance, in 1975, there were 2 million square feet of empty office space – the equivalent of ten Centre Points. Manchester, too, had a precinct centre 75 per cent empty in the same year. Instead of too much money chasing too few goods, it is often too many shops chasing too few people.

But just as local authorities have genuine problems, so do owners, corporate and individual. One can sympathize considerably with those responsible for maintaining the buildings housing London clubs. In a *Country Life* article in February 1976, Marcus Binney pointed out that the London club was becoming one of our fragile national institutions. The last half of 1975 saw the closure of the United Service Club and the St James's Club, and the Guards' Club moving from its own premises to join the Cavalry Club. In 1977, there were less than fifty clubs belonging to the Association of London Clubs and pessimists were suggesting that by 1986 there would be no more than ten surviving. If this happens, the nation will be left with a series of 'architectural albatrosses'. For no less than seven of the clubs are listed as Grade 1 buildings, and another four are Grade 2 – and even some of those that are not listed, such as the Constitutional,[2] are not without their attractions and importance to the streets in which they stand. The loss of Decimus Burton's Athenaeum, or Barry's Reform Club, would be even more significant and regrettable than the demolition of the Euston Arch. The importance of the clubs is all the greater because London has so very few important town houses left, and many of the City livery halls were damaged or destroyed during the War. To quote *Country Life* again, 'The principal rooms of the major clubs form an unrivalled series of nineteenth-century interiors and many contain either original or very appropriate furnishings or paintings . . . Many have major collections of books on particular subjects . . . In present financial circumstances, all these must be threatened by attrition.' Rising staff costs together

2. This closed in 1977, but has now (1978) been taken over by the Freemasons.

with the general inflationary spiral are making it more and more difficult for the clubs to put up subscriptions without losing too many members. The future is bleak and their listing may not save them.

It is possible that these, and other buildings, will feature in a future edition of that alarming book *Goodbye London* (1973). Happily some of the book's warnings of what was at risk were heeded, but there are still in 1978 hundreds of plans large and small affecting every part of the city; and that in London and elsewhere listing is not a sufficient protection is most graphically illustrated in the Save Report. *Save Britain's Heritage*, a committee inspired by, and largely consisting of, environmental journalists, was formed during Architectural Heritage Year to give publicity to proposals for demolishing historic buildings, and although its activities were not without success, the Report they published at the end of 1975 showed that we were still destroying officially listed buildings at the rate of one a day.

In the first six months of 1975, Heritage Year itself, permission was given to demolish no less than 182 buildings in England and Wales, and hundreds more were partially demolished or drastically altered and their setting ruined. The Report says, 'Even given the facts that more buildings are being placed on the lists each year, the loss suggests a disturbing inability to protect the very buildings that they have singled out to be worthy of preservation.' Its obituary on Heritage Year is perhaps a little unkind but its strictures should not go unheeded.

Heritage Year has possibly been unfortunate in coinciding with a year of economic recession unprecedented since the Second World War. As a result, many local authorities simply abandoned their Heritage Year projects. And the Department of the Environment which has so ardently supported the idea of Heritage Year found itself effectively ordering local authorities to ignore it under the guise of cutting out all unnecessary expenditure. The list of projects put forward to celebrate Heritage Year, projects which in any civilized society should have been normal civic activities, makes pathetic reading. The emphasis on spending public money on superficialities was fundamentally mistaken and the campaign should have pressed instead for the use of legal sanctions that now lie dormant and for fiscal reforms that would encourage owners to maintain and use their buildings in the public interest . . . The local authority and the public

91

corporation have assumed the grim mantle of vandalism which once lay on the shoulders of the property developer. For given an alert public opinion and a determined local authority there is precious little which a private property developer can get away with, yet Britain is, alas, cursed with some of Europe's most philistine public officials.

Perhaps some of these words are a little harsh, for the sanctions that can be invoked against those who either pull down listed buildings or allow them to decay were not until very recently at all daunting. But the Save Committee's criticisms are difficult to ignore as one looks through the photographs of some of the buildings which were pulled down during Heritage Year: the Tapestry Factory at Streatham Street, London, pulled down by Town and City Properties; the Church of the Saviour, Bolton, pulled down by the Church of England; Nile Street, Birmingham, pulled down by the Corporation; the former town hall in Leominster, demolished by the Council; the Queen's Hotel, in Micklegate, York, demolished by its owner; Wellington House, Westminster, pulled down by Land Securities; the fabulous nineteenth-century St Enoch's station in Glasgow, destroyed by British Rail; and the loss of the Westminster Palace Hotel, once the finest and largest hotel in London. So the grim list continues with photographs of buildings from Swindon to Aylesbury, Stroud and Wotton-under-Edge, all gone or under threat.

The Save Committee quotes the injunction laid down for German Master Masons: 'When a master dies and another comes he shall not remove the first master's masonry already set nor throw away the unset but hewn stones, that the master whose work has been interrupted by death may not be put to shame.' When one sees the striking Hylands House in Chelmsford, a splendid building dating from the early years of the nineteenth century and the centrepiece of a Repton park, one wishes that those words from medieval Germany would be more closely heeded in some of the council chambers of the land. For Hylands House was allowed to fall into a state of sad dilapidation and three private schemes for restoration were turned down until, because of its parlous state, Chelmsford District Council applied for permission to demolish it. Mercifully, when the Department of the Environment's Inspector considered the application he decided that not enough had been done to find a new use for the house. The Council then acted upon his suggestion and carried out emergency repairs to preserve the house whilst its plight was publicized in the hope of finding a new use for it. Similar stories could, alas, be told about many parts of the country from Buckingham to Hull, from Berkhamsted to Carlisle, from Sutton Coldfield to Merthyr Tydfil. The catalogue – and many detailed examples have been graphically documented by the Save Committee – is a dismal one and, although the Committee's work and warnings have borne fruit in some cases, there are far too many buildings they properly sought to preserve that are still in danger of being transformed into piles of rubble.

And there are many piles of rubble to testify to past destruction. A book about them was published in 1975 – *The Rape of Britain* by Colin Amery and Dan Cruickshank. In his foreword, John Betjeman remarks, 'In my mind's ear, I can hear the smooth tones of the committee man explaining why the roads must go where they do regardless of the old towns they bisect. In my mind's eye, I can see the swish perspective tricked up by the architect's firm to dazzle the local councillors.'

The scenes of rape from Aberdeen to Truro are startling, a dreary commentary on the activities of the soulless and the insensitive. Nowhere have those activities had a more devastating effect than in Bath. Bath was the Queen of English cities and, indeed, unrivalled in Europe as a surviving example of an elegant age, planned with symmetry and sensitivity and nearly untouched for 200 years until, in the 1950s, a development plan was drawn up. Today the results of that plan tower over Bath: an austere, impersonal, square and scaleless hotel squats ugly and depressing on the river bank above Adam's Pulteney Bridge, one of the last of Europe's old town bridges. Where eighteenth-century houses once stood, a modern technical college now dominates. New blocks of flats have replaced Georgian homes, which could have been restored at much less cost and provided more human and attractive dwellings for their occupants, and shopping arcades which might have graced Wigan Pier have replaced bow-fronted stores. As Lord Goodman remarked in the foreword to Adam Fergusson's *Sack of Bath* (1973): 'It is incredible that a city so loved for the character and beauty of its buildings should have suffered the indignities already inflicted on it and should remain exposed to increasing and even lethal risks. If this can happen to Bath, there is no architectural

93

Georgian elegance replaced by twentieth-century ugliness. Southgate, Bath *William Morris*

shrine safe from violation.' John Betjeman writes:

> Now houses are units and people are digits,
> And Bath has been planned into quarters for midgets . . .
> Goodbye to old Bath. We who loved you are sorry.
> They've carted you off by developer's lorry.

But so much was there that in spite of acres of Georgian rubble and in spite of the distortion of scale that has been inflicted upon a gracious city, much does remain. Although 3000 listed buildings have been pulled down there are well over 20,000 left. Bath, one of the towns singled out by Government in 1966 for a special conservation study, now has one of the most vigorous local amenity societies in the land, the Bath Preservation Trust. Every plan is monitored, logged and listed and every application carefully studied and where necessary challenged. Bath City Council has been persuaded that destruction and redevelopment is not the answer to every problem. In 1968 the Buchanan Conservation Study of Bath said: 'In no case has the Corporation bought an unfit dwelling for occupation or re-occupation . . . the emphasis is on closure with a view to demoli-

94

The monstrous Beaufort Hotel, an intruder in a graceful townscape, Bath *William Morris*

tion. Of course, some of the houses pulled down were in a bad state, but many of them could have been rehabilitated and were far from slums. There were small proud Georgian homes, the kind that many people would sacrifice their savings for.'

Though there is far too much urban destruction and decay, and though visitors to Gloucester and Lincoln and Bristol who knew the towns only a few years ago throw up their hands in horror at what has gone, every story is not one of disaster. The character has been ripped out of towns as different as Worcester and Grimsby, but the conservation movement and the coming of the conservation area has brought a new appreciation of our heritage.

The Civic Trust which began in Norwich (where, appropriately enough, one of the most outstandingly successful of Architectural Heritage Year schemes, the Winsom scheme, has brought new life and beauty to an old and neglected area) has burgeoned during the last two decades and been given great encouragement by the passing of the Civic Amenities Act. Indeed it was the President of the Civic Trust, Lord Duncan-Sandys, who piloted that Act through Parliament and whose persistence as much as anything else was responsible for the

Town and Country Amenities Act – the logical successor passed in 1974.

There are now local civic societies in all parts of the country. The Civic Trust makes awards and holds conferences to discuss what is being done. Its publications record some refreshing achievements, such as the protection of traditional street character side by side with new and up-to-date living accommodation in Cirencester, or the way in which the Hammerson group of companies has redeveloped a whole block of shops and offices in the centre of Salisbury and the revival of the Barbican district of Plymouth.

It is perhaps in Edinburgh that one sees the most startling contrast of failure and achievement. There the south side of the city, including much of the medieval town round the castle and the land immediately to the south of it, seems to have been regarded as expendable in the interests of academic expansion and road engineering. The University redeveloped most of George Square and its surroundings and did not exactly put harmony of old and new and the preservation of all that was best at the head of its priorities. The rest of the area was allowed to deteriorate while the ring road controversy continued and the city was unable to decide on an overall shopping policy. At the end of the War many structurally sound and architecturally pleasing houses were allowed to decay and be demolished purely because they did not have bathrooms when their modernization could have been achieved at a fraction of the cost of new houses and the city's appearance, as well as the comforts of residents, would have gained immeasurably. To walk round the old town is to have dismal reminders of what has gone and what is almost certainly going. But the active campaigning of the Cockburn Association – the oldest of all the civic societies – has drawn not only local, but also national, attention to what is at stake and there is a hope that much of what remains of the old town will still be saved. It is incomprehensible that the old town, an essential foil to the new, and containing some architecture of equal distinction, should be neither a conservation area nor a Heritage Year project. Across the city, however, in the New Town, the finest Georgian city in the country after Bath, the story is happily different.

The spacious classical area, designed to accommodate the wealthy citizens of Edinburgh and their servants who wished to move out of the overcrowded medieval city clustering around the castle, remains a living city. Its regularly patterned streets, squares and crescents laid out on sloping ground have a compelling beauty. Charlotte Square was designed by Robert Adam and much of the rest of the new town, almost all designed by Scottish architects, is worthy to rank with the work of the master. By 1970 the condition of many of the buildings after two centuries of northern weather was perilous indeed and in that year the Scottish Civic Trust organized a remarkable conference on the conservation of Georgian Edinburgh. Their initiative was supported by local associations, residents and representatives of the Government and the Corporation and the conference was addressed by, among others, John Betjeman, Professor Buchanan, Lord Halford and Count Sforza, who indicated that Edinburgh was as important to the culture and the civilization of Europe as Venice and said that he had never attended a meeting of similar character that had gathered so large an audience. It was as a result of this conference, that highlighted both the treasures and the problems of retaining them, that the Edinburgh New Town Conservation Committee was formed. The funds were provided, two-thirds from the Government, one-third by the Corporation, for distribution by the Committee for owners to restore walls, roofs and external features.

The largest grants were offered to owners restoring properties with low rateable value. For most of these properties were on the 'scattered fringe' of the New Town where decay was most apparent. Residents were circulated with information such as a leaflet called *Your House is a National Treasure* and inviting applications for grants for restoration. At the headquarters of the Committee, presided over by a genial Dubliner, Desmond Hodges, advice was given on fixtures and fittings from fanlights to door-knockers and every scheme for restoration was carefully examined to make sure that was what done would be authentic. In order to provide a focal point for interest an example of Georgian Edinburgh at its elegant best, 7 Charlotte Square, has been opened by the National Trust for Scotland to show the domestic social conditions of the eighteenth century. An audio-visual show tells the story of the New Town and of the development of Georgian architecture.

The Committee procedure for giving a grant is extremely thorough. When the inquiry is received the property is inspected by the Director or one of his staff. The net annual valuation of all affected properties is listed and averaged (for grant purposes). The category and historical notes of the property are then extracted from the statutory list of buildings of architectural and historical importance and a summary made of all visible defects in the external structure and of all deviations from the original design. When a number of owners are involved in an application a meeting is held and the Director goes through his preliminary reports, discussing the desirable work and explaining the types of grants that might be offered. The applicants themselves are advised to appoint a committee with authority to commission architects and quantity surveyors with a view to finding out exactly what is needed.

The procedure is meticulously set out in a series of guide sheets issued by the Committee, and the very professional approach to the problem is certainly justified by the results so far achieved. In Fettes Road, for instance, where the pilot conservation scheme was launched, some £43,000 of the total £49,000 cost was furnished by the Committee. At 2 Scotlands Street, the Committee provided £116 out of £199 cost. Grants can be as low as £40 because the Committee works on the basis of 'a stitch in time'. If it is allowed to continue its work – financial stringency threatens here as elsewhere – the future of the New Town will be assured, tremendous impetus given to Scottish craftsmanship and a model conservation project will continue to be an inspiration and example to the rest of Europe.

South of Edinburgh and just over the border lies one of the most historic towns in England. Berwick-upon-Tweed, today a town of 12,000 people, has a unique and colourful history. It has been fought over and 'owned' by both the English and the Scots. Because it was normally specifically mentioned in treaties, but was omitted from that which concluded the Crimean War, a local legend persists that the town is still at war with Russia. Border feuding and exciting history apart, Berwick, with its massive walls and fortifications, is a town of enormous charm. One in ten of its houses is listed as being of architectural or historic interest, a higher proportion than anywhere else in the country. Yet Berwick, with its strategic position and its three bridges, had the problems of traffic and industrial stagnation common to many towns of similar size. As the town's fortunes declined, so did the state of its buildings, and many of the citizens moved out to the initially more comfortable housing estates beyond the walls. The process continued without exciting

Above: The ruins of Berwick Castle. Both the castle and walls of Berwick have been imaginatively preserved
Tweeddale Press Ltd

Left: The archway to the famous Vanburgh Barracks at Berwick, the oldest in the country still in use. They are the Regimental Headquarters of the King's Own Scottish Borderers and the head-quarters of the Berwick Preservation Trust
Tweeddale Press Ltd

undue attention until, in the early seventies, it was realized that unless something was done to arrest the process of decay and deterioration, the attractions of Berwick would be memories rather than realities. Luckily the realization did not come too late, although inevitably some demolition had occurred. A Town Preservation Trust was established to arouse public interest, improve standards of planning and urge local authorities to come to the assistance of the preservationists with enlightened planning and financial aid. A sum of £45,000 was spent on restoring the Georgian Town Hall and many of the fine town houses were renovated and repaired with the aid of grants. A special headquarters was set up for the Trust in the old barracks and spurred on by local newspaper proprietor Jim Smail, a New Zealander but with Berwick blood in his veins, the properties around the wall were systematically tackled. Today Berwick presents not only a more pleasing but a more hopeful aspect than a decade ago.

But Berwick is not by any standards a large town and it is perhaps understandable that some of the more notable achievements in conservation have been accomplished in towns of more manageable proportions. There and elsewhere perhaps the greatest contribution towards safeguarding the heritage would be an intensification of the demolition controls that at present exist. For every day up and down the country listed buildings are still being demolished without permission and the fines levied are still an insufficient deterrent. A more effective sanction than the fine might be the French system of refusing any subsequent planning for a site where a building had been demolished without consent.

Another loophole in the legislative protections that has been created is that a building, even if part of a conservation area, is exempt from protection if planning permission was obtained prior to the designation of the conservation area.

It is lack of safeguards such as this that make any visitor to Britain's remaining historic towns and cities change his expression from delight to dismay as he travels on. However, belated recognition in Government White Papers in 1977 of the need for renewing inner cities, coupled with the acknowledgement that the new town does not necessarily offer the best hope for the future, gives encouragement to those who are concerned with Britain's urban dignity.

Chapter Six
Country Town and Village

Most of our larger towns have lost much of the character they once possessed. The pressures of expansion, redevelopment and commercial life have seen to that and the struggle to retain such fine buildings and noble streets as remain is not an easy one.

The larger the town the greater the difficulty of adopting and adapting the old street patterns and buildings to the pressures of modern life. One sees this even in our larger university and cathedral cities and mention has been made of the pillage of Worcester and the rape of Gloucester. Of our two ancient English university cities, Cambridge, which did not suffer massive industrialization, has escaped this process much more satisfactorily than Oxford. However, it would be churlish to deny the magic of an early morning or late evening walk through parts of the old university city, or to withhold unstinted admiration for the spectacular successes of the Oxford restoration scheme of the 1960s, a model of living conservation in action and a stimulating example to everyone who cares about old buildings and their maintenance.

If our smaller towns have mercifully fared much better, this is partly because the changing pattern of industrialization created quiet urban backwaters where life could go on much as before. Indeed, most of our recognized 'historic towns' are county towns, serving rural districts as their market and banking centres with perhaps a little light industry on the fringes, but at the same time retaining a sense of community. Not that we can complacently give thanks and think that all is well, for even in Berwick, given as an example in the previous chapter, it took great effort to stir civic pride into civic action. A graphic brochure was issued with large-scale photographs of a crumbling façade and a questioning title, *What Is So Special About Berwick?*, emblazoned across the front. Yet, in spite of the success achieved, Berwick is still not immune from problems created by road-widening schemes and supermarket development projects.

For though tourists love to wander through quaint streets and admire the scale, proportion and beauty of the buildings, there is not always the same local appreciation of the distinctive or the distinguished. Familiarity in this, as in so many things, can breed indifference. Harassed by a reporter from the Architectural Press, one local mayor exploded, 'I am sick and tired of people going on about the period shop fronts. I see no interest in them. Architecturally they leave me cold.' But even where this attitude does not prevail – and all too frequently it is just beneath the surface – one must have some sympathy with the task of the smaller council elected to administer an historic town, but obliged to satisfy many twentieth-century whims and fancies.

An interesting example of the cruel dilemma often faced by smaller councils was first reported on in *The Times* on the very last day of 1975, when it was revealed that Newark's historic coaching inn, the Old White Hart, might be acquired by the local council unless the owner, the National Coal Board, carried out urgent repairs. The council had decided to apply for a compulsory purchase order, as it is entitled to do under the Civic Amenities Act, after its architect described the building as totally unsafe for use, the owners having failed to comply with the repairs notice. The Coal Board reported that the repairs were the responsibility of the tenants, a multiple store. Whatever the moral rights or wrongs of the situation, the fact was that an historic building in a town of great charm and character was in dire danger. Sir Nikolaus Pevsner, in his book *Buildings of Nottinghamshire*, has described the inn as: 'One of the paramount examples of fourteenth-century timber-framed domestic architecture in England.' It stands in the corner of the market square that has been designated a conservation area and, after the parish church and the ruined castle, it is the oldest building in the town. In seeking to take action the council

102

displayed a very proper sense of civic pride and duty, but the necessary repairs were, at that stage, estimated at over £60,000. Inevitably a district council faced with this bill would have to postpone or curtail other important schemes. In the event the council carried out a feasibility study for a library and then had to drop the plan because of the financial restrictions imposed by central Government. The building was made safe whilst various other plans for its future use were considered, but nearly three years after its plight was first revealed no final solution that would guarantee its preservation had been accepted.

Historic towns have modern problems in large measure. The enormous increase in road transport and the decline of the railway have brought heavy and inappropriate traffic streaming through their centres, a threat not only to lives and limbs on the narrow pavements but to the foundations, and even the super-structures, of many buildings. Not all traffic damage is as spectacular and tragic as that caused by the fish lorry that demolished the only remaining Roman arch in the country – the Newport Arch in Lincoln – in 1967.[1] But damage occurs and often noise, dirt and poor access to old houses along heavily used streets in ancient towns have made those houses unattractive, and understandably so, as homes. This factor has often been the cause of poor maintenance and the reason why the fabric of buildings has begun to decay, thus stimulating demand for redevelopment. These demands have been easy to sustain by those who have argued that the medieval street pattern is inconvenient to modern commercial life and that old buildings cannot easily be converted. By the time these arguments have been advanced the charm and individuality of the area in question has often begun to fade, and this has reinforced the contentions of those who want to demolish and start again.

But smaller historic towns while they have not escaped unscathed have fared much better than larger centres. Their future, too, is brighter, in spite of the financial difficulties involved, and in spite of the obvious necessity of ensuring that market towns remain market towns and are not just conserved as pretty museums of a departed way of life. Fareham in Hampshire furnishes an excellent example of how an historic main street can be conserved alongside a developing shopping centre. The old High Street follows a medieval line, although its buildings are

1. It has since been meticulously reconstructed.

mainly Georgian. It still contains a number of excellent shops, mostly specialized, a club, an hotel and a private school in three of the finest Georgian houses, offices in other converted houses, a pub, and some residential accommodation. Here is a high street conforming to something of a traditional pattern, a community street in the true sense of that much maligned and over-used word. But, not all high streets have been as effectively maintained. Far too often a single blot, like an incongruous modern supermarket, spoils the scale and pattern as in Kinver in the southernmost tip of Staffordshire.

Sometimes the solution for modern problems is to restrict traffic, or even create a pedestrian precinct, as at Harlow Old Town, Essex, where all the old houses have been renovated and repainted. The street is well paved and spacious, the shops inviting and the area served by a well-planned but unobtrusive car park. Far too often, though, main routes take passing traffic through the midst of towns and it is heartening to know that even at a time of economic stringency, when, quite rightly, decisions have had to be taken to cut back the road programme, the Government has indicated (White Paper on Public Expenditure, February 1976) that schemes for the by-passing of historic towns should be given priority. This is a wise human decision, and also a wise economic one. The more attractive the town, the less passing traffic that disturbs it, and the better car parking facilities that serve it, the more tourists will come to see it. And because of the scale and size of these towns parking and walking present few problems as parks can generally be fairly close to the hub of the town's activities.

It is important that those in charge of county structure plans should, so far as possible, ensure that large-scale development takes place away from historic towns. However, at the same time there should be positive encouragement given to as much residential reconversion, in-filling and rehabilitation as possible, for a town is not a town if people do not live in it and a proper community spirit and sense of civic pride and dignity are the best safeguards for these places in the future. An active local community is much more likely to fight not only against insensitive redevelopment but also against the distortion of the old town or village street. By distortion I mean that artificial pattern where one sees nothing but over-restored antique shops selling over-restored antiques cheek by jowl with boutiques and craft shops, and with never a grocer, newsagent or

104

greengrocer in sight. That the boutiques and antique shops should be there is natural enough, and without them many of the finest buildings would have gone before now, but one does not want an artificial atmosphere created by people who have no roots in a place and no real opportunity to sell to the community in whose midst they operate.

Ludlow in Shropshire is one of the best examples of a town which escapes this artificiality. With its dominating position, its fine church of St Lawrence, and its famous and imposing Castle where Prince Arthur died and where the Lords of the Marches held their Court, Ludlow must be on any list of the ten most fascinating and romantic towns in the country. Commanding the wooded valley of the Teme, Ludlow is an enchanting place, with its wide streets of gracious, Georgian town houses, small rows and courts with lesser cottages leading off, a market-place which hustles and bustles with life and real shops selling real things to real people. A day there is a most refreshing urban experience, and one cannot but think of Housman's 'Shropshire Lad':

> Oh, come you home of Sunday
> When Ludlow streets are still
> And Ludlow's bells are calling
> To farm and lane and mill.
> Or come you home on Monday
> When Ludlow market hums
> And Ludlow chimes are playing
> 'The conquering hero comes'.

The town is full of history and full of life: a happy and uncommon combination. Of course, Ludlow has antique shops, including an outstanding one run by Paul Smith. Perhaps the essence of the place is summed up by a visit to his charming shop in a quaint alleyway by the church. Here is a man who sells furniture because he knows and loves it and who is not interested in a mere quick profit from trade deals. He has made his home in the town and served on its council, and become Chairman of the Friends of the Parish Church, even though a Roman Catholic. In his shop you have service with integrity, based on a sound knowledge of the thing sold. And perhaps it is integrity more than anything else that is the hallmark of Ludlow itself: a town which has mercifully escaped the attention of the developers, and which although it would certainly benefit from a by-pass, has a street pattern which to some degree has enabled the local

105

St Mary's church, Louth, seen from Westgate. Only the television aerials and yellow lines are visible intrusions of the twentieth century
Northgate Studio

council to protect the centre from the shakes and the exhaust fumes of a traffic-ridden age.

Shropshire is fairly rich in small towns of character: Bridgnorth, clinging to its cliff above the Severn; the half-timbered Much Wenlock, with one of the most romantic ruined priories in England; and Bishop's Castle, and Clun. Unfortunately, the county town, Shrewsbury, does afford a desperately sad example of how character can be torn out of the centre of even the smaller English town. As for Wellington, that has become the nucleus of the new town of Telford, perhaps the most frightening example of the triumph of the accommodation unit and the planners' whims and fancies over people, scale and needs.

On the other side of England in Lincolnshire, is Louth, once described by Sir John Betjeman as the most beautiful town in England. Nestling in the Lincolnshire wolds and overlooking the coastal marshes, the town has much to preserve. It is rich in historical associations, from the Pilgrimage of Grace to the boyhood of Tennyson, who attended its ancient grammar school and lived a few miles away in the still lovely hamlet of Somersby, where his eccentric scholar father was rector. Everyone who knows and loves English churches knows Louth, with its majestic spire, but it is the rows of distinguished Georgian houses that are its special claim to distinction. Wandering down Westgate calls to mind Keats's memorable description of Winchester in September 1817 when he was writing his 'Ode to Autumn'. Rich in buildings of character, it retains its medieval street pattern. Luckily, too, the centre does not bear the brunt of passing traffic and is a charming oasis just a few yards from the coastal road. Many houses and shops are the subject of conservation orders and a number of owners have taken advantage of grants to repair them. But even in Louth there has been some despoliation. Indeed, the fate of the splendid Wesleyan Chapel hangs in the balance and the skyline, which was once solely dominated by the soaring spire, has been marred by a gigantic box-like factory. But Louth is beautiful and those who know it and love it rather relish the fact that its beauty is not more widely known.

England's country towns are certainly the jewels in a rather tarnished urban crown, many of them worthy of whole chapters in themselves. To spend a day in Cirencester or Tewkesbury, to go to Rye or to Oakham or Olney, Woodstock or Chipping Norton, or Chipping Camden, Southwell or Ripon, is to savour a form and pace of life which is rapidly becoming extinct. To select like this is bound to provoke the wrath of many people who feel that their particular favourite has passed unnoticed. But these are merely quoted as an indication of some of the richness that does remain. Mercifully, their future is probably better secured than most parts of our heritage, although even here there are dangers, for the preservation of our country towns depends not only on vigilant local civic societies and enlightened local councils, but also on the ability of owners to maintain the buildings which give them character. A Wealth Tax which assessed dwelling houses as wealth (as has been advocated) and began at £50,000 or even £100,000 could have serious effects in the future. Already, however, these owners have to grapple with such problems as VAT on maintenance, and old buildings always require more maintenance than new. It would indeed be a great incentive and encouragement to those contemplating taking on a bedraggled house in an old town if there could be some easing on the limit of improvement grants. These grants, which have been responsible for the conservation of many neglected buildings, and their restoration to the housing stock, have been restricted to houses below a certain rateable limit and, such has been the increase in property values, that already even modest houses in London and the larger cities are above that limit. The country town could be the next on the list.

At a time when there are some $1\frac{1}{4}$ million unoccupied or derelict houses in the United Kingdom, many of which could be restored and make a significant contribution to our housing shortage, everything possible should be done to encourage their purchase and restoration. How much better the old, small restored house in Bridgnorth to the worker in nearby Telford than one of the accommodation units into which families are being decanted in that depressing new town seven miles away.

We should not be complacent in any way about the future of country towns for, as was indicated at the beginning of this chapter, they know pressures too. Devizes, for instance, always a market town and still retaining the charm of a town closely allied to the land, was for some years a place of controversy and acrimony over a proposed road with the local authority struggling to satisfy legitimate conservation arguments, whilst seeking to maintain the commercial centre.

Commercial development brings particular problems to the smaller historic town: for the illuminated or plastic sign, which might pass unnoticed in the centre of Manchester, would be most incongruous on a shop front in Dorchester. Within conservation areas, especially, a stringent policy to cover such things as the replacement of windows and door fittings and the colours in which shops and houses are painted, is essential to the maintenance of character and charm. The more intimate the town the easier it is to disturb it and to ruin its atmosphere.

Austerity and charm rarely go together. This is perhaps why so many old Scottish towns seem to have been transformed for the worse in an excess of Presbyterian zeal, which has put utility before character. There are, of course, exceptions, and the university and cathedral city of St Andrews is a notable example. It is one of the most attractive of Scotland's old towns. In its courtyards, garden frontages and the interiors of its buildings, St Andrews has some of the best examples of Scottish domestic architecture. A local preservation trust was founded as early as 1937, and has undertaken some remarkable preservation of traditional Scottish buildings threatened with destruction. Many others have been saved by individual initiative and enterprise and, during the period from 1970 to 1973, the Town Council reconstructed houses in South Street, which dated from the

108

early years of the nineteenth century, in order to provide small flats for elderly people. Not only was the scheme successful in itself, but it has important social implications through showing how old buildings can be renovated for new purposes to the benefit of the community.

It is in Scotland that one sees one of the most spectacular and successful schemes for restoring and rehabilitating old houses: the Little Houses Improvement Scheme, promoted by the National Trust for Scotland. Believing that Scotland's lesser buildings were as significant and evocative in their way as the castles and great houses and that, since they were the homes and stores of merchants, artisans and fishermen and their families, they should be preserved, the National Trust for Scotland started its Little Houses Scheme in 1960. The scheme put to use a new concept based on the purchase of appropriate buildings for restoration and subsequent resale. In 1961, with the aid of the Pilgrim Trust, a revolving fund was established to launch the project. Since then, the fund has increased almost tenfold, refreshed by donations, interest-free loans, legacies and profitable sales. The Trust's objective remains the same: to conserve and assist private owners and local authorities to preserve the best of Scottish vernacular architecture for which there can be a use in the future.

Using what they call 'a country-wide intelligence network', the Trust seeks to identify suitable houses; then, taking into account their intrinsic architectural and historic value, the price and the cost of restoration and their potential saleability, it prepares to acquire the property. A building may be purchased from the Trust and restored by a client using his own architect, but he must observe the Trust's general specifications. Alternatively, a purchaser may invite the Trust to become his restoring agent. In urgent cases – when the building is particularly outstanding – the Trust will immediately undertake restoration at its own expense and rely on the ultimate sale to cover the cost of purchase and work done. Sometimes, it has been assisted by the Historic Buildings Council for Scotland making a special grant. But, whatever method is adopted to restore the property, the eventual purchaser is required to enter into a conservation agreement with the Trust in order to ensure the integrity of the building for the future.

Since its conception, the Little Houses Scheme had been instrumental in restoring nearly 150 old houses, principally in

Above: Before the £100,000 scheme for restoration at Pan Ha', Dysart, Kirkcaldy *National Trust for Scotland*

Below: After the six derelict seventeenth-century houses had been restored, plus five new ones, Pan Ha' is a new community *National Trust for Scotland*

Fife. In addition to this, the National Trust for Scotland had made several interest-free loans to enable local conservation societies to undertake similar work.

Scotland also has perhaps the most moving example in the whole country of a community restoration project launched on the initiative of private individuals with a mission. In the middle of the thirteenth century, just a few years after the death of St Francis of Assisi, the Franciscans came to Haddington in Lothian and built there a 'church of wonderful beauty', the choir of which became known for its elegance, clearness and light as the 'Lamp of Lothian'. A century later, when the Lothians were laid waste by the English armies, the church was destroyed in the 'Burnt Candlemass' of 1356. Another church, St Mary's, was built in its place, but during the 'rough wooing' of 1544, when Henry VIII sought the hand of the infant Queen of Scotland for his sickly son, the church was damaged and the choir ruined. For four centuries it remained roofless, until, in the mid 1960s, the Duchess of Hamilton, who lives in nearby Lennoxlove, one of the most romantic and loveliest of Scottish houses, inspired a local project to restore the church to its former glory as the focus of a revived and re-invigorated community.

The success story of the 'Lamp of Lothian' Project, as it came to be called, is one of the most remarkable in the history of restoration and renewal. Now, the church, derelict for four hundred years, is almost fully repaired with walls, roof and windows restored. The project has brought a new sense of purpose and determination both to the immediate community and to a much wider area. Not only has the church itself been recalled to life, but a group of important buildings around have been tackled with similar zeal. Haddington House, close by the church and built in 1680, had stood derelict for some years. In 1969, it was taken in hand and has now been completely renovated to become the home of the Lamp of Lothian centre, housing the office from which the centre is run. There are rooms for recitals and exhibitions, and even accommodation for visiting artists and musicians. Across the road, Poldrate Mill has been restored to provide a concert room and art gallery, and a youth centre has been established in the seventeenth-century mill workers' cottages that were abandoned on the point of collapse as recently as 1967.

The whole story has brought a vigorous new purpose to the

111

Above: The Lamp of the Lothians: Haddington church, East Lothian, from the south east, before restoration *A. F. Kersting*

Below: Haddington church, now almost totally restored, is the centre of a reinvigorated community *A. F. Kersting*

community and the centre acts as a focus for people from many miles around. More than that, it provides an inspiration, both to those who know that conservation is not a barren exercise undertaken for its own sake, that old buildings can have new life and new uses, but also to those haunted by the seemingly daunting task of raising vast sums in small communities for ambitious projects. The secret of the Haddington scheme – which is continuing with exciting plans for seventeenth-century gardens and other ventures – is leadership, in this case provided by the Duchess of Hamilton, a woman of great determination and great faith. This, in itself, illustrates how important the connection between small community and big house can be, even in the seventies.

Nowhere is local patriotism stronger than in Wales, and it is sadly surprising that the conservation movement has been so slow to take root in the principality. As late as 1974 there were no civic societies in Monmouthshire, Radnorshire, Newport or Merthyr, except for the latter's exceptional society at Aberfan. By the summer of 1977, only 241 conservation areas had been designated in the whole of Wales. However, there are welcome signs of an awakening consciousness, and outstanding areas in remarkable towns like St David's, Fishguard, Haverfordwest and Pembroke itself – all scheduled by the Council for British Archaeology and which had remained virtually unprotected as late as 1976 – are now afforded some official recognition. One district council in Tenby had been fashionably interested in conservation for a long period of time. In 1975, in fact, that town alone contained all eight of Pembrokeshire's designated areas, and for years the council had spent an appreciable amount on the conservation of the town wall and asserted powerful development control in its capacity as ground landlord of much of the old borough. This was regarded as a sensible investment in the discriminating type of tourism on which it pinned its future. One can only hope that examples such as this and recent welcome progress will ensure the proper recognition and protection of most of the remaining areas of historic and architectural interest in Wales.

In all conservation projects, especially in smaller towns and villages, the ingredient of local pride and patriotism is essential. But much invaluable work is still done by national amenity groups and preservation bodies, such as the Georgian Group and the Victorian Society. The latter has a particularly exciting

113

record and has done sterling work in drawing attention to the large number of nineteenth-century buildings which have a special distinction, but, until recently, were totally unregarded and unappreciated. Both the Society and the Georgian Group adopt modern methods of painstaking research. They list developments and potential developments, monitor planning appeals, select cases and make submissions, and, in short, do everything possible to mobilize public opinion, local and national, when retrograde planning decisions have been taken or are about to be taken. Over the years, their annual reports catalogue cases in which they have been involved and furnish model and invaluable documentation: classic case studies of battles won and lost.

Looking at recent developments, one often thinks that there should be an English village and cottage preservation society dedicated exclusively to those objectives. The fate of many English villages has been a less than happy one. Of course, England does still have rural communities which preserve a village character and atmosphere and where many of the inhabitants still look to the land for their livelihood. But this rural orientation of community is becoming increasingly rare, as Robin Page wrote in *The Decline of the English Village* (1975):

> The whole structure and nature of village life is dying and in many villages the old ways and the old character have gone; gardens have now been sold off to squeeze in another building plot and lose their country flavour; there are street lights, footpaths, garages instead of garden sheds; and every Sunday morning, worshippers with wash leather and plastic buckets bow down before their new chromium-plated god. Work and entertainment are found mainly in the towns with the village a dormitory empty during the day and dead during the night.

This dismal epitaph on the English village is all too frequently true, and many villages have been swallowed up in the urban sprawl. To say this, and to lament it, is not to suggest that villages should be preserved in aspic, as it were, or that councils should not give planning permission for new buildings in any circumstances. When a community ceases to grow, it begins to die, but too many councils have in the past forgotten that most important word 'scale', which applies not only to the size and height of buildings in town centres, but also to the number of dwellings in rural communities. They have been far too ready on occasions to shrug off responsibilities and allow featureless houses and flats to replace old cottage homes. The disappearance of the English cottage would be an economic and environmental tragedy. Local authorities could, like St Andrews, make use of their old homes, and convert them into accommodation for old people, young marrieds or those who do not want a large house. Many politicians see people in their advice bureaux who would relish the thought of a cottage rather than a unit in a tower block.

If nothing is done positively to encourage retention, restoration and rehabilitation, the cottage will become either a memory or the exclusive preserve of the rich weekend commuter. Cottages are for people to live in and work from. In England, every parish has its church and generally its manor house, and beyond are the homes of the estate workers, farmers, artisans and craftsmen, sometimes grouped around a green, sometimes straggling along the main road. They could still be used for homes and wherever possible their retention should be encouraged. As Alec Clifton Taylor in his brilliant analysis, *The Pattern of English Building* (1972), points out, 'every part of Britain had its own type of cottage, every community and sub-region, studies in a rich vernacular shelter'.

Perhaps the most authentic villages in scale and size are those which are owned by single families. This is not to suggest that rich men should buy up villages and rename them. But, if one wants to study the English village, one could do far worse than go to Rockingham, Northamptonshire, where development has been carefully controlled, plans vetted and scale maintained, or to a little village like Langton-by-Spilsby, Lincolnshire. Langton is not attached to any big house. The last member of the family to achieve fame was Bennet Langton, and then only because he was a friend of Johnson, who stayed with him in 1764. It is not necessary to advocate feudalism to appreciate this sort of system or to wish for it to remain. The chances of its doing so, however, are remote. As the owner of one of these villages wrote: 'While the estates of these families are small, I do not see how continuity can be maintained, with the imposition of Capital Transfer Tax and the Wealth Tax to follow. By working myself and drawing little to date from the income of the estate, I have managed to tidy up the small village which is in an area of outstanding national beauty and I would like to proceed further.' The great value of this type of association is that, where people care deeply for something, they generally work hard to

115

cherish it. One would like to think that they would be encouraged to continue.

For better or for worse, however, few people will have the opportunity of that sort of landlord and, for better rather than worse, more people, one hopes, will come to own their property and will need advice and encouragement on how best to maintain it and ensure that the area in which it is situated is itself properly regarded. For these people and for local community societies, the Civic Trust has been a great guide, philosopher and friend, doing much to draw attention to improvement schemes and showing how to make something of the apparently most drab town or village street. Owing to its inspiration, buildings all over the country have been scrubbed, houses painted, trees planted, gardens created, rivers and canals cleaned up and obtrusive advertisements removed – in fact, eyesores of all kinds eliminated. Abandoned vehicles have been cleared away, street parking reduced and pedestrian precincts established. In 1972, the Trust published *Pride of Place*, a stimulating little book, which brought together ideas and practical experience of the previous decade and gave advice to those who wanted to improve the appearance and quality of the places where they lived. As the book observes, 'Britain can boast not only a great wealth of architectural masterpieces, but at a lower level, a great number of wonderfully agreeable houses, farms, and groups of town or village buildings . . . In the last fifty years, this heritage has been grievously eroded and only since the middle 1960s has public opinion generally shifted to recognize conservation as desirable and necessary.' That it is desirable and necessary, most readers of this book will readily agree, and that its effect can be spectacular and heartwarming on village green or in old country town is beyond dispute.

Chapter Seven
Our Greatest Legacy

On a late September morning in 1975, the Vicar of Brewood in Staffordshire noticed a fungus-like growth along the base of the wall in the north aisle of his church. Within a few days, his worst fears had been confirmed. There was extensive dry rot and the parochial church council, which had taken good care of the the fabric and had reckoned that no major repairs were on the horizon, suddenly found itself facing bills of some £8000. Brewood is a fairly large parish of about 2000 souls, so the task of raising the money locally was not impossible, though it was a formidable one. What was certain was that the money had to be raised quickly if one of the most important of Staffordshire's churches was to be maintained in good repair and preserved for future generations of worshippers.

Brewood's crisis is typical of many that occur every week throughout the year, for architecture, unlike any other form of art, requires unceasing and costly maintenance. Because the greater number of our cathedrals and churches date from medieval times, the problems caused by crumbling stonework, rotting beams and timbers, and subsiding foundations are common. Surveying the vast wealth of English church architecture, and its importance to landscape and townscape, and reflecting on the costly problem of maintenance, I am reminded of a passage from one of Solzhenitsyn's pieces in *Stories and Prose Poems*:

Travelling along country roads in central Russia you begin to understand why the Russian countryside has such a soothing

117

effect. It is because of its churches. [He talks of them in loving terms, but then goes on] As soon as you enter a village you realize that the churches that welcomed you from afar are no longer living. Their crosses have long since been bent or broken off; the dome with its peeling paint reveals its rusty rib cage; weeds grow on the roofs and in the cracks of the walls . . . People have always been selfish and often evil. But the angelus used to toll and its echo would float over the village, field and wood. It reminded man that he must abandon his trivial earthly cares and give up one hour of his thoughts to life eternal . . . The tolling of the eventide bell . . . raised man above the level of a beast . . . Our ancestors put their best into these stones . . . all their knowledge and all their faith.

Let us hope that no English writer has to pen such an elegy on England's churches. Today they still ensure that the English countryside has the soothing effect of which Solzhenitsyn speaks, an effect which is not dissipated as one enters them. True, England has its ruined churches – there are 250 in Norfolk alone – but for the most part our churches are 'lived in' and loved. For all this, however, there is a frightening chance that many of them will have crumbled into decay and will stand neglected and open to the elements twenty years from now.

England's finest architectural heritage and legacy is in our cathedrals and churches. If the cathedrals bring to life much of the pageantry and high drama of some of the greatest events in our history, the daily round of generations of citizens and villagers, whose lives are the social history of England, is brought to mind in the simple quiet of many a village chancel or in the more spacious and grander naves of the great town churches.

No one knows quite how many churches there are in England but there are over 10,000 listed as being of architectural or historic interest, and most are medieval, as are the greatest of our cathedrals. The problems of maintenance and preservation are seen most dramatically in our great medieval cathedrals. There are twenty-six of these and, until this century, they were not only the greatest but the largest public buildings in the land. They are still the supreme examples of the English architectural genius. All well merit visiting and to select is always to be subjective. However, few could deny that many of our medieval cathedrals stand comparison with any of the greatest buildings of the world and must be ranked among the noblest works of man in Europe.

Above: The great enemy of old woodwork: death-watch beetles crawling over an oak beam *Heather Angel*

Below: Detail of galleries and borings made by the beetle *Heather Angel*

There is the mother church of the Anglican communion at Canterbury, with its wonderful Norman crypt, superb medieval glass, the wall paintings in St Gabriel's and St Anselm's chapels and a wealth of fascinating and evocative monuments. Winchester, the longest of our cathedrals, has a slightly austere exterior, but a magnificent nave and transepts, a lovely Perpendicular reredos, three sets of medieval wall paintings, a font of Tournai marble, and fourteenth-century choir stalls with sixty small but exciting misericords. An hour's drive away is Salisbury, one of the most famous and most remarkable buildings in England, with its marvellous spire.

Each of these cathedrals has known its problems. Salisbury imposed an entrance charge for visitors in an attempt to meet the ever increasing costs of daily maintenance. There was something of an outcry at the time (1973), but the practice is rarely challenged. It is surprising that more cathedrals have not followed Salisbury's example. Surely, Canterbury must be tempted to do so. This vast and glorious building is at present in considerable danger and, if £3 million of repairs are not carried out in the next few years, some at least of its outstanding glass will probably be beyond saving.

As at Canterbury, so at Lincoln. A glory both inside and out, this is perhaps the finest building in England, perched on its limestone ridge and visible for miles around. Yet Lincoln has twice had to launch appeals in recent years. Much of the structure is unsafe and passers-by are warned to beware of falling masonry. Almost everything here is of priceless excellence. The misericords, the carved corbels, the soaring beauty of the angel choir, the thirteenth-century glass and the noble chapter house all contribute to a masterpiece which challenges any of the great continental cathedrals, and which only Chartres surpasses.

Norwich, with its graceful spire, elegant nave and splendid presbytery; Ely, with its enchanting lantern tower; Peterborough, one of the least altered of our great Norman churches; Wells, which has been called 'the most poetic of the English cathedrals . . . the queen among cathedrals', with its incomparable west front, a sculpture gallery unsurpassed in Europe, for which a great appeal was launched in 1977; Exeter, with its 300-foot ribbed vault, among the greatest creations of Gothic architecture – all make a stunning and unique contribution to our heritage.

No reference to English cathedrals could be complete without mentioning York, not only a masterpiece of medieval architecture, but now a masterpiece of the restorers' skill and the engineers' genius. For, at the end of the sixties, York was discovered to be in imminent danger of collapse. The foundations were giving way. For a generation, the west front had been sheathed in scaffolding but the Minster was gradually sinking into the ground and, as it did, was being shaken by the thundering of lorries as they drove within feet of the walls. A massive rescue operation was launched. Two million pounds were raised, new foundations were pumped in. Stainless steel and concrete came to the aid of medieval stone and wood and now York looks better than at any time in the last three centuries. One can go north from York to Ripon and Durham, the finest Norman building in England and probably the finest Romanesque church in Europe. With a site to rival that of Lincoln, it broods with massive majesty over the Wear.

The three cathedrals known for the Three Choirs Festival – Hereford, Worcester and Gloucester – must be visited by any serious lover of cathedral architecture or by any student of music. It is not only the cathedrals themselves which are fighting for survival in an expensive and inflationary world, but many of the traditions they embody and enliven, and especially church music. Music plays a vital part in the life of all cathedrals and, without the daily sung services, they could easily become lifeless monuments. English church music is an important contribution to the arts, and the excellence of its accomplishment owes much to the choir schools attached to most of our cathedrals and to many of the colleges of Oxford and Cambridge. These schools are suffering the pressure felt by all small institutions with limited resources, and they also face an uncertain future as Government policy seeks to sweep aside the old educational system and dispatch into oblivion anything considered to be élitist. The problem of the future of our choir schools is felt acutely by all those who value their standards.

However, the difficulties facing cathedrals are to some extent mitigated by the success of appeals. This does not mean that one can take a detached and relaxed view, for there are more and more good causes clamouring for the fewer pounds left in the wallets of the over-taxed. Surely, though, no government could allow Canterbury or York, Durham, Salisbury or Lincoln to collapse.

But if it is unthinkable to contemplate an England without her cathedrals, it is as painful to imagine her without her ancient

121

parish churches. At their greatest, they bring an almost miraculous glory and dignity to town centre or country scene; and even the humblest furnish an oasis of simple reverence and timeless beauty in a troubled world. But the ravages of time and inflation have not passed them by, and though their plight may not be as dramatic as that which faces the cathedrals, in many ways it is worse; many of them lack the national fame and prominence that enables public, and even international, appeals to achieve, as at York, spectacular success. Our parish churches including, as they do, almost all our medieval buildings still in use, are a national treasure collectively; and individually, almost every one gives a special dimension to the town or village it serves. Many of these churches are, by any standards, great buildings. Some, like Cirencester and Boston, St Peter's, Wolverhampton, and Holy Trinity, Hull, are well known. Others, of equal beauty and importance, like Louth in Lincolnshire, its spire second only to Salisbury in height – and perhaps even more beautiful in proportion – are less so. Lincolnshire, being a sparsely populated county, with a long and fairly rich history, has some remarkable churches, none more so than Stow, the finest Norman parish church in England. But Stow is relatively unknown, and certainly off the beaten track, and any need for massive funds could hardly be met from the very limited local resources of the small, scattered rural population. The same is true of Abbey Dore in Herefordshire. Betjeman calls it a perfect example of early English architecture with seventeenth-century fittings and yet, surrounded by the small orchards of the Golden Valley, this survival of a great conventual church of the Cistercian Order, miles from anywhere, must be in danger.

Indeed, of all the churches mentioned here, the only one able to summon large sums with relative ease has been Boston, whose success has arisen from its American connections. And, whilst it is delightful to think that this grandest of parish churches owes its sound condition and beautifully decorated interior to the Americans' acknowledgement of their heritage, it is of small consolation to those hundreds of incumbents and church councils struggling to maintain the fabrics for which they are responsible. That this should be the fact comes as a surprise to some, who talk glibly of 'the church commissioners and their millions'. It is true that the Church of England has fairly substantial resources and investments, but the income from these is devoted exclusively to the religious work of the church and, in particular, to paying the stipends of the clergy, and no one could argue that they are among the better-paid members of the community. So, if the money cannot be centrally provided for the restoration and maintenance of our churches, local vicars and congregations have to raise it as best they can themselves.

The recent plea of the vicar of a locally notable, but nationally unknown, medieval church – one of three in his charge – is all too typical:

New wooden floors have been put in the nave and in the vestry owing to dry rot. We have had to put a drainage trench round part of the outside wall to cure rising damp. I had hoped for a better response from the parish, and some more should come from our appeal, but agriculture and other businesses are not doing very well at the moment. We shall continue trying, for later we shall have to replace tracery in some of the windows.

This type of problem is geographical as well as financial, for the parish churches of England are suffering from the population shifts that have taken place during the last century. The movement away from the centres of our towns and cities has left parishes depopulated after office hours. In this regard, one thinks of Holy Trinity, Hull, or St Peter's, Wolverhampton, both churches of the first importance but neither with a sizeable resident congregation within the parish. Many of our small villages, also, have parish churches big enough to house not only the whole population of their village but of the last three and the next three generations as well; and even small churches have difficulties. At Aston Eyre, Shropshire, a population of fifty-three and a worshipping congregation of about fifteen suddenly had to raise £6000 to save the tiny thirteenth-century church, with its quite magnificent Norman tympanum. Problems like this have to be tackled, not only against the background of a changed population, but at a time when churchgoing has declined. Although most of our parish churches ring to the voices of the occasionally faithful – the festival Christians at Easter, Christmas and Harvest, or on occasions of private joy or grief – they are almost empty for the rest of the year. And so, the band of willing workers who launch and conduct appeals is often a fraction of a congregation, which itself is a fraction of the population served by the church. This is a very far cry from the early sixteenth century, when the great church of Louth, Lincolnshire, was

123

Above: The magnificent baroque church of Great Witley, Worcester
Vicar and Churchwardens of Great Witley

Below: The interior. Despite having a tiny parish, by 1975 half of the
money needed for restoration had been raised and spent *Vicar and
Churchwardens of Great Witley*

rebuilt of Lancaster stone between 1501 and 1515. The church wardens' book tells us, 'For fifteen years, with scanty labour and scantier means, the work was carried on. They borrowed from the Guilds and the richer inhabitants, they pledged their silver crosses and chalices. From the richest to poorest all seem to have been affected with a like zeal.'

Nowadays more and more people are 'appreciative' of our old churches. They exercise an affectionate hold on many people who, when they come, expect to find the brasses bright and ready for rubbing, the floors polished and the stonework clean. Their protestations would be heartfelt if signs of 'danger' and 'keep out' barred the way to occasional conformity, or to historic or artistic pilgrimage. But few of the visitors, whether infrequent worshippers, eager tourists or both, leave much token of their appreciation. That is why so many of these churches are in danger, not of immediate destruction or sudden collapse, but of the slow and total destruction of decay. It is only the faithful and continuing struggle of often tiny groups, sometimes sustained by the generosity of bodies like the Historic Churches Preservation Trust, that has kept England's medieval heritage intact so far.

Aston Eyre is one of the many churches which has been rescued by grant and loan from the Trust, although its own parishioners made very prodigious efforts and raised well over half the money needed. A glance through some of the Trust's files reveals the true extent of the problem. There is hardly a county in the country that does not contain churches which have been helped by the Trust and recent applications show that problems are increasing rather than diminishing. As the Archbishop of Canterbury, Chairman of the Trust (which is non-denominational and generous to those seeking to preserve any important religious building), said: 'The Trust is striving to help in the preservation of a heritage which can never be replaced. For this reason alone our ancient and beautiful churches must continue to make demands on the sincerity of the admiration which so many say they feel for them.' In recent years its efforts have been increasingly valuable in stimulating local endeavour and local responsibility. It has helped famous churches like St Benet's, Cambridge, and others like Holy Trinity, Elsworth, in the same county, which are not necessarily spectacular but whose collapse would be a true local calamity. Elsworth illustrates just how great the problem can be. It is a good, but not outstanding,

125

fourteenth-century church, serving a parish of 600 of whom forty attend services. In 1975, when it applied to the Trust, it was in need of £6000 to arrest inevitable decay. In the same year St Mary's, Kempley, in Gloucester, turned to the Trust when it had to find an unexpected £3000 for roofing repairs: a large sum for a population of 240, and an even larger one for the average congregation of twenty. In 1976 the Trust stepped in to help St Florence, Whitchurch, which contains one of the most spectacular and superb examples of eighteenth-century English sculpture, the princely monument to the Duke of Chandos. It assisted Hedon, Yorkshire, aptly called 'the king of Holderness', generally reckoned to be one of the finest parish churches in the north of England, dating from the time when Hedon was one of the major shipping centres on the north bank of the Humber. And it contributed to All Saints, Martock, in Somerset, one of the most lovely churches in a county rich in church architecture. In all, many hundreds of churches have benefited from the Trust's bounty during its twenty-five years' work. Week after week, applications from churches all over the country flood into the Trust. Often, the Trust is able to help them but its assistance is, of necessity, limited. And the other bodies, such as the Friends of Friendless Churches, and the many county trusts throughout the country, although they have wonderful achievements to their credit, cannot arrest the surging tide of dilapidation and decay. For the sums needed are frequently tremendous in local terms, and inflation adds to them daily – as does VAT. One fails to see how some of the necessary jobs that are in hand can ever be completed: £20,000 to replace the parapet of a city church when most local effort is understandably directed to saving the crumbling cathedral; £5000 for roof repairs to a fourteenth-century country church in a parish of fifty souls; £3000 for essential first aid to a Norfolk church in a village of sixty people.

It is in Norfolk that the problem is most acute. In medieval times, East Anglia was the richest part of England and the great wool merchants and clothiers gave testimony to their wealth and their faith, and sought to ensure a speedy passage through purgatory, by endowing churches. Throughout Norfolk, Lincolnshire and Suffolk, the great churches rose: Boston, Lavenham, Long Melford, Clare, Salle, Blakeney, Cawston, Cley-next-the-Sea, Great Snoring, Great Walsingham, Erpingham, King's Lynn, Snettisham, All Saints, Sheringham, Walpole St Peter's – perhaps the finest of them all. All but the

126

first four of this list are in Norfolk and they represent but a small proportion of the 659 medieval churches in the county. As John Betjeman wrote in *Norfolk Country Churches and the Future* (1973):

> Their profusion is their greatness . . . Some are miracles of soaring lightness with wooden angels in their high-up roofs; some of painted screens or Georgian box pews; some medieval carved bench ends or ancient stained glass. Each is different from its neighbour even if it is miles off or in the same church-yard. None is without a treasure of some sort be it in wood, stone, iron, tile or glass. Some are famous throughout Britain. Lovers of the Norfolk churches can never agree which is the best. I have heard it said that you are either a Salle man or a Cawston man. Others say that Walpole St Peter's bears the palm. Norfolk would not be Norfolk without a church tower on the horizon or round the corner of the lane. We cannot spare a single Norfolk church. When a church is pulled down the country feels empty like a necklace with a jewel missing. Every Norfolk church that is left standing today, however dim, neglected and forgotten, its looks are loved by someone, or it would have disappeared long ago.

That is certainly true, for in addition to the 659 to which John Betjeman refers there are 250 medieval churches which are in ruins. It is because of this local recognition and love of the county's churches, that the Norfolk Society's Committee for Norfolk Churches came into being. A small group of people, led by the indefatigable Lady Harrod from Holt, and fired with a determination to ensure that as many churches as possible should be enjoyed and worshipped in by future generations, set about the task of raising money, fighting suggestions of redundancy, giving encouragement to local efforts and stimulation to local enthusiasts. The Committee has produced booklets on the problem in general and on the glass and the furnishings of the churches. Lady Harrod states her aims in simple but moving terms:

> We feel, that with the rapidly increasing population of East Anglia, the enormous interest in church architecture, and the new and strongly expressed desire for religion on the part of young people, there are real indications that all our major churches should and could be kept for religious use . . . We can offer legal

Above: The church
of St Margaret
Cley-next-the-Sea,
Norfolk, is typical
of many such in
Norfolk, serving a
small community
Eastern Daily Press

Left: The topping
out ceremony on
a 'new' medieval
tower at Wyghton,
Norfolk. The old
tower collapsed, but,
thanks to a Canadian
benefactor, was
replaced *Eastern
Daily Press*

advice, practical suggestions for money raising, historical research, manual work and even a little money to prime the pump. We are involved already in rescue operations for six churches.

One of their great successes has been Warham St Mary Magdalene. Let Lady Harrod tell the story in her own words:

At Warham there are two [churches] both medieval and both of interest. All Saints had very thorough late-Victorian restoration and has lighting and heating. St Mary Magdalene has a Georgian interior but no lighting. If any church could be called 'superfluous' it was this one; so it is not surprising that in 1960 when the architect's estimate of £3450 for repairs was received, a suggestion was made to close it. No doubt the very fine stained glass, and the three-decker pulpit could have been transferred elsewhere but a committee called the Friends of St Mary's was formed and the required money was raised. In order not to deprive All Saints, no general appeal was made in the village, though a few devoted families there gave time and money. The Historic Churches Preservation Trust made a grant of £250 and the Pilgrim Trust paid £1100 for the restoration of the glass. The rest came from families who had ancestors or friends connected with the church. Endowments from these families, added to the donations of patron, worshippers or visitors, and the sale of leaflets enables us to keep the church in proper repair. It is used throughout the year, twice each month for the weekday service of Holy Communion, and there is always a festival evensong for the Saint's Day in July. The box pews keep us warm in winter when the service is read by candlelight, and there are always 'two or three gathered together', to carry out the purpose for which our ancestors built this beautiful little place.

Lady Harrod and her Committee are motivated by love and scholarship. They love the churches for their own sake and for what they represent, for the faith they have kept alive and can still sustain. But their approach is far from sentimental. They see themselves as guardians of an ecclesiastical architecture of national importance. They recognize how vital it is that methods of building should be fully understood and are anxious that research should be done on the relationship between the great cathedral churches and the abbeys, priories and the parish churches. 'Our understanding of such major and internationally important buildings would be greater if the work of known

129

masons can be more clearly defined.' Above all perhaps, they see themselves as trustees of wood and stone and glass for future generations. Their work is echoed in Norwich itself – outside their scheme of things – where the ancient city, with its many fine churches, has its own preservation committee. In Norwich, the local authority has worked with the committee, and local authorities do have power to assist with grants. Some, notably the GLC, have very good records; others, such as Staffordshire, have acknowledged their county responsibility, albeit only in small measure. But local authorities are generally reluctant to commit the ratepayers' money to what they think will not be a very popular cause. What is needed is State aid for churches in use.

The plight of our churches and chapels was most dramatically and movingly underlined in another splendid exhibition at the Victoria and Albert Museum in the summer of 1977, entitled 'Change and Decay – the Future of Our Churches'. This exhibition sought to do for the churches what 'The Destruction of the English Country House' had done for houses in 1974. The first section of the 1977 exhibition revealed just what had been lost. As pictures flashed upon a screen one felt a sense of frustration, deprivation and anger: since 1945 450 chapels and churches demolished, 141 in London alone. As a stark note observed: 'Not all these buildings were outstanding in national terms but all lent distinction, individuality or charm and gave character.' The figures for the non-conformist chapels, perhaps the least regarded but the most interesting legacy of the last two centuries, were particularly alarming. Between 1960 and 1970, 3000 Methodist chapels were closed and, in July 1977, 220 of the 2200 United Reform churches in Britain were up for sale. Some of these chapels, like that of the evangelical Countess of Huntingdon's Connection built two centuries ago in Worcester, were superb and evocative landmarks of religious history.

One of the largest sections of the exhibition dealt with the treasures of our churches. In them most of our greatest English sculpture resides – effigies in wood and stone of regal distinction or quaint charm which tell the story of men and women who moulded districts and, sometimes, shaped the destiny not only of village and county, but of nations. 'Even the plainest and most forbidding church can almost always boast some work of art or craftsmanship of quality and of interest', and with examples of church furnishings and vestments, together with some of the incomparable plate in which our churches are so rich, the exhibition demonstrated this. There was a gloomy series of newspaper cuttings recounting the stories of treasures sold to mend the odd hole in the roof or allow a reorganization of the interior. This is one of the saddest, if one of the most understandable, by-products of the pressures on incumbent and congregation. For, not only do the treasures have an aesthetic importance of their own, they were given to be held in perpetuity for particular and solemn purposes. In a letter to *The Times* in March 1976 (on show at the exhibition), James Lees Milne reflected sadly on the church treasures that filled market stalls in Italian towns as parish priests obeyed the dictates of guilt-ridden superiors. Let us hope that no American tourist in the Portobello Road will be able to pick up Georgian or Victorian chalices sold to meet the pressures of the moment.

Not that all treasures, fixtures and fittings are of great intrinsic worth. Some of the most moving things on view at the V & A most certainly were not, like the watercolour entitled 'Salem', showing a small rural community deep in simple devotion, or the delightful 'Love Feast' set – a simple potter's jug and cups to remind us of that communal meal of bread and water that was taken 'to accompany discussion of religious experiences', an ancient custom revived by Wesley. And then there was the Parson's Hutch, a rough and simple sentry box, in which the priest would await the arrival of the coffin in inclement weather.

From the treasures one moved through to the 'future', pausing to look at a delightful cartoon sequence, one of which showed a church 'closed for desecration'. Photographs and posters illustrated the variety of new uses, from offices to flats, to which certain churches and chapels had been put. Some of them were hardly appropriate, and one wonders what the Unitarians who solicited subscriptions in the early nineteenth century would think of the Watney's Red Barrel sign that replaced a more sublime inscription. But at least the façades had been preserved. However, churches and chapels are often capable of entirely suitable conversion to concert hall, to theatre or exhibition centre. Few could claim that York or Norwich could still support all their medieval churches as churches (although earlier generations and smaller populations did), and no one who has been to St John's, Smith Square, or to the new library of Lincoln College, Oxford, could deny that church buildings *can* be splendidly re-used. But by far the happiest solution is to try to retain these buildings for their original purposes. Sometimes this can be done by vesting in the Redundant Churches Fund, whereby occasional worship is still allowed and fixtures and fittings remain. Sometimes a sensitive transfer to another denomination is the answer. More often than not it is by following the example of Lady Harrod and encouraging often dwindling but deeply devoted congregations to struggle to maintain the buildings they love and are desperately keen to conserve.

This is where State aid comes in. Until 1977, Britain was the only country in Europe that discriminated against churches in the grants that it gave to historic buildings. In 1974, it was agreed that £1 million per year should be made available (at 1973 prices) in grants to religious buildings in use. But it was not until July 1977, an agreed scheme having been worked out eighteen months previously in consultations between Church and State, that the Secretary of State for the Environment announced that he would be prepared to receive *some* applications from churches in greatest need, though not to award the full million for another two years.

Since 1968, the State has been able to assist with grants to redundant churches through the Redundant Churches Fund, but the redundant churches scheme, as devised in 1968, cannot begin to tackle the problems revealed in 'Change and Decay'. Between 1969, when the Fund came into operation, and March 1977 the Church of England had declared redundant no less than 639 churches – in eight years one in twenty-seven parish churches, many of them worshipped in for centuries, were closed. One hundred and fifty had been demolished and others vandalized, or gutted as a consequence of arson (like St Clement's, Sheepscar, Leeds). Indeed the redundancy provisions have been criticized as providing a 'vandal's charter' because of the stipulation that a church, once it has ceased to be used for worship, must remain empty for a year before its fate is finally determined. However, some of our very finest endangered churches have been vested in the Fund. Churches like Shotely, in Northumberland; Upton Cresset, in a quiet and lonely Shropshire valley; St George, on the Isle of Portland; Friarmere, on a windswept Pennine hilltop; Skidbrooke, set in a clump of trees in an empty expanse of Lincolnshire marshland. These and others now have an assured future thanks to the Fund, although it is sad that they can be used for worship only once a year.

Nevertheless that would not necessarily be a cause for major concern if the Fund could cope with the number of churches which are being declared redundant and which do contribute significantly to town or country scene. The Fund's finances, however, are based on its accepting twenty churches a year, and at the time of the V & A exhibition there were at least fifty major churches of sufficient quality to merit vesting in the Fund. Many of them did not lend themselves to conversion, by virtue of their internal structure or their geographical location, and so many will be demolished. For the Pastoral Measure (approved by Parliament in 1968) insists that if neither vesting nor conversion is a possibility demolition must inexorably follow. The fear of what redundancy means to many who are reluctant to accept that a dwindling congregation will inevitably set in train the long and complicated process that might lead to demolition was spelt out by Lady Harrod. 'Until now churches could slumber away in their churchyards until they crumbled away to romantic ruins like Egmere, or were restored to life like Branford (and many others). Now under the Pastoral Measure all that has changed. Once a church has been made redundant, if it does not qualify for preservation by the Redundant Churches Fund and if no suitable use has been found it must, by law, be demolished. The waste of this asset would be regrettable, but if a church is converted to an alternative use, such as a dwelling-house, what has been saved? The landscape value, hopefully the tower, walls and windows, but not the setting – the grave-yard must go – not the furnishings, not the monuments, nor carved grave slabs, not the historical links. Not, in fact, the essence of the church which is its intrinsic worth.'

Whether one goes all the way with Lady Harrod or not, the fact is that the Fund *cannot* provide the answer for most of our churches that stand at risk, and equally it cannot be denied that most of those churches are not, in terms of love and affection and importance to their locality, truly redundant. Yet if more of our great medieval buildings are not to be demolished, or altered beyond recall, if the many fine seventeenth- and eighteenth-century churches that are in danger, and that wealth of churches from the nineteenth century whose architectural distinction is only now being fully recognized, are to be saved, the State *must* play a more active rôle in helping those indi-

133

viduals, congregations and Trusts that are struggling to preserve them.

These churches are among our foremost architectural assets. Centres and places of pilgrimage, focal points in town and country, in a very real sense they embody the soul of the nation. And, at a much lower, but perhaps more easily understood, level, they are among our greatest tourist assets. Furthermore the tide of destruction can be turned back, the process of decay can be halted. In national terms the sums involved are tiny in comparison with what is at stake. A small investment now is certain to bring a greater reward hereafter, whatever one's belief.

Chapter Eight

Artists and Craftsmen— the Rescue of the Past

No Act of Government, however harsh, can quench the creative spirit of man. The arts will survive, however 'cabin'd, cribb'd, confin'd', so long as man survives. Our ancestors adorned their caves with colourful and ritualistic paintings and, even if a nuclear holocaust engulfed us, the last survivors in the fall-out shelters would no doubt do likewise. But, though the creative spirit will persist, the arts need encouragement and stimulation in order to flourish; and individual crafts and techniques, unless they are sustained and the knowledge behind their execution kept alive, will die.

Genius and penury have often gone together and the artist needs recognition and patronage if he is to escape poverty. There are probably fewer full-time artists of repute today – artists earning a living entirely from their creative works – than for many decades. This is sad, for while it is by no means destructive of talent that an artist should spend some time in teaching, if he is to pursue his skills with any degree of commitment he must have time to devote exclusively to art. That time can normally only be paid for by those who purchase his works and it would be a grim prospect indeed, if the sole purchasers were institutional ones, right as it is that industrial patronage should be encouraged and that public institutions should show the works of living artists. The collector, who relies on his knowledge, judgement and discernment, and that almost indefinable attribute we call taste, is a very necessary being in the field of patronage.

On 10 September 1975, thirty-three of Britain's foremost artists wrote to *The Times* urging the Minister for the Arts to intercede with the Chancellor so that the Wealth Tax should not apply to them. Their reason was a fear that:

It [the Wealth Tax] will discourage discriminating patrons from purchasing the works of any artists if an enhancement in their value – even if the purchaser has no intention of selling the work – involves taxation. Survival of an artist is difficult enough without the creation of new difficulties and problems by the very Minister that should regard himself as charged with the duty of aiding and not impeding their careers.

These artists recognized from common, and no doubt often painful, experience that without the private collector prepared to take a chance and indulge a fancy many a career would have been blighted. Thus it has been through history, and, indeed, it could be argued that the private patron can save the public purse, for his judgement may be rejected by the 'experts', and far better that his money should be spent than the public purse raided.

In their letter to *The Times* the artists, who included Francis Bacon, Reg Butler, Frederick Gore, Ivor Hitchens, Henry Moore, Ben Nicholson, Victor Pasmore, John Piper, Ruskin Spear and Feliks Topolski, observed that:

The Minister has made a point that the works of young artists are not purchased by people of wealth. It is happily the case that quite a number of people of limited wealth do buy the works of young artists and have always done so. It is also the case that wealth by no means destroys taste or discrimination and a number of people of considerable wealth continue to support young artists. Artistic discrimination is not a matter of money or speculation.

At a time when increased economic pressures no doubt seduce many an embryonic artist from his course, it is depressing that any Government should take steps further to discourage or penalize artistic progress. What is needed is a positive encouragement, to both individuals and institutions, to purchase the works of artists, and it would be no bad thing if fiscal incentives, such as are available in the USA, were introduced into this country. There, the patron who wishes to give to a public institution can

Craftsmen laying a new floor at Little Moreton Hall, Cheshire
National Trust

offset the purchase price of the work against his tax. Alas, the chances of such a scheme being introduced in this country do not seem very great.

Of course, some artists are in a worse situation than others. The work of a young silversmith, for instance, is liable for $12\frac{1}{2}$ per cent VAT. From April 1975 until April 1976 he had to pay 25 per cent, a figure that made the 8 per cent that other artists have to charge seem like a positive blessing, although that VAT should be applied to the work of any living artist is unfortunate. One might argue that the silversmith is a craftsman rather than an artist but, whatever the outcome of such a debate, one thing is abundantly clear: many of the crafts are in acute danger of disappearing. One of the more depressing ironies of recent years is that, although the conservation movement has grown, the supply of craftsmen has tended to diminish. One faces the absurd prospect of a situation where the crafts and skills necessary for the effective discharge of a sensible conservation policy will not be available. For automation, which has brought many blessings in its wake, has also produced casualties, and far too often the craftsman is the first of these. The 'true' craftsman loves his work and lavishes thought and care upon it, as the

137

Above: Craftsmen working slate to re-roof the market hall at Chipping Campden, Gloucestershire *National Trust*

Below: The art of re-moulding at Blickling in Norfolk *National Trust*

craftsmanship of the past (often executed in the face of extra-ordinary odds) testifies. Perhaps British craftsmanship is at its best in our great cathedrals, but if these buildings are to be preserved, more young men will have to be recruited and trained in ancient crafts.

The recruiting and training of craftsmen is a slow and laborious process. Craftsmanship itself can never be hurried and is therefore expensive in time and materials; and in much of twentieth-century architecture, not needed. The individual who cherishes his work, loves and knows his materials and solves the problems that arise in their use, is not required on most modern building sites. Since the end of the Second World War, methods and techniques of production and materials have changed and superseded traditional skills. As a result, most skilled craftsmen are in the last years of their working life and the new generation of builders and carpenters – even though they may have served apprenticeships – are rarely proficient enough to cope with the intricate problems of repairing and maintaining historic buildings, be they cathedrals or cottages, for we should not forget the inestimable contribution to the quality of rural life and landscape made by the country craftsmen. The trend towards industrial building is bound to continue and so the conservation craftsman will become a special creature whose work will have to be valued for its own sake.

The man who has done more than anyone else to pinpoint a need and suggest solutions is Bernard Fielden, formerly Cathedral architect at York (where he inspired the most remarkable architectural restoration of the century), Norwich and St Paul's until his appointment to a senior UNESCO post in Rome. For several years he has been urging a recognition of the 'craftsmanship crisis' and it is gratifying to know that he is now in a position to bring many of his brilliant and imaginative ideas to the notice of governments throughout the world and, one hopes, to fruition. He acknowledges that the few craftsmen to be found in modern firms, generally retained for special assignments, are often an uneconomic proposition as far as their employers are concerned. As he sees it, 'The problem is twofold, firstly, to organize a steady supply of work and secondly to find a means of paying for the cost of any craft work or to make this cost more palatable to the public.' Bonus schemes and work study techniques are almost impossible to apply to the case of craftsmen. He suggests that the level of demand for each trade in each region should be assessed and that there would be a case for setting up regional or national crafts trusts on a trade by trade basis. He instances the York Glaziers Trust, established to cope with the enormous problems involved in the maintenance and restoration of the medieval stained glass of York.

The cathedrals could well provide an ideal basis for regional craft centres. Like the Forth Bridge, they are in constant need of attention and so many of the skilled crafts are constantly called for that a cathedral base would be both sensible and economical. Craftsmanship is always bound to be expensive, and with so many intensive labour activities, it is in danger of being priced out unless some form of sensitive subsidy scheme can be devised.

All this is not to suggest that nothing is being done. There are a number of cathedrals with their own resident staff, though the inflationary pressures of recent years have already led to some redundancies. Perhaps the whole subject, with the problems and the achievements that are possible, can best be understood by looking in some detail at the restoration of a great cathedral. The story of Canterbury is less well known than that of York, but it provides an almost equally good example of the restoration drama and the central rôle of the craftsman: the stone-mason, who must replace features eroded by pollution, shattered by water and frost and split by iron; the cathedral plumber, who has to be a specialist in working lead, responsible for roof coverings and dispersal of rainwater; the carpenter, who has to work in the maze of medieval beams and struts; the glazier, who has to cope with the problems caused by the eroding iron bars which hold the great windows together.

Canterbury is the cradle of English Christianity and one of the largest and loveliest of our cathedrals, its glass ranking with that of Chartres. The central tower is the finest in the land and the nave a masterpiece of earlier Perpendicular style. Long a place of pilgrimage, its history and associations still hold a powerful fascination for all Englishmen with a sense of history, and for Anglicans throughout the world. The history of the cathedral mirrors much of the turbulence and joy of our chequered past. The first cathedral was consumed by fire in 1069 and the second was the work of the great Lanfranc, appointed by the Conqueror. On 5 September 1174, just four years after the murder of Becket, his cathedral, too, suffered the ravages of fire. A detailed description of that catastrophe was written by one of the monks,

140

Gervase, and so Canterbury is better documented at the time of destruction and rebuilding than any other English cathedral.

Fire has always been a hazard – even in recent years – and most English cathedrals, at some stage in their history, have suffered from it to a greater or a lesser degree. The destruction of Canterbury was in 1174 when 'the grief and distress of the sons of the church were so great that no one can conceive, relate, or write them; but to relieve their miseries they fixed the altar, such as it was, in the nave of the church where they howled, rather than sang, matins and vespers'. (This quotation is from a translation by Charles Cotton of Gervase's record.)

In place of Lanfranc's church there rose one of the glories of early English Gothic architecture. Under William of Sens the choir was built and then another architect, known as William the Englishman, built eastwards, transepts, Trinity chapel, corona. It was to this new cathedral that the remains of the canonized 'holy, blissful martyr' were carried in 1220 and placed in the shrine, which became one of the greatest places of pilgrimage in the medieval church. This was the shrine of which Erasmus wrote in 1512, 'I saw St Thomas's tomb all over bedecked by a vast number of jewels of an immense price . . . The holy man, I am confident, would have been better pleased to have his tomb adorned with leaves and flowers.' A quarter of a century later the jewels had gone and the religious houses of England were dissolved and plundered. History was rewritten, Becket proscribed, the monastic foundation destroyed, and in its place the Dean and Chapter established.

Canterbury's treasures were further plundered during the great rebellion of the seventeenth century. Glass, statues, vestments and rich hangings perished and the inadequate work of replenishment at the Restoration cost some £10,000. But, through trials and tribulations, the cathedral has survived. As John Shirley wrote, 'The cathedral has stood through the changes and chances of this mortal life, sometimes damaged, sometimes near destroyed, whether by fire or invading armies or the zeal of reformers and iconoclasts. Today it stands in all its calm majesty witnessing to the spiritual and the eternal, as it stood in the fateful first week of June 1942 when fifteen high explosive bombs were rained on its precincts and many hundred incendiary bombs.'

Now Canterbury faces perhaps its greatest danger, for it is struggling with the problem of preservation, a problem

141

consequent upon the erosion of decades and exacerbated by mounting inflation. To rouse the nation, and the Anglican community, to the dangers faced by glass, stone and timber, and in the knowledge that there would be no money forthcoming from Government sources to help maintain this famous and valuable national asset, a Cathedral Appeal Trust Fund was set up under Lord Astor of Hever. The trustees include the Prince of Wales, Lord Armstrong, the former head of the Civil Service, Lord Selwyn Lloyd, the former Speaker of the House of Commons, Lord Clarke (of *Civilization*) and Lord Hailsham of St Marylebone. The special needs were outlined by the Dean: 'The preservation and conservation of the stained glass, the restoration of much of the fabric, and the establishment of adequate bursary funds for apprentices in our glassworks and masons' yard, and for the forty-four members of the musical foundation.' The intention of those responsible for the Appeal was to ensure that there would be adequate craftsmen to maintain the building well after the immediate dangers had been removed and also to ensure that the living heritage of music, to which the English church has made such a valuable and individual contribution, should continue.

Overall responsibility for the restoration rests with the Surveyor to the Fabric, Peter Marsh, a highly qualified professional architect and surveyor, who stresses that the immediate problems, though grave, are not the consequence of past indifference or neglect. Canterbury has been lovingly cared for through the centuries and, because it was built over a period of four centuries, the deterioration and decay does not affect every part of the structure to the same degree. The greater part of the cathedral is faced with Caen stone, brought from Normandy by boat in the Middle Ages, and used throughout south-eastern England as it was generally more accessible than the stone from most of our own quarries. Today, Caen stone is hard to acquire and, although Clipsham stone provides a good substitute and has been used in the restoration of Canterbury and other cathedrals, the policy of saving materials to save costs has been adopted at Canterbury and, wherever possible, the old stone is re-used. Indeed, no piece of masonry is discarded out of hand: recycling is the order of the day. After all, those entrusted with restoring a great cathedral must be cost-conscious. Labour costs in particular are daunting and far outstrip that of materials. In the old days, the reverse was true.

142

The head mason, Keith Newing, makes zinc templates, or patterns, to enable the masons to fashion each block of replacement stone to the shape of the old *Canterbury Cathedral*

The task faced by the Surveyor was a daunting one. The stonework had been badly affected by corrosive elements. Outside, crumbling masonry was everywhere apparent, even to the casual observer; inside, there was evident damage to upper stonework and the ribs of the vaults were in an uncertain condition in many places. There were cracks in the south-east tower and the south-east transept and, although the whole interior needed to be cleaned before the full extent of the damage could be ascertained, it was quite clear that only the most comprehensive programme of cleaning and repair, stone replacement and maintenance would ensure the preservation of the building. Repairs to Bell Harry Tower were started as early as 1963 after inspection had disclosed that the tower, though structurally sound, was suffering from erosion of the stone facing – the core was of English brick – and that this was endangering the roof of nave and transept. Initially, Clipsham stone was used for replacement, but this was believed unsuitable, and so the quarries of Normandy were surveyed and stone imported, which it was hoped would nearly match the original Caen stone of William of Sens. The work on Bell Harry took some nine years and occupied the attentions of five masons and four apprentices under the supervision of a head mason. It became increasingly apparent that the cathedral could not expect to find a body of skilled craftsmen in the future and they took active steps to encourage the training of apprentices. Working conditions within the precincts were unsuitable and so the Dean and Chapter established a masons' yard a mile and a half away at Broad Oak, Here, there was plenty of space for the delivery, storage and working of stone. Given the success of the current Appeal, the cathedral should now be able to have a continuing supply of skilled masons to ensure proper maintenance for many years ahead, but the capital outlay on a project such as this is considerable.

An even greater problem facing Canterbury is the preservation of the incomparably beautiful stained-glass windows, which constitute the finest body of medieval glass in the country. This glass has survived the dangers of war and iconoclasm and now faces the much more perilous hazards of decay and corrosion. These windows, which include the genealogical sequence depicting the descent of Christ from Adam, the Apse windows with scenes from Christ's life and Passion, were begun in 1178. They told some of the great Bible stories to the untutored pilgrims in medieval times, and represent as varied and as historically important a collection as in almost any cathedral outside Chartres.

In the early 1970s, it suddenly became apparent that this unique collection was so mutilated by the passage of time and the pollution of the modern atmosphere that its survival was at risk. The extent of the damage only became apparent after scaffolding had been erected for a close inspection of the west and south-west transept windows in 1970 to 1971. As a result of this inspection, it was arranged that the eighth colloquium of the Corpus Vitrearum Medii Aevi, the greatest concentration of international expertise on medieval glass, should be held in part at Canterbury to examine the windows. The genealogical panel, 'Adam Delving', and one window from the south choir clerestory were taken down and mounted in frames in the crypt, where they were scrutinized by seventy of the leading scientists, historians and restorers of Europe and America. Other early windows were examined from the scaffolding inside the cathedral at clerestory level. The unanimous decision of the delegates was that the condition of the early glass was critical. Dr Frenzel of Nuremberg called it 'catastrophic' and added that the glass could not survive in its present state for twenty years. Another

144

German expert said that none of his European colleagues had ever seen glass in such poor condition. The rapid decline during recent years is very largely due to the accumulation of chemicals in the atmosphere. The combined effects of sulphur dioxide, together with a moist climate, had created a corrosive acid that had eaten into the surface of the glass, a problem of course, not unique to Canterbury. At Augsburg, photographs taken in 1947 revealed little more than slight blemishes to the surface of the glass, but by 1972, this was so deeply eroded as to be almost opaque and four panels alone would, it was estimated, take four years to stabilize and restore at a cost of £40,000.

At Canterbury, the decay is worse even than that of Augsburg and the area involved some fifty times greater, yet the problem is being tackled. A modern studio workshop is established in the precincts and glass in a dangerous condition is restored in a thermostatically controlled strong-room and treated by the most scientific techniques and aids. A Stained Glass Advisory Committee has been appointed, consisting of experts from Europe as well as from this country, and including cathedral officials, and help is being sought from leading specialists in glass history and glass technology. The idea is that some of them will be invited to become research fellows.

Faced with the task of establishing an order of priorities, the salvation of the glass is of necessity first on the list. However, unless work on the fabric is maintained, its condition could be as grave as that of the glass ten years from now. And, added to the problem of arresting decay and disintegration, there is the ever-present worry of future damage and the Surveyor is especially concerned about fire risks. Every large and old building is at risk from fire, as the fire at Malines in Belgium sadly emphasized. As part of the current programme, therefore, Canterbury is taking urgent measures to reduce the possibility of outbreaks and to contain them if they should occur.

Of necessity, any major restoration project must depend to some degree on outside contractors working on particular tasks, and the whole operation must be planned with military precision. In Canterbury, a comprehensive plan has been evolved which will take the restoration and conservation up to 1982. The work is all concurrent, designed to save costs and to make the most flexible and practical use of available labour. The hope is that, by 1982, the urgent tasks will all have been accomplished and then the permanent staff will be able to concentrate on the continuing problems of routine maintenance. A project of these dimensions affords opportunity for research and development of techniques which can be of use to other cathedrals and great churches. Although, luckily, Canterbury does not face such grave problems as there were at York, where the whole foundations were at risk, design faults are constantly being discovered and research into their correction carried out. Scientific research and application has been concentrated upon the need for discovery of new materials with weathering properties to help prolong the life of the stone. The use of plastics is being investigated, particularly with regard to whether they can help protect the windows from pollutants. To date, these materials have shown a tendency to yellow in time and plain glass protection is out of the question as it would seriously detract from the artistic glories of the medieval glass.

Canterbury, because it is a national and international symbol, found that its Appeal met with initially striking success. By mid 1977, over £2 million had been raised or promised. The target, however, is over £3 million – at 1975 prices. The burden of cost is becoming increasingly heavy and even Canterbury may be glad of some Government aid. Surely, no Government could deny the request if it were made but, in fact, there is no criticism of Government for not stepping in immediately. There is indeed deep feeling that spontaneous giving and local control over spending is of fundamental importance. Peter Marsh fears that any legislative intervention could lead to 'less interest, love and care'. There would seem little danger of any diminution of love and care at present. The case for Canterbury has been put with force and public figures of great eminence have rallied to its support, not only in Britain, but elsewhere, irrespective of religion. There is, too, a happy relationship with local voluntary pressure groups, such as the Canterbury Amenity Group and the local archaeological trust.

The media have all been helpful in publicizing the dangers to the cathedral. The Prince of Wales went on television to talk about it and there is a fervent hope among those conducting the Appeal that anything they may achieve will help other cathedrals with similar problems. Peter Marsh is confident of succeeding. As he told me, 'We are getting on top of the problem. Until the Appeal we were losing out.' He sees his task in graphic terms: 'We have no option in my view. We are the caretakers of our heritage. We must see to it that we pass it on in the state we inherited it. The sum of money can do more than just ensure speedy repairs. It can enhance the quality of the building if it is spent wisely.' The $2\frac{1}{2}$ million people who pass through Canterbury every year must surely share his determination and pray his optimism is justified.

Chapter Nine

Treasures on Earth—
Private Patrons and
Public Collections

Man's acquisitive instinct is as old and as natural as his desire for security and, from the earliest times, those in positions of authority and responsibility have sought to surround themselves, both in life and in death, with the most beautiful objects their fellows could create. Perhaps the most remarkable collections of ancient times were those which the Egyptian pharaohs accumulated to support them in the next world, and everyone who has seen just something of the fabulous treasures of Tutankhamen, which have survived the pillaging of grave-robbers, must be grateful to the religious beliefs of Ancient Egypt.

Collecting for collecting's sake, however – the acquisition of works of art and beautiful objects to attract and adorn – began on a significant scale in Greece and by the second century BC had spread to Rome. Throughout the period of the Roman Empire there was a constant searching of the East for masterpieces of great art, for their possession was a proud symbol of prestige with wealthy Romans. Many of the most notable figures in Roman history were avid collectors of Greek art – Atticus, Pompey and Julius Caesar, and those equally remarkable but very different Emperors, Hadrian and Nero. Rome itself produced a fine flowering of artistic elegance, and sometimes genius, as any visitor to Rome or Pompeii, or a thousand outposts of the Roman Empire, can testify. But the desire to collect is universal and the hallmark of every civilization; long before the concept of fine art was recognized in Europe, the

Chinese Emperors were amassing vast collections of objets d'art. Unfortunately, many of these collections perished with the overthrow of the dynasty that had accumulated them. The Greek and Roman empires passed away but the successive civilizations of China went on while Europe was plunged into the Dark Ages. And, during that same period, great collections were made in Japan. On another continent and in a third world, the royal rulers of Ife and Benin in Africa employed artists to adorn and beautify their courtly surroundings. In medieval Europe the great patron was the Church, and the monasteries of Italy, France and England became the treasure-houses of western Christendom, full of paintings and sculptures, rare and beautiful manuscripts, sacred relics, precious stones, and all manner of lovely and curious things. War and religious upheavals led to the dispersal of many of these treasures, but in Aachen and Cologne, and in some of the individual glories of the medieval age, one senses just what richness did belong to monasteries and churches throughout Europe.

Among the earliest secular collectors of precious objects were the dukes of Burgundy but it was in the Italy of the Renaissance with the glittering acquisitions of the humanist princes – the Medici, the Este, the Gonzaga, and many of the popes – that the first great collections of post-medieval times came into being. This is not the occasion to dispute their morals or politics, but it is indisputable that these men, both as collectors and as patrons, helped to create a whole new civilization and attitude of mind.

England's Elizabethan Renaissance, also, depended largely on the discernment and vanity of the private patron and benefactor, but one of the first important English collectors was Charles I. He bought most of the paintings and antiquities that had been gathered together by the dukes of Mantua. However, his collection (one of the finest that Europe had ever known) hardly outlived him, and the stern rulers of the Commonwealth were glad to disperse it for cash to Mazarin, Philip IV of Spain, the Archduke of Austria and many others. With the Restoration, collecting again became an acceptable and fashionable pursuit and paved the way for its greatest age in England: the eighteenth century.

The succession was assured, internal strife – save for two brief flurries in 1715 and 1745 – was over and, as great magnate and local squire settled down in an attitude of national and parochial superiority and turned their attention to their houses and estates, they also turned their minds to beautifying and adorning them. By the middle of the century the Grand Tour was beginning to be thought of as the natural conclusion of any young gentleman's education; and when he travelled he bought, and brought back, antiquities, pictures and other things that took his fancy. If his scholarship was real, or he was well advised, he collected masterpieces, but whether his foreign acquisitions were genuine or dubious, he turned his attention to housing them properly and giving them a setting worthy of their true or alleged lineage. He patronized the great cabinet-makers of the day, silversmiths who had come over from France when Louis XIV revoked the Edict of Nantes, and the new generation of portrait painters. Every family had to have its likenesses displayed on the walls. The public museum was on the way because, proud of what he had gathered, the duke, or even the squire, was often eager that his collection should be accessible to an interested public, and by the middle of the century some of the more spectacular country houses were open on specific days of the week.

Not all looked upon patronage kindly. We all know of Johnson's unhappy experience which led him to write one of the bitterest and saddest letters in the English language to the Earl of Chesterfield, when he spurned that nobleman's tardy recognition of its genius and wrote that a patron was 'one who looks with unconcern on a man struggling for his life in the water and, when he has reached the ground, encumbers him with help'. A patron, he thought, was 'commonly a wretch who supports with insolence and is payed with flattery'. But Johnson's experiences were not, happily, universal.

One would have thought that patron and collector would have had their day with the growth of public galleries and museums in the nineteenth century. However, not only were most of these galleries and museums indebted for their very existence to private benefaction, but the continuing existence of the private collector was never more important than when 'official taste' dominated the selection and display of pictures and works of art in public places. Academic judgement is often blinkered, and committees seldom make adventurous decisions. It is therefore sad, but understandable, that almost all the creative movements in the arts in the nineteenth century took place in spite of public patronage rather than because of it. The arch example is that of the Impressionists, and the Post-Impressionists, who were excluded from official exhibitions. They and their successors

151

depended almost entirely on private buyers, and sometimes on dealers, and their works found their way into public collections only after their position had been established, and then only because there were private holdings of their works to be donated for public display.

The rôle of the private collector was not restricted to his patronage of contemporary art. His was the interest that focused attention on Japanese colour prints, African sculpture, pre-Columbian American art, in fact, on almost everything that added to the aesthetic vision of the nineteenth century. It was he who created a new awareness for some of the more obscure periods of European art. Fifteenth-century Italian paintings were in private hands long before any national gallery was interested in them. Collectors such as Sir Hugh Lane and the famous Misses Davies owned superb French nineteenth-century paintings which official hands were reluctant to take when offered. In this century the same trends have continued and it is to collectors and scholars, led by Denis Mahon, that we owe the rediscovery of Italian seventeenth-century paintings, and most of the celebrated collections in that field are still in private hands.

So it is in Britain today that many of the most distinctive and stimulating collections are not owned by the State, local authorities or other public bodies. This fact is recognized and positively welcomed by the directors of almost every public gallery and museum. They, above all, know that the private collection of today may well become the public collection of tomorrow, and they know, too, that without the private collection most of the exhibitions which attract attention to their galleries could never be held. Also, of course, the public itself has a greater chance of seeing beautiful things, in a variety of settings throughout the country, if collections are preserved and the private collector encouraged. Many of our greatest private collections are on display for at least half the year for anyone who wishes to see them and there are very few which cannot be viewed by the serious student at any time, provided adequate notice is given and proper arrangements made. It is this accessibility in the stately homes and country houses of England that gives them such a special status.

Much has been said about the English country house already, but two points can readily be made here. First of all, it is surely not desirable that works of art should only be accessible in the big cities, and in London in particular. Far better that there should be beautiful things to see, and in beautiful, non-institutional settings, in obscure corners of Lincolnshire, Shropshire, Suffolk and Bedfordshire than that everything should be displayed in the often clinical atmosphere of a museum or gallery. Secondly, not everything that gives pleasure and enchantment in a country house would be suitable for a museum. Vast numbers of topographical pictures and family portraits are interesting and enlivening in their natural setting, but are often of very little interest when removed from it. That many will be moved, together with their surrounding domestic trappings, the unrivalled collections of English furniture and porcelain, silver and tapestries that make up the contents of so many of our country houses, is only too likely. Throughout the twentieth century, country houses have been abandoned and their contents dispersed. We have seen, too, how the threat to the houses is greater than ever, but if the threat to the houses is great, the danger to their contents is acute. For who, faced with the necessity of maintaining a family, would sell a productive field or woodland in order to retain a Rembrandt or a Reynolds?

It is this threat of extinction by taxation that faces the private collection, and continuing private patronage, and calls for the most spirited defence of collections and collector. Such a defence can best begin by a careful examination of just how dependent our public collections have been upon private benefaction and loan and how dependent they still are on these sources. In a paper submitted in 1975 to the Select Committee examining the proposals for the Wealth Tax, the Museums Association, which represents the governing bodies of the country's museums and art galleries, and also the staff working in them, pointed out that there are some 950 public museums and galleries in this country and that just under half of these are administered by national or local government bodies. Their acquisitions have been built up to a large extent by outright gifts from private collections. One thinks instinctively of the Wallace Collection, the Iveagh Bequest at Kenwood or the Courtauld Gallery, but these are in a special category and recognized as such – they were bequests to the nation. It is when looking at the country's other museums that one becomes aware of how vital a rôle private benefaction and private loan has played in their growth. For instance, in Wolverhampton 75 per cent of the works on show have been given; in Liverpool the Walker Art Gallery, one of the most important provincial galleries in the

A treasure at risk: 'Racehorses Exercising' by Stubbs, who painted
many pictures while staying at Goodwood in 1759–60. Having always
hung in the Long Hall, the room for which they were painted, they
should not be lost from there *Trustees of the Goodwood Collection*

world, owes 90 per cent of its works to private generosity and
private purchase appeals. In the Ashmolean, Oxford, 90 per cent
of the coin room has been given, 80 per cent of the antiquities,
98 per cent of the Eastern art, 95 per cent of the silver, 80 per cent
of the paintings. From Bristol to Leeds, Manchester to Hull,
in all of these places the figures are startling. And, even where the
objects themselves have not been given, it is private endowment
that has enabled the museum to continue. In Hull, for instance,
80 per cent of the purchases of the Ferens Art Gallery have come
from an endowment fund established by Thomas Ferens when
he founded the gallery. These figures illustrate just how little of
the purchase money comes from public sources. The Fitzwilliam Museum in Cambridge, for example, one of the finest
of all university museums, has official annual purchase funds of
less than £10,000.

Apart from provincial collections that owe either their existence or their chief attractions to non-public sources, of the
5890 works owned by the Tate Gallery, 71 per cent were bequeathed or given, 1049 purchased with Government money and
593 bought out of privately subscribed funds. In the National
Gallery, founded with a private bequest, 55 per cent of the

154

paintings have been given or bequeathed. At the National Portrait Gallery the figure is almost as high. At Edinburgh, the National Gallery of Scotland is heavily dependent upon the pictures lent by the Duke of Sutherland, and at Cardiff in the National Museum of Wales, 95 per cent of the ceramic collection, 90 per cent of the glass, 83 per cent of the Impressionist and modern paintings, have been given or lent. The same applies to the recently established specialist museums, such as the National Army Museum, or the RAF Museum, which rely very heavily on material and financial help from private sources.[1]

Perhaps the greatest artistic bequest the nation ever received was Turner's. When he died in 1851, he left a complex will, but its essential purposes were clear: £140,000 was to be devoted to establishing a charity for impoverished artists (alas, a frustrated wish) and a bequest of 20,000 works was left to the nation, including 100 completed oils, 182 unfinished (but often significant, beautiful and important) paintings, and over 19,000 drawings and sketches including 300 superb water colours. A condition of Turner's bequest, however, and a condition that was recognized by the greatest lawyer of the day, and also by a House of Commons Select Committee, was that the works should be kept together in a separate gallery known as the Turner Gallery. Since the great bicentenary exhibition of 1975, increasing attention has been focused on the nation's failure to honour Turner's wishes, and it can only be hoped that shortly the works languishing in the cellars of the Tate and out of sight in the British Museum will at last be on view. Somerset House has been suggested as an appropriate home for the Turner Gallery, and it was, after all, the Royal Academy that Turner knew and loved and served so faithfully. One of the attractions of housing Turner at Somerset House would be the relatively low cost, a factor that ought to appeal to Government, which, like local authorities, has repeatedly shown itself reluctant to commit proper resources to this particular public good.

Local authorities in fact have a very shabby record, and as late as 1975 there were only two local authorities, Birmingham and Manchester, which gave their galleries and museums purchase funds of £20,000 or more and if that be thought to indicate that all was well in Birmingham and Manchester, it should be

1. See the list supplied by the Standing Commission on Museums and Galleries as an appendix to their evidence to the Select Committee on the Wealth Tax in 1974.

noted that only nine of the seventeen picture galleries in Birmingham are available for display of paintings and barely a quarter of the collection of oil paintings can be shown at any one time. Three galleries have in fact been converted into store-rooms, but even these are insufficient to house the paintings under tolerable conditions and many pictures are on long-term loan to offices and colleges for want of adequate storage. This highlights the fact that, if there were a flood of acceptable works of art released on to the market by owners who could no longer afford to hold them, and if Government refused to allow any of them to be exported, very few could be displayed. There is a real crisis of accommodation in the nation's museums and many notable works of art hardly see the light of day from one decade to the next. Even if the maintenance of museums and art galleries to a defined minimum standard became a statutory liability upon local authorities, it would be at least a couple of generations before those works already owned could be properly displayed, let alone quantities of new ones. It is not only a question of storage and display; perhaps the most acute crisis facing provincial museums is the problem of conserving their collections. There are almost no galleries which have sufficient conservators on their staff adequately to maintain them.

All of these facts underline the importance of enabling collections in houses as different and as far apart as Belton and Woburn, Castle Howard and Goodwood, Weston Park and Lennoxlove, to be maintained by their owners without the public purse being embarrassed in any way. Not only are the Woburn Canalettos as well preserved and displayed as ever they could be in their historic setting, and visited by as many people as would see them in any public gallery, but also there is surely no point in seeking to take them into public ownership while eight galleries in Birmingham remain closed, the Tate has an enormous store of paintings never on public view, and while the new extension at the National Gallery can hardly cope with those which it already has to display. It is for these reasons that, when the Select Committee on the Wealth Tax was receiving submissions and hearing evidence, the almost unanimous plea, not only from collectors but from those knowledgeable about the state of our national museums, is that the private collector has a continuing rôle to play in maintaining and enhancing our heritage.

The Museums Association, for instance, made the point that

loans from private collections are vital, for in many instances the loans are semi-permanent and if withdrawn can have a devastating effect on a collection (as would have happened if the Harewood Titian had not been bought by the National Gallery in 1974). Of course, if fiscal impositions mount, an owner would be sorely tempted to sell something that is not even adorning his own walls as the line of first resort when confronted with a tax bill. Mr Hugh Leggatt, who owns the famous Beechey portrait of Nelson on show in the National Portrait Gallery, has made it plain that, much as he would like that picture to be regarded as a permanent part of the heritage, it would be one of the things he would sell first if he were in dire straits as a result of the taxman's incursions. Many short-term loans form the basis of exciting and unique exhibitions. Without the willing private lender, the Tate could not have held the superb Constable bicentenary exhibition in 1976, nor the Royal Academy the Turner exhibition of 1975. In the field of contemporary art, especially, the private collector is often prepared to take risks in his purchases which public museums, accountable to the public purse, may not feel justified in taking. With the extraordinary nature of much 'Modern Art' this is a good thing in more ways than one. For example, those who deplored the Tate Gallery's acquisition of a pile of bricks for a sum reputed to be well over £1000 in February 1976 would merely have raised their eyebrows or shrugged their shoulders had some eccentric made the purchase out of his own pocket.

The Museums Association warned about the possible outcome of the Wealth Tax and suggested that it would result in the depletion of existing private collections, the withdrawal of loans from museums and the drying up of private patronage, not to mention the end of outright gifts of money and objects. One of the Association's prime anxieties was that the operation of export controls as such works came on the market would be inadequate. They felt it likely that, wherever restrictions were introduced, there would be a considerable increase in the activities of overseas buyers. And it must not be forgotten that, currently, the Reviewing Committee on the Export of Works of Art cannot consider objects costing less than £4000, and many of those can have either a local or a national significance.

All of these points were underlined, and many more made, in the submission produced by the Standing Commission on Museums and Galleries itself. This Commission, whose members are appointed by the Prime Minister, and which reports to the Secretaries of State for Education for Scotland and Wales, has a statutory duty to advise generally on questions 'relevant to the most effective development' of museums and galleries of all kinds. It was set up 'to stimulate the generosity of those who aspire to become public benefactors'. In its Report the Commission said:

> The role of the private collector can never be replaced by the State. This is even the case with old master works which are subject to fashion . . . But it is illustrated most clearly in the case of modern, and especially contemporary art. In comparison with Germany, Switzerland and the USA, this country is not rich in pictures and sculptures of this and the late nineteenth century, particularly the works of modern foreign artists. If it had not been for the gifts and bequests of Sir Hugh Lane and Samuel Courtauld to London and the Misses Davies to Wales and Alexander Aitkin to Scotland, the country would have owned virtually no Impressionist paintings.

The Standing Commission's conclusion, also, was that a Wealth Tax, in conjunction with a Capital Transfer Tax, even with some sort of exemption for chattels, would deplete existing private collections of museum objects. The museums could only benefit from this if their funds for purchases, exhibition and conservation were most substantially increased and this, in turn, would involve considerable expenditure from public funds. They went on to say that the definition of a museum object, given the needs of different museums both now and in the future, was bound to be arbitrary and affected by changes in fashion, and the application of the definition to many thousands of objects year by year would be difficult, uncertain and irksome. It would be far better to exempt all art and scientific objects or archives whatever their individual merit. Since this would include furniture and silver, as well as pictures, books and manuscripts, it would probably mean exempting all household goods.

All of this was reinforced by a letter to the Chancellor of the Exchequer by the Chairman of the Standing Commission: 'The past importance of private collections to public collections cannot be overstressed.' He then quoted some of the examples already mentioned and made the additional point that all the great foundation collections of early books and manuscripts in the British Library became public property as a result of

private generosity. He also observed that, 'The future importance of private collections at home is no less vital for our
public collections as future acquisitions from abroad are now
virtually impossible.'

That such a Commission should have to spend its time urging
Government not to do what it recognized should not be done
when it appointed the Commission in the first place is particularly absurd, the more so in that in recent years there has been
an increasing recognition in Government circles of the importance of private benefaction. This was recognized when gifts of
property and other bequests to public collections were exempted
from Estate Duty and Capital Gains Tax. When these concessions were made, many felt that the way was open for an adoption of the American fiscal incentives, whereby those giving
money or works of art to museums are allowed to offset their
expenditure against taxable income. If such a system were adopted here it would undoubtedly act as a spur towards an industrial participation in the arts, which has in this country been
lamentably behind that of many of our neighbours, and is in any
event almost entirely restricted to sponsorship of the performing arts. Once cannot but think that, if the incentive were there,
more companies and individuals would feel inclined to be generous. Then we might see an early implementation of some of
the Gulbenkian and Wright Reports' recommendations on conservation and the display of collections. The record of public
subscription to meet existing contingencies, let alone to enhance
our collections, has not been notably spectacular in recent years.
The Radnor Velazquez would probably have remained in the
country if contributions towards its retention could have been
offset against tax and, if that sort of concession had been allowed,
the National Gallery would not have had to pawn its future
purchasing grant to retain the Titian.

The Reviewing Committee on the Export of Works of Art
feels alarmed about recent fiscal developments. In 1975 they
said, 'We feel that the threat of such a tax [i.e. the Wealth Tax]
may at any moment start a rush to sell which could lead to chaos
in the world of art and scholarship, and to the breakdown of the
present control system with greater or lesser national treasures
leaving the country never to return.' Certainly, the art market has
not suffered from the fluctuating fortunes of the Stock Market
or the property market and there has been an increasing
number of foreign buyers during the last three years. That

London should continue to be the centre of the art market is obviously desirable from every point of view, whether one looks at it through the spectacles of scholarship, or is motivated by concern for the balance of payments. In the past, however, a vast amount of the goods bought in the London auction houses were bought by British dealers and came to rest in British homes, but 1975 and 1976 saw a distinct change in this pattern. More and more works were being bought for foreign buyers, especially in the Middle East.

This disturbing trend is likely to continue, and the fears of the Reviewing Committee realized, unless there is a very sharp change in Government policy, for, although the Budget of April 1976 gave extended Capital Transfer Tax exemption to works of art, the exemptions only applied to works of art owned for twenty years. There could be hardly less of an inducement to the British collector of today than this. Again, the exemption would, at the time of writing (April 1976), only seem to apply to works of art readily accessible to public view. Whilst one can understand the reasons behind such a policy, it must be recognized that not all collectors live in mansions and that there are, as Denis Mahon, a great scholar collector, said in a letter to the *Accountant*, April 1975:

> ... innumerable collections or even more or less isolated objects, situated (in very considerable quantities in the aggregate) in houses or indeed flats, which cannot reasonably be expected to be accessible on a similar basis to those in the great historic houses ... Moreover there exist great quantities of works of art and items of cultural and historic importance which ought not to be dispersed overseas but which are of interest to specialists rather than to the general public. This would include, to take but a single category, manuscripts, archival material and libraries. These have problems of conservation as do, for example, certain drawings (and particularly water colours) which can be quite literally consumed if they are subjected to light on more than infrequent intervals.

Many of those who would support the 'qualified' exemptions would do so because of a mistaken idea that most people who buy works of art at the present time are speculators and investors assisted by avaricious dealers but, although this is a travesty of the truth, that has not prevented its being given circulation in numerous agitatory articles. It is undeniable that some people buy works of art because they believe they keep their value better than other things, but very few people buy them purely as investments. The great auction houses and well-established London and provincial dealers represent a core of men and women whose integrity and contribution to the heritage is considerable, and without them most of the great collections of the twentieth century would never have been assembled. A healthy and flourishing art market, organized by people who know their subjects and care for them, is an integral part of a cultured community. Without the pre-eminence of Christie's and Sotheby's, and the fame and often the altruism of the great dealers, many of Britain's public institutions would be poorer, and great works of art, which we now accept as integral parts of the heritage, would never have reached this country, or would have left it for ever.

In spite of all the uncertainty, great works do still pass from private to public collections. In 1975, for instance, the National Portrait Gallery acquired Reynolds's superb portrait of Sterne, and the British Museum a beautiful Holbein drawing, possibly of Anne Boleyn. In 1976, the National Gallery purchased Rembrandt's haunting portrait of Hendrickje Stoffels, and the Tate an enchanting seventeenth-century painting of the Soltonstall family of Chipping Campden; the Victoria and Albert Museum was able to acquire Donatello's bronze relief of the Madonna and Child in the same year; and, in 1977, the National Gallery used its purchase grant to add Drouais's portrait of the ageing Madame de Pompadour from Mentmore to its collection. But most of these were acquired for the public as a result of the willingness of their owners to forgo the possibility of a spectacular price, accepting the very limited advantage of the tax concessions that the State currently allows. The portrait of Sterne, for example, was acquired for £50,000 and that of Anne Boleyn for £70,000. In the open market 'on a good day' the Reynolds could well have reached £200,000 and the Holbein substantially more. The temptation to go for the big price will increase as the fiscal burden on owners becomes heavier. A Wealth Tax, coupled with the Capital Transfer Tax, could quickly reduce our remaining great collections. As one museum director remarked to me:

No one is going to hold on to and retain works of art either by heritage or by purchase to pay rent to the State and finally as a

161

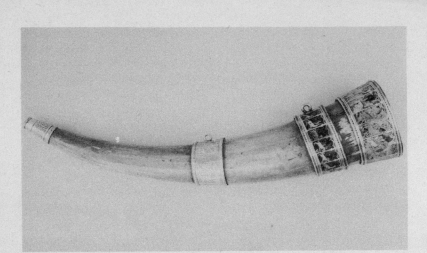

Above: A superb
example of medieval
craftsmanship in
silver, the Savernake
Horn, purchased
with a grant from
the National Art
Collections Fund in
1975 *Trustees of the
British Museum*

Left: Holbein's
drawing of a lady
of King Henry VIII's
court, sometimes
said to be Anne
Boleyn, bought by
the British Museum
for £70,000 in 1975
*Trustees of the
British Museum*

gracious gesture be allowed by the State to wipe out his tax arrears by giving it to a museum. It is astounding that words such as 'encourage' and phrases such as 'it is highly desirable to ensure that the rich benefit which public collections have attained from private munificence be continued' can be used in a series of proposals designed to produce precisely the opposite effect.

With the exception of a few Marxist art historians, everyone giving evidence to the Select Committee on the Wealth Tax agreed that the future of the private collection and the private patron is gravely in doubt because of the oppressive level of current taxation, and the threats of new taxes. Recognition of the realities by a sensitive Government would go far to remove the threat and restore incentives to collectors, and thus provide an investment for the public collection of the future. The Government of the Republic of Ireland seems to have recognized this, for its Finance Act of 1975 contained provision for a wealth tax that would exempt all works of art to which there are reasonable facilities for viewing by members of the public or recognized bodies, And reasonable facilities should not be taken to mean constant availability or display. For much has been achieved by the small collector devoting his time, talents and resources to the acquisition and study of works that would otherwise have been lost or forgotten. As the then Chairman of the National Arts Collection Fund said in 1975, 'Great wealth is not essential for the creation of outstanding collections but if a collector happens to be wealthy this does not preclude that he may be a man of taste, a man with an eye, or a man with a sense of public responsibility to boot.'

This view is not shared, of course, by those who see any possessions, particularly durable ones, as evidence of some sort of social immorality. During the debate on the Wealth Tax, one of the leading advocates of its application to works of art was a certain Marxist art historian called Peter Fuller. He and a group of colleagues said that they took their stand, 'because such a measure would be in the social and cultural interests of the majority of the population of this country. We are also certain that it will advance the interest of the increasing number of people who enjoy looking at painting and sculpture rather than hoarding them or trading in them . . .' It was very sad that the only person who was seen to accept this line of argument was the then Minister for the Arts, Mr Hugh Jenkins.

163

But Fuller was a political nonentity, and one can only hope and indeed trust that his view of the heritage will never prevail. If 'public wealth' in the arts is an object of those who devise Government policy for the arts, there must be a conscious and determined effort to safeguard not only the great private collections but the collecting instinct as such.

Chapter Ten

A Wider Heritage

The heritage that we cherish in Britain is part of a wider heritage, that of western Christendom, which itself has cultural roots in Greece, Rome and Judaism. The pattern of our landscape, the temples of our faith, our houses great and small, all have a distinctive native quality about them, yet they are none of them insular in the fully isolated sense of the word. Though Romanesque architecture evolved far from the banks of the Wear, we owe to it Durham Cathedral. To the brilliance of the ancient world filtered through the Italian Renaissance, we owe the Banqueting Hall in Whitehall. To the acquisitive instinct in action on the Grand Tour, we owe many of our finest collections of works of art. Indeed, there is hardly a notable expression of our civilization that does not betray, if not portray, its European roots: though the plants may be indigenous to our soil the seeds were nurtured across the Channel.

With more and more people from these shores flocking to the Continent every year, our television screens making many of the landmarks of Europe as familiar as our own and Britain now fully involved in the European Economic Community, it is appropriate to look briefly at some aspects of this wider heritage and to see how problems common to its effective appreciation and preservation are dealt with in other European countries. And it is particularly appropriate, in the aftermath of the 1975 European Architectural Heritage Year, which saw a common expression of concern – a desire to educate, and a desire to co-ordinate and concert effective action to preserve the best of our architectural heritage. That many of the problems are common, and that each nation can teach its neighbours something about effective solutions, was most graphically demonstrated in the Architectural Heritage Year film, *Europa Nostra*. But it is surprising, when one comes to look in detail at the question, how little work has been done of a comparative nature, seeking to analyse the approaches to heritage problems in neighbouring countries. Much of what follows will, in so far as it concerns architecture, lean heavily on the work of Dennis Rodwell, a young Scottish architect who has done some of the most valuable pioneering work in this field.

'Out of evil cometh good.' This has certainly been true of the way in which the efforts of civilized men and women all over Europe have been directed in recent years towards saving Venice. 'Venice in Peril', an international fund, has focused attention on the dire plight of this European city, whose influence as a city state reached out across nations and frontiers and touched indirectly the life of so many courts and communities in the fifteenth and sixteenth centuries. When it became widely known that Venice was in danger of sinking beneath the waters that have given it its distinctive, indeed unique, character, the common cry went up, 'Venice must be saved'. Funds were established and in many countries, scholars, connoisseurs, architects, restorers (including some from the Victoria and Albert Museum) and statesmen have been at work to assist the efforts of the Italian Government. Unfortunately, whilst this united action was a moving testimony to international co-operation, it became increasingly obvious that all would depend upon the will of the Italian Government, in its determination in imposing, and its financial commitment in underwriting, a solution which would preserve Venice into the twenty-first century.

The problems facing any Italian Government are enormous as Italy has so much of the European heritage, not only in Venice; Florence, Rome, Assisi, Pisa and Naples and . . . one could go on through a whole catalogue of historic cities and noble buildings, all of them important landmarks in the history of European civilization. Provisions for safeguarding them are enshrined in a series of laws passed between 1892 and 1971. As a result of these, about 100,000 individually important buildings have statutory protection and may not be altered or demolished without permission. This provision is separate from those seeking to guarantee the protection and restoration of certain important historic towns. They are safeguarded by separate legislation; for instance, there are special laws for Venice itself and Assisi and Siena, and Urbino. Under a law of 1968, regional authorities are given power to establish strict regulations for safeguarding historic zones within their areas and there is provision for the awarding of grants. Over and above the statutory protection that is afforded and the grants that are made available – up to 50 per cent for restoration to listed buildings – there is the powerful pressure group known as Italia Nostra, founded in 1954, and now having over a hundred local branches or chapters, and a membership of some 20,000 in Italy and 50,000 abroad.

Some of the successes and failures, and continuing problems, facing the planning authorities are most clearly seen in Naples. The hills around the city bear witness to the inadequacy of past Italian planning regulations. They have been defaced and despoiled by thousands of featureless slabs of housing blocks. Historic and romantic landscape has gone for ever, buried under the undistinguished architectural excreta of the post-War developers. The heart of the old city, however, remains, dowdy and dingy, but largely inviolate and, though the vagaries of Italian drivers make a walk through the narrow courts and alleys a hair-raising experience, the street patterns and buildings have for the most part survived. But enormous sums of money will have to be spent if they are going to last beyond the end of this century. The city, however, pulsates with life and there seems an encouraging resolve that the ghastly mistakes on the hills around, based on a fraudulent falsification of the 1939 city plan, should not be repeated. The new city plan, resembling in intention that of 1939, limited the city's population to 1,100,000 and has among its features an intention to remove oil refineries and chemical works from the city. All remaining open spaces are to be preserved and the conservation area within the city enlarged from 170 hectares – the ancient centre – to 750 hectares, to protect the Spanish, Baroque and nineteenth-century extensions.

There is, though, all the difference between a plan and an achievement, especially in Italy, and the latest plan has not been widely accepted, still less welcomed, in every quarter. But plans are important. They show that people who care think, and they can often point the way for others in similar circumstances and in different countries. The low-cost housing plan in the

167

historic centre of Bologna has many features which could commend it to local authorities throughout Europe. The idea is based upon a belief that the town depends for its life on people of all classes being able to afford to live in it. The Bologna Council considered this an indispensable element in the active preservation of the centre of their city and wisely sought the co-operation of small proprietors, so that there would be no danger of their selling out to speculators, and no need for compulsory acquisition, which always slows up any work, in order to restore and conserve.

With a population of $13\frac{1}{4}$ million and expenditure of some 84 million guilders on preservation and restoration projects in Heritage Year, the Netherlands have one of the most encouraging records in the field of heritage, preservation and protection. A Government Commission was founded to prepare an inventory of historic monuments as long ago as 1903. The State Office for the Protection of Monuments was founded in 1918, and laws to ensure their protection were passed in 1940 and 1950, though the present comprehensive system was enacted as recently as 1965. Overall responsibility for the preservation of historic buildings and of town and village views rests with the Ministry of Cultural Affairs, Recreation and Social Work. Working through the State Service for the Preservation of Monuments and advised by the Monuments Council, an independent body established by statute, the provincial authorities are responsible for the provision of grants and the general maintenance of monuments within their territory. A number of the provinces have special by-laws for the purpose, and have also appointed local qualified inspectors to supervise their implementation. A similar situation exists in regard to the larger towns, and special restoration departments have in fact been established in some of these, such as Amsterdam, Haarlem and Utrecht. In the Netherlands, there is a proliferation of voluntary organizations working closely with local and central government. As in Britain, some of these organizations are of a general nature whereas others are specifically concerned with certain types of monuments, such as castles or windmills, and some restrict their activities to specific regions or towns. The State Service for the Preservation of Monuments is concerned with the grading of restoration projects and the provision of expert advice in cases where alterations to buildings are envisaged. It acts as a clearing-house for applications and gives information to applicants on how to obtain grants for maintenance, conversion and alteration. It has been instrumental in the establishment of a Documentation Centre on Dutch Architecture in Amsterdam, which is intended to form the nucleus of a future national museum of architecture. The Service has on its staff not only inspectors, but architects and town planners, art historians, artists and craftsmen and other specialists.

The Monuments Act of 1961, which the Service seeks to interpret and enforce, specifies monuments as 'those objects and sights, no less than fifty years old, which are of public interest because of their beauty and significance to science, ethnological value or historical association'. Under the Act, not only single monuments but groups of buildings can be designated. All the buildings listed under the Act are entered into a Monuments Register, which in 1975 contained some 40,000 entries, ranging from 27,800 private dwellings to 135 inns and including Government buildings (600), churches and other ecclesiastical buildings (2200), castles (250) and diverse monuments (a special category covering statues, gates, signposts, etc). In 1974, an additional register was compiled, which included 136 churches and 18 railway stations built between 1825 and 1924, as well as 25 archaeological sites in Friesland. Once a building has been listed, the owner is subject to certain restrictive provisions and must obtain permits for alteration or demolition. Similarly, he is eligible for grants of up to 70 per cent towards the cost of approved restorations.

As a result of these carefully constructed and monitored provisions, many thousands of houses throughout the Netherlands are restored each year and the budget for grants is certainly high compared with other countries. In spite of this, funds are not adequate to cover all authorized restoration projects and there is a substantial backlog of work. However, projects are always tackled with typical Dutch thoroughness and this is no doubt why so many Dutch towns preserve an individual identity very much more successfully than those in neighbouring countries. One of the by-products of the Dutch policy has been the discovery, as in the ancient city of Middleburg, that renewing a modest residential heritage can cost far less than its demolition and replacement by new accommodation. Tourists sometimes criticize Dutch restoration as being more in the nature of complete rebuilding but the results are so pleasing to the eye that most would discount this criticism as academic. They have also been particularly adept at finding new uses for old buildings, as in Amsterdam. where the round Lutheran Church, a fine example of Dutch classicism, has become a reception centre for a new hotel. They have set great store on maintaining the scale of street building, too, so that old and valued scenes are not unduly distorted by a skyline dominated by out-of-scale buildings.

As long ago as 1950, the famous Gowers Report on English Country Houses carried a special appendix on the protection of historic buildings and their contents in France. This pointed out that among other things the most important of French châteaux, *monuments classés*, qualified for repair grants of up to 50 per cent and could claim 50 per cent relief on tax on repair and maintenance expenditure.[1] The owner of a major French château is in a more advantageous position with regard to tax than the owner of a British stately home, but although the French system affords considerable protection to the greatest of its ancient buildings, many of the rest are in a somewhat dilapidated state.

France appointed its first Inspector General of Historic Monuments in 1830 and established its first Historic Monuments Commission in 1837. The original list of such monuments was drawn up in 1840 and, by 1841, a framework of control and grants to major cathedrals and other large monuments had been prepared. In this century, a whole series of laws has been passed between 1913 and 1975. The Historic Monuments Law of 1913, the basis of all subsequent legislation, provided for the strict control of a limited number of buildings and enacted the grant and tax provisions which the Gowers Report extolled. Under this law, some 75,000 movable objects – paintings, sculptures, etc. – were also listed. In 1930, a Sites Law, which established a list of protected town and country sites and parks eligible for grants, and which restricted development and building heights, was enacted and in 1945 came the concept of a protected zone of up to 50 metres radius around all designated monuments and sites. The seminal act of recent years was the Malraux Law of 1962, which designated some fifty protected areas and twenty-three action areas for which detailed conservation plans had to be made up and implemented. Loans of up to 60 per cent and a further grant of 20 per cent in the case of

1. When one considers how empty most of the great châteaux are in contrast to our great houses one realizes how foolish it is not to do everything possible to keep our houses and their contents together.

action areas were made available and under this law some 5300 buildings have already been restored at a cost of some hundred million francs in special grants. In France, all is very much under the eye of the central authorities and every action is carefully logged and monitored. The work that has been carried out, especially since the Malraux Law, has often been fascinating and spectacular. In Chartres and in Lyons, whole streets have been completely restored and in the Marais district of Paris buildings have been transformed from objectionable and filthy slums into luxurious apartment buildings and museums.

The disadvantage of the French system, however, is that, while certain selected buildings are subjected to the most thorough and comprehensive treatment on restoration, many pleasant and important vernacular buildings, such as the less important châteaux, and many villages and farm buildings, are left entirely without protection and are in danger of disappearing altogether. There is also a noticeable lack of public participation and involvement in conservation: either the State does it or no one does. There is, therefore, an urgent need for a reappraisal of the system which will enable more buildings to be helped and private initiative to be encouraged. Another criticism is that the expensive restoration often results in a situation whereby the working people who lived in an area cannot afford to return to their old homes at the new rents.

The contrasting of Ghent and Bruges shows the patchiness of approach and success in Belgian conservation issues. In Ghent, a project supported by the Ministry of Transport and the Ministry of Public Works among others, envisaged the filling-in of 10 kilometres of waterways to allow for the construction of an express highway through the city. This, in spite of the fact that the beauty of Ghent relies on the association of the buildings with the water. The same is true of Bruges, but there a beautiful and ancient city has been very successfully safeguarded. Canals in the centre of the city have been cleaned and the residential quarters attained a new attraction. The local authority is now backing the scheme, initiated by a private trust, and at present newly restored houses can be rented, but not bought, so that the authority has a tighter control over the character of the residential population. Belgium, however, is not a success story in the sphere of conservation. A law of 1931 does provide for the protection of monuments and sites and includes provision for control and grants for a limited number of the more outstanding

171

buildings, but with notable exceptions, such as that of Bruges (and at Louvain where the Grand Beguinage has been restored for use by the university). Belgium has few outstanding successes of which it can boast.

The Federal Republic of Germany, too, presents a strangely disappointing picture. One always thinks of Germany in terms of efficiency and, of course, some of their restoration projects, such as the *Rathaus* in Bonn, have been remarkably successful. However, there is no special protection for monuments in the federal laws although there are sections in the Federal Building Law which require developers to take into account 'cultural necessities' when producing plans. A number of the German Landes have no statutory provision for the protection of buildings either (Berlin, Bremen, Hamburg, Lower Saxony). In general, there seems no appreciation or implementation of the conservation area approach and towns as famous as Lubeck and Heidelberg seem remarkably vulnerable. In Lubeck there is already much disruption of the scale of the centre of the town by inappropriate modern building, and at Heidelberg little seems to have been achieved in the way of permanent protection, save the listing of some of the more important buildings.

In Bavaria, the picture is much more encouraging. Although, until recently, the protection of historic buildings had been achieved largely through voluntary agency, the State authorities have a record of consistent sympathy with conservation and the State has some examples of which any country could be proud. In the historic town centre of Nuremberg, where 90 per cent of the 2560 historic buildings were destroyed, there has been a painstaking reproduction of the old; there have been some magnificent reconstructions of war-damaged cathedrals and churches and castles; the old town of Rothenburg, a notable centre, has been exceptionally well preserved. Regensburg is another notable example of a revived and attractive historic city, and Munich itself has been pedestrianized to a greater extent than almost any other major European city.

The most outstanding examples of complete reconstruction, however, come from behind the Iron Curtain, and no story is more moving than Warsaw's. Warsaw was devastated during the Second World War; and in 1945, when half the population was living in tents or rubble houses and with hunger bordering on famine proportions, it was decided to rebuild this historic capital of Poland. It was seen as a national gesture of faith and

172

the results have been remarkable. With painstaking accuracy, whole areas arose with their former glories and the opportunity of rebuilding allowed for more open space and therefore a better setting for many of the great public buildings. The Russians adopted a similar policy, especially in Leningrad, and the opportunity has been taken to encourage craftsmanship and to inspire the young with a particular regard for the treasures of the past. There is something contrived and clinical in all this rebuilding, but the results have been astonishing and ought to act as a spur to those of us in the West who have so many genuine old buildings that demand our careful attention if they are to be safeguarded and appreciated into the next century. We also have the added incentive of being able to restore buildings that are still being used for their original purpose. If a purely aesthetic appreciation of what is pleasing and a dispassionate regard for certain versions of the nation's history is sufficient to prompt the Russians to erect their wooden churches in open-air museums, then our motivating force should be even greater with the opportunity to preserve a living history and tradition. But this should not allow us to belittle the achievements of Eastern Europe, nor to denigrate the genuine regard which has prompted these feats of rebuilding, restoration and preservation.

Whole volumes could be written on this subject, and this one can only afford the passing reference. A similar reference, however, must obviously be made to the United States of America where in the bicentenary year of 1976 a cherishing of the past and a re-enactment of selected portions of it became both a national preoccupation and a national industry. The lavish protection afforded to the great national shrines in and around Washington is second to none and the loving care with which chapters of the nation's past have been rebuilt at Jamestown and Williamsberg is quite remarkable. Williamsberg, in particular, is a startlingly successful recreation of an old colonial capital, based on the restoration of what had survived and the rebuilding of what had been lost. This centre of national pilgrimage and historical entertainment could easily have become trivialized, especially as all the restored shops do business and all the inns serve food and drink. But restrained good taste prevails and to walk through the town is like taking a step back in time and to have an acuter appreciation than anywhere else of just what the eighteenth-century colonial capital was like. There is certainly nothing quite like this anywhere in

Europe. However, the concept of preservation in the USA has only recently begun to replace the old frontier mentality of exploiting resources and then moving from one locality to the next without much regard for what was left behind. Now, prompted by such bodies as the Council for Environment Equality, established in 1970, there is a concerted attempt to ensure that what remains of the American past is properly regarded and maintained. In 1975, Senator Henry Jackson promoted a Land Use Bill which had, as its major objective, a regulation of the somewhat chaotic planning structure, the establishment of an order of priorities which would obviously go far towards safeguarding the best of the past.

The problems of the USA over conservation of historic buildings are small in comparison with those faced by most European nations. However, it is in America that one sees twentieth-century civilization at its ultimate, with all the benefits and pitfalls that its impedimenta generate; and much of the American experience can act as a warning to all of us who lag behind in adopting the gagetry and gimmickry of a 'throw-away' society. Perhaps the acutest twentieth-century problems with which Americans have to cope are those of pollution. The average American family produces 4lb of domestic refuse per person per day, twice the current British rate, and in many parts of the USA, and indeed in almost any town of any size, the problems of pollution are manifest and manifold. (One does not merely have to think of the Los Angeles smog or the stagnant waters of the Great Lakes.) Both Federal and State authorities have, in the last decade, begun to battle with some success on the pollution front, and thus water and air pollution control legislation, which includes provision for 'citizen participation', are now on the Federal Statute Book.

Parts of Europe can make us feel fairly satisfied with the level of our own pollution problems and the measures taken to redress them. The Mediterranean, for instance, is a heavily polluted zone along much of its coastline and, although those like Lord Ritchie Calder and Jacques Cousteau are perhaps unnecessarily pessimistic in forecasting doom and stagnation for this brightest of European seas, the débris of the industrial nations around its shores – sewage, oil and industrial waste – which cause disease and destroy marine life do present enormous hazards. It is reckoned, for instance, that 90 per cent of all sewage flowing into the Mediterranean is untreated, that 300,000

174

tons of oil is dumped into the Sea every year; that the Rhône alone discharges 500 tons of pesticides and 1250 tons of detergent each year. It would be unjust to suggest that the Mediterranean countries are doing nothing, but their programmes do seem to lack a necessary degree of international co-operation and urgency. The magnitude of the problem though, is illustrated by the fact that the new sewage plants for the Bay of Naples alone cost something over £100 million.

Britain's record, in comparison with her neighbours, is not a bad one but much can be learnt from the thoroughness with which the Dutch tackle their problems. In the Netherlands, there is a greater emphasis on the importance of history and appreciation of art, and secondary school pupils are given a thorough grounding in these subjects. As a result there is a close liaison between schools and museums, and the directors of the national museums and representatives of the Department of Archaeology and Nature Conservation and the Ministry of Cultural Affairs Recreation and Social Work meet several times a year to discuss common interests and how they can best work together. But of the 400 museums in the country only eighteen are national museums and the Government provides advisory services and grants to many of the rest. There is a Government Inspector for National Works of Art and his office makes recommendations to the governing bodies of these museums and galleries not owned by the State. It acts as an information centre, organizing travelling exhibitions and, in its registry, records works of art that are not housed in State museums but which belong to the State. In addition, the office functions as a centre for the collection of works of art that were recovered from Germany after the War and which could not be returned to their original owners. The registry is also responsible for paintings and drawings and other works of contemporary artists who receive financial assistance from the State. The Netherlands, too, is a pioneer in the concept of the open-air museum. Near Arnhem, a large and representative collection of Dutch buildings that would have otherwise been lost – windmills, houses, shops, etc. – have been reassembled in open-air settings and have for many years given not only delight, but a clear insight into methods of building and types of housing fast disappearing in parts of the country.

There are now open-air museums in Britain, and perhaps our most spectacular venture is at Iron Bridge on the Severn Gorge.

This exciting experiment in industrial archaeology, a new but an increasingly fascinating and, until recently, a sadly neglected field, is attracting considerable numbers of visitors. In 1977, the Iron Bridge Gorge Museum won the coveted Museum of the Year award. This in itself showed the properly increased recognition given to the importance of industrial archaeology, especially as in 1976 the award had been won by another exciting, privately financed, industrial museum: the Gladstone Pottery Museum at Stoke-on-Trent. That was the product of the foresight of a small group who, in the early 1970s, suddenly realized that the whole of the history of the Potteries would be confined to photographs and the printed page, as all the old kilns were demolished to make way for advanced technology. It was decided to save one of these old potteries and to turn it into a living museum where people could see how the area had acquired both its name and its prosperity. Thus the Gladstone Pottery Museum was born, and today thousands of people, and especially children, get a new pride in their industrial origins as they visit the static demonstrations and the living workshops, and examine the old kilns and processes. A similar attempt to preserve the industrial past of a nation can be seen at Englesberg, a tiny village of about 200 inhabitants some 160 km north-west of Stockholm. This is in Bergslagen, the traditional centre of the Swedish mining and iron-working industry. A number of buildings have been preserved, renovated and restored and Englesberg has been declared an historic area under an Act of the Swedish Parliament of 1960.

There is, in this part of Sweden, the potential for a vast industrial museum where appropriate historic monuments in their original settings could illustrate the old techniques and the development of the mining and metal-making process. Although some of the installations and buildings have been listed as monuments, and some converted to other uses, many of the old workshops and houses are derelict and in danger of demolition and others are falling down as the result of years of neglect. This is something of a tragedy, for Sweden has more monuments connected with the mining and metal industry than any other country in Europe, an industry going back to the twelfth century and reaching its climax in the nineteenth.

As elsewhere, sophisticated techniques and the march of technology had their casualties and the reminders of the foundations on which the Swedish iron industry was built

176

diminished rapidly in number during the last century, although the last charcoal furnace did not cease operation until 1966. And so, as the iron industry progressed, the old iron works were abandoned or closed down and reminders of a former greatness disappeared. Still, Sweden is rich in monuments and many of them are worth maintaining, because of their intrinsic attractiveness as buildings and because they form a vital part not only of Swedish but of European industrial history. Alas, their future is far from secure and therefore Englesberg was chosen as one of the pilot projects in European Architectural Heritage Year in the hope that it would stimulate debate on the necessity of retaining the whole Bergslagen district as a vast conservation area. In this, as in so much else, finance plays a vital part. Many of the buildings and installations in question are still the properties of industrial companies and of necessity their first priority must be towards production and continued prosperity. Thus, with a government decision to reduce the contribution from central finance for all conservation work, the future of Sweden's industrial heritage is at risk.

Throughout Europe, adequate conservation of the heritage depends on effective partnership of government and private, individual and industrial co-operation. There is a need for harnessing business and commercial sponsorship of the arts in all their forms. And there is a need for giving adequate incentive and special consideration to those who, through accident of birth and inheritance, have the duty of guarding much of a country's history and heritage. Although this is recognized by many European governments in their taxation structure, it is particularly depressing to note that, whereas this country has more of its heritage dependent on an enlightened guardianship, and where the record of that stewardship is second to none, the burdens of taxation on the stewards are heavier and administered in a more insensitive way here than almost anywhere else in the free world.

Most governments do not create the same fiscal problems for the agriculturalist, the owner of the country house or the collector of works of art as does the British Government. For instance, the highest rate of personal Income Tax in the United Kingdom is 98 per cent, whereas in Germany it is 56 per cent, in France 60 per cent and even in Italy – our closest challenger in this field – 82 per cent. And it is not just in Income Tax that the United Kingdom heads the league. In March 1975,

177

the Chancellor of the Exchequer was asked if he would set out a table showing the maximum rate of tax on a gratuitous transfer of capital by a man on his death to his son, for Germany, Belgium, France, Holland, Italy and the UK. The table produced in answer made fairly stark reading. In the UK the percentage could be as high as 75 per cent whereas in Belgium and Holland the highest rate was 17 per cent, in France 20 per cent, in Germany 35 per cent, and in Italy 31 per cent. Similar figures apply to lifetime gifts.

On top of Britain's penal rates of Income Tax and high level of Capital Transfer Tax, it is the intention[2] of the British Labour Party to introduce a Wealth Tax as soon as they have a stable Parliamentary majority. Many countries already have such a tax and in Belgium the rate can be as high as 72 per cent and in Ireland 70 per cent, down to Denmark, where it is 39.6 per cent. However, Denmark, the Netherlands, Sweden and Norway give total exemption to works of art, and Germany partial exemption. Favourable treatment, too, is given to the owners of historic houses. In Denmark, the only part of the house taken into account is that which is actually lived in; in Germany, houses and estates which are open to the public are exempt and other historic houses are charged at 40 per cent of the full rate. In the Netherlands, estates designated as preservation areas and open to the public are charged at 25 per cent of the value of the parkland and, in Sweden and Norway, there are no special concessions, but Wealth Tax valuation on historic houses is very low and there is exemption in Norway for land that is under statutory protection by reason of scientific or historic interest. Agriculture, too, has special treatment in Denmark, Germany, the Netherlands, Sweden and Norway. Comparative figures and tables are always difficult to compile, for they do tend to change from year to year, but what emerges quite clearly, from even the most perfunctory study, is that the incidence of taxation in the UK is already much higher than in most of Europe, even without the added imposition of a Wealth Tax. It is equally apparent that most European countries make more concessions for the heritage than Britain does.

One of the other keys to the preservation and survival of the heritage is the adequate encouragement of conservation techniques and of those who practise them. The inadequate facilities in most European countries for the training of architects and

2. Reaffirmed as recently as December 1977.

178

craftsmen in conservation is alarming. In an admirable article in the Heritage Year publication, *Architectural Conservation in Europe* (1975), Bernard Fielden and Derek Linstrum of York University make this observation:

> Taking it [conservation] in its widest architectural sense, as the method of ensuring continuity to a building, it is clear that whether this is achieved by preservation, restoration, consolidation, adaptation, rehabilitation (or even at times reconstruction or imagination), that it must be a part of a large number of general architectural purposes and should be regarded as a normal professional skill which might need at times a specialist's knowledge and experience. It is equally clear that the conservation of great monuments, cathedrals, castles and ruined abbeys, country houses and public buildings, is another professional obligation. Whether it is undertaken by public or private practice, it must continue as a service to the public.

Fielden and Linstrum, surveying the provision of training facilities available to undergraduate architects in Europe, come up with the depressing information that 'only in Louvain, Delft, Copenhagen, Aarhus and Stockholm are there facilities for the study before graduating of the restoration of historic monuments or the problems of historic town centres'. Bearing in mind the vast dimensions of the problem, and the number of historic buildings which need expert attention, this is a depressing statistic and it is made all the more so when one considers that there are few postgraduate courses on conservation either. France has its well-established ones in the *Centre d'Etudes Supérieures d'Histoire et de Conservation desMonuments Anciens*, whose qualifications are essential for any wishing to practise in the field of conservation. There are also postgraduate courses in Madrid, Segovia, Copenhagen, Rome and Naples. Most of these courses are intended to serve the countries in which they are situated but, as Fielden and Linstrum point out, none is exclusively national and they suggest that a possible new rôle for UNESCO could be in co-ordinating and strengthening the links already existing between these courses and those in Britain and North America and, potentially, in Central and South America as well.[3] The situation in architecture is mirrored in the state of craftsmanship in general throughout the Continent. Because the building industry has become ever more

3. Happily, Fielden was appointed to do this job for UNESCO in Rome in 1977.

dependent on the techniques of mechanization, the need for higher standards of workmanship has tended to diminish, and so the truly proficient carpenter, bricklayer, mason, plasterer and glazier are in very short supply.

The old-fashioned edifice of the City and Guilds Craft Training and the five years' apprenticeship has been simplified and condensed by the wishes of the building industry. The skills required by the present-day building industry are now inadequate for conservation work, where the craftsman needs the ability to be able to think out problems for himself, based on the knowledge of traditional techniques and materials.

Fielden and Linstrum suggest the whole organization and incentives of the construction industry militate against the encouragment of craftsmanship, and this is a European problem.

This chapter has merely touched on some of the problems, but what it has possibly illustrated is that the problems are common, and that, although some other nations might have things that they can teach us, especially in the way most of their tax systems operate, the difficulties facing the heritage are similar throughout Europe and demand the same blend of sensitivity and patience and positive commitment if they are to be solved. The wider heritage is worth fighting for, and all over Europe there is greater realization of this fact. European Architectural Heritage Year was not an unqualified success, but that it ever happened at all should give cause for rejoicing, and real optimism to all of those new people who now realize that without their active interest and their constant cajoling of government, their heritage will not merely be in danger – it will disappear.

Chapter Eleven

Some Solutions –
the Preservation
of the Heritage

It would be very easy to end on a gloomy and despondent note. Much of the finest of our past has disappeared and the threat of decay or destruction hangs over much of what remains. But much does remain and there is no reason why, given public will and Government resolve, our heritage should not be progressively enhanced and our descendants two centuries from now have as rich and varied an inheritance as we enjoy today.

Enhancement implies addition and it would be a mistake to think purely in terms of preserving monuments and works from the past. A heritage, if it is to have meaning and inspire affection, is something that is being added to constantly, and added to not only by acts of preservation but by new works of creative genius.

Though the dedication of individuals and the activities of voluntary societies, and schools and other institutions, will always have a vital part to play in the conservation field, the central rôle inevitably, if regrettably, belongs to Government. Given the backing of authority there is little that cannot be achieved, but if Government is negligent or uninterested the erosion of our history, the impoverishment of our landscape, and the disappearance of our finest buildings will continue. Understandably, the provision of hospitals and schools, roads and sewers and other public services will always take priority over the preservation of the landscape and historic buildings, or the encouragement of the arts. But these are not the only amenities essential to the living of a well-ordered and comfortable life.

One of the phrases politicians are particularly fond of using is 'the quality of life'. If challenged, most of us would say that it is our duty to protect quality where it exists and to promote it where it does not. But definitions of this 'quality' are not so easily supplied. Pledging oneself to protect and promote the quality of life must mean something more than the incantation of a favourite slogan. It must mean, in particular, having a clearly developed strategy for the defence of the national heritage and promotion of the arts. For much that is best and most enjoyed in this country is symbolized by, and enshrined in, the landscapes and buildings and great collections that constitute our heritage, and much that is most excellent and vigorous in our national life is represented by our achievements in the arts.

To say that Government must have such a strategy is not to suggest that it should be the rôle of any politician to advocate the creation of an all-embracing ministry of culture on the Eastern European model, with the unhappy and stultifying connotations of 'State Art' that such a creation brings to mind. But politicians do have it in their power to create conditions where things can happen, and it should be a foremost aim to create conditions where things that are excellent are safe from harm, and talents that are creative and imaginative are positively encouraged. In no field of policy are such conditions easier, or cheaper, to create than in that of the heritage and the arts, and nowhere is it more important that they should be created, and created quickly. That things could so easily be put right – and at little cost – is both a tragedy and a challenge. A sensitive and imaginative Minister could do for the nation what Myra Hess did for Londoners during the last War – lighten the darkness and inspire the weary. But the most sensitive and imaginative person can only be an effective Minister if he has the authority to reveal his sensitivity and the opportunity to display his imagination.

That is why we should be thinking in terms of appointing a Cabinet Minister with total responsibility for the heritage and the arts, a Minister with the chance to formulate a strategy and the muscle to ensure its effective execution. At the moment, much of the heritage is in the hands of the Department of the Environment and most of the arts are under the jurisdiction of the Department of Education and Science. The junior Ministers who, often valiantly, fight for both can easily be divided and conquered, or just ignored, by a Chancellor besieged by Cabinet colleagues with demands on more spectacular fronts. Even within their own departments the responsibilities of these Ministers are often reckoned to be of relatively minor importance.

A Minister who had an overall responsibility for seeing that Canterbury cathedral did not collapse nor Wilton House become a deserted ruin; that London remained the theatre capital of the world; that true craftsmanship and artistry was stimulated; and that our great collections did not evaporate before the dragon breath of the taxman, would be in a powerful position when arguing with his colleagues. He would be powerful not only because of the obvious and recognized importance of his job, but because he could discharge his responsibilities to much benefit at little cost.

The benefit is not difficult to demonstrate. Forgetting for a moment the vital educative and civilizing rôle of the arts in any society, and the importance of a national heritage to a nation's culture, it does not take much forensic skill to argue that our heritage and arts represent much of our wealth in the full financial sense of the word. Tourists who come to Britain, and without whose money we would already be both the poor and the sick man of Europe, do not come especially to bask in our sunshine or sample our cuisine. They come to marvel at our history and share in our heritage, and to enjoy, in London in particular, our drama, our opera and our ballet. In 1977 alone, overseas visitors spent something over £2300 million within the UK and another £600 million in fares on British air and shipping lines. In 1976, when there were over 10 million visitors, our balance of payments benefited to the tune of some £640 million.[1]

Tourism is, in fact, one of the fastest growing earners of foreign currency for Britain, and all sections of the community benefit from tourist spending. Yet it is not only overseas tourists who

1. During the year 1976–7, total Government expenditure on the arts amounted to £79,7 million, including expenditure on construction works and the maintenance of buildings at the national museums and galleries. During the same period £3.1 million was spent on grants for the repair of historic buildings and for the preservation and enhancement of conservation areas. Local authorities spent a further £750,000 on historic buildings. Total national and local authority expenditure on conservation since 1953 amounts to some £21 million. These figures do not include expenditure on buildings and monuments in the care of the Department of the Environment.

help to prime the pump of the national economy. In 1976, 50 million holiday trips of four nights or more were undertaken by British citizens and 40 million of those were taken within the United Kingdom. British citizens spent some £1750 million on these holidays and many of them included in their itinerary at least one historic house or museum or cathedral; 15 million separate visits were paid to historic houses in private ownership during 1976.

It is surely quite extraordinary that, given these figures, we should have a situation where many of the attractions that delight these tourists should be fighting for survival. What then should be the policies and priorities of a Government enlightened enough to create an important and co-ordinating Ministry for the Heritage and the Arts?

Its responsibilities for the landscape would inevitably not be absolute for, as we have seen, the landscape depends so much upon farming, and farming obviously would remain the responsibility of the Ministry of Agriculture. However, there is no reason why the Minister for the Heritage should not have an overall responsibility for the national parks and for the designation of areas of natural beauty. He could do much, too, to encourage those industrialists and architects who are becoming increasingly aware of their responsibility towards the creation of a pleasant environment for industry by supporting the technically feasible and generally very successful large tree transplanting operations which have already done much to transform the landscape in industrial areas. He could also, no doubt in concert with the Minister of Agriculture, realizing how much the landscape depends upon the farmer, encourage the Chancellor to provide a legislative framework for an owner of agricultural land to 'dedicate' it for agriculture on the lines of the forestry dedication scheme and receive tax concessions if he did so. The advantage of such a scheme would be to give inducement to landscape preservation to owners who now find themselves preoccupied with fiscal worries.

One also finds it difficult not to believe that an active Minister for the Heritage would not have sought to inspire a more active Government fight against the scourge of Dutch Elm disease as it ravaged and rampaged through most of England. Certainly he could have a stimulating rôle in ensuring that proper encouragement and incentives were given to farmers and landowners, both public and private, to replace with good English trees, as so

184

many have done, the elms that have been lost. This Minister could work closely with the Countryside Commission and do much to encourage such valiant and imaginative schemes as Enterprise Neptune, one of the most splendid ventures ever promoted by a non-Governmental agency or association. Enterprise Neptune has already added 175 miles of outstanding coastline to the 190 in the possession or the protection of the National Trust. But many more hundreds of miles are in danger of despoliation or 'threatened' with improvement, and they surely constitute an emotive and valuable part of the heritage of an island race.

He could stand up, too, for the National Trust in its struggle to preserve the principle of the inalienability of the National Trust land, endangered, for instance, by the West Sussex County Council's plan to relieve Petworth's town traffic problem by building a by-pass through the grounds of Petworth House, so threatening perhaps the finest example of Capability Brown's genius. For such a Minister could do much to ensure that the powers of local authorities were supervised and controlled in a field where they have so frequently been misused by the shortsighted, the indifferent, or the frankly hostile.

These attitudes have taken their toll of some of our finest townscapes and buildings, and there is certainly a need in this regard for a stronger Governmental presence. Perhaps the Government should give serious attention to designating some of our finest remaining towns as 'heritage towns', so as to ensure that special resources are made available to assist in their preservation and that not all of the decisions about their future are left to local councils, for local councils can, as we have seen, make great mistakes. Although there has been a considerable extension of sensible and protective legislation over the last few years there are still grave threats facing many of our historic buildings, and of these perhaps the gravest is the cost of maintenance and repair.

The Historic Buildings Council administers Government grants and loans toward the upkeep of Grade 1, and sometimes Grade 2, buildings, and buildings in outstanding conservation areas. Owners of other Grade 2 buildings, however – those buildings often of vital importance to the preservation of a whole street or town or village scene – do not normally qualify for any assistance, despite current legislation that can prevent them from demolishing or altering a building they cannot afford to maintain. A Minister for the Heritage would obviously have some added weight if he sought to widen the Historic Buildings Council's terms of reference so that proper assistance could be given to Grade 2 buildings, and indeed there is something to be said for the theory that the very act of listing could include some entitlement to a grant.

It might be argued, of course, that the Local Authority (Historic Buildings) Act of 1962 was intended to help the owners of any historic building, and especially those outside the scope of the Historic Buildings Council. In fact, local authorities very rarely use their powers to give grants: there always seems to be something more pressing on the agenda and more justifiable to the ratepayer. I sought to introduce an Historic Churches Preservation Bill in successive sessions of Parliament and this did include a clause to enforce the provisions of the 1962 Act. The Government felt unable to accede to it then, but perhaps this is something that could be achieved with an Exchequer subsidy towards local authority expenditure, along the lines of the successful 'town schemes' in which central and local Government pay joint grants towards the repair of buildings and selected urban areas of outstanding interest.

But provision of extra Government finance, as desirable and welcome as it would be, is not necessarily the most important form of aid and incentive that could be given. As long ago as 1950, the Gowers Committee's Report recommended that owners of historic houses should be entitled to certain types of tax relief if they opened their houses to the public, including income tax and surtax in respect of expenditure on the house and relief from death duties on the house, land and property, to provide an income for maintenance. Although they have frequently been advocated these recommendations have never been implemented.[2]

Now we have seen that with the additional burden of the Capital Transfer Tax, and the still present threat of Wealth Tax hanging over their heads, the owners of historic buildings are in a siege condition. They certainly need a powerful Minister to point out to his colleagues that it would cost little to achieve much, to ensure that neither Capital Transfer Tax nor Wealth Tax so distorted social priorities that in seeking equality they destroyed what all our people now have the opportunity to

2. Changes introduced in the 1976 Finance Act do not begin to tackle this problem effectively.

enjoy: Britain's country parks with their houses and the collections they contain. The National Trust would certainly be the first to pass a vote of thanks to any Minister who achieved this for, as they said in their annual report for 1975: 'Believing that the private owner looks after these properties best, and at the lowest cost, the Trust will continue its efforts to ensure that the issues at stake are fully understood and will press for policies that will make this possible.'

The further fiscal burden that menaces not only private owners but those entrusted with the preservation of our ancient churches is that of VAT. This is chargeable on the repair and maintenance of buildings and it has been calculated that if it were lifted in respect of historic buildings in order to help owners and others to keep them in good condition the total cost to the Government in lost revenue would be very modest. It is difficult to justify a situation where those who give – many of them are small givers – to bodies like the Historic Churches Preservation Trust, are inadvertently supporting the Chancellor of the Exchequer, and it is ridiculous that grants from the Historic Buildings Council should be diminished in their value because of the imposition of VAT on the repairs they make possible. One of the ironies of the situation that was brought out in the 'Change and Decay' exhibition, was that in 1976 repairs on Church of England buildings brought more than £1 million to the Exchequer at a time when the Government was protesting that it could not afford to make a similar sum available in State aid for Churches.

Of course, if the intentions of its founder had been truly honoured, the National Land Fund would be there to provide the rescue resources so often needed to safeguard a great building or fine landscape, or prevent a notable work of art from being exported. But the deficiencies of the Land Fund, or rather the inhibiting interpretation of its function, insisted upon by the Treasury, were most graphically demonstrated during the Mentmore saga. Indeed, one of the most farcical aspects of the whole story was the debate over the precise nature of the Land Fund.[3] The Fund was established by Dr Dalton in 1946, with £50 million from the sale of war stores, the idea being to create a

3. By the autumn of 1977 such was the concern in Parliament and outside at the way in which the fund was being operated, and at the decision not to use it to save Mentmore (see page 73) that the House of Commons Select Committee on the Environment began a detailed investigation of its workings and promised to report to the House in the spring of 1978.

fund which could be used for a variety of purposes connected with the preservation of historic buildings and landscapes of outstanding natural beauty. He thought that it would be 'a thank offering for victory and a war memorial which, in the judgement of many, is better than a work of art in stone or bronze.' Unfortunately, his imaginative idea has not lived up to his hopes, and although the Fund has been used for the acceptance of chattels and a number of fine houses, the Treasury rules which hedge its operation prevented it from being used to save either Stonor or Mentmore. During the Mentmore debate the Treasury was quite adamant that its use was a charge upon the Public Purse, as it involved selling securities and therefore borrowing money. This in spite of the fact that it was also made plain in Parliamentary answer that it is possible for individuals to give to, or to bequeath to, the Land Fund, actions which they take presumably because they believe that its founder's intentions will be honoured. Again, according to Parliamentary answer, the Fund stood at almost £18 million at the spring of 1977, and in every year but one, since it had been raided by the Macmillan administration and reduced from £50 million to £10 million, it had earned more than it had spent. This wrangling must end. There is a necessity for a true contingency fund; a fund, moreover, that would, as Private Members' Bills in both the Commons and Lords advocated in 1977, be administered or supervised by a body of trustees able to take decisions on the true merits of each case. A contingency fund fed by annual grant, and available to ensure that no outstanding building crumbles into ruin for lack of assistance, and no outstanding work of art leaves these shores for lack of funds, would be a real insurance against future Mentmore-type disasters.

Listed buildings are still being demolished without permission because fines for demolition, although they can be severe, are in practice rarely penal. A more effective sanction might be the adoption of the French system of refusing any subsequent planning permission for a site where a building has been demolished without consent. There is another loophole in the law in that a building, even though it is part of a conservation area, is exempt from protection if planning permission was obtained prior to the designation of the area. This means that a building totally out of scale and character can sometimes be erected after the importance of an area has been officially recognized.

188

Another measure that is sorely needed to preserve scale and character is one designed to restrict the heights of buildings in sensitive areas – in order to protect grand views and noble vistas. Their protection was, indeed, one of the original aims of the founders of the Civic Trust in 1957 but legislative action was not taken. In 1977 I presented a Skyline Protection Bill to Parliament which sought to draw attention to the problem and to indicate some possible remedies. The Bill did get an unopposed Second Reading[4] but there was not sufficient Parliamentary time to enact it. However, the fact that it had significant all-Party support, and attracted the sponsorship of two former Secretaries of State for the Environment (Peter Walker and Geoffrey Rippon), gives me grounds for hoping that something along these lines, a logical and sensible extension of the Conservation Area concept, will be enacted before the Civic Trust celebrates its silver jubilee.

Other threats to conservation areas are the building of roads or motorways, as has been seen at Petworth, and at Chillington – perhaps the classic case. There, a six-lane motorway is to be driven through the finest Capability Brown park in the Midlands, even though the local authority, Staffordshire County Council, had the imagination and foresight to declare the whole of the Chillington grounds a conservation area, and even though the Inspector at the Public Inquiry acknowledged that enormous environmental damage would be done and recommended the consideration of alternative routes.

In London a listed building can still deliberately be neglected by an owner in order to redevelop the site. Under the London Buildings (Amendment) Act if a building is declared unsafe and a Dangerous Structure Notice is issued by the District Surveyor, a court can order its demolition regardless of every protection given by planning laws. In 1975, Sir George Dobry's final Report on 'The Review of the Development Control System' emphasized the need for tighter control in special environmental areas, including conservation areas. It was recommended that this control could be achieved through a more extensive use of existing powers, although the same Committee's interim report on Control of Demolition suggested that some further control was necessary.

The Save Report in December 1975 suggested that listed buildings should be presumed 'innocent' and condemned only

4. Though the Government was less than warm in its enthusiasm.

if an overwhelming case against them had been proved: 'Otherwise they should be discharged unconditionally. The burden of proof should rest with the applicant who should be required to give reasons for demolition – the test should be why demolish? not, why save?' Another deficiency in the present system highlighted in the Save Report is that the public notices for an application to demolish need be only a small notice outside the building in question, and a paragraph on the announcements page of the local newspaper. It is very rare that photographs of the threatened building are published, or even available for inspection, and owners and architects can, and frequently do, refuse the Press permission to reproduce plans of such new buildings or alterations as are proposed. The Report suggests that all notices of applications for listed building consent should be accompanied by proper photographs.

It is in matters like this that Government direction is needed for most of the laws relating to historic buildings are administered by local authorities and the powers they have, though extensive, are rarely used. A Minister for the Heritage could take a much stronger line on these matters and could perhaps do something to ensure that where local authorities fail to discharge their obligations they are called to account. The very last thing a Minister for the Heritage would do would be to imply, by suggestion of Government omnipotence, that voluntary effort was neither required nor necessary. Nowhere is this truer than in the case of historic churches. Here it is vital that communities should contrive to have a congregational responsibility and voluntary aid should continue side by side with State aid. Churches must not become mere museums because of State assistance in restoring them.

There is definitely a vital rôle for Government in ensuring that this priceless heritage of largely medieval architecture survives. One often ignored factor is that our churches contain within them some of the most interesting and irreplaceable parts of our heritage and the national funding of a survey and the listing of individual objects of special merit in parish churches, as is the practice with historical monuments in France, has much to commend it.

The present intention is not to assist cathedrals with State funds but Government aid in the setting up of cathedral workshops that would combat the serious shortage of craftsmen would be a welcome step. Indeed, Government encouragement and subsidizing of regional craft workshops based upon our cathedrals would be a constructive move. But these buildings are of supreme national importance and must have a properly recognized eligibility for assistance from central funds.

State funds are, of course, already provided for redundant churches but so far only for the Anglican ones. As Marcus Binney has suggested, the Redundant Churches Fund could well be extended to become a National Trust for Churches. Its aid could then be available to unwanted churches, chapels and kirks of all denominations throughout the United Kingdom and it could recruit members to augment its resources and to enlist public support of a voluntary nature.

There is something very sad, however, about the word 're-dundant' when applied to churches, and with the proper encouragement of bodies such as the Historic Churches Preservation Trust and the Friends of Friendless Churches and with fiscal aid (by the removal of VAT) to local congregations, and a provision of State aid in cases of real need, the redundancy solution would not be invoked as lightly as it has been in some dioceses. Imaginative alternative uses such as the transforming of suitable churches into concert halls should continue to be encouraged, but it must be recognized that churches of significant value architecturally are frequently unsuitable for conversion; those that are and cannot be kept in a state of good repair by the Fund should be allowed to fall into ruin rather than be bulldozed into oblivion as the present regulations demand. There are, of course, a number of ruined churches and where these are of any worth they could be registered with the Ministry of the Heritage as ancient monuments and opened to the public in the same way that our ruined abbeys and castles are.

As long ago as 1971, the Civic Trust approached the Department of the Environment and advocated the setting up of a National Building Conservation Fund. It pointed out that the initiative for setting up such a fund would have to come from the Government and suggested as a first step exploratory consultation with such bodies as the British Tourist Authority and the CBI, leading chambers of commerce, building societies and insurance companies. There is a rôle for such commercial and industrial involvement and recently an Association for Business Sponsorship of the Arts, under the chairmanship of Lord Goodman, was established. It should be encouraged in every possible way.[5] It should not need Government funds, but it could do much to encourage commercial and industrial participation in the preservation of the heritage and the patronage of the arts. Whether we will ever adopt in Britain the full range of fiscal incentives that exist in the USA, where it is permissible to deduct from taxable income the value of donations of money or works of art to public institutions, is possibly doubtful. But it is noticeable that the American scheme has played a very large part, and a very constructive part, in the establishment in the United States of some of the finest collections in the world. It is surely not anti-social or reprehensible to give tax concessions to those companies and individuals who are prepared to support public projects and adorn public collections. The sponsorship of the performing arts and the collection of objects of beauty should be seen as laudable aims in themselves – as laudable as any other form of industrial or private investment or saving.

Both sides of industry could play a particularly valuable part in helping our public museums to maintan and increase their collections. The grants for extensions to museums and for acquisitions of new works are, as we have seen, grossly inadequate. When a great work comes on to the market, a public appeal is invariably the one means of saving it for the nation, but what incentive is there when, as in the case of the 'Donatello Relief', saved for the Victoria and Albert Museum in the early part of 1976, an appreciable part of the money subscribed finds its way back to the Exchequer? In this instance, a commercial concern produced silver replicas of the relief and the entire profits were given to the purchase fund. However, silver is liable for $12\frac{1}{2}$ per cent (25 per cent until April 1976) VAT and so far from giving money towards the purchase the Government found itself £26,000 the richer as a result.[6] A strong and central Ministry could surely do something to ensure that this sort of anomaly did not exist; and to ensure that local authorities did not starve, or treat as mere Cinderellas, the museums and collections in their

5. In a letter to the *Financial Times*, 29 May 1976, Brenda Capstick, Secretary of the Museums Association, expressed the need for private and business sponsorship and welcomed the idea of lotteries to provide 'desperately needed' additional funds for provincial museums and galleries.

6. In 1975–6, VAT receipts from the sale of antiques and fine arts, and the sales of works by living artists, authors, and composers amounted to £8 million – over three times the amount the Government spent on grants and loans to historic buildings.

The techniques of a new age used to preserve the
beauties of an old: work on the new foundations of
York Minster. *Shepherd Building Group Ltd*

The church of St Faith, Little Witchingham as the Trust found it.
Peter Newbolt, for the Norfolk Churches Trust

St Faith's church, Little Witchingham after part of the medieval wall paintings had been discovered. *Peter Newbolt, for the Norfolk Churches Trust*

Right: Natural disaster: one of two spirelets of Peterborough Cathedral blown down by the great gales of January 1976. *Dean and Chapter of Peterborough Cathedral*

The ravages of time: stained glass from the panel, 'Adam Delving', showing the damage caused by acids from atmospheric pollution. *Canterbury Cathedral*

The face of Adam from the same panel shows pitting, erosion and fracturing. *Canterbury Cathedral*

The empty shell: stripped of its contents Mentmore faces
an uncertain future. *Strutt and Parker*

The Stone Hall, Houghton Hall, Norfolk, opened to the public
for the first time in 1976. *Sydney W. Newbery, for* COUNTRY LIFE

An example, in Dysart, of the National Trust for Scotland's Little Houses Scheme: before the restoration. *National Trust for Scotland*

(Above)
After restoration: the house of John McDouall Stuart, the explorer. *National Trust for Scotland*

Stubbs' *Reapers* saved for the Nation. One of the two great pictures (the other being *The Haymaker*) bought by the Tate Gallery after a massive appeal to 'top up' the government's share. The appeal included a lottery and celebrity action. *Tate Gallery*

care – in short, that standards of excellence were nationally and rigorously upheld.

The condition of our museums causes concern to everyone with an intimate knowledge of the arts and an appreciation of the vital rôle which the public museum and gallery must play in preserving the heritage and in educating people so that they can enjoy it to the full. The great national museums in London are models of what museums should be but they are not exactly over-burdened with resources by generous governments. For instance, between 1965 and 1975 the total expenditure on acquisitions by all our national collections amounted to a fraction over £12 million – perhaps the value of the collection at Chatsworth – an interesting thought for those who would like to see the State take over our great houses. Furthermore, although the National Gallery has recently opened a splendid new extension there is no exhibition space spare in any of our national museums or galleries.

Our national museums have, however, achieved remarkable success and attained a new popularity during the years since the Second World War, partly owing to the splendid occasional exhibitions that they have staged. In this context, one cannot escape mention of the invigorating presence on the museum scene of Dr Roy Strong who, first as Director of the National Portrait Gallery and now as Director of the Victoria and Albert Museum, has been responsible for some of the most vital and lively presentations ever seen in this country – exhibitions such as 'The Age of Pepys' at the Portrait Gallery, 'The Destruction of the English Country House' or the less significant, but captivating display of English fashions in the early decades of this century at the V & A. The Tate staged a series of set-piece exhibitions which linger in the memory of those who were fortunate enough to see them: exhibitions such as 'The Age of Charles I', 'The English Landscape', 'Hogarth' and, more recently, 'Constable' – perhaps the finest exhibition ever devoted to a single artist. The Royal Academy, also, has played a great part in the exhibition field. Perhaps its most spectacular success – vying in popularity with the Treasures of Tutankhamen at the British Museum – was its presentation of 'The Arts of Ancient China' in 1973.

Although the national museums have their problems, it is the museums in the provinces which give cause for alarm. It is not that they are staffed by unqualified, unimaginative people:

193

quite the contrary. Whether one is thinking of the great provincial and university museums, or the local collections of limited interest but of importance to understanding the English past, the truth is that many are starved of resources and administered by authorities which place them very low in their order of priorities.

A Minister of the Heritage could give special status to the great provincial museums. These are exceptional by virtue of the excellence of their collections and often, too, by virtue of the difficulties under which they operate: Bristol, with an art gallery and museum crammed onto one site; Birmingham, with display facilities of some 20 per cent less than at the end of the First World War; Manchester, where an extension has been deferred since before the First World War; Leeds, where the buildings are unsafe;[7] Glasgow and the Ashmolean at Oxford, both severely under-financed; and the Fitzwilliam at Cambridge, faced with a serious problem of staff and display facilities. These and the other important provincial museums, Liverpool, Leicester, Norwich and Sheffield, deserve to be elevated to become National Museums in the Provinces, given a proper degree of Government support, and administered under a trustee system (with, of course, local government representation) as our other great national museums are.

But beyond these outstanding museums, it would be advisable for local authorities to be obliged to have an efficient museum service, administered preferably at county level, and possibly supervised by a national museums council. Far too often museums are merely part of a local authority's leisure services and a poorly regarded part of them at that. A capital and central fund of as little as £1 million a year to provide grants for improving facilities, to encourage the development of conservation scholarships and conservation centres, within the context of a ten-year plan designed to bring all museums up to minimum acceptable standards, would revolutionize the museum-world. And if it were allied to a new and improved system of training, designed to provide a national career structure (where there could be a staff interchange, of a regular nature, between national and provincial museums), the museum service would offer an attractive and challenging career to the able and industrious

7. There is a novel plan for a small extension over a basement pub but Leeds' major galleries have been closed since 1974 and are likely to remain so for many years.

194

undergraduate. Unless steps along these lines are taken, the danger is that all but a few of our museums will by the turn of the century be slum depositories of objects badly secured, inadequately housed and conserved, and poorly displayed.[8]

Great as the need is for a more forceful co-ordinating Government strategy for the preservation of the heritage and the encouragement of the arts, there is a limit to what Government can do, and rightly so. 'At a stroke', Government could remove the threat that is posed by the ubiquitous VAT and it could do much to generate the development of policies already suggested, but at the end of the day without a lively and widespread public concern and participation the rôle of Government could become an oppressive and directional one. Without alert and active local amenity societies we would have very little heritage to safeguard and the price of our heritage, as of our liberty, will increasingly be eternal vigilance on the part of these bodies. It is heartening, however, to read about the number of rescue and restoration stories that are already shining examples of what local effort and initiative can achieve. One thinks of the restoration of Bateman's Mill recounted in a 1976 issue of the National Trust Newsletter:

> Kipling's Mill, celebrated in Puck of Pook's Hill, is busy again after seventy years disuse . . . During its long idleness the whole of the mill's ground floor had disappeared, the wheel pit was full of mud and rubble to shaft level and the evidence of the ravages of the woodworm and beetle was everywhere. An outside inspection revealed considerable damage to the lower part of the mill where the brickwork had collapsed. In addition, the mill leaked. The mill pond and tail race were blocked with silt and the river bank and its surroundings overgrown with luxuriant vegetation . . . The primary need was for repairs to the building's structure so that volunteers could work without fear of injury. The crumbling brickwork was restored, a complete ground floor laid, new roof joists fitted to the west roof, the rickety stairway renewed . . . undergrowth was removed from banks and approaches, the silt removed from the pond and mill and the sluice put in order. Now the streams are filling the pond at need . . . and the mill which 'has ground their corn and paid their tax ever since Doomsday Book' will be grinding and paying once more.

8. In 1976 local authorities spent a total of £214,915 on conserving their collections. National collections employed only 125 conservationists with a further thirteen in training.

Jobs that can be done by volunteers of all ages whose enthusiasm is harnessed to a common cause, are innumerable. Even the dearth of expert craftsmen can in some cases be compensated for by the activities of devoted and conscientious volunteers. The National Trust's Annual Report for 1974, dealing with textile conservation, observed:

> A number of the Trust's properties contain fine textile hangings and furnishings. Their condition is delicate and they are now increasingly threatened by the effects of light and dirt. A scheme was devised at Knole to make a systematic start on the restoration of the famous gold and silver thread and other furnishings in the King's Room. The task is being carried out by a large number of volunteer embroiderers who have generously put their time and skill at the disposal of the Trust to work under an expert supervisor.

Much can be done to arouse the interest of schools and one of the pleasantest and most successful features of Architectural Heritage Year in this country was the way in which the enthusiasm of youth was channelled and directed. There was a series of awards sponsored for youth groups which furthered the aim of the Heritage Year. In Winchester the famous College, in conjunction with St Swithin's Girls' School and the Winchester Consumer Group, planned a Town Trail. At Stow, the boys helped restore the famous Kent and Capability Brown landscape gardens. The Department of Education and Science sponsored a special course at Bath College of Education and the National Institute of Adult Education held courses aimed at increasing the number of tutors in environmental and architectural heritage studies. Following on the success of these schemes, the Historic Houses Association and the National Trust, backed by a grant from the Department of the Environment, decided to designate the year from March 1977 to March 1978 as Education Heritage Year, the aim being to interest school teachers throughout the country, and through them their pupils, in our heritage, in its potential as an incomparable teaching medium. Conferences were held in many parts of the country, in country houses, and already, by the summer of 1977, thousands of children were being involved in projects and pageants.

The Chiltern Society, one of the largest and most enthusiastic of local amenity societies, set up a Chiltern Conservation Volunteers Bureau in 1975 and in the first ten months of its existence it had offers of help from sixty-two organizations, including twenty-five schools and twelve scout groups. Indeed, most of the offers came from young people and youth organizations – all of them anxious to improve the Chiltern countryside. The vice-chairman, Mr Don Gresswell, in a letter to *The Times* in August 1975 said:

> There is great scope to carry out projects that would otherwise never be accomplished. Our society has never sought to 'save the rates' but to do those tasks that the authorities would not tackle, e.g. surveying and clearing 1500 miles of Chiltern footpaths, restoring a windmill, both taking five or six years to accomplish . . . I am sure that the youth of this country would welcome the spirit of adventure and the feeling of comradeship and opportunities to improve our environment and our countryside and this would bring no additional cost to the taxpayer.

Don Gresswell's words should remind us that there is still a rôle for the individual. By joining societies such as his, any man or woman can play a part in preserving and enhancing what he values. And the individual, too, can, without the backing of societies or even membership of them, be vigilant and speak out through the columns of his local press or in letters to his Member of Parliament or to his local amenity society if he sees trees being needlessly sawn down, cottages vandalized, hedges uprooted. Perhaps his initiative will not be rewarded, but a danger foreseen can often be a disaster prevented. As a positive encouragement to those with initiative, the Save Group joined forces with the Lesser Group of companies in the summer of 1977 to launch a new £2000 award scheme, for the imaginative re-use of old buildings. The award was specifically designed to help voluntary groups involved in the practical reclamation of old buildings, the idea being to reward initiative and help preserve for future use buildings which would otherwise disappear. A notable feature of the scheme was the stipulation that no prize money should go to individuals, architects or consultants; corporate or society effort was what it was designed to encourage.

The increase in membership of conservation and amenity societies and the number of extremely imaginative new societies and groups that have been set up has been heartening in recent years. Perhaps the most exciting of these has been the Landmark Trust, the brainchild of John Smith, former Member of Parliament for the Cities of London and Westminster. The Trust set out to rescue smaller but significant buildings which would otherwise crumble into decay and to make them available for people to live in and enjoy for holiday periods. Now, a Martello Tower at Aldeburgh, the Gothic temple at Stow, an abandoned railway station at Alton in Staffordshire and Clytha Castle in Wales are booked up through the year by people who enjoy a period of peace and recreation, and a chance to appreciate their heritage.

There is certainly scope for the Landmark Trust to increase its invaluable work and plenty of scope for other similar trusts. In the Netherlands they have played an invaluable part in the re-habilitation of many noteworthy buildings and have done so for many years. The first in the field there, the Hendrick Dekyser Association, was founded in 1918 and today has some 2500 members and donors and owns about 200 buildings, 67 in Amsterdam and the remainder in 54 other towns and cities. Then there is an investment company specializing in the restora-tion of old houses in which the Amsterdam City Council itself has a shareholding. It owns over 200 houses in Amsterdam alone, many of them on important corner sights on the central canals. These and other trusts have undertaken some vitally important conservation work, work which would almost cer-tainly not have been done by central or local government agencies. The most distinctive contribution has been the way they have restored to entirely suitable modern uses ancient and apparently obsolete buildings.

It is this sort of work – for instance, the restoration of a group of seventeenth-century Dutch alms houses into a quarter for students, flats for single teachers and a few homes for old people – which is the best type of answer to those who are sceptical of the value of conservationists. These people, and there are many of them, tend to decry the desire to conserve because they see it as a desire to preserve every scrap of existing fabric no matter what its potential use or worth. Their attitude was well summed up in an article in the journal *Built Environment* in January 1975: 'The idea of function has a very different meaning in the vocabulary of the environmental critic from the connota-tion which would be familiar to a Social Scientist. Thus New Scotland Yard, for all that it is unusable as an office for ordinary people to work in, must at all costs be preserved as a monument to Norman Shaw.'

198

In fact, the north Norman Shaw building has already been completely restored and transformed and now provides the best offices available for Members of Parliament and their secretaries – and this at a fraction of the cost that would have been incurred had the grandiose project for a new parliamentary building been allowed to proceed. That building, with its acres of tinted glass, sauna baths, and luxurious facilities, would not only have been difficult to justify to the taxpayer; its size and construction would have been totally incongruous in Parliament Square.

It is appropriate to end in Parliament Square. The decisions of Government touch our lives more nearly, and more often, as each year passes and it is these decisions which can do most to increase, or to remove, the many dangers to our heritage. Those who care should strive to influence those who decide; to impress upon Parliament and, through Parliament, upon Government, the need to maintain those things that are 'honest, lovely and of good report'. It is a cause that can succeed for it is capable of arousing great passions – without party rancour.

Those who know Kilvert's *Diary* – one of the best of all bedside books – may remember a joyful description of a cloud that hung heavy over Clyro till it became a rainbow. There is really no reason why the cloud that hangs heavy over our heritage should not be similarly transformed.

Countryside Conservation
(courtesy of the Countryside Commission)

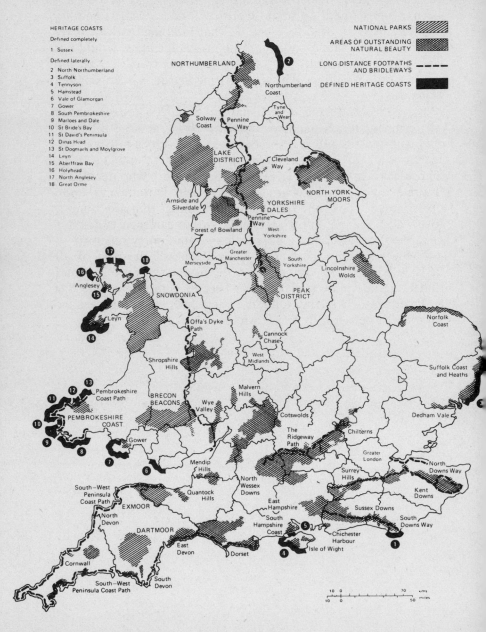

HERITAGE COASTS

Defined completely

1 Sussex

Defined laterally

2 North Northumberland
3 Suffolk
4 Tennyson
5 Hamstead
6 Vale of Glamorgan
7 Gower
8 South Pembrokeshire
9 Marloes and Dale
10 St Bride's Bay
11 St David's Peninsula
12 Dinas Head
13 St Dogmaels and Moylgrove
14 Leyn
15 Aberffraw Bay
16 Holyhead
17 North Anglesey
18 Great Orme

NATIONAL PARKS

AREAS OF OUTSTANDING
NATURAL BEAUTY

LONG DISTANCE FOOTPATHS
AND BRIDLEWAYS

DEFINED HERITAGE COASTS

NORTHUMBERLAND

Northumberland
Coast

Solway
Coast

Pennine
Way

Tyne
and
Wear

LAKE
DISTRICT

Cleveland
Way

Arnside and
Silverdale

YORKSHIRE
DALES

NORTH YORK
MOORS

Forest of Bowland

Pennine
Way

West
Yorkshire

Merseyside

Greater
Manchester

South
Yorkshire

Lincolnshire
Wolds

Anglesey

Leyn

SNOWDONIA

PEAK
DISTRICT

Offa's Dyke
Path

Cannock
Chase

Norfolk
Coast

Shropshire
Hills

West
Midlands

Pembrokeshire
Coast Path

BRECON
BEACONS

Malvern
Hills

Suffolk Coast
and Heaths

PEMBROKESHIRE
COAST

Wye
Valley

Cotswolds

Dedham Vale

Gower

The
Ridgeway
Path

Chilterns

Mendip
Hills

Greater
London

North Downs Way

North
Wessex
Downs

Surrey
Hills

Kent
Downs

South—West
Peninsula
Coast Path

Quantock
Hills

East
Hampshire

Sussex Downs

South
Downs Way

EXMOOR

North
Devon

South
Hampshire
Coast

Chichester
Harbour

DARTMOOR

East
Devon

Dorset

Isle of Wight

Cornwall

South
Devon

South—West
Peninsula Coast Path

10   0   70   kms
10   0   50   miles

A Gazetteer of
the Heritage
County by County

This Gazetteer cannot claim to be totally comprehensive, but it does endeavour to give the enquiring visitor an idea of the riches that remain. It lists our national parks and officially designated areas of national beauty and also those historic houses, castles, gardens, museums and galleries that were open to the public at the end of 1977. It also lists a selection of the more notable historic buildings and ancient monuments. The biggest problems of selection have been created by the wealth of ecclesiastical treasures. However, all of our cathedrals are given, together with a list of some of the more interesting parish churches in each English county.

The problems presented by Wales and Scotland (in Scotland, for instance, there are no national parks) of necessity mean that there is a bias in favour of England. This is based not on chauvinism but on the fact that there is more information readily available for England than for either of its beautiful neighbours.

The new, post-1974, boundaries have been used throughout, with apologies to those who abhor the mutilation of Lincolnshire and Somerset, the amalgamation of Herefordshire and Worcestershire, and the emergence of such unromantic sounding counties as the West Midlands. One thing the list does indicate very clearly is just how many areas would be impoverished if historic houses in private ownership were closed.

*denotes open by appointment

ENGLAND

AVON
AREAS OF OUTSTANDING NATURAL BEAUTY
Cotswolds (part)
Mendip Hills (part)

CASTLES AND HISTORIC HOUSES
Badminton House, *Badminton* (His Grace the Duke of Beaufort, KG, GCVO)
Built for the 1st Duke in Charles II's reign. Altered by Kent c. 1740.
Clevedon Court, Nr *Clevedon* (National Trust)
14th-century manor house incorporating 12th-century tower and 13th-century hall with terraced 18th-century garden, rare shrubs and plants.
Dodington House, *Chipping Sodbury* (Major S. F. B. Codrington)
Last great 18th-century classic house to be built. Magnificent staircase. Architect James Wyatt. 700 acres of parkland landscaped by Capability Brown.
Dyrham Park, Nr *Bristol and Bath* (National Trust)
Late 17th-century house in remarkable setting. Blathwayt furniture and Dutch paintings in fine series of panelled rooms.
Horton Court, *Horton* (National Trust)
Cotswold manor house restored and altered in 19th century. 12th-century hall and Renaissance ambulatory.
*Little Sodbury Manor, *Chipping Sodbury* (Gerald Harford, Esq)
15th-century manor house with fine great hall and scenes of William Tyndale work.
Priory Park College, *Bath*
Georgian mansion built by John Wood the elder, c. 1735. Now Roman Catholic public school.
No. 1 Royal Crescent, *Bath* (Bath Preservation Trust)
Georgian house as it was when built by John Wood the Younger in 1767.
*Royal Fort House, Tyndall Avenue, *Bristol* (University of Bristol)
18th-century house with historical associations with the Civil War.
St Vincent's Priory, *Clifton* (G. Melhuish, Esq)
Small Gothic revival house, built over caves which were traditionally a Christian sanctuary.

CATHEDRALS AND CHURCHES
Backwell (St Andrew)
Fine fabric of 12th–17th century. 15th-century tower repaired in 17th century. 15th-century chancel and tomb. Early 16th-century screen, 18th-century brass chandelier.

Banwell (St Andrew)
14th and 15th century. Notable 15th-century roof, vaulted screen, bench ends, pulpit and painted glass.
Bath Abbey (St Peter and St Paul)
Perpendicular monastic church. Nave completed in 17th century. Restored by Sir Gilbert Scott, 1864–73.
Bristol (All Saints)
Late Norman and perpendicular nave. Georgian tower. Magnificent Colston monuments.
Bristol Cathedral
Only eastern half wholly medieval, nave mainly Victorian. Chapter-house with rich non-figurative ornamentation. Choir has good lierne vault and, over aisles, vaulting of unique design.
Bristol (Lord Mayor's Chapel)
Dates from 13th century. Perpendicular tower, 1487. Early 16th-century fan-vaulted Payntz chantry. Important tombs.
Bristol (St Mary Redcliffe)
Abbey-like size and plan mainly early perpendicular. Stone vaults and bosses. Medieval tombs; brasses; brass eagle; lectern, 1638; Baroque iron screen; 3 fonts.
Bristol (St Stephen's)
Mainly perpendicular. Magnificent tower, monuments.
Iron Acton (St James The Less)
Perpendicular. 15th-century memorial cross. 19th-century mosaic floors, reredos and chapel screen by Eden, old glass, Laudian altar rails, Jacobean pulpit, effigies.
Redland (no dedication)
Classical with Ionic façade. Fine woodwork, busts by Rysbrack.
Westbury-on-Trym (Holy Trinity)
Mainly 13th century with 15th-century chancel. Perpendicular apse. 15th-century tower. Georgian monuments.
Wrington (All Souls)
Fine tower. 15th-century nave and aisles. Notable roofs, screens, 15th-century font, stone pulpit, 1860.
Yate (St Mary)
Fine perpendicular tower.
Yatton (St Mary)
Central tower with truncated stone spire. Good 14th–15th-century monuments.

GARDENS
*Vine House, *Henbury* (Professor and Mrs T. F. Hewer)
2 acres. Trees, shrubs, irises, water garden, bulbs, naturalised garden landscape.
Zoological Gardens, *Clifton Down*
Extensive gardens with animals, reptiles, fish.

HISTORIC MONUMENTS
Hinton Priory, *Hinton Charterhouse*
Ruins of Carthusian priory founded 1232.
Kings Weston Roman Villa, *Lawrence Weston*
Mosaics and walls of villa occupied AD 270–370.
Stoney Littleton Barrow, Nr *Bath*
Neolithic communal burial chamber. Rebuilt 1858.
Temple Church, *Bristol*
14th- or 15th-century ruin.

MUSEUMS AND GALLERIES
American Museum in Britain, Claverton Manor, Nr *Bath*
American decorative arts (from late 17th century and mid-19th century) seen in a series of furnished rooms and galleries of special exhibits.
Bath Carriage Museum, Circus Mews, *Bath*
Comprehensive collection of horse-drawn vehicles.
Bath Roman Museum, Abbey Churchyard, Nr *Bath Abbey* (Bath City Council)
Adjoins extensive remains of Roman baths, and includes material from that and other Roman sites.
Beckford's Tower, Lansdowne Road, *Bath*
Built for William Beckford by H. E. Goodridge in Neo-classical style, 1827. Small museum of Beckfordiana.
Blaise Castle House Museum, Henbury, *Bristol* (Bristol Corporation)
Collections in an 18th-century house, dealing with objects illustrating English life.
Bristol City Art Gallery, Queen's Road, *Bristol* (Bristol Corporation)
Permanent and loan collections of paintings; applied art with particular emphasis on English and Oriental ceramics.
Bristol City Museum, Queen's Road, *Bristol* (Bristol Corporation)
Collections of Egyptology, British archaeology, ethnography, industrial history and technology, natural history with geology. Chief attention is given to the history and natural history of West of England.
Chatterton House, Redcliffe Way, *Bristol* (Bristol Corporation)
Birthplace of Thomas Chatterton.
Georgian House, 7 Great George Street, *Bristol* (Bristol Corporation)
Georgian House exhibiting furniture and fittings of that period.
Holburne of Menstrie Museum, Great Pulteney Street, *Bath* (University of Bath)
Exhibits displayed in elegant 18th-century building.
Museum, Burlington Street, *Weston-super-Mare*
Local history including archaeology, folk-life costume and natural history. Frequent special exhibitions.

Museum of Costume, Assembly Rooms, *Bath* (Bath City Council)
Founded on collection of Mrs Langley Moore. Comprises every
aspect of fashion from the 17th century to current year.
Red Lodge, Park Row, *Bristol* (Bristol Corporation)
Elizabethan house with early 18th-century alterations and furnishings
of these periods.
St Nicholas Church and City Museum, St Nicholas Street, *Bristol*
(Bristol Corporation) (A redundant church)
Church plate and vestments, watercolours and medieval antiquities
related to local history. Hogarth altarpiece.
Victoria Art Gallery, Bridge Street, *Bath* (Bath City Council)
Exhibitions from permanent collections changed monthly.

BEDFORDSHIRE
AREAS OF OUTSTANDING NATURAL BEAUTY
Chilterns (part)

CASTLES AND HISTORIC HOUSES
Luton Hoo, *Luton* (Wernher Family)
Exterior commenced by Robert Adam, 1767. Interior remodernized
in 18th-century French style early this century. Art collection includes
Fabergé jewels and unique Russian collection. Park landscaped by
Capability Brown.
Woburn Abbey (Trustees of the Bedford Estates)
Great 18th-century house remodelled by Flitcroft c. 1747 and Henry
Holland 1802. Famous collection of paintings together with collec-
tion of French and English 18th-century furniture and silver. 3000
acres of park designed by Repton. Game reserve.

CATHEDRALS AND CHURCHES
Chalgrave (All Saints)
Fine 13th-century carving of nave arcade capitals; 15th-century
traceried bench-ends. Wall paintings.
Dunstable Priory (St Peter)
Fine Norman nave. Norman and early English west front with
notable 13th-century north-west door. Norman vaulting re-created
in south aisle.
Eaton Bray (St Mary the Virgin)
Exterior is 15th-century reconstruction. 13th-century interior with
very fine nave arcades. 13th-century font. East windows on south
aisle are well detailed. 13th-century ironwork on south door.
Elstow (St Mary and St Helen)
West front begun in 13th century, never finished but restored.
Coeval 13th-century bays at west end, remainder is fine Norman
work.

Felmersham (St Mary the Virgin)
Fine Early English. Arcaded west front. Notable interior with clustered piers of crossings contrasting with 15th-century screen.
Leighton Buzzard (All Saints)
13th–15th century with fine spire and magnificent timber roofs. Complete collegiate chancel of late 15th century. Kempe windows.
Luton (St Mary)
13th–15th century Wenlock chapel and monuments. 14th-century baptistry. Fine tower.
Marston Moretaine (St Mary the Virgin)
14th–15th century interior with bold detailing, and interesting screen paintings. Detached bell tower.
Odell (All Saints)
15th century; noble tower, rood screen, stained glass, arcades.
Pavenham (St Peter)
Fine Jacobean woodwork installed in 19th century. Good fabric with 14th-century canopied work.
Totternhoe (St Giles)
14th–16th century, fine exterior with pinnacled roof line.
Wymington (St Lawrence)
14th-century ornamented tower and spire. Fine nave roof, remains of 'Doom', old pewing, some colour still on capitals and arches.

GARDENS
Lodge Reserve, *Sandy* (Royal Society for the Protection of Birds)
Over one hundred acres. Variety of birds can be seen in natural habitat. Nature trail and nature discovery room.
Stagsden Bird Gardens, *Stagsden* (Mr and Mrs R. E. Rayment)
Bird zoo and breeding establishment for birds. Collection of shrub roses.
Wrest Park, *Silsoe* (Department of the Environment)
Fine example of a formal canal garden.

HISTORIC MONUMENTS
Houghton House, *Ampthill*
Ruins of Jacobean house.

MUSEUMS AND GALLERIES
Bedford Museum, The Embankment, *Bedford*
Local antiquities, local history and national history.
Bunyan Collection, Public Library, Harpur Street, *Bedford*
Library and exhibits devoted to life and works of John Bunyan (Mott Harrison Collection).
Bunyan Meeting Library and Museum, Mill Street, *Bedford* (Trustees of Bunyan Meetings)
All surviving personal relics of John Bunyan. World-famous collection of Bunyan's works in 165 languages.

Cecil Higgins Art Gallery, Castle Close, *Bedford*
English and continental porcelain and outstanding collection of
English watercolours. Handley-Read collection of Victorian and
Edwardian decorative art.
Elstow Moot Hall, *Bedford*
Medieval market hall containing 17th-century collections associated
with John Bunyan.
Luton Museum and Art Gallery, Wardown Park, *Luton* (Borough of
Luton)
Bedfordshire archaeology and history, rural trades and crafts, social
and domestic life, furniture, woodwork, decorative and fine arts.
Costume, needlework accessories. Doll and furniture collection.
The Shuttleworth Collection, Old Warden Aerodrome, *Old Warden*
40 specimens of historical types of aeroplanes, cars, carriages and
bicycles – many unique and in flying and running order.

BERKSHIRE
AREAS OF OUTSTANDING NATURAL BEAUTY
North Wessex Downs (part)

CASTLES AND HISTORIC HOUSES
*No. 25 The Cloisters, Windsor Castle, *Windsor* (Dean and Canons
of Windsor)
Privately occupied medieval house with remains of medieval wall
painting in main bedroom.
Swallowfield Park, *Swallowfield* (Mutual Households Association
Ltd)
Built by 2nd Earl of Clarendon in 1678. Now converted into flats.
Windsor Castle, *Windsor* (Royal Residence)
Largest inhabited castle in the world. It is largely medieval, Stuart
and Regency. State apartments contain many historic treasures.

CATHEDRALS AND CHURCHES
Avington (St Mark and St Luke)
Mostly Norman with rich carving.
Bradfield (St Andrew)
1847, rebuilt by Gilbert Scott.
Hurst (St Nicholas)
Norman and later 17th-century woodwork. 17th- and 18th-century
tombs.
Lambourn (St Michael or All Saints)
Norman with 15th–16th-century chapels. 16th-century tombs,
brasses and remains of glass.
Maidenhead (All Saints), *Boyne Hill*
1854–8 by G. E. Street. Rich interior.

207

Padworth (St John the Baptist)
12th-century Norman. Plastered exterior. Semi-domed apse, Norman chancel arch and south doors, remains of wall paintings, 18th-century monuments.
Shottesbrooke (St John the Baptist)
14th-century decorated. Interior with fine carved 14th-century detail, founder's tomb, sedilia, brasses and pieces of 14th-century glass.
Warfield (St Michael and All Angels)
Mostly 14th-century decorated. Fine east window, remains of 14th-century glass, 15th-century wooden screen and loft, 19th-century stone screen by Street.

GARDENS
Old Rectory, *Burghfield* (Mr and Mrs R. R. Menton)
Roses, hellebores, lilies, rare Japanese plants, old-fashioned cottage plants, autumn colour.
Savill Garden, *Windsor Great Park* (Crown Property)
35 acres of woodland garden. Large range of plants throughout the season, of horticultural and botanical interest.
Valley Gardens, *Windsor Great Park* (Crown Property)
300 acre woodland garden adjoining Virginia Water lake.
Wexham Springs, *Wexham* (Cement and Concrete Association)
Large informal garden with mixed shrubs and lake. Formal area, with courtyards, terraces, patios, walling and paving.

HISTORIC MONUMENTS
Donnington Castle, *Donnington*
Late 14th-century gatehouse. Earthworks from Civil War sieges, 1643–44.

MUSEUMS AND GALLERIES
Eton College Natural History Museum, *Eton*
British birds, entomological specimens, mammals, reptiles and fossils.
Guildhall Exhibition, High Street, *Windsor*
Collections including implements, documents, pictures. The Guildhall, dating from 1689, contains collection of royal portraits.
Henry Reitlinger Bequest, Oldfield, Riverside, Guards Club Road, *Maidenhead*
Chinese, European, Italian, Persian pottery. Paintings, sculpture, drawings and glass.
Household Cavalry Museum, Combermere Barracks, *Windsor*
Uniforms, weapons, horse furniture, and armour of Household Cavalry from 1685 to present. Series of terrain models depicting Life Guards and Royal Horse Guards campaigns.

Museum and Art Gallery, Blagrave Street, *Reading* (Reading Corporation)
Natural history and local archaeology. Roman collection from Silchester. Changing art exhibitions each month. Thames Conservancy collection of prehistoric and medieval metalwork. Historical collections.
Museum of English Rural Life, Whiteknights Park, *Reading* (University of Reading)
National collection of material relating to history of English countryside.
***Museum of Greek Archaeology (Faculty of Letters),** Whiteknights, *Reading* (University of Reading)
Greek antiquities, mainly pottery.
Newbury Museum, Wharf Street, *Newbury*
Local collections covering Paleolithic to Saxon and Medieval to recent periods, natural history.
Royal Electrical and Mechanical Engineers' Museum, Meat House, *Arborfield*
REME history and equipment; vehicles, models, weapons, photographs, uniforms, etc.
Stanley Spencer Gallery, King's Hall, *Cookham-on-Thames*
Paintings, drawings, sketches and personalia of the artist.

BUCKINGHAMSHIRE
AREAS OF OUTSTANDING NATURAL BEAUTY
Chilterns (part)

CASTLES AND HISTORIC HOUSES
Ascott, *Wing* (National Trust)
Anthony de Rothschild collection of fine pictures, French and Chippendale furniture, Oriental porcelain. 12 acres of grounds. Garden contains unusual trees, flower borders, topiary sundial, naturalized bulbs and water lilies.
Chicheley Hall, *Newport Pagnell* (Trustees of the Hon. Nicholas Beatty)
Baroque house and gardens built 1719–23. Fine panelling, naval pictures, and mementos of Admiral Lord Beatty.
Claydon House, Middle Claydon, Nr *Winslow* (National Trust)
Built mid-18th century as addition to an earlier house. Magnificent rococo state rooms, including Florence Nightingale Museum, her bedroom and sitting-room.
Cliveden, Nr *Maidenhead* (National Trust)
Fine tapestry and furniture. Gardens contain temples of Giacomo Leoni. Box parterre, fountain, formal walks. Historic open air theatre, water garden, rose garden, herbaceous borders.

209

Dorton House, *Brill* (Governors of Ashford School)
17th–18th-century house with later alterations. Now Ashford School.
Hartwell House, *Aylesbury* (House of Citizenship)
Jacobean with 18th-century front and decorations.
Hughenden Manor, *High Wycombe* (National Trust)
Home of Benjamin Disraeli. Small garden. The Disraeli Museum.
Manor House, *Chenies* (Lt-Col and Mrs Macleod Matthews)
Early home of Russell (Bedford) family. Tudor house and garden.
Milton Cottage, *Chalfont St Giles* (Milton's Cottage Trust)
Preserved as it was in 1665, cottage where Milton completed
'Paradise Lost' and began 'Paradise Regained'. Contains many relics
and library with first and early editions.
Nether Winchenden House, *Aylesbury* (J. G. C. Spencer Bernard, Esq)
Tudor manor house with 18th-century additions. Home of Sir
Francis Bernard, Governor of New Jersey and Massachusetts, 1760.
Waddesdon Manor, Nr *Aylesbury* (National Trust)
English, Dutch, Flemish and Italian paintings, French decorative
art and drawings from 17th and 18th centuries and other works from
earlier centuries. Mementos of Rothschild family. Grounds include
18th-century aviary and small herd of Sikka deer.
West Wycombe Park, *West Wycombe* (National Trust)
Palladian house with frescoes and painted ceilings. 18th-century
landscape garden with lake and various classical temples.
Wotton House, Nr *Aylesbury* (Administrator Mrs Patrick Brunner)
Built 1704 on the same plan as Buckingham House. Interior remodelled by Soane in 1820. Wrought iron by Tijou and Thomas Robinson.
Capability Brown landscape.

CATHEDRALS AND CHURCHES
Bledlow (Holy Trinity)
Nave arcades with carved capitals, c. 1200; Aylesbury font, frag-
ments of wall paintings, 13th–14th-century south doorway with
traces of original colour.
Chenies (St Michael)
Very fine Russell monuments, 14th–20th century.
Chetwode (St Mary and St Nicholas)
Choir and chancel of priory. Notable 13th-century work. 14th-
century north chapel.
Clifton Reynes (St Mary the Virgin)
13th–15th century. 14th-century font; medieval Reynes monuments.
Victorian restoration has removed ancient plaster.
Dinton (St Peter and St Paul)
Norman door with inscribed lintel.
Dorney (St James)
Tudor brick tower and architecture of every period from Norman to
19th century. Note 12th-century font; west gallery, 1634; south porch,

1663; 15th-century stalls and base of screen; 17th-century communion rails and other woodwork; Gerrard monument, 1607.

Edlesborough (St Mary the Virgin)
Complete screen, stalls, pulpit and tester, and roofs of 15th century; transverse arches in aisles; brasses.

Gayhurst (St Peter)
1728, Classical. Tower with urns at corners and cupola in centre. Interior with good plasterwork, pews, pulpit and panelling, monument to Speaker Wright and his brother by Roubiliac.

Hillesden (All Saints)
Mainly 15th century. Contemporary roofs, seats, screen and glass and Te Deum frieze in chancel. Monuments. Fine canopy over stair turret.

Langley Marish (St Mary)
17th-century Kederminster and Seymour transept, pew and library.

Little Kimble (All Saints)
Fine early 14th-century wall paintings.

North Marston (St Mary)
Remains of 14th-century shrine; late 15th-century 2-storied vestry and chancel. Fine nave.

Pitstone (St Mary)
13th-century capitals, 15th-century nave arcades. 12th-century font. Jacobean pulpit and tester beneath 18th-century 'sentences' over chancel arch.

Quainton (Holy Cross and St Mary)
Magnificent Renaissance sculpture by Grinling Gibbons, Roubiliac, Rysbrack and others.

Stewkley (St Michael and All Angels)
Fine Norman, particularly west front.

Stoke Poges (St Giles)
14th-century porch, 13th-century tower; Hastings chapel with 17th–18th-century glass.

Willen (St Mary Magdalene)
1670s, Classical pilasters, urns, high pews, pedestal font.

GARDENS

Boarstall Duck Decoy, Nr *Brill*
Ancient working duck decoy.

Dorneywood Garden (National Trust)
Given to the Trust as official residence for a Secretary of State, or Minister of the Crown.

Stearthill, *Little Horwood* (Mrs R. S. G. Close Smith)
Old and modern roses set in formal and shrub gardens. Herbaceous borders, water garden and tropical greenhouse.

Stowe (Stowe School), *Buckingham* (Governors of Stowe School)
Famous 18th-century house (not open). Garden and garden buildings by Bridgeman, Kent, Gibbs, Vanbrugh and Capability Brown.

MUSEUMS AND GALLERIES

Buckinghamshire County Museum, Church Street, *Aylesbury* (Buckinghamshire County Council)
County geology, natural history, archaeology and history; new rural life gallery; costume; collection of paintings. Temporary exhibitions.

Cowper and Newton Museum, Market Place, *Olney*
Personal belongings of William Cowper and Rev. John Newton, manuscripts and other items of local interest.

Royal Army Educational Corps Centre and Museum, Wilton Park, *Beaconsfield*
History of education in army since mid-18th-century.

Wycombe Chair and Local History Museum, Castle Hill, *High Wycombe* (Wycombe District Council)
Collection of chairs of most periods, but mainly directed to Windsor chair. Unique collection of local tools and equipment, Bucks lace and local items.

CAMBRIDGESHIRE

CASTLES AND HISTORIC HOUSES

Angelsey Abbey, Nr *Cambridge* (National Trust)
Founded in reign of Henry I. Elizabethan manor created from remains by Fokes family. Fairhaven collection of art treasures. About 100 acres of grounds.

Hinchingbrooke House, *Huntingdon* (Hinchingbrooke School)
Early 13th-century Nunnery converted mid-16th-century into Tudor house with additions, late 17th century and 19th century.

Kimbolton Castle, *Kimbolton* (Governors of Kimbolton School)
Tudor manor house, completely remodelled by Vanburgh.

King's School, *Ely* (The Governors of King's School)
Built in 12th and 14th centuries.

Longthorpe Tower, Nr *Peterborough*
Fortified 13th–14th century, belonged formerly to de Thorpe family. Rare wall paintings.

Northborough Castle, *Northborough* (Mr Roy Genders)
Early 14th-century house with great hall and solar. Rose garden and herbaceous borders.

Peckover House, *Wisbech* (National Trust)
Example of early 18th-century domestic architecture. Victorian garden contains rare trees, flower borders, roses.

University of Cambridge (In most Colleges, only Chapels and Halls are open)
   Gonville and Caius College, Trinity Street (1348)
   Christ's College, St Andrew's Street (1505)
   Clare College, Trinity Lane (1326)
   Corpus Christi College, Trumpington Street (1352)

Downing College, Regent Street (1800)
Emmanuel College, St Andrew's Street (1584)
Jesus College, Jesus Lane (1496)
King's College, King's Parade (1441)
Magdalene College, Magdalene Street (1542)
Pembroke College, Trumpington Street (1347)
Peterhouse, Trumpington Street (1284)
Queen's College, Queen's Lane (1448)
St Catherine's College, Trumpington Street (1473)
St John's College, St John's Street (1511)
Sidney Sussex College, Sidney Street (1596)
Trinity College, Trinity Street (1546)
Trinity Hall, Trinity Lane (1350)

CATHEDRALS AND CHURCHES

Alconbury (St Peter and St Paul)
Note 13th-century chancel with 15th-century roof. Good broach spire.

Babraham (St Peter)
Noble 13th-century tower. 17th-century Bennet monuments.

Bottisham (Holy Trinity)
14th century with indent for brass of Elias de Bekyngham, one of Edward I's judges. Stone chancel screen and wooden parcloses. Monuments.

Burwell (St Mary the Blessed Virgin)
Good perpendicular. Lower stages of tower, 12th century.

Chesterton (St Michael)
18th century, Roman chancel, chancel screen, Jacobean Beville monument.

Ely Cathedral
Richly arcaded but incomplete west front, with south-west transept. Majestic interior with octagon unique in Gothic architecture.

Fleeton (St Margaret)
Notable Saxon carvings, Norman work.

Great Paxton (Holy Trinity)
12th century. Great arches of crossing.

Harlton (Blessed Virgin Mary)
Decorated-perpendicular transition. 17th-century Fryer monument.

Hildersham (Holy Trinity)
13th century. Effigies, c. 1300; brasses, glass.

Isleham (St Andrew)
Decorated. Panelled nave. Clerestory with notable roof. 17th-century communion rail. Good brasses.

Kirtling (All Saints)
16th-century North family chapel with monuments. Norman and early English features.

213

Landwade (St Nicholas)
15th century, later extended. Medieval fittings. Cotton monuments.
Leighton Bromswold (St Mary)
Nave and tower rebuilt, 1626, by George Herbert. Notable roof, 17th-century furnishings; twin pulpits, choir stalls and chancel screens.
Leverington (St Leonard)
Fine 15th-century glass, especially Jesse Tree window.
Little Gidding (St John)
Mainly early 18th-century fabric. Classical arcading in timber. Ribbed and panelled barrel ceiling. Lectern, font and chandelier.
Peterborough Cathedral
One of the least altered great Norman churches. Painted wooden roof to nave, c. 1220, unique west front; only Galilee porch and spires are later than 1220. Fan-vaulted retrochoir, c. 1500.
Ramsey (St Thomas of Canterbury)
Perpendicular nave with late 12th-century arcades. Late Norman chancel with Angevin vault.
St Neots (St Mary)
15th-century fine tower.
Sutton (St Andrew)
14th-century fine tower. Notable window tracery.
Thorney (St Mary and St Botolph)
Fragment of Romanesque abbey with east end added by Blore, 1840–41.
Trumpington (St Mary and St Nicholas)
14th century. Famous brass of Sir Roger de Trumpington, 1289.
Westley Waterless (St Mary the Less)
Decorated. Good 14th-century brass to Sir John and Lady Creke.
Whittlesey (St Mary the Virgin)
Fine tower and spire. Sub-modern stained glass. Monuments.
Wimpole (St Andrew)
14th century rebuilt by Flitcroft, 1749. Fine heraldic glass and monuments.
Wisbech (St Peter and St Paul)
Wall monument by Nollekens; reredos by Salviati, 1885; detached bell tower.
Yaxley (St Peter)
Fine steeple. Wall paintings. 15th-century chancel screen. East window, altar and reredos by Comper.

GARDENS
University Botanic Garden, *Cambridge* (Cambridge University)
Fine specimen trees and shrubs. Founded 1761.
Wildlife Trust, Nr *Peterborough*
Large collection of living wildlife in wooded setting.

HISTORIC MONUMENTS
Duxford Chapel, *Duxford*
14th-century hospital chapel.
Buckden Palace, *Buckden*
Ancient palace. Once residence of Archbishcp of Lincoln.
Wandlebury Ring, Nr *Cambridge*
Hill fort on Gog Magog hills.

MUSEUMS AND GALLERIES
Cambridge County Folk Museum, 2–3 Castle Street, *Cambridge*
Museum occupying the former White Horse Inn, contains domestic and agricultural bygones.
Cromwell Museum, Market Square, *Huntingdon* (Cambridgeshire County Council)
Concerned with the Cromwellian period, displaying contemporary portraits, Cromwelliana and documents.
Farmland Museum, High Street, *Haddenham*
Agricultural implements, rural crafts.
Fitzwilliam Museum, Trumpington Street, *Cambridge*
Picture gallery of cld and modern masters. Collections of antiquities, ceramics and applied arts, coins, drawings and prints. Collections of music and medieval manuscripts and art library.
Norris Library and Museum, The Broadway, *St Ives* (St Ives Town Council)
Local collections. Prehistory to bygones. Local literature.
Peterborough Museum and Art Gallery, Priestgate, *Peterborough* (Peterborough City Council)
Local archaeology, history, geology and natural history. Small collection of paintings and ceramics.
Scott Polar Research Institute, Lensfield Road, *Cambridge*
Current scientific work in the Arctic and Antarctic. Expedition relics and equipment. Eskimo and general polar art collections.
Sedgwick Museum of Geology, Downing Street, *Cambridge*
Fossils and subordinate collections of rocks, building stones and ornamental marbles.
University Archives, University Library, West Road, *Cambridge*
Manuscripts dating from 13th century. Charters of privilege, statutes, Royal letters and mandates, Grace books, matriculation books, university accounts and many cther classes of records.
University Collection of Aerial Photographs, 11 West Road, *Cambridge*
Aerial photographs illustrating different aspects of agriculture, archaeology, geography, geology, history, vegetation, and the social and economic past and present of the United Kingdom.
University Museum of Archaeology and Ethnology, Downing Street, *Cambridge*
Archaeological collections illustrating Old Stone Age in Europe,

Asia and Africa, Britain from Prehistoric to Medieval times, Pre-
historic America, Ethnographical material fom America, Africa,
South East Asia and Oceania.
University Museum of Classical Archaeology, Little St Mary's
Lane, *Cambridge*
Representative collection of casts of Greek and Roman sculpture.
University Museum of Mineralogy and Petrology, Downing Place,
Cambridge
Comprehensive collection of minerals and rocks.
University Museum of Zoology, Downing Street, *Cambridge*
Zoological specimens used in teaching and research.
Whipple Museum of the History of Science, Free School Lane, *Cam-
bridge*
Collection of historic scientific instruments mainly of the 16th, 17th
and 18th centuries.
Wisbech and Fenland Museum, Museum Square, *Wisbech*
Fenland and Natural History, Archaeological and Antiquarian
Collections. Pottery and porcelain, bygones.

CHESHIRE
CASTLES AND HISTORIC HOUSES
Adlington Hall, *Macclesfield* (Charles Legh, Esq)
Great Hall dates from 1450. Elizabethan half-timbered 'black and
white' portion 1581.
Bishop Lloyd's House, *Chester*
Restored half-timbered house (1615) rich in carvings. Associated
with Yale University and New Haven in America.
Capesthorne, *Macclesfield* (Lt-Col Sir Walter Bromley-Davenport)
Built by John Wood of Bath in 1722, with later alterations by Blore
and Savin. Pictures, furniture, Americana.
Chorley Old Hall, *Alderley Edge* (Mr and Mrs M. W. Burling)
Small moated 14th-century hall with 16th-century Elizabethan wing.
Medieval screens, passage with stone arches. Squint in solar.
Churche's Mansion, *Nantwich* (Mr and Mrs R. V. Myott)
Elizabethan tanner's half-timbered mansion house, built by Thomas
Clease in 1577 for Richard Churche. Original plan. Fine oak
panelling.
Dorfold Hall, *Nantwich* (R. C. Roundell, Esq)
Jacobean country house (1616). Plaster ceilings and panelling.
Gawsworth Hall, *Macclesfield* (Raymond Richards, Esq)
Tudor half-timbered manor house with tilting ground. Former home
of Mary Fitton, Maid of Honour at the Court of Elizabeth I, and
supposed 'dark lady' of Shakespeare's sonnets. Pictures, sculpture
and furniture.

Little Moreton Hall, *Congleton* (National Trust)
16th-century moated half-timbered building. Remarkable carved gables.

Lyme Park, *Disley* (Leased to Stockport Metropolitan Borough Council by the National Trust)
House dating from Elizabethan times. Impressive Palladian exterior (1720) by Giacomo Leoni. Home of Leghs for 600 years. Grinling Gibbons carving. Extensive garden. Parks of 1320 acres. Herd of red deer.

Peover Hall, Over Peover, *Knutsford* (Randle Brooks)
Dates from 1585. Tudor stables, famous magpie ceiling.

Stanley Palace, *Chester* (English Speaking Union)
Half-timbered house dates from 1591, former house of Stanleys, Earls of Derby. Now local headquarters of English Speaking Union.

Tatton Park, *Knutsford* (National Trust [financed, maintained and administered by the Cheshire County Council])
Seat of late Lord Egerton of Tatton. Georgian house by Samuel and Lewis Wyatt. 2000 acre park. 50 acre garden.

CATHEDRALS AND CHURCHES

Acton (St Mary)
Mostly 13th–14th century. Stone seats around inner walls; 15th-century canopied wall tomb, 17th-century effigies. Late 17th-century chancel furnishings. 18th-century Gothic tower.

Astbury (St Mary)
Detached mid-14th-century spire. 15th-century stalls, screen, wooden eagle lectern, and roofs with pendants; 17th-century altar rails, royal arms and font cover. Restored by Sir Gilbert Scott, 1862.

Baddiley (St Michael)
Interesting tympanum: pre-Reformation with paintings of 1633.

Bunbury (St Boniface)
14th-century collegiate. Early alabaster effigy, other effigies and fine early 17th-century tomb, interesting fittings. Successful restoration after damage in Second World War.

Chester Cathedral
Suffered greatly from Victorian restoration. Fine stalls in choir, c. 1380, with figure carving and 48 misericords.

Congleton (St Peter)
1742. Galleries, box pews; William III arms; 18th-century glass, font and altar rails; good brass candelabrum, 1748.

Great Budworth (St Mary and All Saints)
14th–15th-century fabric. Some medieval stalls, monuments. 16th-century roof and supporting stone shafts.

Harthill (All Saints)
Early 17th-century screen.

217

Lower Peover (St Oswald)
Timber with stone tower. Box pews, Jacobean rails, altar and screen.
Malpas (St Oswald)
Mainly 15th century. Two family chapels. Fine screenwork, few old stalls, monuments, vestry and churchyard gates attributed to Vanbrugh.
Mobberley (St Wilfred)
Late medieval. Rood screen, 1500; good roof, some ancient glass, wall paintings; tower screen, 1683.
Nantwich (St Mary)
Extensive rebuilding, 1885, but exterior still impressive and fine chancel. 14th-century canopied choir stalls.
Over Peover (St Lawrence)
Mainly 1811. Two earlier side chapels, each with fine monuments, medieval glass and 17th-century heraldic glass.
Shotwick (St Michael)
Twin naves separated by low arcade, box pews, 3-decker pulpit, notable canopied seat, 2 fine quatrefoil 14th-century lights.
Winwick (St Oswald)
14th-century notable roof, Legh monuments and Pugin chancel.
Wrenbury (St Margaret)
Early 16th century. Box pews, hatchments, monuments, west gallery.

GARDENS
Arley Hall Gardens, *Northwich* (Viscount and Viscountess Ashbrook)
Topiary, rhododendrons, azaleas, herbaceous border, shrub roses.
Bridgemere Wild Life Park, *Bridgemere*
Birds and waterfowl in landscape of pools and marsh land.
Cholmondeley Castle Gardens, *Malpas* (Marquess of Cholmondeley)
Gardens and farm.

HISTORIC MONUMENTS
Beeston Castle, *Beeston*
Ruined 13th-century fort.
Chester Castle, *Chester*
Large square tower of once great castle.
Roman Amphitheatre, *Chester*
Half-excavated amphitheatre of 12th Legion.
Sandbach Crosses, *Sandbach*
9th-century carved stone crosses.

MUSEUMS AND GALLERIES
Cheshire Military Museum, Chester Castle, *Chester*
Exhibits from Cheshire Regiment, Cheshire Yeomanry and Carabineers.
Chester Heritage Centre, St Michaels Church, *Chester*
Exhibition of Chester architectural heritage.

Grosvenor Museum, Grosvenor Street, *Chester*
Roman antiquities from legionary fortress, including a large number
of inscribed and sculptured stones. Special gallery illustrating the
Roman army. Natural history and bygones.
King Charles Tower, City Walls *Chester*
Dioramas and exhibits illustrating Chester in Civil War.
Lancashire Regiment Museum, Peninsula Barracks, *Warrington*
Museum of South Lancashire Regiment from 1717.
Museum and Art Gallery, Bold Street, *Warrington* (Warrington
Borough Council)
Natural history, bctany, geology, ethnology, anthropology, bygones
and small arms. Art gallery contains collections of early English
water colours, pottery and pcrcelain and local glass. Temporary
exhibitions.
Norton Priory Museum, Warrington Road, *Runcorn* (Norton Priory
Museum Trust)
Recently excavated remains of monastic house. Set in woodlands
and gardens.
The Shaw Museum, Cross Street, *Runcorn* (Halton District Council)
Pictures and photographs of Runcorn and some excavated historical
objects.
West Park Museum and Art Gallery, Prestbury Road, *Macclesfield*
(Macclesfield Corporation)
Important Egyptian collection, local exhibits, oil paintings and
watercolour drawings.

NATIONAL PARKS
Peak District (part)

CLEVELAND
CASTLES AND HISTORIC HOUSES
Ormesby Hall, Nr *Middlesbrough* (National Trust)
Mid-18th-century house. Contemporary plasterwork. Small garden.

CATHEDRALS AND CHURCHES
Hartlepool (St Hilda)
Early English. Particularly fine tower and buttresses. Chancel
restored by Caroe, 1931. 19th–20th-century glass. Fittings of high
standard.
Skelton (St Giles)
Fine proportions and spatial relations. Completed prior to 1247.
Notable font, gable crosses, bell-cote and buttresses.

HISTORIC MONUMENTS
Gisborough Priory, *Gisborough*
Remains of east end of 14th-century church of Augustinian priory.

MUSEUMS AND GALLERIES

Billingham Art Gallery, *Billingham* (Stockton Borough Council)
Modern and forward-looking gallery with monthly changing exhibitions.

Captain Cook Birthplace Museum, Stewart Park, *Middlesbrough* (Middlesbrough Borough Council)
Illustrating Cook's life and adventures, Australasian ethnography and natural history.

Chapel Beck Gallery, *Gisborough* (Langbaurgh Borough Council)
Changing exhibitions with emphasis on local history of Cleveland and work of locally based artists and craftsmen.

Dorman Museum, Linthorpe Road, *Middlesbrough* (Middlesbrough Borough Council)
Social, industrial and natural history of the area. Changing exhibitions, specialist collections.

Gray Art Gallery and Museum, Clarence Road, *Hartlepool* (Hartlepool Borough Council)
19th- and 20th-century paintings, oriental antiquities. Museum displays illustrate archaeology, social history and natural history of the district.

Maritime Museum, Northgate, *Hartlepool* (Hartlepool Borough Council)
Maritime history of town.

Middlesbrough Art Gallery, Linthorpe Road, *Middlesbrough* (Middlesbrough Borough Council)
Contemporary British paintings. Monthly changing exhibitions.

Newham Grange Farm, Off the Parkway, *Middlesbrough* (Middlesbrough Borough Council)
Leisure-educational farm, featuring agricultural museum and interpretive centre.

Preston Hall Museum, Preston Park, Eaglescliffe, *Stockton-on-Tees* (Stockton Borough Council)
Arms, armoury personalia, local pottery, toys, ivory period rooms.

Redcar Museum of Shipping and Fishing, King Street, *Redcar* (Borough of Langbaurgh Museum Service)
Graphic and three-dimensional material, illustrating the history of Tees shipping and fishing, including ships and *The Zetland*, oldest surviving lifeboat in the world.

Stockton and Darlington Railway Museum, *Stockton-on-Tees* (Stockton Borough Council)
Historic pictures and relics of world's first paid-passenger railway.

NATIONAL PARKS

North York Moors (part)

CORNWALL
AREAS OF OUTSTANDING NATURAL BEAUTY
Cornwall (part)

CASTLES AND HISTORIC HOUSES
Antony House, *Torpoint* (National Trust)
Home of Sir John Carew Pole, Bt. Built for Sir William Carew from 1711 to 1721. Unaltered Queen Anne house, panelled rooms, fine furniture.
Cotehele House, *Calstock* (National Trust)
Fine medieval house. Former home of the Earls of Mount Edgcumbe. Armour, furniture, tapestries. Terraced garden falling to valley, ponds, stream, unusual shrubs.
Ebbingford Manor, *Bude* (Mr and Mrs Dudley-Stamp)
Cornish manor house dating from 12th century with walled garden.
Godolphin House, *Helston* (S. E. Schofield, Esq)
Tudor House. Colonnaded front added 1635. Former house of Earls of Godolphin.
Lanhydrock, Nr *Bodmin* (National Trust)
17th-century picture gallery. Fine plaster ceilings. Family portraits 17th to 20th centuries. Formal garden laid out in 1857.
Mount Edgcumbe, Nr *Plymouth* (City of Plymouth and County of Cornwall)
Home of Earl of Mount Edgcumbe. Fine gardens and park.
Pencarrow House and Gardens, *Bodmin* (Molesworth-St Aubyn Family)
Georgian mansion. Fine collection of 18th-century paintings. English, French and Oriental furniture and china. Large formal garden and woodlands, with granite rockery, ancient encampment and lake. Specimen conifer collection.
St Michael's Mount, *Penzance* (National Trust)
Home of Lord St Levan. Medieval and early 17th century, with considerable alterations and additions in 18th and 19th centuries.
Tintagel, Old Post Office (National Trust)
Miniature 14th-century manor house with large hall.
Trerice, *St Newlyn East* (National Trust)
Small Elizabethan house, plaster ceilings and fireplaces, newly planted garden.
Trewithen, Probus, Nr *Truro* (Mrs G. H. Johnstone)
Early Georgian house. Landscaped garden of camellias, magnolias, rhododendrons and other rare plants.

CATHEDRALS AND CHURCHES
Altarnun (St Nonna)
15th century. Fine 16th-century bench-ends. Norman font. Notable rood screen and early 17th-century panels on east wall.

221

Bisland (St Protus and St Hyacinth)
15th-century granite tower. Old carved wagon roofs, few old carved bench-ends, nave with slate floor, Georgian wine-glass pulpit and rich screen and loft restored by F. C. Eden. Altars by Comper.

Chacewater (St Paul)
Sedding, 1892. Noble tower, wagon roof to nave, 5-light east windows. Interior with unplastered stone walls, granite arches and shafts of Polyphant stone.

Kilkhampton (St James)
Mostly 16th century, but retains notable Norman doorway. Fine arcades, wagon roofs and carved bench-ends. Grenville monuments; organ c. 1775.

Laneast (St Michael or St Sidwell)
13th century, enlarged and refashioned in 15th century. Early 16th-century pulpit, bench-ends, screen, remains of painted glass.

Lanteglos-by-Fowley (St Willow)
14th century, refashioned in 15th century. 13th-century font, 16th-century bench-ends, 15th-century altar tomb and brasses.

Launcells (St Andrew)
Unrestored interior. Old plaster, ancient roofs, fine bench-ends, box-pews, pulpit, 3-sided altar rails, reredos, organ case, Norman font with 17th-century cover.

Launceston (St Mary Magdalene)
Early 16th century. Exterior with panelled ornament; scraped interior with 16th-century pulpit; 17th- and 18th-century monuments; 18th-century organ case.

Mullion (St Melan)
Mainly late medieval. Interior restored and adorned by F. C. Eden. Wagon roofs and old bench-ends.

Probus (St Probus and St Gren)
Very fine early 16th-century tower. Notable arcades; 3 great east windows; early 16th-century brass; mural monument, 1766.

St Endellion (St Endelienta)
Three altars, including 15th-century table tomb; Norman font; unstained glass; old roofs.

St Keverne (St Keveran)
Fine tower and spire. 15th-century interior, wall painting, bench-ends.

St Neot (St Neot)
Decorated tower, buttressed 16th-century double-aisled exterior. 15 windows of medieval glass renewed in 1829; rood screen, old roofs.

GARDENS
County Demonstration Garden and Arboretum, *Probus*
Displays of aspects of garden layout, plant selection, effect of weather. Exhibitions, etc.

Glendurgan Gardens, *Helford River* (National Trust)
A valley garden overlooking the estuary, with fine trees and shrubs.
Giant's stride and maze.
Penjerrick Gardens, Nr *Budock* (Mrs J. M. K. Fox)
Sub-tropical gardens.
Trelissick Garden, Nr *Truro* (National Trust)
Beautiful wooded park at head of Falmouth harbour. Woodland
walks. Particularly rich in rhododendrons and hydrangeas.
Tremeer, *St Tudy* (Major-General E. G. W. Harrison)
6-acre garden with water, closely planted with rhododendrons,
camellias and other shrubs. Aviary of budgerigars.
Trengwainton Garden, *Penzance* (National Trust)
Large shrub and woodland garden. Fine views. Series of walled
gardens containing rare sub-tropical plants.

HISTORIC MONUMENTS
Ballowall Barrow, *St Just*
Prehistoric barrow.
Chysauster, Nr *Madron*
Excavated Roman hamlet.
Cromwell's Castle, *Tresco* (Scilly Isles)
Mid 17th-century castle.
Duputh Well Chapel, Nr *Callington*
Most complete of many well chapels in Cornwall.
Harry's Walls, *St Mary's* (Scilly Isles)
Tudor coastal battery.
Hurlers, *Minions*
Three prehistoric stone circles.
King Charles's Fort, *Tresco* (Scilly Isles)
16th-century fort.
King Coniert's Stone, Nr *St Cleer*
Two 9th-century broken stone bases.
Launceston Castle, *Launceston*
11th-century castle motte; 13th-century tower.
Pendennis Castle, *Falmouth*
Fort built by Henry VII.
Old Blockhouse, *Tresco* (Scilly Isles)
Late 16th-century coastal battery.
Restormel Castle, Nr *Lostwithiel*
13th-century ruins.
St Catherine's Castle, *Fowey*
Ruined 16th-century castle.
St Mawes Castle, *St Mawes*
16th-century fort.
Tintagel Castle, *Tintagel*
Remains of 13th-century castle and 5th–9th-century Celtic monastery.

MUSEUMS AND GALLERIES
Barbara Hepworth Museum, *St Ives*
House where artist lived. Sculpture, photographs, letters, documents, etc.
Barnes Museum of Cinematography, *St Ives*
Items relating to history of cinematography and photography.
Cornish Engines, East Pool Mine, Pool, *Cambourne* (National Trust)
The 30-in rotative beam winding engine (1887) and the 90-in beam pumping engine (1892) stand complete in their houses.
Cornish Museum, Lower Street, *East Looe* (Museum Enterprises)
Representing life and culture of Cornwall, including unique collection of relics dealing with witchcraft, charms and superstitions.
County Museum and Art Gallery, River Street, *Truro* (Royal Institute of Cornwall)
Local antiquities and history. Ceramics and art. Cornish minerals.
Folk Museum, *Mevagissey*
Local crafts, seafaring, agricultural and mining items.
Helston Borough Museum, Old Butter Market, *Helston*
Folk museum dealing with all aspects of local life in Lizard Peninsula.
Lawrence House, Castle Street, *Launceston* (National Trust)
Local museum.
Military Museum, *Bodmin*
Duke of Cornwall's Light Infantry.
Museum of Nautical Art, *Penzance*
Gold and silver treasure from undersea wreck of 1707. Man-of-war display.
Museum of Smuggling, *Polperro*
Past and present smuggling activities.
Museum of Witchcraft, *Boscastle*
Customs of witches and their implements.
Newlyn Art Gallery, *Newlyn*
Exhibitions of contemporary works by leading West Country artists. Collection of Newlyn School paintings, 1880–1930.
Old Mariners Church, Norway Square, *St Ives* (St Ives Society of Artists)
Exhibitions of St Ives Society of Artists.
Paul Corin Playing Music Collection, Mill House, *St Keyne*
Organs and other musical instruments.
Penlee House Museum, Penlee Park, *Penzance*
Archaeological, local history and tin-mining exhibits.
Public Library and Museum, The Cross, *Cambourne*
Collections of archaeology, mineralogy, local history and local antiquities.
Thorburn Museum and Gallery, *Dobwalls*
Paintings, sketches, prints, books, letters, photographs, etc., by bird painter Archibald Thorburn (1860–1935).

Town Museum, *Bodmin*
Local history collection.
Valhalla Maritime Museum, Tresco Abbey, *Tresco* (Isles of Scilly)
(R. A. Dorrien-Smith)
Figureheads and ships' ornaments from ships wrecked in Isles of
Scilly.
Wayside Museum, Old Millhouse, *Zennor*
Archaeology and folk collections.
West Cornish Museum of Mechanical Music, *Goldsithney*
Including collections of Douglas R. Berrymen and Graham Webb.
Wheal Martyn Museum, Nr *St Austell*
Open-air museum of china clay industry.

CUMBRIA
AREAS OF OUTSTANDING NATURAL BEAUTY
Arnside and Silverdale (part)
Solway Coast

CASTLES AND HISTORIC HOUSES
Belle Island, *Bowness-on-Windermere* (E. S. C. Curwen, Esq)
Built in 1778. Interior by Adams brothers. Portraits, furniture.
Dalemain, Nr *Penrith* (Mr and Mrs Bryce McCosh)
Medieval, Elizabethan and Georgian house. Countryside park.
Hilltop, Nr *Sawney* (National Trust)
17th-century house where Beatrix Potter wrote Peter Rabbit books.
Contains her furniture, china, pictures, and some original drawings.
Holker Hall, *Cark-in-Cartmel* (Hugh Cavendish)
Dates from the 16th century with 19th-century additions. Exhibition,
gardens and deer park.
Hutton-in-the-Forest, *Penrith* (Lord and Lady Inglewood)
14th-century Pele tower with later additions. Pictures, tapestries and
furniture. Gardens and terraces dating from 17th century. Park and
woodlands. Specimen trees.
Levens Hall, *Kendal* (O. R. Bagot, Esq)
Elizabethan house with fine plasterwork, panelling and notable
furniture. Famous topiary garden laid out in 1689.
Muncaster Castle, *Ravenglass* (Sir William Pennington-Ramsdem, Bt)
Seat of Pennington family since 13th century. Rhododendron and
azalea gardens.
Rydal Mount, *Ambleside* (Lt-Cdr and Mrs P. P. R. Dane)
Wordsworth's home from 1813–59. Family portraits, furniture,
many of poet's personal possessions, and first editions of his works.
Garden with rare shrubs and trees.
Sizergh Castle, *Kendal* (National Trust)
Home of Stricklands for 700 years. 14th-century Pele tower. 15th-
16th- and 18th-century additions.

Townend, *Troutbeck* (National Trust)
17th-century lakeland farmhouse with original furnishings. Home of the Brownes for 300 years.
*Whitehall, *Mealsgate* (Mrs S. Parkin-Moore)
14th-century Pele tower.
Wordsworth House, *Cockermouth* (National Trust)
Built 1745, birthplace of Wordsworth.

CATHEDRALS AND CHURCHES
Brougham (St Ninian)
1669. Plain, whitewashed, oak box and canopied pews, pulpit with sounding board, seats and screens. Brasses.
Brougham (St Wilfred)
Very fine woodwork, including magnificent 15th-century carved altar piece.
Carlisle Cathedral
Only 2 out of 7 bays of Norman nave survive. Impressive choir, rebuilt after 1292. Richly moulded decorated windows. Well preserved early 15th-century stalls.
Cartmel (St Mary the Virgin)
Basically late 12th-century transitional. Renaissance screens and stall-canopies. Memorials, good brass chandeliers.
Crosthwaite (St Kentigern)
16th century with 14th-century arches. Unique set of consecration crosses. 14th-century font, 15th-century effigies.
Grasmere (St Oswald)
11th, 13th and 17th centuries. 2-storied continuous arcade dating from 17th century. Wordsworth's burial place.
Greystoke (St Andrew)
Collegiate (1382). Mainly 15th-century tower and chancel rebuilt; 19th-century misericords; fine old glass in chancel east windows.
Isel (St Michael)
Mainly Norman. 15th-century window, with 3 sundials, 2 pre-Norman stones.
Kirby Lonsdale (St Mary the Virgin)
Fine Norman work. Chancel fittings and pulpit, 1619.
Kirby Stephen (St Stephen)
Rebuilt 13th and 15th century. Cathedral-like nave, early English in style. 15th- and 16th-century monuments.
Lanercost (Priory of St Mary Magdalene)
Transitions and early English. Notable clerestory, west front, undercroft with vaulted roof, 13th-century pillars and Roman fragments.
Millom (Holy Trinity)
Mostly rebuilt, 1322. Fine Norman work. Mainly 15th-century chancel with 5-light eastern windows. Fine black-and-white roof

to nave. Notable old roof to south aisle and modern screen.
Over Denton (no dedication)
Saxon. Original Roman chancel arch.

GARDENS
Acorn Bank, *Temple Sowerby* (National Trust)
Spring bulbs, walled garden with herbaceous plants, herb garden.
Red sandstone house, part 16th century (*not open*).
Graythwaite Hall, *Ulverston* (Major M. E. M. Sandys)
7 acres of landscaped gardens. Rhododendrons, azaleas and other
shrubs.
Lingholm, *Keswick* (Viscount Rochdale)
Large rambling garden, woodland, rhododendrons, azaleas, etc.
Stagshaw, *Ambleside* (C. H. D. Acland, Esq)
Woodland garden, bulbs, trees and shrubs.
White Craggs Garden, *Clappers Gate*
Shrubs, heathers, rhododendrons, azaleas. Fine views.
Wild Life Country Park, *Lowther*
Deer, cranes, rare breeds of cattle in natural setting.

HISTORIC MONUMENTS
Bewcastle Castle and Cross, *Bewcastle*
Remains of castle built from materials from Hadrian's Wall. 7th-
century cross with Runic carvings.
Brough Castle, *Brough*
Dates from 12th century. Repaired in 17th century.
Carlisle Castle, *Carlisle*
Remains of keep date from 1170. 13th-century outer gatehouse.
Castlerigg Stone Circle, *Keswick*
Neolithic or Bronze Age religious centre.
Furness Abbey, *Barrow-in-Furness*
Ruins of Cistercian Abbey, founded in 1123.
Hardknot Roman Fort, Nr *Boot*
Remains of square fort.
King Arthur's Round Table and Mayburgh, *Eamont Bridge*
Pair of Neolithic or Bronze Age religious monuments.
Lanercost Priory, *Brampton*
Remains of house of Augustinian Canons, founded 1166.
Penrith Castle, *Penrith*
Ruins of late medieval castle, modernized in 1470s.
Shap Abbey, *Brampton*
Ruins of house of Premonstratensian Order, 1201–1540.

MUSEUMS AND GALLERIES
Abbot Hall Art Gallery, *Kendal* (Lake District Art Gallery Trust)
18th-century furnished rooms and modern galleries with pictures,
sculpture, furniture and pottery. Changing exhibitions.

227

Abbot Hall Museum of Lakeland Life and Industry, *Kendal* (Lake District Museum Trust)
Period rooms, costumes, printing, weaving, local industries, farming.
Barrow-in-Furness Museum, Ramsden Square, *Barrow-in-Furness* (District Council)
All aspects of area. Vickers-Armstrong collection of model ships. Findings from prehistoric sites, mainly Bronze Age. Lake District bygones.
Brantwood, *Coniston*
The home of John Ruskin from 1872 to 1900. Pictures by Ruskin and his associates, his coach, boat, furniture and other associated items.
Dalton Castle, *Dalton* (National Trust)
14th-century Pele tower houses collection of armour and documents.
Dove Cottage, *Grasmere*
The early home of Wordsworth from 1799 to 1808.
Fitz Park Museum and Art Gallery, Station Road, *Keswick*
Original Southey, Wordsworth and Walpole manuscripts. Local geology and natural history.
Hawkshead Court House, *Hawkshead* (National Trust)
Building dating from 15th century now used as museum of rural life.
Helena Thompson Museum, Park End Road, *Workington*
Local material mainly of family association.
Kendal Borough Museum, Station Road, *Kendal* (Kendal Corporation)
Collection of mammals and birds, area geology and Kendal bygones.
LYC Museum and Art Gallery, *Banks*
Roman and other antiquities. Works of international artists.
Maritime Museum, *Maryport*
Maritime models and artifacts. Photographic display of Maryport's history.
Millom Folk Museum, St George's Road, *Millom* (Millom Folk Museum Society)
Unique full-scale model of a drift of the former Hodbarrow iron ore mine.
Museum and Art Gallery, Tullie House, Castle Street, *Carlisle* (Carlisle Corporation)
Jacobean town house with Victorian extension having regional collection rich in prehistoric and Roman remains, Lakeside birds, mammals and geology. Bottomley Bequest of Pre-Raphaelite paintings, Williamson Bequest of English porcelain.
Priory Gate House, *Cartmel* (National Trust)
Gallery and local Museum.
The Ruskin Museum, *Coniston*
Life and work of John Ruskin. Also local history, scenery and industries.
The Wordsworth Museum, *Grasmere*
Manuscripts, first editions and collection of objects illustrative of rural life in Wordsworth's time.

NATIONAL PARKS
Lake District (part)
Yorkshire Dales (part)

DERBYSHIRE

CASTLES AND HISTORIC HOUSES
Chatsworth, *Bakewell* (Trustees of the Chatsworth Settlement)
Built by Talman for 1st Duke of Devonshire 1687–1707. Books,
furniture, pictures and drawings. Gardens with elaborate waterworks
surrounded by great park.
Foremarke Hall, *Milton* (Governors of Repton School)
Georgian house built 1762 by David Hiorns. Now a school. School
museum by appointment.
Haddon Hall, *Bakewell* (His Grace the Duke of Rutland)
Medieval and manorial house. Terraced garden.
Hardwick Hall, Nr *Chesterfield* (National Trust)
Built 1591–97 by Bess of Hardwick. Notable furniture, needlework,
tapestries. Gardens with yew hedges and borders of shrubs and
flowers. Extensive collection of herbs.
Kedleston Hall, *Derby* (Viscount Scarsdale, TD)
Probably finest Robert Adam house in England, with unique marble
hall, contemporary furniture and fine pictures.
Melbourne Hall, *Melbourne* (Marquess of Lothian)
Pictures, furniture and works of art. Garden by Wise, in style of Le
Notre. Wrought-iron pergola.
Winster Market House, Nr *Matlock* (National Trust)
Stone market house of the late 17th or early 18th century.

CATHEDRALS AND CHURCHES
Ashbourne (St Oswald)
Very fine tower and spire. Decorated with early English chancel,
perpendicular windows, monuments.
Chesterfield (St Mary and All Saints)
13th and 14th century. Notable east end with high altar and 4
chapels, one with polygonal apse. Alabaster tombs in Lady chapel.
Medieval screens. Jacobean pulpit, 18th-century candelabra of
wrought-iron. Stained glass by Comper and Webb.
Derby (All Saints)
Classical with perpendicular tower. 18th-century wrought-iron
screen, 17th–18th century plate, tombs, Comper furnishings.
Melbourne (St Michael and St Mary)
Norman. 2 west towers and crossing tower, stone-vaulted narthex
and circular apses to chancel and aisles. Interior little changed with
fine Norman workmanship.

229

Morley (St Matthew)
Norman south arcade, remainder 14th–15th century. Glass from Dale Abbey. Fine brasses, monuments and incised slabs.
Norbury (St Mary and St Barloke)
Notable 14th-century chancel with fine windows and much original glass. 2 Saxon cross shafts, palimpsest brass, altar tombs.
Sandiacre (St Giles)
Norman nave, decorated chancel, Norman chancel arch and south porch with much carving, fine tracery in chancel, sedilia.
Tideswell (St John the Baptist)
14th century. Fine chancel, perpendicular tower, wood carving, tombs and brasses.
Trusley (All Saints)
1713. Brick with stone-edged windows and pedimented doorway. Contemporary interior.
Wirksworth (St Mary)
13th century, much added to and restored. Sculptured 9th-century coffin lid. 2 fonts, Norman and 17th century. Brasses, monuments, medieval sculpture.
Youlgreave (All Saints)
Perpendicular tower. Fine Norman work. Notable late medieval alabaster monuments.

GARDENS
Ednaston Manor, *Brailsford* (S. D. Player, Esq)
Rare trees, shrubs, roses and alpines, woodland.
Lea Rhododendron Gardens, *Lea* (Mrs Tye and Miss Colyer)
Species and hybrid rhododendrons and azaleas in woodland setting.

HISTORIC MONUMENTS
Arbor Low, *Youlgreave*
Prehistoric stone circle.
Bolsover Castle, *Bolsover*
Norman castle, rebuilt in 1613.
Hob Hurst's House, *Beeley*
Prehistoric barrow.
Nine Ladies, *Stanton Moor*
Prehistoric stone circle.
Peveril Castle, Nr *Castleton*
Ruins dating from 11th century.

MUSEUMS AND GALLERIES
Buxton Museum, Terrace Road, *Buxton* (Derbyshire County Council)
Local history. Pleistocene and later animal remains from local caves. Local rocks, minerals, fossils and stones. Blue John and Ashford Marble ornaments. Paintings, prints, pottery, glass.

Derby Museum and Art Gallery, The Strand, *Derby*
The museum: archaeology, social history, ethnography, coins and medals, zoology, geology. Bonnie Prince Charlie Room (1745 rebellion). Art gallery: paintings by Wright of Derby, Derby porcelain, costumes.
Derbyshire County Museum, Sudbury Hall, *Sudbury* (National Trust)
Permanent exhibition: 'Exploring Childhood'. Temporary exhibitions. Charles II house with fine plasterwork and wood carving. Lakeside garden.
*Heathcote Museum, Birchover, *Matlock*
Finds from Bronze Age barrows on Stanton Moor.
Industrial Museum, Silk Mill, off Full Street, *Derby*
Rolls-Royce collection of historic aero engines and introductory gallery to Derbyshire industries.
Lecture Hall, Library Centre, New Square, *Chesterfield* (Borough of Chesterfield)
Exhibitions of art, photography, etc.
Old House Museum, Cunningham Place, *Bakewell* (Bakewell Historical Society)
Early Tudor house. Costumes, kitchen utensils, craftsmen's tools, etc.
Regimental Museum, The Strand, *Derby*
9th/12th Lancers.
Revolution House, Old Whittington, *Chesterfield* (Borough of Chesterfield)
An old inn connected with the plotting of the 1688 revolution. 17th-century furnishings.
The Tramway Museum, Matlock Road, Crich, Nr *Matlock* (Tramway Museum Society)
Horse, steam and electric tramcars and associated equipment.

NATIONAL PARKS
Peak District (part)

DEVON
AREAS OF OUTSTANDING NATURAL BEAUTY
East, North and South Devon

CASTLES AND HISTORIC HOUSES
Arlington Court, *Barnstaple* (National Trust)
Regency house furnished with collections of late Miss Rosalie Chichester, including shell, pewter and model ships. Display of horse-drawn vehicles. Victorian formal garden.
Bickleigh Castle, Nr *Tiverton* (Mr and Mrs O. N. Boxall)
Home of heirs of the Earls of Devon. Great hall, armoury. Thatched Jacobean wing. Early Norman chapel, moat and garden.

231

Bradley Manor, *Newton Abbot* (National Trust)
15th-century manor house with great hall, screen passage, buttery and perpendicular chapel.

Buckland Abbey, Nr *Plymouth* (National Trust, administered by Plymouth Corporation)
13th-century Cistercian monastery altered by Sir Richard Grenville in 1576. House of Drake. Drake's relics. Folk gallery.

Cadhay, *Ottery St Mary* (Lady William-Powlett)
Elizabethan manor house built about 1550.

Castle Drogo, Nr *Chagford* (National Trust)
Granite castle designed by Sir Edward Lutyens. Standing at over 900 feet, overlooking gorge of River Teign. Terraced gardens and walks.

*Castle Hill, Filleigh, *Barnstaple* (Lady Margaret Fortescue)
Palladian mansion built c. 1730–40. Fine 18th-century furniture, tapestries, porcelain and pictures. Ornamental garden, large shrub and woodland park, and arboretum.

Chambercombe Manor, *Ilfracombe* (Mr and Mrs H. R. Sirett)
Small 14th- and 15th-century manor house. Mainly Tudor and Jacobean furniture. $1\frac{1}{2}$ acre garden.

Compton Castle, Nr *Paignton* (National Trust)
Fortified manor house. Restored great hall.

Flete, Ermington, *Ivybridge* (Mutual Households Association Ltd)
Built around an Elizabethan manor.

Hayes Barton, Nr *Otterton*
Thatched and plastered 16th-century house. Birthplace of Sir Walter Raleigh.

Kirkham House, *Paignton* (Department of the Environment)
Interesting example of 15th-century architecture.

Lawrence Castle, Nr *Exeter* (Dale family)
Triangular turreted tower. Fine ballroom.

Oldway, *Paignton*
19th-century house containing replicas of rooms at Palace of Versailles. Gardens.

Powderham Castle, Nr *Exeter* (Earl and Countess of Devon)
Medieval castle built c. 1390, damaged in the Civil War, and restored and altered in the 18th and 19th centuries. Music room by Wyatt. Park stocked with deer.

Saltram House, *Plymouth* (National Trust)
George II house built around and incorporating remnants of late Tudor house, in landscaped park. 2 fine rooms by Robert Adam. Furniture, pictures, fine plasterwork and woodwork. Garden with orangery and octagonal summerhouse.

Shute Barn, Nr *Axminster* (National Trust. Tenant: Patrick Rice, Esq)
Remains of manor house built over centuries and completed in the 16th century.

Tiverton Castle, Nr *Tiverton* (Mr and Mrs Ivar Campbell)
Historic fortress of Henry I. Joan of Arc Gallery. Clock collection. Chapel of St Francis.
Torre Abbey Mansion, *Torquay*
House with pictures and furniture. Abbey ruins and tithe barn.
Watersmeet Cottage, Nr *Lynmouth* (National Trust)
Fishing lodge furnished in 1832, used for recruiting and information.
Youlston Park, Nr *Barnstaple* (J. J. C. Clarke, Esq)
Former Chichester home. 18th century with fine ceilings and staircase and Chinese wallpaper. Lake and woodland garden.

CATHEDRALS AND CHURCHES

Ashton (St John the Baptist)
15th century. Medieval screens, glass and wall paintings, and carved woodwork. Elizabethan pulpit with canopy; 17th-century altar rails; wooden monument, 1657; wagon roofs.

Atherington (St Mary)
Perpendicular. Notable screens, wagon roofs and 15th-century bench-ends. Original rood loft. Medieval effigies, some medieval glass.

Bere Ferrers (St Andrew)
Mostly rebuilt, 14th century. Early 14th-century glass. Norman font, early 16th-century benches, Ferrers tombs. Table tomb to Lord Willoughby de Broke, 1522.

Bridford (St Thomas à Becket)
Perpendicular. Late medieval glass and woodwork. Very fine rood screen, c. 1530.

Chittlehampton (St Urith or Hieritha)
Late perpendicular with fine tower. Medieval stone pulpit, monuments.

Coldridge (St Mary)
15th–16th century with some Norman work. Medieval screens, carved pulpit, bench-ends, tiles, glass, wagon roofs with carved bosses. 16th-century table tomb of Sir John Evans.

Crediton (Holy Cross)
12th century remodelled in 14th–15th century. Notable clerestory. Muniment chest, c. 1420. Monuments.

Cullompton (St Andrew)
15th–16th century perpendicular. Fan traceried roof and exterior carvings, coloured roof and rood screen. Jacobean west gallery.

Exeter (St Mary Arches)
Norman. 18th-century altar arrangement. 16th–18th century memorials.

Exeter Cathedral
Towers are Norman, most other important aspects are decorated, 1275–1369. Elaborate west front but badly worn statues. Interior Gothic tierceron ribbed vault, 300 ft long. Richly moulded piers

233

and arches, carved corbels and bosses. Original pulpitum, 1325. Notable decorated carving on stone sedilia and oak Bishop's Throne. Choir stalls with earliest misericords in England, 1260–80.

Gittisham (dedication unknown)
Perpendicular. 18th-century furnishings. 16th–18th-century mural monuments.

Haccombe (St Blaize)
Fine 13th–17th-century effigies and brasses. Some 14th-century glass. 19th-century stone screen, pulpit and reredos.

Harberton (St Andrew)
14th–15th century. Fine late medieval rood screen, rich vaulting and cornices. 15th-century pulpit with 17th-century figures in panels. Norman font.

Hartland (St Nectan)
14th century with late 15th-century embellishments. Norman font; carved bench-ends, 1530; wagon roofs. 15th-century rood screen, priest's chamber, monuments.

High Bickington (St Mary)
12th century with later additions. Original wagon roofs and magnificent Gothic and Renaissance bench-ends.

Kentisbeare (St Mary)
Perpendicular checkered tower. Fine early 16th-century rood screen. West gallery, 1652, carving on arcade. Tombs.

Kenton (All Saints)
Late 14th century. Fine tower and south porch. Arcade with carved capitals. Notable rood screen, medieval pulpit, reredos by Kempe. Monuments.

Ottery St Mary (St Mary)
13th century with Dorset aisle, 1520. Fine fan-vaulted roof, 14th-century clock, canopied tomb, choir stalls, altar screen, sedilia, minstrels' gallery and gilded wooden eagle. 18th-century pulpit. Monuments.

Parracombe (St Petrock)
Unrestored Georgian interior. Some 16th-century benches. Early English chancel, remainder plain perpendicular.

Sampford Courtenay (St Andrew)
Mostly early 16th century. Much clear glass, good arcades, screen, Norman font, carved bosses and wall plates in roof.

Sutcombe (St Andrew)
15th–16th century with some Norman work. Early 16th-century carved bench-ends, late medieval floor tiles, restored rood screen, some medieval glass.

Swimbridge (St James)
14th-century tower and spire, 15th-century remainder. Medieval stone pulpit, c. 1490; 15th-century rood screen. Renaissance font cover, some bench-ends, wagon roofs.

Tawstock (St Peter)
Mainly 14th century. Splendid Bath monument. Ceilings of Italian plasterwork, medieval glass, 16th-century gallery. Renaissance memorial pew of earls of Bath.

Torbryan (Holy Trinity)
Perpendicular 15th-century rood screen, pulpit and altar, 18th-century box pews, clear glass.

GARDENS

Bickham House, *Roborough* (Lord Roborough)
Shrub garden, camellias, rhododendrons, azaleas, cherries, bulbs, trees.

Combe Head, *Bampton* (Mr and Mrs A. D. Baxter)
Aboretum in 25 acres of fine old trees and walled garden.

The Garden House, Buckland Monachorum, *Yelverton* (Mr and Mrs L. S. Fortescue)
Trees, lawns, terraces. Up-to-date collection of flowering shrubs, ornamental cherries etc.

Killerton Garden, Nr *Exeter* (National Trust)
Lovely throughout year. 19th-century chapel and ice house.

Knightshayes Court, Nr *Tiverton* (National Trust)
Garden of interest at all seasons. House by William Burges (1870), decorated by J. D. Crace.

Lee Ford, *Budleigh Salterton* (Mr and Mrs N. Lindsay Fynn)
40 acres of parkland with Adam pavilion. Georgian house.

Marwood Hill, Nr *Barnstaple* (Dr J. A. Smart)
Camellias, daffodils, rhododendrons, flowering shrubs, rock and alpine garden, rose garden and waterside planting.

Rosemoor Garden Charitable Trust, *Torrington* (Col J. E. and Lady Anne Palmer)
Rhododendrons, ornamental trees and shrubs, primulas, species of roses, scree and alpine beds.

Staplers, *Sticklepath* (Mrs M. Lees)
Garden with lilies, crocus display and rare plants.

Tapeley Park Gardens, *Instow* (Christie Estate Trust)
Home of the late John Christie, founder of Glyndebourne. Italian style garden.

HISTORIC MONUMENTS

Blackbury Castle, *Southleigh*
Well preserved hill fort.

Dartmouth Castle, *Dartmouth*
15th-century castle designed for coastal defence.

Hound Tor, *Manaton*
Remains of medieval hamlet used for summer grazing.

Lydford Castle, *Lydford*
Remains of 12th-century stone keep built on site of Saxon fortress town.

Okehampton Castle, *Okehampton*
Chapel, keep and hall dating from 11th–14th century.
Totnes Castle, *Totnes*
Ruined 13th–14th-century castle with shell keep and curtain walls.

MUSEUMS AND GALLERIES
Ashburton Museum, 1 West Street, *Ashburton*
Local antiquities, weapons, period costumes, lace, implements, lepidoptera, American Indian antiques, bygones.
Bicton Countryside Museum, Bicton Gardens, *East Budleigh* (Clinton Devon Estates)
Items dealing with countryside.
Bideford Museum, Municipal Buildings, *Bideford* (Bideford Town Council)
North Devon pottery, shipwright's tools, geological specimens, maps and prints.
Burton Art Gallery, Victoria Park, Kingsley Road, *Bideford*
Hubert Coop collection of paintings and other *objects d'art.*
Butterwalk Museum, *Dartmouth*
Half-timbered 17th-century row with small maritime and nautical museum.
City Museum and Art Gallery, Drake Circus, *Plymouth* (Plymouth Corporation)
Collections of paintings and English porcelain. Cottonian collection of English and Italian drawings. Reynolds family portraits and early printed books. Local and natural history collections. Ships' models.
Cookworthy Museum, The Old Grammar School, 108 Fore Street, *Kingsbridge*
William Cookworthy and story of china clay. Victorian kitchen and scullery. Local history. Trade and shipbuilding tools, rural life, early photographs, costume and prints.
The Elizabethan House, 70 Fore Street, *Totnes* (Joint Committee)
Period furniture and costumes, local tools, toys, domestic articles and archaeological exhibits. Documents from local collections. Computer exhibition. Local reference library.
Elizabethan House, 32 New Street, *Plymouth* (Plymouth Corporation)
16th-century house in Plymouth's historic quarter, furnished according to period.
Exeter Maritime Museum, The Quay, *Exeter* (International Sailing Craft Association)
Working craft, many afloat, from all over the world.
Fairylynch Arts Centre and Museum, *Budleigh Salterton*
Exhibits of local interest in 18th-century house.
Guildhall, High Street, *Exeter*
One of the oldest municipal buildings in the country. Main structure

medieval, Tudor frontage, and oak door added in 1593. City regalia, silver and historic portraits.

Honiton and Allhallows Public Museum, High Street, *Honiton*
Collections of local interest including Honiton lace, local implements, and a complete Devon kitchen; bones of hippopotamus, straight-tusked elephant, ox and red deer.

Ilfracombe Museum, Wilder Road, *Ilfracombe*
British botany, North Devon birds, reptiles and insects. Early engravings, pictures, maps, arms, Victoriana. Ships' models and marine life.

Lyn and Exmoor Museum, *Lynton*
History and life of Exmoor.

Morwellham Quay, Morwellham, Nr *Tavistock* (Morwellham Recreation Company)
Museum of industrial archaeology, copper port of the 19th century with incline planes, harbours, quays and water wheels.

Museum of Shellcraft, *Buckfast*
Worldwide collection of shellcraft.

The North Devon Anthenaeum, The Square, *Barnstaple*
North Devon geological specimens. Cryptograms, local antiquities, and library.

Rougemont House Museum, Castle Street, *Exeter*
Archaeology and local history from Exeter and Devon.

Royal Albert Memorial Museum and Art Gallery, Queen Street, *Exeter*
English paintings, watercolours, ceramics and glass, Exeter silver, costume, natural history and anthropology. Temporary exhibitions.

St Anne's Chapel Museum, St Peter's Churchyard, High Street, *Barnstaple*
Antiquities and exhibits of local interest.

St Nicholas Priory, The Mint, Fore Street, *Exeter*
Fine monastic guest house including a Norman crypt, and a 15th-century guest hall.

Sharpitor, *Salcombe* (National Trust)
Museum of local interest and of special appeal to children. Gardens.

Sidmouth Museum, *Sidmouth*
Local history.

South Molton Museum, Town Hall, *South Molton* (South Molton Town Council Friends of the Museum Committee)
Local history, pewter weights and measures, documents, bygones.

Topsham Museum, 25 The Strand, Topsham, *Exeter*
History of port and trade of Topsham.

Torquay Natural History Society Museum, Babbacombe Road, *Torquay*
Collections illustrate Kent's Cavern and other caves. Devon natural history, local folk culture.

Underground Passages, entrance in Princesshay, *Exeter*
City medieval aqueducts.

NATIONAL PARKS
Dartmoor (part)
Exmoor (part)

DORSET
AREAS OF OUTSTANDING NATURAL BEAUTY
Dorset (whole)

CASTLES AND HISTORIC HOUSES
Athelhampton, *Athelhampton* (Robert Cooke Esq, MP)
One of finest medieval houses in England. 10 acres of formal and
landscaped gardens. Chinese deer.
Barneston Manor, Nr *Church Knowle*
13th–16th-century stone manor.
Clouds Hill, Nr *Wareham* (National Trust)
The home of T. E. Lawrence (Lawrence of Arabia) after First World
War.
Dewlish House, *Dewlish* (J. Anthony Boyden, Esq)
Queen Anne house built 1700.
Forde Abbey, Nr *Chard* (Trustees of G. D. Roper, Esq)
12th-century Cistercian monastery. Famous Mortlake tapestries,
25 acres of gardens.
Hardy's Cottage, *Higher Bockhampton* (National Trust)
Birthplace of Thomas Hardy (1840–1928).
Manor House, Sandford Orcas (Col F. Claridge)
Tudor mansion furnished with antiques, period furniture, pictures,
silver, glass, maps, china.
Milton Abbey, Nr *Blandford* (Governors of Milton Abbey School)
Georgian Gothic house built 1771, on site of 15th-century abbey.
Fine hall and ceilings. Abbot's hall completed 1498. Ceilings in house
were designed by James Wyatt.
Parnham House, *Beaminster* (J. Makepeace, Esq)
Tudor manor house with additions by Nash. Tile panelling, heraldic
plasterwork and leaded windows. Formal and informal gardens.
Woods and parkland.
Purse Caundle Manor, *Purse Caundle* (R. E. Winckelmann, Esq)
Medieval manor house. Period furniture. Lawns, roses.
Sherborne Castle, *Sherborne* (Simon Wingfield Digby, Esq)
16th-century mansion in continuous occupation of Digby family
since 1617.
Smedmore, *Kimmeridge* (Major J. C. Mansel)
18th-century manor house. Dutch marquetry furniture. Antique
dolls. Views.

No 3 Trinity Street, *Weymouth* (E. Walmsley Lewis, Esq, FRIBA)
Converted Tudor cottages, now one house. Completely furnished
with 17th-century objects.
Wolfeton House, *Dorchester* (Capt N. T. L. Thimbleby)
Fine medieval and Elizabethan manor house with magnificent
stonework, great stairs, Jacobean fireplaces and ceilings. 17th-
century furniture.

CATHEDRALS AND CHURCHES
Abbotsbury (St Nicholas)
Mainly 15th century. Chancel with 18th-century plastered barrel
ceiling and altar-piece. 15th-century painted glass; stone effigy;
Jacobean pulpit.
Bere Regis (St John the Baptist)
Fabric of 12th century refashioned and enlarged 13th–15th century.
Elaborate timber roof of nave. Note arcades, some mid-16th-
century seating and Purbeck marble monuments.
Blandford (St Peter and St Paul)
Georgian design in ashlar, 1731–9. Interior retains galleries, font,
pulpit, box pews and mayoral seat.
Bradford Abbas (St Mary)
Embattled parapets, pinnacled tower and large windows. Fine
panelled roof, stone rood screen, late 15th-century bench-ends,
17th-century pulpit.
Cattistock (St Peter and St Paul)
Mostly rebuilt by Sir Gilbert Scott in 19th century. Superb tower,
porch, north aisle, and vestry; pre-Raphaelite stained glass.
Cerne Abbas (St Mary)
Late 13th century rebuilt 15th–16th century with 15th-century tower.
Stone screen, 14th-century wall paintings, 11th-century pulpit, east
windows.
Chalbury (dedication unknown)
Fabric of 13th-century origin with 14th-century east windows.
Plastered walls and timber bell-cote. Note box pews, 3-decker
pulpit, west gallery and clear 19th-century glass.
Charlton Marshall (St Mary)
Rebuilt 1715 except for late medieval tower. Interior with Georgian
atmosphere. Clear glass, altar rails and fine canopied pulpit.
Christchurch (Christ Church)
Norman nave with good ribbed plaster vaulting, 1819–20; perpendicu-
lar spire. Great screen with Tree of Jesse; Tudor Renaissance Salisbury
chantry; fine misericord seats; rich Norman turret of north transepts.
Hazelbury Bryan (St Mary and St James)
Mainly 15th century with embattled parapets and sturdy west tower.
Note 13th-century font with 18th-century cover, canopied pulpit,
remains of 15th-century painted glass.

Hilton (All Saints)
Late Gothic. 15th-century windows, fan-vaulted porch, 16th-century painted panels.
Kingston (St James)
One of Street's latest and best churches. Much beautiful ironwork.
Milton Abbey (St Mary, St Michael, St Sampson and St Branwaleder)
Mainly 14th century with 15th-century detail in tower and north transepts. 14th-century pulpitum and sedilia, 15th-century reredos and pyx canopy, 16th-century Tregonwell monument. Milton effigies, 1775.
Puddletown (St Mary)
Fine panelled roof to nave. Note beaker-shaped font, probably 11th century; box pews, canopied pulpit and gallery; 15th and 16th-century brasses and monuments; Comper glass in south chapel.
Sherborne (St Mary)
Norman fabric, transformed in 15th century, but with slight Saxon remains. Very fine fan vaults of nave and quire. Monument to Earl of Bristol, and his 2 wives, 1698. Note 15th-century painted glass in Leweston chapel; 12th- and 13th-century abbatial effigies; Elizabethan Horsey and Leweston monuments; 18th-century mural tablets.
Studland (St Nicholas)
Most complete Norman church in Dorset. Much good 12th-century detail. Chalice-shaped 12th-century font and mutilated 18th-century pulpit. 13th-century east windows.
Trent (St Andrew)
Lateral tower with stone spire. 13th-century fabric enlarged and refashioned in 14th–15th century. Much restoration and refitting, c. 1840. Fine rood screen. Pulpit of continental origin. Old painted glass in east window. Fine early 16th-century bench-ends.
Whitchurch Canonicorum (St Candida and Holy Cross)
Mainly 12th and 13th century. Fine 15th-century west tower. Unique in that it retains relics of patroness in 13th-century shrine. Note late 12th-century font, early 17th-century pulpit, fragments of 15th-century painted glass, 16th- and 17th-century monuments.
Wimbourne Minster (St Cuthberga)
Formerly collegiate church. 12th-century central tower and part of arcade, remainder 13th–15th century. Drastically restored. Good Georgian painted glass. Remains of Jacobean screen and stalls. Medieval and later monuments. Notable clock of 14th-century origin.
Worth Matravers (St Nicholas)
Norman. Fine 14th-century east window. External corbel tables, inner south doorway and chancel arch.
Yetminster (St Andrew)
Late 13th-century chancel, rest rebuilt in 15th century with embattled parapets and good roofs retaining much original colour decoration.

240

Some early 16th-century seating and good brass of 1531. Table tombs and headstones, late 17th–18th century, in churchyard.

GARDENS

Compton Acres Gardens (J. R. Brady, Esq)
Gardens with valuable bronze and marble statuary and ornaments. 7 separate secluded gardens.

Cranborne Manor Gardens, *Cranborne* (Marquess of Salisbury)
Walled gardens, yew hedges and lawns, wild garden with spring bulbs, herb garden, Jacobean mount garden, flowering cherries and collection of old-fashioned and species roses.

Hyde Crook, *Dorchester* (Major P. R. A. Birley)
Flowering trees and shrubs, Japanese cherries, magnolias, camellias, azaleas, daffodils, orchids, narcissi.

Mapperton, *Beaminster* (Victor Montague, Esq)
Terraced and hillside gardens. 18th-century stone fish-ponds and summerhouse. Tudor manor house, enlarged by Charles II.

Melbury House, Nr *Yeovil* (Lady Teresa Agnew)
Large garden, very fine arboretum, shrubs and lakeside walk; beautiful deer park.

Minterne, *Dorchester* (Lord Digby)
Rhododendrons, azaleas, and trees.

HISTORIC MONUMENTS

Abbotsbury Abbey and St Catherine's Chapel, *Abbotsbury*
Gable of one of minor buildings of abbey and hill-top chapel.

Christchurch Castle, *Christchurch*
Motte with 14th-century tower.

Corfe Castle, *Corfe Castle*
12th–16th-century stronghold.

Jordan Hill Roman Temple, Nr *Preston*
Few fragments remain.

Knowlton Circle and Church, Nr *Cranborne*
Ruined Norman church in centre of prehistoric henge monument.

Maiden Castle, *Dorchester*
Large prehistoric triple ramparted camp with extensive plateau on summit.

Ninestones, *Winterbourne Abbas*
Prehistoric stone circle.

Poor Lot Barrows, *Winterbourne Abbas*
Large number of barrows.

Sherborne Old Castle, *Sherborne*
12th-century ruin. South-west gate still stands 4 storeys high.

MUSEUMS AND GALLERIES

Abbey Ruins Museum, Park Walk, *Shaftesbury*
Objects from excavations of Church of Benedictine Nunnery founded by Alfred the Great.

Bournemouth Natural Science Society's Museum, 39 Christchurch Road, *Bournemouth*
Local natural history and archaeology.
Brewery Farm Museum, *Milton Abbas*
Brewing, farming and village bygones, from the Dorset countryside.
Bridport Museum and Art Gallery, South Street, *Bridport* (West Dorset District Council)
Collection of local interest. Antiquities and natural history. Collection of paintings, drawings and sketches.
Corfe Castle Museum, *Corfe Castle*
Old village relics
Dorset County Museum, *Dorchester* (Dorset Natural History and Archaeological Society)
Regional museum whose collections cover Dorset geology, natural history and prehistory, bygones and history with Thomas Hardy Memorial Room. Temporary exhibitions.
Dorset Military Museum, The Keep, *Dorchester*
Exhibits of Dorset Regiment, Dorset Militia and Volunteers, Queen's Own Dorset Yeomanry and Devonshire and Dorset Regiment (from 1958).
Gallery 24, Bimport, *Shaftesbury*
Art gallery with changing exhibitions of paintings by new and internationally known artists. Also work of potters and unusual crafts.
Guildhall Museum, Market Street, *Poole* (Poole Borough Council)
18th-century ceramics and glassware. Curiosities, changing exhibitions.
Local History Museum, Gold Hill, *Shaftesbury*
Maritime Museum, Paradise Street (Poole Borough Council)
14th-century town cellars portraying the wealth of Poole's medieval maritime trade and commerce.
Philpot Museum, Bridge Street, *Lyme Regis*
Old prints and documents, fossils and coins, old Sun fire engine of 1710.
Portland Museum, Avice's Cottage, Wakeham, Nr *Easton*
Objects of local, historical and folk interest, natural history.
Priest's House Museum, High Street, *Wimborne Minster*
Local archaeology and general history. Tudor building with garden.
Red House Museum and Art Gallery, Quay Road, *Christchurch* (Hampshire County Museums Service)
Regional museum with natural history and antiquities. 19th-century fashion plates, costume dolls and bygones. Art exhibitions frequently changed. In Georgian house with herb and other gardens.
Rothesay Museum, 8 Bath Road, *Bournemouth* (Bournemouth Corporation)
Lucas collection of early Italian paintings and pottery; English

porcelain; 17th-century furniture; Victorian bygones and pictures; ethnography; arms and armour; marine rooms; local and exotic butterflies and moths.

Royal Armoured Corps Tank Museum, *Bovington Camp*
Armoured fighting vehicles from 1915.

Royal Signals Museum, *Blandford Forum*
History of army signalling methods. Also photographs, paintings and uniforms.

Russel-Cotes Art Gallery and Museum, East Cliff, *Bournemouth* (Bournemouth Corporation)
17th–20th-century oil paintings, tempera, watercolours, sculpture, miniatures, ceramics, Japanese, Burmese, Chinese, theatrical (Irving).

Scalpens Court (Old Town House), High Street, *Poole* (Poole Borough Council)
14th-century merchant's house displaying archaeological and local history of Poole, including industrial archaeology.

Sherborne Museum, Abbey Gate House, *Sherborne* (Trustees)
Local geology and history, including abbey, founded AD 705. Sherborne missal AD 1400, and 18th-century local silk industry.

Weymouth Local History Museum, *Weymouth* (Weymouth and Portland Borough Council)
Local illustrations and bygones, shipwrecks and transport.

CO DURHAM

CASTLES AND HISTORIC HOUSES

Durham Castle, *Durham* (University of Durham)
Norman castle of prince bishops has been used by the University since 1832.

Raby Castle, Staindrop, *Darlington* (Lord Barnard, TD)
Principally 14th century, alterations made in 1765 and mid-19th century. Fine pictures and furniture. 10 acre garden.

CATHEDRALS AND CHURCHES

Brancepeth (St Brandon)
12th–17th century. Magnificent 17th-century woodwork. 2 fragments of medieval rood screens. Fine Flemish carved chest. Royal arms of James I. Jacobean north porch.

Chester-le-Street (St Mary and St Cuthbert)
Early medieval with good spire. Lumley effigies.

Darlington (St Cuthbert)
Early English. Medieval stalls with good misericords. Gothic font cover, chancel arch with stone rood-loft or pulpitum.

Durham Cathedral
England's noblest Norman cathedral. Only eastern transepts, 3

towers and cloisters later than 12th century. Unique Galilee chapel with slender piers and chevron decoration. Impressive nave with non-figurative decoration. Original early 12th-century vaults over nave and transepts. Neville screen.

Escombe (dedication unknown)
Saxon, little altered. Inscribed stone from Binchester Roman font. Sundial.

Haughton-le-Skerne (St Andrew)
Norman chancel arch. Woodwork, box pews, font cover, pulpit and reading desk in post-Reformation manner. Saxon and medieval carved stones.

Pittington (St Lawrence)
Late Norman carved pillars in nave, fragments of wall paintings, Jacobean font cover, carved 13th-century tombstone.

Roker (St Andrew)
1906–7 by E. S. Prior. Fittings and ornaments in style of Arts and Crafts movement.

Sedgefield (St Edmund)
Medieval. Fine tower. Good woodwork of 17th century. 1708 epitaph on tablet in chancel. 13th-century carved capitals in nave. Organ case and font, c. 1708.

Staindrop (St Mary)
Saxon window above nave arcading. Pre-Reformation stalls and chancel screen. 2-storied priest's dwelling. Neville tombs and effigies. 18th-century monument.

HISTORIC MONUMENTS

Barnard Castle, *Barnard Castle*
11th–13th-century ruin with circular 3-storied keep.

Bowes Castle, *Bowes*
Norman keep in angle of Roman fort of 'Lavatrae'.

Egglestone Abbey, Nr *Barnard Castle*
Remains of poor house of Premonstratensian Canons, founded 1189.

Finchale Priory, Nr *Durham*
Considerable remains of 13th-century church of Benedictine priory.

MUSEUMS AND GALLERIES

Bowes Museum, *Barnard Castle* (Durham County Council)
Main collections are representative of European art from late medieval period to 19th century.

Darlington Art Gallery, Crown Street, *Darlington*
Local exhibitions, loan exhibitions and selections from permanent collection.

Darlington Museum, Tubwell Row, *Darlington*
Stockton and Darlington and North Eastern Railway history, local and natural history.

Dormitory Museum, The Cathedral, *Durham*
Relics of St Cuthbert, Anglo-Saxon sculptured stones, medieval seats, vestments and manuscripts.
Durham Light Infantry Museum and Art Centre, Nr County Hall, *Durham*
History of Regiment and a wide variety of constantly changing exhibitions.
Gulbenkian Museum of Oriental Art and Archaeology, Elvet Hill, *Durham* (University of Durham)
Northumberland collection of Egyptian and Mesopotamian antiquities; Malcolm MacDonald collection of Chinese pottery and porcelain; Sir Charles Hardinge collection of Chinese jade and other hand stone carvings; part of Sir Victor Sassoon collection of Chinese ivories. Chinese textiles, ancient Near-Eastern pottery, Indian sculpture, Japanese and Tibetan art.
North of England Open Air Museum, Nr Stanley, *Beamish*
Museum representing the industrial development and social history of the North of England.
Timothy Hackworth Museum, Hackworth Cottage, *Shildon*
Home of Timothy Hackworth, first manager of Stockton-Darlington railway. Furniture from 1830s, Hackworth's papers and personal trivia, Stockton and Darlington items, etc.

EAST SUSSEX
AREAS OF OUTSTANDING NATURAL BEAUTY
Sussex Downs (part)

CASTLES AND HISTORIC HOUSES
Alfriston Clergy House, Nr *Seaford* (National Trust)
Pre-Reformation parish priest's house, c. 1350.
Bateman's, *Burwash* (National Trust)
Built 1634. Rudyard Kipling lived here. Watermill, garden, yew hedges, lawns, daffodils.
Battle Abbey, *Battle*
Founded by William the Conqueror.
Beeches Farm, Nr *Uckfield* (Mrs Vera Thomas)
16th-century tile-hung farm house. Lawns, yew trees, borders, sunken gardens, roses, fine views.
Brickwall House, Northiam, *Rye* (Frewen Educational Trust)
Home of the Frewen family since 1666. 17th-century drawing-room with richly decorated plaster ceiling. Family portraits.
Bull House, *Lewes* (Sussex Archaeological Trust)
Half-timbered 15th-century house, home of Tom Paine in 18th century.
Charleston Manor, Westdean, *Seaford* (Lady Birley)
Norman, Tudor and Georgian architecture. Famous Romanesque window in Norman wing.

Durbar Hall, *Hastings* (Hastings Borough Council)
Indian Palace (Punjab and Bombay) built for Indian and Colonial Exhibition 1886. Acquired by Lord Brassey. Contains collections of Oriental and Primitive art based on those of Lord and Lady Brassey.

Firle Place, Nr *Lewes* (Viscount Gage, KCVO)
Italian, Dutch and English pictures. Sèvres china, French and English furniture and objects of American interest.

Haresmere Hall, *Etchington* (Jacqueline, Lady Killearn)
Early 17th-century manor house. Minstrel staircase, panelled Great Hall, carved doors and Flemish fireplace. Furniture and collection of rugs, ornaments, pottery, plates from Middle and Far East. Terraced garden.

Holy Cross Priory, *Cross-in-Hand*
Built in 1866 by Sir Matthew Digby Wyatt. Large mansion in extensive grounds. Now old people's home.

Glynde Place, Nr *Lewes* (Mrs Humphrey Brand)
Beautiful example of 16th-century architecture. Pictures, bronzes, needlework, historical documents, pottery.

Great Dixter, *Northiam* (Quentin Lloyd, Esq)
15th-century half-timbered manor house in a Lutyens designed garden.

*Kidbrooke Park, *Forest Row* (Council of Michael Hall School)
Sandstone house and stables built in 1730s with later alterations.

Lamb House, *Rye* (National Trust)
Georgian house with garden. Home of Henry James from 1898 to his death in 1916.

Michelham Priory, Nr *Hailsham* (Sussex Archaeological Trust)
Founded in 1229, Augustinian priory surrounded by moat. Elizabethan wing and 14th-century gatehouse. Special exhibitions and events. Tudor barn.

The Old Minthouse, *Pevensey* (Mr and Mrs J. C. Nicholson)
Mint house c. AD 1342. Occupied by King Edward VI and Andrew Boarde. Coins struck on this site AD 1076. Flowered courtyard.

Preston Manor, *Brighton* (Borough of Brighton)
Georgian house. Macquoid bequests of fine furniture, pictures, etc.

Royal Pavilion, *Brighton* (Borough of Brighton)
Unique building by Henry Holland and John Nash, built for the Prince Regent.

Sheffield Park, Nr *Uckfield* (Mr and Mrs P. J. Radford)
Tudor house remodelled by James Wyatt, 1775–8. Dickens's letters, rare books, weapons.

Standen, *East Grinstead* (National Trust)
Built in 1894 by Philip Webb. William Morris wallpapers and textiles. Furniture, paintings, garden.

CATHEDRALS AND CHURCHES

Alfriston (St Andrew)
14th century, transition from decorated to perpendicular. Piscina, sedilia, Easter sepulchre.

Ashburnham (St James)
Rebuilt 1663 except for Tudor tower. Box pews, gallery, pulpit, font, tower staircase, altar rails, painted altar piece, 1676. Iron railings. Armour and tombs of Ashburnhams.

Brighton (St Bartholomew)
1874. Chancel never built. Baldachino silver side altar. Baptistry mixture of Art Nouveau and Byzantine, by H. Wilson.

Etchingham (St Mary and St Nicholas)
14th century. Note chancel and east window. Old glass, screen, carved stalls, misereres, brasses.

Glynde (St Mary)
Classical, 1764–5. Complete interior but overlaid with later 19th-century embellishment.

Penhurst (dedication unknown)
Perpendicular with tile-capped tower. Interior with walls scraped but old fittings remain: perpendicular screen, 17th-century pulpit, lectern, altar rails and font cover. Nave has oak seating with 17th-century doors and panelled walls.

Rotherfield (St Denys)
Wall paintings, wagon roof to nave, font cover, 1533. Canopied pulpit, c. 1630. Glass by Burne-Jones, Georgian Royal Arms.

Winchelsea (St Thomas the Apostle)
Completed early 14th century. Only choir and aisles. Glass by Strachan, richly canopied sedilia and piscina. Canopied tombs.

GARDENS

Bentley, Halland, Nr *Lewes* (Mrs Gerald Askew)
Wildfowl Gardens. Swans, geese, duck, flamingoes, peacocks, and pheasants.

Horsted Place Gardens, Nr *Uckfield* (Lord Rupert Nevill, DL, JP)
Charming Victorian garden, rose borders, rhododendrons, shaded walks.

Sheffield Park Garden, Nr *Uckfield* (National Trust)
Large gardens with series of lakes linked by cascades, and great variety of unusual shrubs.

The Spring Hill Wildfowl Collection, *Forest Row* (R. A. and D. M. Pendry)
15th-century farmhouse (*not* open). 10 acres, ponds, shrub and terraces. Rare geese, swans, flamingoes, cranes, peacocks, and pheasants.

HISTORIC MONUMENTS
Bayham Abbey, Nr *Lamberhurst*
Ruins dating from 13th century including part of church, cloistrial building and gatehouse.
Pevensey Castle, *Pevensey*
3rd-century Roman fort of Saxon Shore with Norman and 13th-century additions.
Wilmington Priory, Nr *Polegate*
Remains of 12th-century priory.

MUSEUMS AND GALLERIES
Anne of Cleves' House, High Street, Southover, *Lewes* (Sussex Archaeological Society)
Half-timbered house, containing collection of household equipment, furniture, bygones, the Every collection of Ironwork and Firebacks and Lewes collection.
Barbican House Museum, High Street, *Lewes* (Sussex Archaeological Society)
Prehistoric, Romano-British and medieval antiquities relating to Sussex. Prints and watercolours of Sussex.
Battle Museum, Langton House, *Battle* (Battle and District Historical Society)
Battle of Hastings diorama, Roman-British remains from local sites. Sussex iron industry collection of ores and cinders.
Bexhill Manor Costume Museum, Manor House Gardens, Old Town, *Bexhill*
Bexhill Museum, Egerton Park, *Bexhill*
Natural history and archaeology of district.
Bodiam Castle Museum, Nr *Hawkhurst* (National Trust)
Relics found during excavations of this example of medieval architecture.
Booth Museum of Natural History, Dyke Road, *Brighton* (Brighton Borough Council)
Display of birds, mounted in their natural habitat, also reference collections of eggs, insects, minerals, palaeontology, osteology, bird and mammal skins and herbaria.
Brighton Museum and Art Gallery, Church Street, *Brighton* (Brighton Borough Council)
Old master paintings, watercolours, furniture and ceramics; Willitt collection of English pottery and porcelain; Edward James collection of surrealist paintings; fine and applied art of the Art Nouveau and Art Deco periods; ethnography and archaeology; musical instruments, Brighton history, special exhibitions.
Fisherman's Museum, Rock-a-nore, *Hastings*
All the exhibits in the museum are donations. Among them is a large picture of the presentation to Sir Winston Churchill of a golden winkle

at The Enterprise on Winkle Island, September 1955.

Grange Art Gallery and Museum, *Rottingdean* (Brighton Borough Council)
Georgian house, adjacent to Kipling's home, displays, letters, books and illustrations of author, Sussex folk-life collection, and large display of toys from Toy Museum. Frequent temporary displays in the Brighton Art Gallery.

Hove Museum of Art, 19 New Church Road, *Hove* (Hove Borough Council)
English fine and applied art of 18th and 19th centuries – paintings and prints, English, Continental and Oriental ceramics. Furniture, silver, glass, watches, coins and medals, dolls, local history items, and galleries for special exhibitions.

Museum and Art Gallery, Cambridge Road, *Hastings* (Hastings Borough Council)
Local history, archaeology, zoology and geology; Sussex ironwork and pottery; English, European, Oriental and primitive art, especially ceramics; Durbar Hall; temporary exhibition gallery.

Museum of Local History, Old Town Hall, High Street, *Hastings* (Hastings Borough Council)
Local history, folk-life, topography and archaeology; maritime history.

Norton's Farm Museum, *Seddlescombe*
Farm machinery and tools from carthorse era.

Royal National Lifeboat Institution Museum, Grand Parade, *Eastbourne*
All types of lifeboats from earliest date to present time. Various items used in lifeboat service.

Rye Museum, Ypres Tower, *Rye*
Local history collections housed in 13th-century tower. Medieval pottery from the Rye kilns, Cinque Ports material, militaria, shipping, dolls, toys and glass.

Tower 73 (The Wish Tower), *Eastbourne*
A restored Martello tower. Displays show historical background, disposition, building and manning of these defence forts, together with examples of equipment, weapons, uniforms and documents relating to the building.

The Towner Art Gallery, Manor House, 9 Borough Lane, *Eastbourne*
British painters of 19th and 20th centuries, contemporary original prints. Temporary exhibitions. Collection of Sussex pictures. Georgian caricatures. Original drawings by British book illustrators. Bell collection of British butterflies.

The Toy Museum, The Grange, Rottingdean, *Brighton* (National Toy Collection)
Over 20,000 toys and playthings from many lands.

Wilmington Museum, *Wilmington Priory* (Sussex Archaeological Society)
Collection of old agricultural implements and farmhouse utensils.
Winchelsea Museum, Court Hall, *Winchelsea*
History of Cinque Ports. Handcrafts, archaeological specimens, models, maps, documents.

ESSEX
AREAS OF OUTSTANDING NATURAL BEAUTY
Dedham Vale (part)

CASTLES AND HISTORIC HOUSES
Audley End House, *Saffron Walden* (Department of the Environment)
Palatial Jacobean mansion begun in 1603 on site of Benedictine abbey. State rooms and hall.
Blue Bridge House, *Halstead* (Mr and Mrs B. E. Pleydell-Bouverie)
Small Queen Anne house.
Castle House, *Dedham*
Home of late Sir Alfred Munnings, KCVO, President of the Royal Academy (1944–9). Many paintings, drawings, sketches and other works.
Gosfield Hall, *Halstead* (Mutual Households Association Ltd)
Fine Tudor gallery.
Hedingham Castle, *Castle Hedingham* (Miss Musette Majendie, CBE and Dr Margery Blackie)
Great Norman keep and Tudor bridge.
Layer Marney Tower, Nr *Colchester* (Major and Mrs Gerald Charrington)
1520 Tudor brick house with 8-storey gate tower. Terracotta dolphin cresting and windows. Formal yew hedges, rose bushes and lawns.
Paycocke's, *Coggeshall* (National Trust)
Richly ornamented merchant's house dating from about 1500.
St Osyth's Priory, *St Osyth* (Somerset de Chair)
Group of 13th–18th-century buildings. Gardens, 13th-century chapel, abbots tower. Great gatehouse houses works of art including Chinese jade and ceramics.

CATHEDRALS AND CHURCHES
Blackmore (St Laurence)
Norman. Elaborate 15th-century timber bell tower. Broach spire.
Brightlingsea (All Saints)
Fine 15th-century tower. Fragments of medieval painting, brasses.
Castle Hedingham (St Nicholas)
Norman. Fine 12th-century doorways, 16th-century hammer beam roof. 14th-century rood screen, 15th-century stalls with misericords, 16th-century altar tomb.

Chelmsford (St Mary the Virgin)
(Now enjoys Cathedral status following post-1850 Diocesan re-organization.) 15th century with 18th–19th-century alterations. Gothic ceiling. Fine south porch and west tower with 18th-century spire.

Copford (St Michael and All Angels)
Continuous vaulted nave and chancel. Important wall paintings dating from mid-12th century.

East Horndon (All Saints)
16th-century Tyrell chantry; incised stone slab, 1422.

Finchingfield (St John the Baptist)
Good Norman work. Tower with 18th-century cupola. 2 fine screens. 16th-century tomb.

Great Baddow (St Mary)
Fine 16th-century brickwork, 17th-century pulpit with panelled back and sounding board.

Great Bardfield (St Mary the Virgin)
Mainly 14th century. Magnificent stone rood screen.

Great Bromley (St George)
Mainly 15th century. Fine tower and south porch. Double hammer beam roof to nave. Fine brass.

Great Warley (St Mary the Virgin)
1904. Art Nouveau, furnishings by Sir William Reynolds-Stevens.

Greensted-Juxta-Ongar (St Andrew)
Only surviving example of timber Saxon Church. Early 16th-century chancel. Drastically 'restored' in 19th century.

Hatfield Broad Oak (St Mary the Virgin)
Good 14th- and 15th-century work with fine tower. Notable sculptured monument, 1221; 18th century woodwork. Library with books given in 1680.

Ingatestone (St Mary the Virgin and St Edmund)
Excellent late 15th-century brick tower. Norman church with 15th–17th-century additions. Monuments.

Lawford (St Mary)
Notable 14th-century stone carving.

Layer Marney (St Mary)
Fine Tudor brickwork, notable early Renaissance monuments, wall paintings, medieval screens.

Little Maplestead (St John the Baptist)
c. 1340. One of 5 round churches in England. Hexagonal nave separated from circular aisle by 14th-century arcade much restored in 1850.

Newport (St Mary the Virgin)
13th–16th century. 13th-century portable altar with lid which becomes reredos, when open, with early paintings. Pre-Reformation lectern. Early 15th-century chancel screen. Fragments of old glass.

251

Rivenhall (St Mary and All Saints)
Very fine medieval glass.
Saffron Walden (St Mary the Virgin)
15th–16th century. Note stone workmanship in arcades. Drastically 'restored'.
Thaxted (St John the Baptist, St Mary the Virgin and St Laurence)
14th–16th century. Fragments of old glass, 2 windows by Kempe, late 15th-century font case and cover, notable 17th-century carved pulpit, roofs, and 18th-century communion rails.
Tilty (St Mary the Virgin)
13th–14th century. East window of chancel has notable tracery. Fine sedilia and piscina. Belfry with 18th century cupola. Brasses.
Waltham Abbey (Holy Cross and St Laurence)
Splendid Norman nave. 14th-century Lady chapel with fragmentary painting. Monuments. Much 19th-century restoration.

GARDENS
Hyde Hall, Nr *Rettendon* (Mr and Mrs R. H. M. Robinson)
Trees, shrubs, bulbs, cherry trees, roses, irises and greenhouse plants.
White Barn House, *Elmstead Market* (Mrs B. Chatto)
3-acre garden landscaped with unusual plants in wide range of conditions.

HISTORIC MONUMENTS
Hadleigh Castle, *Hadleigh*
Founded in 1231 and rebuilt in 14th century. Retains 2 of original towers.
Lexden Earthworks, *Colchester*
Massive earthworks around Camulodunum, tribal capital of the Catuvellauni.
Mistley Towers, *Mistley*
Plain Georgian church was embellished in 1776 with porticoes and pair of domed towers. Only towers remain, designed by Robert Adam.
St Botolph's Priory, *Colchester*
Ruined nave of church of Augustinian monastery, with early Norman arches made of Roman brick.
St John's Abbey, *Colchester*
Fine flint work on gatehouse of Benedictine abbey.
Waltham Abbey, *Waltham Abbey*
14th-century gatehouse and bridge with cloister entrance dating from 12th century.

MUSEUMS AND GALLERIES
Bardfield Cottage Museum, *Great Bardfield*
16th-century thatched cottage with exhibition of Essex farming history.

252

Beecroft Art Gallery, Station Road, *Westcliff-on-Sea* (Borough of Southend-on-Sea)
Municipal, Thorpe Smith and Beecroft collections. Monthly loan exhibitions.

Chelmsford and Essex Museum, Oaklands Park, Moulsham Street, Chelmsford (Incorporating Essex Regiment Museum) (Chelmsford District Council)
Archaeological material from Chelmsford and Essex, bygones, coins, costume, paintings, ceramics, natural history and geology. Temporary exhibitions.

Colchester and Essex Museum, *Colchester* (Colchester Borough Council)

The Castle
Norman keep standing on site of Roman temple. Contains archaeological material of all kinds from Essex, and the finds of Roman Colchester.

The Holly Trees
1718 house used as museum of later social history.

Museum of Natural History, All Saints Church, High Street
Natural history of Essex.

Holy Trinity Church, Trinity Street
Country life and crafts.

Dutch Cottage Museum, *Canvey Island*
17th-century thatched octagonal cottage of Dutch design. Exhibition of furnishings and models of shipping used on Thames from earliest times. Collection of corn dollies.

Finchingfield Museum, Guildhall, *Finchingfield*
Local history from Roman times onwards.

Ingatestone Hall, *Ingatestone* (Lord Petre and Essex County Council)
Exhibition of Essex documents and pictures.

Minories Art Gallery, High Street, *Colchester* (Victor Batte-Lay Trust)
Monthly exhibitions.

Prittlewell Priory Museum, Priory Park, *Southend-on-Sea* (Borough of Southend-on-Sea)
Originally Cluniac monastery, now a museum of local and natural history.

Saffron Walden Museum, Museum Street, *Saffron Walden*
Local archaeology, natural history, geology, local building methods, ceramics, glass, costumes, toys, ethnography.

Southchurch Hall, Southchurch Hall Close, *Southend-on-Sea* (Borough of Southend-on-Sea)
Moated timber-framed manor house early 14th century with small Tudor wing, open hall furnished as a medieval manor. Exhibition room.

Thurrock Local History Museum, Central Library, Orsett Road, *Grays* (Thurrock Borough Council)
Prehistoric, Romano-British and pagan Saxon archaeology. Social, agricultural and industrial history of locality.

GLOUCESTERSHIRE
AREAS OF OUTSTANDING NATURAL BEAUTY
Cotswolds (part)
Malvern Hills (part)
Wye Valley (part)

CASTLES AND HISTORIC HOUSES
Ashleworth Tithe Barn, Nr *Hartpury* (National Trust)
15th-century tithe barn with 2 projecting porch bays and fine roof timbers with queenposts.
*Barnsley Park, *Cirencester* (C. M. Henderson)
Georgian baroque mansion built 1720–31. Early 18th- and 19th-century decoration. Nash conservatory. Fine vistas. 400 acres of parkland.
Berkeley Castle, Nr *Bristol* (Mr and Mrs R. J. Berkeley)
Historic castle over 800 years old and still lived in by Berkeleys. Scene of murder of Edward II (1327).
Buckland Rectory, Nr *Broadway* (The Rev. Michael Bland, MA)
England's oldest rectory. 15th-century great hall with contemporary stained glass. Earlier staircase and house. Associations John Wesley.
Chavenage, *Tetbury* (David Lowsley-Williams, Esq)
Elizabethan Cotswold manor house with Cromwellian associations. 2 tapestried rooms. Also medieval Cotswold barn.
Clearwell Castle, Nr *Coleford* (B. Yeates, Esq)
A 'mock Gothic castle' reputed to be the oldest in Britain. Regency interior restored from ruin over past 20 years. 8 acres of formal gardens. Still under restoration.
Court House, *Painswick* (Mrs L. O. Collett)
Cotswold Manor. Original court room and bedchamber of Charles I. Handsome panelling. Collection of antique furniture.
Elmore Court, Nr *Gloucester*
Elizabethan and Georgian house. Furnishings, manuscripts and paintings.
Kelmscott Manor, Nr *Lechlade* (Society of Antiquaries of London)
Cotswold style manor of 16th and 17th centuries. Summer home of William Morris from 1871 until death in 1876. Original Morris possessions and examples of his designs. Small formal garden.
Prinknash Abbey and Bird Garden, Nr *Cranham Woods*
14th-century and early 16th-century house, now abbey for Benedictine monks. Bird park.

Snowshill Manor, *Broadway* (National Trust)
Tudor manor house with a later façade containing a 'magpie' collection of musical instruments, clocks, toys, etc. Terraced garden.
Sudeley Castle, *Winchcombe* (Mrs Elizabeth Dent-Brocklehurst)
12th-century house, home of Katherine Parr. Rich in art treasures. Gardens highlighted by historic Elizabethan garden.
Upper Slaughter Manor House, *Cheltenham* (E. Turrell, Esq)
Elizabethan manor house with typical Edwardian rose and herb gardens.

CATHEDRALS AND CHURCHES
Berkeley (St Mary the Virgin)
Fine early English nave and west front. 15th-century chapel. Monuments.
Bishops Cleeve (St Michael and All Saints)
Magnificent late 12th century. 17th-century gallery. Striking Norman west front and south porch. Decorated chancel with fine window. Fine monument, 1639.
Bledington (St Leonard)
Mainly perpendicular. 15th-century glass. Chantry chapel. Transitional Norman south arcade, Norman bellcote, early English east window.
Buckland (St Michael)
13th-century nave arcades with perpendicular clerestory. 17th-century oak panelling. 15th-century glass, 16th-century silver mounted bowl, 15th-century pall.
Chipping Campden (St James)
Great perpendicular 'wool' church with magnificent tower. Monument to Lord and Lady Noel (1664), one of Joshua Marshall's finest works.
Cirencester (St John the Baptist)
Largest and most splendid of Cotswold 'wool' churches. Fine exterior; nave and aisle have parapets with ornamental embattlements with tracery and pinnacles. 3-storey porch. 2-storey oriel windows. Clerestoried nave of great height. Wine-glass pulpit, c. 1450, early 18th-century Bristol brass candelabra, Lady chapel monuments, fine fan vaulting in St Katherine's chapel, and 15th-century glass in east window.
Daglingworth (Holy Rood)
Saxon with 15th-century tower. Notable sculptures.
Deerhurst (St Mary)
Saxon, dating from 9th century. Best preserved Saxon font in existence.
Duntisbourne Rous (St Michael)
Saxon with Norman chancel and crypt. 17th-century box pews and misericords.

Elkstone (St John the Evangelist)
Famous Norman church. Tall perpendicular tower at west. Richly carved south doorway.

Fairford (St Mary the Virgin)
Complete perpendicular church. Exterior with embattled parapets and pinnacles. Best 15th–16th-century glass in England.

Gloucester Cathedral
Norman nave. Early perpendicular choir with huge windows. Early example of lierne vault. Large eastern window with much original glass. Perpendicular Lady chapel. Fan-vaulted cloister.

Hailes (dedication unknown)
Unspoilt interior, Elizabethan benches, 17th-century pulpit and tester, 15th-century tiles, glass and screen, 14th-century wall paintings.

Kempley (St Edward the Confessor and St Mary)
By Randall Wells, 1903. Notable fittings and sculpture. Beside it is old church of St Mary with Norman nave and chancel and important Romanesque frescoes.

Kempsford (St Mary the Virgin)
Noble tower with perpendicular north and south windows. Victorian stained glass, chancel aisle by Street, 1858.

Leonard Stanley (St Swithun)
Part of Norman priory. Good Norman arches particularly in chancel.

Newland (All Saints)
13th–14th century restored in 18th century. Fine pinnacled west tower; recumbent effigies.

North Cerney (All Saints)
Norman with early English upper stage to saddle-back west tower. Some 15th-century glass. Interior by F. C. Eden.

Northleach (St Peter and St Paul)
Perpendicular 'wool' church. Fine south porch with pinnacles and statue-filled niches.

Oddington (St Nicholas)
Doom painting, clear glass, William IV arms, Jacobean pulpit.

Rencomb (St Peter)
Late perpendicular. 16th-century screen, Norman font, old glass.

Tetbury (St Mary)
Early Gothic revival by Francis Hirone, 1781. Surrounded by enclosed cloister. Box-pews and gallery.

Tewkesbury (St Mary the Virgin)
Abbey church with proportions of cathedral. Grand Norman nave, west front and tower, early 14th-century apsidal choir with chapels forming chevet, vaulting to nave and transepts, 1349–59. 14th-century monuments.

Toddington (St Andrew)
Good example of G. E. Street's work. Rich decorated style. Purbeck marble columns and 19th-century marble effigies of Lord and Lady Sudeley by Lough.
Winchcombe (St Peter)
Perpendicular 'wool' church. Finest weather-cock in England, gargoyles, fine brass candelabrum, 1753. Late 17th-century organ case, painted Royal Arms of George III.

GARDENS
Barnsley House Garden, Barnsley, Nr *Cirencester* (Mr and Mrs D. C. W. Verey)
Laid out in 1770, trees planted 1840. Replanned 1960. Many spring bulbs. Laburnum avenue (early June). Lime walk, herbaceous and shrub borders. Ground cover. Knot garden. Gothic summer house 1770. Classic temple 1780.
Batsford Park Arboretum, *Moreton-in-Marsh* (Batsford Estates Company)
Over 1000 different species of trees. Oriental garden of peace.
Hidcote Manor Garden, *Hidcote Bartrim* (National Trust)
Beautiful English garden.
Kiftsgate Court, Nr *Chipping Campden* (Mrs D. H. Binny)
Garden with many rare shrubs and plants including collection of species and old-fashioned roses.
Lydney Park, *Lydney* (Viscount Bledisloe)
Gardens and woodland garden. Deer park. Roman Temple site and museum.
Misarden Park, Nr *Stroud* (Mrs Huntley Sinclair)
Herbaceous borders.
Westbury Court Garden, *Westbury-on-Severn* (National Trust)
Formal water-garden with canals and yew hedges, laid out 1696–1705 – the earliest of its kind remaining in England.
Westonbirt Arboretum, *Westonbirt* (Forestry Commission)
Landscaped collections of maples, rhododendrons, birches, conifers, etc.
Wildfowl Trust, *Slimbridge*
Founded by Peter Scott. Large collection of ducks, geese and swans in wild area.

HISTORIC MONUMENTS
Belas Knap Long Barrow, *Charlton Abbots*
Very complete Neolithic burial ground.
Chedworth Roman Villa, *Chedworth*
Fine villa, AD 150–350 with mosaic pavements.
Hailes Abbey, *Hailes*
Ruins of Cistercian abbey founded in 1246.

Hetty Pegler's Tump, *Uley*
Fairly complete long barrow.
Notgrove Long Barrow, Nr *Cheltenham*
Group of 5 badly ruined Neolithic burial chambers set round central passage.
Odda's Chapel, *Deerhurst*
Rare Saxon chapel dating back to 1056.
Witcombe Roman Villa, Nr *Birdlip*
Large courtyard Roman Villa. Hypocaust and mosaic pavements.

MUSEUMS AND GALLERIES
Bishop Hooper's Lodging, 99–103 Westgate Street, *Gloucester* (Gloucester Corporation)
3 Tudor timber-framed buildings. Collections illustrate bygone crafts and industries of country, agriculture, Severn fishing, local history and history of Gloucestershire Regiment.
Canal Museum, *Chalford*
Museum of derelict Thames and Severn Canal in former lock-keeper's cottage, c. 1783.
Cheltenham Art Gallery and Museum, Clarence Street, *Cheltenham* (Cheltenham Borough Council)
Baron de Ferrieres Gallery of Dutch paintings and permanent collection of oils, watercolours, etchings and local prints. Museum: English pottery and porcelain, Chinese porcelain, furniture, social history material relating to Cheltenham and Cotswolds and archaeology. Temporary exhibitions.
City Museum and Art Gallery, Brunswick Road, *Gloucester* (Gloucester Corporation)
Local archaeology, natural history, geology and numismatics; English period furniture and barometers, pottery, glass, silver and costume. Temporary art exhibitions.
City Wall and Bastion, entrance in King's Walk, *Gloucester* (Gloucester Corporation)
The Roman and medieval city defences in an underground exhibition chamber.
Corinium Museum, Park Street, *Cirencester* (Cotswold District Council)
Redevelopment museum for Cotswold region, includes collection of Roman antiquities from site of Corinium Dobunnorum.
Down Ampney House and Art Exhibition, Nr *Cirencester*
Annual exhibition of paintings by local artists in Tudor and later house with restored mid-15th-century hall.
*Filkins and Broughton Poggs Museum, *Filkins*
Domestic articles, folklore, tools.
Folk Museum, Town Hall, *Winchcombe*
Objects of local interest.

Hailes Abbey Museum, Hailes Abbey, *Winchcombe* (Department of the Environment)
Medieval sculpture and other archaeological fragments found in Abbey ruins.
Holst Birthplace Museum, 4 Clarence Street, *Cheltenham* (Cheltenham Borough Council)
Regency house with period rooms containing Gustave Holst memoralia and reference collections.
Jenner Museum, *Berkeley*
Commemorates Edward Jenner (1749–1823) who discovered small-pox vaccination.
Stroud Museum, Lansdown, *Stroud* (Cowle Trust)
Geology, archaeology, local crafts and industrial archaeology, farming and household equipment, ceramics, dolls, etc, paintings, photographs and records of local houses and mills.
Tewkesbury Museum, Barton Street, *Tewkesbury* (Tewkesbury Borough Council)
Archaeology, costumes, furniture, military and local history.

GREATER MANCHESTER
CASTLES AND HISTORIC HOUSES
Foxdenton Hall, *Chadderton*
Restored house dating from 1665 and c. 1700.
Newton Hall, *Hyde* (William Kenyon and Sons Ltd)
Restored cruck-framed manor hall, built 1380. Original cruck beams and spurs with side wall. Park.
Smithills Hall, *Bolton* (Bolton Metropolitan Borough)
14th- and early 16th-century timbered hall. Tudor panelling. 17th-century furniture.
Wythenshawe Hall, *Northenden* (Manchester City Art Galleries)
Half-timbered manor house in fine parkland. Seat of the Tatton family for over 500 years. Furniture and pictures of 17th century. Royal Lancastrian pottery, local history material and modern pottery.

CATHEDRALS AND CHURCHES
Ashton-under-Lyne (St Michael)
Important painted glass, c. 1500.
Manchester (St Ann)
1709–12 in style of Wren. East apse with good carving. Arcaded, galleried interior with flat coved ceiling. Much original woodwork. Marble font, 1711. Late Victorian and Edwardian glass. Monuments.
Manchester (St Luke), *Cheetham*
1839. Clerestoried Gothic by Atkinson. Unspoilt galleried interior.

Middleton (St Leonard)
Perpendicular. Wooden bell chamber, brasses, glass.
Pendlebury (St Augustine)
1874 by Bodley and Garner.
Stand (All Saints)
1822–6 by Sir Charles Barry. Galleried interior, plaster rib-vaulting, rood screen, glass.

MUSEUMS AND GALLERIES
Art Gallery, Esplanade, *Rochdale* (Rochdale Metropolitan District Council)
Contemporary British art-craft gallery. British paintings, Victorian to modern.
Art Gallery and Museum, Union Street, *Oldham* (Oldham Metropolitan Borough)
Frequently changed exhibitions. Early English watercolours, British paintings of 19th and 20th centuries, and contemporary art. British glass. Oriental collection.
The Astley Cheetham Art Gallery, Trinity Street, *Stalybridge* (Stalybridge Town Council)
Athenaeum, Princess Street, *Manchester*
Museum of ceramics.
Bramall Hall, *Bramhall*
15th- and 18th-century house with fine timber and plasterwork, containing a museum.
Bury Art Gallery and Museum, Moss Street, *Bury* (Metropolitan Borough of Bury)
Museum: local history. Art Gallery: permanent collection and Wrigley collection of oil and watercolour paintings.
The City Art Gallery, Moseley Street, *Manchester*
Designed by Sir Charles Barry (1824). Paintings, sculpture, silver and pottery. Assheton Bennett collection of silver and Dutch 17th-century pictures, and Greg collection of English pottery.
Faculty of Art and Design Galleries, Cavendish Street, All Saints, *Manchester* (Manchester Polytechnic)
Temporary exhibitions, chiefly of contemporary art and design.
Fletcher Moss, *Didsbury* (Manchester City Art Galleries)
Old parsonage of late Georgian, early Victorian character, housing best part of city art galleries' collection of English watercolours.
Hall-I'-Th'-Wood, *Bolton* (Bolton Metropolitan Borough)
Folk museum in half-timbered house, 1485, with stone wing, 1591 and 1648.
Heaton Hall, *Prestwich* (Manchester City Art Galleries)
Designed by James Wyatt, 1772; former home of Earls of Wilton. Unique decorated interior, furniture and displays of English porcelain, Wedgwood, glass and oil paintings. Samuel Green organ, 1792.

Local Interest Centre, Greaves Street, *Oldham* (Oldham Metropolitan Borough)
Local studies, library, local history museum, small gallery.
Manchester Museum, The University, Oxford Road, *Manchester*
Geology, botany, zoology, entomology, archaeology, Egyptology, ethnology, numismatics.
Monks Hall Museum, 42 Wellington Road, *Eccles* (City of Salford)
Nasmyth machine tools, temporary exhibitions including art, science, bygones.
Municipal Museum, Vernon Park, Turncroft Lane, *Stockport* (Metropolitan Borough of Stockport)
Local history, natural history, geology, ceramics, Victoriana. Temporary exhibitions.
Museum, Sparrow Hill, *Rochdale*
Local history, natural history (vivarium), furniture, costume.
Museum and Art Gallery, Civic Centre, *Bolton* (Bolton Borough Council)
Museum: Botany, zoology and prehistory, Egyptian collection, aquarium. Art Gallery: paintings and sculpture of English and European schools, English watercolours, 18th-century English pottery.
Museum and Art Gallery, The Crescent, Peel Park, *Salford* (City of Salford)
L. S. Lowry paintings and drawings; 'Lark Hill Place', 19th-century 'street' of shops and period rooms.
Ordsall Hall Museum, Taylorson Street, *Salford* (City of Salford)
Manor house with fine 15th-century spere truss in great hall; furniture, kitchen equipment and local history items.
Park Bridge Museum, *Ashton-under-Lyne* (Medlock and Tame Valley Conservation Association)
Industrial, natural and social history of Medlock Valley and Park Bridge.
Platt Hall, *Rusholme* (Manchester City Art Galleries)
Gallery of English costume – clothing from 17th century to present – in Georgian country house of early 1760s designed by John Carr of York.
Queen's Park Art Gallery and Military Museum, Rochdale Road, *Manchester*
1878 purpose-built Victorian gallery hung with large Academy works. Paintings by Manchester School and Adolphe Valette. Museum of Manchester Regiment and 14th/20th Hussars.
Regimental Museum The 20th Lancashire Fusiliers, Wellington Barracks, *Bury*
History of regiment from 1688 to present.
Rochdale Co-operative Museum, Toad Lane, *Rochdale*
Original store of Rochdale Co-operative Pioneers containing

261

documents, pictures and other material of British and international co-operative interest.

Sandleworth Museum, *Sandleworth*
Part of old woollen mill converted into museum of local, domestic and industrial interest.

Swinton Memorial Art Gallery, Central Library, Chorley Road, *Swinton* (City of Salford)
Temporary art exhibitions.

Tonge Moor Textile Machinery Museum, Tonge Moor Road, *Bolton*
Historic textile machines, including Crompton's Mule, Hargreave's Jenny and Arkwright's water frame.

Turnpike Gallery, *Leigh* (Metropolitan Borough of Wigan)
Small watercolour collection. Major touring exhibitions.

War Memorial Art Gallery, Wellington Road South, *Stockport* (Metropolitan Borough of Stockport)
British artists, mainly watercolours. Epstein's head of Yehudi Menuhin.

Whitworth Art Gallery, Oxford Road, *Manchester* (University of Manchester)
English watercolours. Old master drawings, Post-Impressionist and 20th-century Continental drawings. Contemporary paintings and sculpture. Prints, ranging from Renaissance period to the present day, including Japanese colour wood-cuts. Textiles.

Wigan Museum, Station Road, *Wigan* (Metropolitan Borough of Wigan)
Local geology, archaeology, history, coal-mining, pewter, bell-founding, clogging, local art collection, Rimmer collection of musical instruments.

NATIONAL PARKS
Peak District (part)

HAMPSHIRE
AREAS OF OUTSTANDING NATURAL BEAUTY
Chichester Harbour (part)
East Hampshire
North Wessex Downs (part)
South Hampshire Coast (part)

CASTLES AND HISTORIC HOUSES
Avington Park, *Winchester* (J. B. Hickson, Esq)
Red brick house in Wren tradition.

Beaulieu Abbey and Palace House, National Motor Museum, *Beaulieu* (Lord Montagu of Beaulieu)
Cistercian abbey founded 1204. Palace house originally great gate-house of abbey converted 1538. Historic car, motor cycle and cycle museum.

Breamore House, Nr *Fordingbridge* (Sir Westrow Hulse, Bt)
Elizabethan manor house, 1583, with paintings, tapestries, furniture. Countryside museum. Carriage museum.
Grove Place, Nursling, *Southampton* (Northcliffe School Trust Limited)
Elizabethan House. Contents for boys' boarding school.
Jane Austen's Home, *Chawton* (Jane Austen Memorial Trust)
Jane Austen's home, personal relics of herself and her family.
Mottisfont Abbey, *Mottisfont* (National Trust)
Originally a 12th-century Augustinian priory. South front 18th century. Drawing-room by Rex Whistler. Fine lawns and trees. Walled gardens with old-fashioned roses.
Stratfield Saye House, *Reading* (Trustees of the Duke of Wellington)
1630 house filled with Great Duke's possessions.
Vyne, *Basingstoke* (National Trust)
Early 16th-century house with classical portico added 1654. Tudor panelling, 18th-century ornamented staircase. Extensive lawns, lake, trees, herbaceous border.
*West Green House, *Hartley Wintney* (National Trust)
Red brick early 18th-century house in walled garden.

CATHEDRALS AND CHURCHES
Avington (St Mary)
Built 1768–71. Interior with all its mahogany fittings and working barrel organ.
Basing (St Mary)
15th–16th century. Statue of Virgin and Child on west front. Paulet tombs.
Beaulieu (St Bartholomew)
Early English. Notable reader's pulpit, coloured roof with wooden bosses.
Breamore (St Mary)
Saxon, c. 1000. Note double-splayed windows, 'long and short' work quoins and stone rood.
Crondall (All Saints)
Tower, 1658. Transitional-Norman interior with impressive clerestoried nave and vaulted chancel. Scraped and refurnished in 19th century.
East Meon (All Saints)
Mainly Norman fabric with 15th-century rebuilding. Tournai marble font. Glass and fittings by Comper.
Idsworth (St Hubert)
Small Norman 16th-century chapel. 18th-century bell turret. Nave has Georgian and 1913 fittings, Royal Arms. 1913 stucco ceiling and pictorial panels with 14th-century painting in chancel.

Pamber (dedication unknown)
Early English quire and Norman central tower. 15th-century screen
and pews. Purbeck marble coffin slabs, set of oil lamps, wooden
cross-legged effigy of Knight, c. 1270.
Romsey (St Mary and St Ethelfleda)
Grand Norman architecture. Early 16th-century painted reredos,
Saxon rood and carving of crucifixion, fine 13th-century Purbeck
marble effigy of a lady. St Barbe monument by Thomas Stanton,
1660; east window of north nave by Kempe; image of Our Lady
by Martin Travers.
Silchester (St Mary)
Norman-perpendicular Jacobean pulpit with domed canopy. 15th-
century screen, 14th-century effigy of a lady. Early English chancel
with coeval painted patterning on south window splays.
South Hayling (St Mary)
Early English 'Tree of Life' glass in chancel by Bryans.
Stoke Charity (St Michael)
North chapel with old plaster and clear glass holds. Hampton and
Waller monuments and brasses. Sculpture of The Mass of St Gregory.
Fragments of 15th-century glass.
Winchester (St Cross)
Originally chapel to Hospital, 1160–1345. Gradual transition in style
from rich Norman at east end to decorated west end. Notable old
wall paintings, glass and tiles. Renaissance woodwork and stone
brasses.
Winchfield (St Mary)
Norman restored in 1849. Note chancel arch with fine sculpture.
Some original windows, Jacobean pulpit, old oak seats.
Winchester Cathedral
Europe's largest Gothic church. Superb nave, combination of Nor-
man and perpendicular. 3 sets of medieval paintings; font, c. 1180,
of black Tournai marble. Virgin and Child, c. 1480, in choir. Notable
stalls of c. 1320 with 60 misericords. Retrochoir with most extensive
medieval tiled floor in country. Tombs.

GARDENS
Bohunt Manor, Nr *Liphook* (Lady Holman)
Woodland gardens. Lakeside walk, water garden, roses, herbaceous
borders and wildfowl.
Exbury Gardens, *Exbury* (E. L. de Rothschild, Esq)
Woodland gardens, azaleas, rhododendrons and other flowering
shrubs.
Furzey Gardens, Minstead, Nr *Lyndhurst* (H. J. Cole, Esq)
Heathers, azaleas, rhododendrons, bluebells, peonies, tree peonies,
irises and roses and many other plants.

Hurst Mill, *Petersfield* (Mr and Mrs Willoughby Norman)
Waterfall, mill stream and bog garden, flowering shrubs, forest and ornamental trees.
Jenkyn Place, *Bentley* (G. E. Coke, Esq)
Old fashioned and species roses, herbaceous borders, collection of shrubs.
Spinners, *Boldre* (Mr and Mrs P. G. G. Chappell)
Azaleas, rhododendrons, primulas and woodland plants.

HISTORIC MONUMENTS
Basing House, Nr *Basingstoke*
Ruins of great Tudor palace, 1530, built on site of former Saxon fortress, later a Norman castle.
Bishops' Waltham Palace, *Bishops' Waltham*
Flint ruins of palace of bishops of Winchester dating from 12th century and 15th century.
Hurst Castle, Nr *Milford-on-Sea*
Fortress built by Henry VIII. Restored in 1873.
Netley Abbey, Nr *Hamble*
Extensive remains of Cistercian abbey, founded in 1239.
Porchester Castle, *Porchester*
4th-century Saxon fort with 12th-century keep and Assheton's tower, 1367.
Portsmouth Garrison Church, *Portsmouth*
Ruins of hospital built in 1212 on lines of church.

MUSEUMS AND GALLERIES
Airborne Forces Exhibition, Browning Barracks, *Aldershot*
Weapons from Second World War, captured enemy arms, airborne vehicles, dioramas of actions, scale models, equipment, photographs, and medals.
Bargate Guildhall Museum, High Street, *Southampton* (Southampton Corporation)
Local historical exhibits and changing exhibitions, in former hall of guilds above medieval north gate.
Calleva Museum, Rectory Grounds, *Silchester Common*
Roman objects from site of Calleva.
City Museum and Art Gallery, Museum Road, *Portsmouth* (City of Portsmouth)
English furniture, pottery and glass; contemporary and topographic paintings and prints. Local history galleries. Temporary exhibitions.
Cumberland House Museum and Aquarium, Eastern Parade, *Southsea*, Portsmouth (City of Portsmouth)
Natural history and geology of Hampshire basin.
Curtis Museum, High Street, *Alton* (Hampshire County Council)
Local geology, botany, zoology, archaeology and history; craft

tools, pottery and dolls, toys and games. Museum Annexe and Allen Gallery (10 and 12 Church Street) contain respectively a collection of sporting firearms and selections of paintings from W. H. Allen collection and loan exhibitions.

Dickens's Birthplace Museum, 393 Commercial Road, Mile End, *Portsmouth* (City of Portsmouth)
House where Dickens was born in 1812.

Gilbert White Museum and the Oates Memorial Library and Museum, The Wakes, *Selborne*
Relics of Gilbert White, pioneer naturalist, Capt. L. E. G. Oates, Antarctic explorer and Frank Oates, African explorer.

God's House Tower Museum, Town Quay, *Southampton* (Southampton Corporation)
Early 15th-century fortification, now museum of archaeology.

Gosport Museum, *Gosport* (Gosport Borough Council)
Local geology, history and natural history.

Guildhall Picture Gallery, High Street, *Winchester* (Winchester City Council)
Local topographical pictures and loan exhibitions.

Gurkha Museum, Queen Elizabeth's Barracks, *Church Crookham*
Gurkha history since 1815.

Maritime Museum, Buckler's Hard, *Beaulieu*
Collection of models and exhibits of ships built at Buckler's Hard for Nelson's fleet.

Maritime Museum, Wool House, Bugle Street, *Southampton* (Southampton Corporation)
14th-century wool store, now museum of shipping.

The Portsmouth Royal Naval Museum, HM Naval Base, *Portsmouth*
Situated adjacent to HMS *Victory* and containing personal items of Nelson, his officers and men. Ships models and figureheads and 'Panorama of Trafalgar'. The Nelson-McCarthy collection of commemorative material.

Royal Corps of Transport Museum, Buller Barracks, *Aldershot*
Uniforms and badges of Royal Army Service Corps and predecessors, and models and photographs of vehicles used from 1795 to present.

Royal Green Jackets Museum, Romsey Road, *Winchester*
Material relating to Royal Green Jackets and regiments from which it stemmed.

Royal Hampshire Regiment Museum, Serle's House, *Winchester*
Regimental museum in Baroque style 18th-century house.

Royal Marines Museum, Eastney, *Portsmouth*
History of Royal Marines from 1664 to present.

Southampton Art Gallery, Civic Centre, *Southampton* (Southampton Corporation)
Specializes in British painting, particularly contemporary; French 19th-century and continental masters.

Southsea Castle, Clarence Esplanade, *Portsmouth* (City of Portsmouth)
Local and military history of Portsmouth. Permanent exhibition on *Mary Rose*. Archaeology.
Tudor House Museum, St Michael's Square, *Southampton* (Southampton Corporation)
16th-century Tudor mansion containing historical and antiquarian exhibits.
The Westgate Museum, High Street, *Winchester* (Winchester City Council)
Medieval west gate of city. Exhibits illustrate civic history of Winchester; city moot horn (13th century) and collection of medieval and later weights and measures.
The Willis Museum and Art Gallery, New Street, *Basingstoke* (Hampshire County Council)
Local collections of archaeology, natural history, geology; Basingstoke canal, horology and watch and clock-makers' tools, pottery. Temporary exhibitions. New town history gallery.
Winchester Cathedral Treasury
Church silver and additional pieces from parishes and other sources in Hampshire.
Winchester City Museum, The Square, *Winchester* (Winchester City Council)
Archaeology of Winchester and central Hampshire.
Winchester College Museum, *Winchester*
Collections of Greek pottery, English watercolours.

HEREFORD AND WORCESTER
AREAS OF OUTSTANDING NATURAL BEAUTY
Cotswolds (part)
Malvern Hills (part)
Wye Valley (part)

CASTLES AND HISTORIC HOUSES
Berrington Hall, *Leominster* (National Trust)
Built 1778–81 by Henry Holland. Painted and plaster ceilings. Capability Brown parks.
Brilley, Cwmmau Farmhouse, *Whitney-on-Wye* (National Trust)
Early 17th-century timber-framed and stone-tiled farmhouse.
Burton Court, *Eardisland* (Lt Cmdr and Mrs R. M. Simpson)
14th-century great hall. European and Oriental costume and curio exhibition.
Croft Castle, Nr *Leominster* (National Trust)
Welsh border castle. Inhabited by the Croft family for 900 years.
Dinmore Manor, Nr *Hereford* (C. Ian Murray, Esq)
14th-century chapel; also cloisters, music room and rock garden.

Eastnor Castle, Nr *Ledbury* (The Hon. Mrs Hervey-Bathurst)
Excellent specimen of 19th-century castellated architecture containing armour, pictures, etc. Arboretum.
Eye Manor, *Leominster* (Mr and Mrs Christopher Sandford)
Built 1680. Renaissance interior with plasterwork, furniture, pictures, period costumes, books, art and crafts, secret passage.
*The Greyfriars, *Worcester* (National Trust)
Timber-frame house built 1480 for adjoining Franciscan friary.
Hanbury Hall, Nr *Droitwich* (National Trust)
Red brick house, c. 1700. Only Thornhill's painted ceilings and staircase and 2 furnished rooms are shown.
Harvington Hall, *Kidderminster* (Roman Catholic Archdiocese of Birmingham)
Moated Tudor manor house containing priests' hiding places. Catholic associations.
Hellen's, *Much Marcle* (Pennington-Mellor-Munthe family)
Manorial house lived in since 1292.
*Kentchurch Court, *Hereford* (Lt-Cmdr J. H. S. Lucas-Scudamore)
Fortified border manor house altered by Nash. Gateway and part of original 14th-century house still survive. Pictures and Grinling Gibbons carving. Owen Glendower tower.
Little Malvern Court, *Little Malvern* (T. P. Berington, Esq)
14th-century prior's guest hall.
Lower Brockhampton, *Bromyard* (National Trust)
Small half-timbered manor house c. 1400.
Moccas Court, *Moccas*
House under restoration; designed by Adam and built by Keck in 1775. Park laid out by Capability Brown.
Pembridge Castle, *Welsh Newton* (R. A. Cooke, Esq)
17th-century moated border castle.
Sutton Court, *Mordiford*
Small Palladian mansion by Sir James Wyatt. Park by Repton. China, lace embroideries and watercolours.

CATHEDRALS AND CHURCHES
Abbey Dore (Holy Trinity and St Mary)
Early English with 17th-century fittings and glass. Very fine great oak screen, 1634.
Aymestry (St John the Baptist and St Alkmund)
Very fine 16th-century rood screen.
Bredon (St Giles)
Mainly 12th century with central tower and spire. Old glass, medieval heraldic tiles, early tombs, 17th-century monument recording heart burial.
Brinsop (St George)
14th-century screen, 14th-century glass, carved Norman tympanum,

268

alabaster reredos and glass by Comper, windows in memory of Wordsworth.

Broadway (St Eadburgh)
12th–17th century. Note altar rails, 15th-century pulpit.

Brockhampton-by-Ross (All Saints)
W. Lethaby, 1902. Central tower and thatched roof. Temple of Arts and Craft Movement.

Castle Frome (St Michael and All Angels)
Notable 12th-century carved font. 17th-century alabaster effigies.

Chaddesley Corbett (St Cassian)
Fine 14th-century work, 12th-century font, early 14th-century monuments.

Croome (St Mary Magdalene)
Gothic, 1763. Magnificent Coventry monuments.

Dudley (St Thomas)
By Brooks, 1817–19. Regency Gothic. Spire, plaster work, marble, altar, carving by Samuel Joseph.

Eardisley (St Mary Magdalene)
Notable 12th-century carved font.

Eaton Bishop (St Michael and all Angels)
Fine 14th-century glass in east window.

Elmley Castle (St Mary)
Medieval. Tower with gargoyles, 12th- and 15th-century font, Savage and Coventry monuments.

Great Witley (St Michael)
Finest Baroque church in England. Plaster work by Pergotti, painted ceiling, probably by Laguerre, painted glass by Price, 19th-century woodwork.

Hereford (All Saints)
Mostly 13th–14th century, chained library, spire, fine choir stalls.

Hereford Cathedral
Small cathedral. 14th-century tower collapsed in 1786 and led to punitive restoration by Wyatt. Noble central tower, c. 1325, and handsome north porch. Interesting interior to north transept with almost triangular arches. Early English Lady chapel with lancet windows set within shafted frames.

Kilpeck (St Mary and St David)
Rich example of late Romanesque style with fine carving. Some medieval windows.

Leominster (St Peter and St Paul)
Fine Norman arches, decorated windows, tower with 12th-century doorway.

Madley (The Nativity of St Mary the Virgin)
13th–14th century. Long arcaded nave and apsidal chancel with 14th-century glass in east window.

269

Malvern (St Mary and St Michael)
Mainly 15th century. Note glass, tiles and choir stalls.
Martley (St Peter)
12th–15th century. Early painted wall decoration. Mortimer effigy, 1459.
Moccas (St Michael and All Angels)
12th-century Norman rounded apse. Some 14th-century glass.
Much Cowarne (St Mary the Virgin)
Early English arcade. 17th-century effigies of Sir Edmund Fox and wife.
Much Marcle (St Bartholomew)
13th century. Very fine 14th- and 17th-century monuments.
Pembridge (St Mary)
Fine early decorated. Detached belfry.
Pershore (Holy Cross)
Notable 13th-century arcading of presbytery. Early monuments.
St Margaret's (St Margaret)
Very fine carved pre-Reformation screen and rood loft.
Shobdon (St John the Evangelist)
Mid-18th-century Rococo-Gothic.
Strensham (St John the Baptist)
Painted rood-loft front, 13th–19th-century monuments, 15th-century floor tiles.
Worcester (St Swithun)
1736. Untouched 18th-century furnishings. Ceiling vaulted in plaster in Gothic manner.
Worcester Cathedral
Norman crypt and chapter house. 2 Transitional west bays of nave. Finest portion is early English choir and retrochoir. Decorated and perpendicular 7 bays of nave, north porch and central tower. Carved misericords date from 1379.

GARDENS
Abbey Dore Court Garden, Nr *Hereford* (Mrs C. L. Ward)
River and walled garden specializing in ferns.
Broadway Tower Country Park, *Broadway* (Batsford Estates Company)
18th-century folly. Exhibitions. Natural history centre.
Hergest Croft Garden and Park Wood, *Kington* (W. L. and R. A. Banks, Esq)
Trees, shrubs, rhododendrons and azaleas from all over the temperate world.
Spetchley Park, *Worcester* (Mr and Mrs R. J. Berkeley)
Trees, shrubs and plants. Ornamental waterfall. Red and fallow deer in park.
The Weir, *Swainshill* (National Trust)
Spring garden with fine views from cliff garden walks.

HISTORIC MONUMENTS
Arthur's Stone, *Dorstone*
Neolithic long barrow.
Clifford Castle, *Clifford*
Remains of 11th-century castle.
Goodrich Castle, *Goodrich*
Mainly late 12th-century ruins.
Llanthony Priory, *Llanthony*
Mainly 12th–13th-century remains of Augustinian foundation, c. 1108.

MUSEUMS AND GALLERIES
Almonry Museum, Vine Street, *Evesham* (Vale of Evesham Historical Society)
Roman-British, Anglo-Saxon, medieval and monastic remains. Agricultural implements and general exhibits of local historic interest.
Art Gallery, Market Street, *Kidderminster*
Loan exhibitions, Brangwyn etchings, small permanent collection.
*****Avery Historical Museum,** Smethwick, *Warley*
Machines, instruments, weights, records, etc, relating to the history of weighing.
The Avoncroft Museum of Buildings Ltd, Stoke Heath, *Bromsgrove*
Open-air museum containing buildings of great variety from reconstructed Iron Age hut to 15th-century merchant's house.
Bewdley Museum, The Shambles, Load Street, *Bewdley* (Wyre Forest District Council)
18th-century market converted to folk museum of Bewdley and Wyre Forest.
Churchill Gardens Museum, Venn's Lane, *Hereford* (Hereford District Council)
Costume, fine furniture, watercolours and paintings by local artists. Brian Hatton Gallery.
City Museum and Art Gallery, Worcester (Worcester City Council)
Local history, archaeology, geology and natural history illustrating man and his environment in the Severn Valley region with particular reference to City of Worcester.
Dyson Perrins Museum of Worcester Porcelain, The Royal Porcelain Works, Severn Street, *Worcester* (Dyson Perrins Museum Trust)
Finest and most comprehensive collection of old Worcester in the world.
Elgar's Birthplace Museum, Lower Broadheath, Nr *Worcester*
Scores, photographs, letters and personalia.
Hereford and Worcester County Museum, Hartlebury Castle, *Hartlebury* (Hereford and Worcester County Council)
Changing displays including archaeology and geology, crafts and

271

industries of county, restored cider mill, furniture, glass and costume and horse-drawn vehicles, including gypsy caravans.

Hereford City Museum and Art Gallery, Broad Street, *Hereford* (Hereford District Council)
Archaeology and natural history, costumes, toys, embroidery, textiles, military equipment and agricultural bygones. Pictures by local artists and examples of applied art, silver, pottery and porcelain in Art Gallery.

Museum, *Kidderminster*
Local studies and archaeology. Official repository for Kidderminster and District Archaeological and Historical Society.

Norton Collection, *Upton Warren*
Victorian music boxes, gramophones, wireless and crystal sets, organs, kitchenware, lamps and Victoriana. Crafts and industries, local history. Costume and chemist's shop.

Old House, High Town, *Hereford* (Hereford District Council)
Preserved and furnished as Jacobean period museum.

Playthings Past Museum, Beaconwood, Beacon Lane, Nr *Bromsgrove*
Antique and period dolls, dolls' houses, toys and automata.

St John Coningsby Museum, Widemarsh Street, *Hereford*
Dining hall and chapel, c. 1170, of Knights of St John with chapel hospital and almshouses added in 1614 by Sir Thomas Coningsby. Remains of Blackfriars' priory and preaching cross at rear.

Tudor House Museum, Fair Street, *Worcester* (Worcester City Council)
Permanent and temporary displays illustrating the domestic and working life of City of Worcester.
Also houses the **Museum of the Worcestershire Regiment,** and the **Museum of the Worcestershire Yeomanry Cavalry.**
Art Gallery contains travelling exhibitions and the permanent collection.

HERTFORDSHIRE
AREAS OF OUTSTANDING NATURAL BEAUTY
Chilterns (part)

CASTLES AND HISTORIC HOUSES
Ashridge, *Berkhamsted* (Governors of Ashridge Management College)
Early Gothic revival. Begun 1808 by James Wyatt for the Earl of Bridgwater. 17th-century crypt. Tudor barn. Gardens landscaped by Repton.

Gorhambury House, *St Albans* (Earl of Verulam)
Mansion built 1777–84 in modified classical style by Sir Robert Taylor. 16th-century enamelled glass and historic portraits.

Hatfield House, *Hatfield* (Marquess of Salisbury)
Jacobean house and Tudor palace, childhood home of Elizabeth I.
House built by Robert Cecil, first Earl of Salisbury, in 1611. Fine
portraits, furniture and relics of Elizabeth I. Fine gardens and large
park. Exhibition including facsimiles and transcripts of Tudor papers
in archives and costumes from portraits of Elizabeth I and her
courtiers.

Knebworth House, *Knebworth* (The Hon. David Lytton Cobbold)
Tudor mansion started in 1492. External decoration in the Gothic
style by Sir Edward Bulwer-Lytton in 1843. Gardens.

Moor Park Mansion, *Rickmansworth* (Three Rivers District Council)
Palladian house reconstructed in 1727 incorporating house of 1670.
Interior by Verrio, Thornhill and others. Under restoration.

Picotts End, Medieval Murals, *Hemel Hempstead* (A. C. Lindley, Esq)
Hall house containing 15th-century wall paintings.

Salisbury Hall, *London Colney* (W. J. Goldsmith, Esq)
18th-century house surrounded by medieval moat. Fine staircase,
panelling. Beautiful fireplaces. Prototype de Havilland Mosquito,
Vampire, Venom.

Shaw's Corner, *Ayot St Lawrence* (National Trust)
Home of George Bernard Shaw, 1906–50.

CATHEDRALS AND CHURCHES

Anstey (St George)
Lower stages of central tower, c. 1200, show transformation from
Romanesque to Gothic. 13th-century chancel with 16th-century
stalls and misericords and unusual sedilia and piscina. 14th-century
nave with clerestory and 15th-century roof. 15th-century lych-gate.

Ashwell (St Mary)
14th century. Fine tower. Timber and lead spirelet. 15th-century
screens and sedilia, 17th-century pulpit and communion table.

Bishop's Stortford (St Michael)
15th century. Original roofs with fine spandrels and corbels. Rood
screen, choir stalls, misericords.

Broxbourne (St Augustine)
Fine 16th-century roofs. Note Say tombs, 17th-century south door.

Great Gaddesden (St John the Baptist)
12th-century core, later enlarged. Note south nave arcade. Halsey
monuments.

Hemel Hempstead (St Mary)
12th-century central tower and 14th-century timber spire. Elaborate
decoration of nave and transepts. Chancel with early ribbed vault.

Much Hadham (St Andrew)
12th-century core with later rebuilding. Note roofs, 15th-century
screen and chancel stalls, brasses.

St Albans Cathedral
Imposing interior with grand Norman arches. Remains of 13th-
and 14th-century wall paintings in nave, stone rood screen, painted
wooden roofs over choir and presbytery, reredos of 1484, oak
watching-loft, c. 1400.
Stanstead Abbots (St James)
Unspoilt interior with 18th-century box pews and 3-decker pulpit.
16th-century brick north chapel, 12th-century nave, 13th-century
chancel, 15th-century tower and timber south porch, 19th-century
memorials.
Ware (St Mary)
14th–15th century. Note nave arcades, fan arch between chancel
and south chapel, font, 1380, 17th-century woodwork and communion rails.
Watford (St Mary)
13th and 15th century. Essex chapel, 1595, with Tuscan arcade and
Morryson tombs. Good woodwork.

GARDENS
Royal National Rose Society's Gardens, Chiswell Green Lane, *St
Albans*
Rose garden and trial ground for new varieties.

HISTORIC MONUMENTS
Berkhamsted Castle, *Berkhamsted*
Remains of 11th-century motte and bailey castle with later circular
keep. Former home of Black Prince.

MUSEUMS AND GALLERIES
Ashwell Village Museum, Swan Street, *Ashwell* (Trustees)
Life and work in the village from Stone Age to present. Folk
museum.
City Museum, Hatfield Road, *St Albans*
County biology and geology. Salaman collection of tools to illustrate
local crafts and trades. 19th-century glass and pottery.
Hertford Museum, 18 Bull Plain, *Hertford* (Hertford Town Council)
Local archaeology, history, geology and natural history.
Hitchin Museum and Art Gallery, Paynes Park, *Hitchin* (North Herts
District Council)
Archaeology, local and natural history, costume, Hertfordshire
Yeomanry room; pictures by Samuel Lucas, special exhibitions.
Letchworth Museum and Art Gallery, Town Square, *Letchworth*
(North Herts District Council)
North Hertfordshire archaeological material, natural history,
history of first garden city. Monthly art exhibitions.
Rhodes Memorial Museum, *Bishop's Stortford*
Collections illustrating life of Cecil Rhodes in house in which he was

born. Illustrations of Southern and Central African history.

Royston Museum, Town Hall, *Royston*
Old photographs, paintings and other historical material from the town.

St Albans Organ Museum, Camp Road, *St Albans*
Collection of automatically operated organs and other musical instruments.

Stevenage Museum, New Town Centre, *Stevenage*
Local archaeology, local and natural history, live animals, etc.

The Verulamium Museum, St Michael's, *St Albans* (St Albans District Council)
Stands on site of Roman city of Verulamium and houses material from Roman and Belgic cities, including several mosaics in Britain, one of which is preserved in situ in the 'Hypocaust annexe'.

Watford Art Collection, Central Public Library, Hempstead Road, *Watford*
Local prints, paintings, fossils, flints, etc. Exhibitions.

Zoological Museum, British Museum (Natural History), Akeman Street, *Tring*
Mounted specimens of animals from all parts of the world.

HUMBERSIDE
AREAS OF OUTSTANDING NATURAL BEAUTY
Lincolnshire Wolds (part)

CASTLES AND HISTORIC HOUSES
Blaydes House, *Hull* (Georgian Society for East Yorkshire)
Restored mid-Georgian merchant's house, fine staircase and panelled rooms.

Burton Agnes Hall, *Bridlington* (Marcus Wickham Boynton, Esq, DL)
Elizabethan country house. Old and French impressionist paintings, carved ceilings and overmantels.

Burton Constable, Nr *Hull* (J. Chichester Constable, Esq)
Elizabethan house, built 1570. Interior by R. Adam ,Wyatt, Carr and Lightoler. Beautiful gardens, lakes, park, laid by Capability Brown.

Maister House, *Hull* (National Trust)
Rébuilt 1744 with staircase-hall, designed in Palladian manner.

Normanby Hall, *Scunthorpe* (Scunthorpe Corporation)
Regency mansion by Sir Robert Smirke, furnished and decorated in period. Costume displays, garden and deer park.

Old Rectory, *Epworth* (Trustees of World Methodist Council)
Built 1709. Birthplace and former home of John and Charles Wesley.

Sledmere House, *Driffield* (Sir Richard Sykes, DL, JP)
Georgian house built 1787. Adam ceilings, fine collection of furniture and paintings, famous 100ft long library. Gardens and park by Capability Brown.

CATHEDRALS AND CHURCHES

Aughton (All Saints)
Tower, 1536. Norman chancel arch and font. Baluster altar rails.

Barton on Humber (St Mary)
Originally chantry chapel. Elaborate Norman north arcade, early 14th-century south arcade, 15th-century clerestory, memorials.

Beverley (St John of Beverley)
Very fine Gothic. Decorated nave, early English choir and main transepts. Perpendicular west front and towers. 14th-century altar screen. Decorated Percy tomb. West door by Hawksmoor.

Beverley (St Mary)
Rich exterior. Nave and tower rebuilt after 1520. Minstrel's pillar, 1530. Reredos by J. Oldrid Scott. 14th-century stalls with misericords, 15th-century font. Lodger stones and matrices of brass. Wrought-iron altar table, 18th-century monuments, painted roofs.

Birkin (St Mary)
Rich, complete Norman church. Fragments of medieval glass, 14th-century effigy, 18th-century pulpit.

Bottesford (St Peter's Chains)
Long lancet windows in chancel, bronze sanctuary bell.

Boynton (St Andrew)
Late 14th-century tower. Classical structure with Gothic details. Strickland mortuary chapel contains family monuments. East window by William Peckitt. Tower with 'Gothick' plaster vault and gallery. Unusual lectern and font cover.

Bridlington (St Mary)
Nave of Augustinian priory. Note 13th- and 14th-century arcades with triforium and clerestory, north porch, Frostenley marble font, Tournai marble tomb slab.

Burton Agnes (St Martin)
13th- and 14th-century nave and aisles. Late 15th-century tower. Chancel rebuilt, c. 1840. Remains of Georgian squire's pew, and gallery front. Box pews, monuments.

Cadney (All Saints)
Mainly early 13th century with late Norman south arcade. Perpendicular east window. Norman font, very fine parclose screen, 12th-century stone coffin lid.

Eastrington (St Michael)
Norman with 12th- and 13th-century work and 15th-century additions. 15th-century altar tomb, incised alabaster slabs, crane to 17th-century font cover.

Hendon (St Augustine)
Early English transepts and chancel with perpendicular east window. Early English arcading on interior west wall of vestry. 15th-century tower. Fine elevation to north transept. Decorated nave with reticulated windows. 14th-century font. Elizabethan Royal Arms, 1585.

276

Holme-upon-Spalding Moor (All Saints)
Mainly 15th–16th century with 17th-century parapets and porch.
Remains of medieval screen, Jacobean pulpit with tester, 18th-
century gallery with 17th-century barrel-organ, early 19th-century
Gothic pews. 15th-century roofs, crown glass, Elizabethan black
letter texts on east wall. In tower rich ancient crowned figure holds
souls in sheet.

Howden (St Peter)
13th–14th century. Geometric west window flanked by pierced
hexagonal turrets. 15th-century stone pulpitum with medieval
statues. Metham and Saltmarshe tombs. Fragmentary brasses.

Hull (Holy Trinity)
Early medieval brickwork in decorated choir and transepts. 15th-
century central tower and nave. Much old screenwork, 18th-century
Rococo altar and reredos, good 19th-century pewing and poppy-
heads. Remains of chantries. De la Pole tombs, 15th-century brass
and ledger stones in choir. 14th-century font.

Lockington (St Mary)
Decorated chancel. Remains of Norman chancel arch. Estoft chapel,
1634. Monuments.

North Newbald (St Nicholas)
Fine Norman fabric. Early English belfry. Chancel rebuilt in 15th
century. Note south doorway. 13th-century font with 17th-century
cover.

Patrington (St Patrick)
Mainly decorated with flamboyant tracery to aisle windows and
carved foliated capitals to nave. Rose window in south gable. Reredos to Lady Altar, restored medieval screen. 17th-century pulpit.
Easter sepulchre. Gilded reredos in memory of King George V.

Swine (St Mary)
Fragment of priory. Important early 16th-century screen. Carved
misericords. Fine alabaster altar tombs. Rococo 'Gothick' font.

Welwick (St Mary)
14th-century remodelling of early Norman church with 15th-
century clerestory. 17th-century brick porch. Flamboyant tracery.
Jacobean pulpit. Much restored chancel screen. Tomb with effigy
of medieval priest.

GARDENS
Burnby Hall Gardens, *Pocklington* (Stewart's Burnby Hall Gardens
and Museum Trust)
Museum housing Stewart collection of animal heads and native
objects.

HISTORIC MONUMENTS
Howden Church, *Howden*
Ruined chancel and chapter house of medieval church.

277

Skipsea Castle, *Skipsea*
Earthworks of large Norman motte and bailey castle.
Thornton Abbey, *Thornton*
14th-century gatehouse and 13th–14th-century remains.

MUSEUMS AND GALLERIES
Bayle Museum, *Bridlington*
14th-century priory gatehouse with museum of local antiquities.
Beverley Art Gallery and Museum, Champney Road, *Beverley*
(Beverley Borough Council)
Museum of local antiquities. Art gallery includes work by Beverley
artist, F. W. Elwell, RA.
Borough Museum and Art Gallery, Oswald Road, *Scunthorpe*
(Scunthorpe Corporation)
Important prehistoric collections; Roman and later archaeology,
geology, natural history, local industry. Bygones, period rooms.
John Wesley collection. Art exhibitions.
Bridlington Art Gallery and Museum, Sewerby Hall, *Bridlington*
(North Wolds District Council)
Permanent collection and local artist exhibition. Amy Johnson
exhibition. Local and natural history and archaeology. House built
1714–20 with 1803 additions.
Central Library, Town Hall Square, *Grimsby* (Humberside County
Council)
Travelling and local exhibitions.
Doughty Museum, Town Hall Square, *Grimsby* (Grimsby Corpora-
tion)
Model ships, especially fishing vessels; china constituting Doughty
bequest, with supplementary exhibits.
Ferens Art Gallery, Queen Victoria Square, *Hull* (Hull City Council)
Old masters, English 18th- and 19th-century portraits, Humberside
marines, modern collection. Visiting exhibitions.
Georgian Houses, High Street, *Hull* (Hull City Council)
Merchant's house with furniture, silver and costumes.
Stewart Collection, Burnby Hall Gardens, *Pocklington*
(Stewart's Burnby Hall Gardens and Museum Trust)
Collection of animal heads and native objects.
Town Docks Museum, Queen Victoria Square, *Hull* (Hull City Coun-
cil)
Exhibition of Whales and Whaling; further displays devoted to
fishing and shipping industries.
Transport and Archaeological Museum, 36 High Street, *Hull* (Hull
City Council)
Collection of coaches and motor cars. Archaeology of East York-
shire. Roman mosaics of Humberside.

Wilberforce House, High Street, *Hull* (Hull Corporation)
17th-century mansion. Birthplace of Wilberforce, slave emancipator.
Local history museum and memorial.

ISLE OF WIGHT
AREAS OF OUTSTANDING NATURAL BEAUTY
Isle of Wight (whole)

CASTLES AND HISTORIC HOUSES
Arreton Manor, *Arreton* (Count L. H. Slade De Pomeroy)
17th-century manor house, early and late Stuart furniture. Toys,
doll and folk collections, King Charles I relics. Wireless Preservation
Society Museum.
Norris Castle, *East Cowes*
Built by James Wyatt in 1795. Period furniture, paintings, tapestries,
armour.
Nunwell House, *Brading* (D. Oglander, Esq)
Home of Oglanders since 1522. Paintings, antique furniture and
documents dating back to Middle Ages. Family museum with dis-
plays of dolls and children's books. Garden being restored.
Osborne House, *East Cowes* (Department of the Environment)
Queen Victoria's favourite residence.

CATHEDRALS AND CHURCHES
Carisbrooke (St Mary)
Fine 15th-century west tower and trans-Norman arcade. Common-
wealth pulpit, 1658; tomb of Lady Margaret Wadham, c. 1620.
Godshill (All Saints)
Mostly perpendicular, 15th century. Interior with old plaster and
much clear glass. Canopied tomb, wall paintings in south transept,
mainly 18th-century monuments, large painting attributed to
Rubens.
Shorwell (St Peter)
15th-century perpendicular stone pulpit with Jacobean tester,
monuments, wall painting of St Christopher, poppy-headed pews.

GARDENS
Robin Hill Country Park, *Downend*
Variety of animals in down and woodland.

HISTORIC MONUMENTS
Appuldurcombe House, *Wroxhall*
Roofless shell of 18th-century mansion in ornamental gardens.
Brading Roman Villa, *Brading*
Includes hypocaust and mosaic pavements.
Newport Roman Villa, *Newport*
Built at end of 2nd century AD. Baths and mosaic floors.

St. Catherine's Chapel, *Chale*
Hill-top tower of medieval lighthouse chapel.
Yarmouth Castle, *Yarmouth*
Built by Henry VIII. Repaired in 1609 and 1632.

MUSEUMS AND GALLERIES
Blackgang Chine Museum, *Chale*
Local and national museum. Large garden.
Maritime Museum and Public Library, *Cowes*
Ships' models, photographs, paintings, books, etc., showing maritime past of the island.
Museum of History of Smuggling, *Ventnor*
Smuggling of past 600 years.
Museum of Isle of Wight Geology, High Street, *Sandown* (Sandown and Shanklin Urban District Council)
Collection of fossils from secondary and tertiary strata of the island.
Natural History Collection, *Godshill*
British and tropical butterflies, tropical seashells, marine and tropical aquarium, precious and semi-precious stones.
Osborne-Smith's Wax Museum, *Brading*
Cameos of island history with authentic costume, war figures, period furniture and harmonious settings. Displayed in the island's oldest house, AD 1228.
*The Ruskin Gallery, Bembridge School, *Bembridge*
Large collection of pictures and manuscripts by Ruskin and his contemporaries.

KENT
AREAS OF OUTSTANDING NATURAL BEAUTY
Kent Downs

CASTLES AND HISTORIC HOUSES
Allington Castle, Nr *Maidstone* (Order of the Carmelites)
13th-century castle. Former home of Tudor poet, Thomas Wyatt, restored by Lord Conway in early part of this century. Collection of icons and Renaissance paintings.
Aylesford – The Friars, Nr *Maidstone* (Order of the Carmelites)
Restored 13th-century friary and shrine of Our Lady. Original 14th-century cloisters. Sculpture and ceramics by contemporary artists. Pottery, rose garden.
Black Charles, Nr *Sevenoaks* (Mr and Mrs William Temple)
14th-century home of John de Blakecherl and his family 1317–1746. Wealth of old oak beams, Elizabethan panelling, Tudor fireplaces and other interesting features, furniture, etc. Old-world garden.
Boughton Monchelsea Place, Nr *Maidstone* (M. B. Winch, Esq)
Grey stone, battlemented Elizabethan manor house with views over 18th-century landscaped park and fallow deer.

Chartwell, *Westerham* (National Trust)
Home of Sir Winston Churchill for many years.
Chiddingstone Castle, Nr *Edenbridge* (Denys E. Bower, Esq)
Pictures and furnishings. Royal Stuart and Jacobite collection;
ancient Egyptian collection; Japanese lacquer, swords, netsuke.
Cobham Hall, Nr *Rochester* (Westwood Educational Trust Ltd)
Gothic and Renaissance architecture with good examples of the work
of James Wyatt. Now girls' public school.
Down House, *Downe* (Royal College of Surgeons of England)
Home of Charles Darwin for 40 years.
Eyhorne Manor, *Hollingbourne* (Mr and Mrs Derek Simmons)
Early 15th-century timber-framed house. Galleried chimney.
Laundry museum. Herbs and old-fashioned roses.
Finchcocks, *Goudhurst* (Mr and Mrs Richard Burnett)
Early 18th-century house. Keyboard instrument collection.
Godinton Park, *Ashford* (Alan Wyndham Green, Esq)
Mainly Jacobean house, interior containing panelling and carving,
portraits, furniture and china. Formal gardens.
Great Maytham Hall, *Rolvenden* (Mutual Households Association
Ltd)
Built in 1910 by Sir Edwin Lutyens.
Hever Castle, Nr *Edenbridge* (Lord Astor of Hever)
Formal Italian garden with statuary and sculpture, lake and 13th-
century moated castle.
***Ian Ramsey College, Brasted Place,** Nr *Westerham* (The Principal)
Clergy training college housed in Brasted Place (Robert Adam
1784).
Ightham Mote, *Ivy Hatch* (C. H. Robinson, Esq)
One of most complete remaining specimens of an ancient moated
manor house.
Knole, *Sevenoaks* (National Trust)
One of largest private houses in England, dating mainly from 15th
century.
Jacobean interior and fine collection of 17th- and 18th-century
furnishings.
Leeds Castle, Nr *Maidstone* (Leeds Castle Foundation)
Castle of medieval queens of England. Water and woodland gardens,
ducks, aviary.
Lullingstone Castle, *Lullingstone* (Guy Hart Dyke, Esq)
Family portraits, armour, Henry VII gateway. Church.
Lympne Castle, Nr *Hythe* (Henry Margary, Esq)
14th-century building restored in 1905. Once owned by the arch-
deacons of Canterbury. Terraced gardens.
Manor House, *Minster-in-Thanet*
One of oldest inhabited houses in Kent. Some 11th-century work.

281

Old Soar Manor, Nr *Borough Green* (National Trust, under guardianship of Department of the Environment)
Solar block of late 13th-century knight's dwelling.
Owletts, *Cobham* (National Trust)
Red brick Carolean house with contemporary staircase and plasterwork ceiling.
Owl House, *Lamberhurst* (Maureen, Marchioness of Dufferin and Ava)
16th-century half-timbered tile-hung wool-smuggler's cottage. Garden with roses and woodland walks.
*Pattyndenne Manor, *Goudhurst* (Mr and Mrs D. C. Spearing)
Wealden Manor, built 1470. Exceptional timbering. Remains of 13th-century stone prison. Associated with Henry VIII and Catherine of Aragon.
Penshurst Place, *Tunbridge Wells* (The Rt Hon. Viscount De L'Isle, VC, KG)
House, including the Great Hall, dates from 1340. There are later additions but whole house conforms to English Gothic style in which it was begun.
Quebec House, *Westerham* (National Trust)
Probably early 16th century in origin, now mainly 17th century. Relics of General Wolfe.
Saltwood Castle, Nr *Hythe* (The Hon. Alan Clark, MP)
Medieval castle, subject of quarrel between Thomas à Becket and Henry II. Grounds and parts of castle, including battlement walk, undercroft, armoury.
Sissinghurst Castle, *Sissinghurst* (National Trust)
Famous garden created by late V. Sackville-West and Sir Harold Nicholson. Tower and long library are also open.
Squerryes Court, *Westerham* (J. St A. Warde, Esq)
William and Mary manor house. Period furniture, paintings, tapestries and china. Objects of interest connected with General Wolfe. Attractive grounds with lake, fine display of spring bulbs, rhododendrons and azaleas.
*Stoneacre, *Otham* (National Trust)
A yeoman's half-timbered hall house, c. 1480.
Warden Manor, *Isle of Sheppey* (Voluntary and Christian Service [Trustees])
Small manor house built 1468.
Wool House, *Loose* (National Trust)
15th-century half-timbered house, formerly used for cleaning wool.

CATHEDRALS AND CHURCHES
Badlesmere (St Leonard)
18th-century interior. Box pews, 3-decker pulpit, choir stalls, twin east lancets.

Barfrestone (St Nicholas)
Norman. Fine carved decoration. Much restored in 19th century.
Brook (St Mary)
Unaltered early Norman. 11th-century and later paintings, screen, pulpit, old tiles.
Brookland (St Augustine)
13th century and later. Detached timber belfry with conical cap. 12th-century lead font. Crown-post roofs, box pews, clear glass.
Canterbury Cathedral
Outstanding Norman crypt. Fine late 12th- and early 13th-century stained glass in choir and Trinity chapel. 12th-century wall paintings in St Gabriel's and St Anselm's chapels. Many interesting monuments.
Nave is masterpiece of early perpendicular. Central tower is finest in England.
Collection of heraldic bosses in perpendicular cloisters.
Charing (St Peter and St Paul)
Late 15th-century tower. Mainly 13th- and 15th-century interior restored in 17th century. Vaulted porch and 17th-century bench-ends.
Cliffe-at-Hoo (St Helen)
13th century with later additions. Magnificent 14th-century sedilia, stalls and screen.
Cobham (St Mary)
Finest collection of brasses in Kent. 16th-century carved and painted 'altar' tombs.
Elham (St Mary the Virgin)
Restored by Eden. 13th-century arcades pierced through Norman walls; perpendicular clerestory; early English chancel; corbels; old tiles; text-boards.
Graveney (All Saints)
Norman in origin, now chiefly 14th century and later. Good nave roof; old tiles; screens; sedilia; Grinling Gibbons' pulpit; chest; stalls; box pews; brasses.
Hythe (St Leonard)
Norman fabric largely rebuilt in 13th century and later. 18th-century tower. Good early English work in chancel.
Ivychurch (St George)
Mainly late decorated but tower later.
Lullingstone (St Botolph)
Mainly 14th-century fabric. Early 16th-century wood screen. Decorated plaster ceiling. Old English and foreign painted glass monuments.
Mereworth (St Lawrence)
C. 1740. Tuscan nave and west portico. Doric interior with painted barrel vault to nave and plaster ceilings in aisles; carved tombstone; 18th-century armorial glass.

Minster-in-Thanet (St Mary the Virgin)
12th- and 13th-century fabric. Stone vaulting in chancel and transepts.
Stalls with misericords.
Newington-on-the-Street (St Mary the Virgin)
Mainly 13th and 14th century. Noble tower. Tombs, screens, wall
paintings and capitals in chancel. 13th-century tomb of Saint
Robert le Bouser.
New Romney (St Nicholas)
Mostly Norman and 14th century. Fine tower and west door; geo-
metric tracery of east window, Norman arches to nave.
Rochester Cathedral
Façade and nave basically Norman, remainder early English.
Notable 12th-century west door showing marked French influence.
Raised choir with crypt under. Fine mid-14th-century doorway from
south-east transept to chapter room.
St Margaret-at-Cliffe (St Margaret of Antioch)
Fine Norman work.
Stone (St Mary)
13th century. Richly decorated. Chancel work by Street. Mural
paintings, 16th-century tomb, brass of 1408.
Tunbridge Wells (King Charles the Martyr)
1676 with later enlargement. Magnificent plaster moulded ceiling by
Doogood.
Upper Hardres (St Peter and St Paul)
Medieval glass, fine west gallery, good roof, monuments.
Westwell (St Mary)
13th century with later alterations. 16th-century timber-framed porch.
Vaulted chancel. Sedilia; remains of painted glass and stalls.
Woodchurch (All Saints)
13th century with later alterations. Arcades with alternate round and
octagonal columns. Triple lancets at east end with banded marble
shafts. Late Norman font. 13th-century glass and manorial pew.
Priest's brass, 1320.

GARDENS
Bedgebury Pinetum, Nr *Goudhurst* (Forestry Commission)
Landscaped collection of conifers with rhododendrons and other
trees.
Chilham Castle, Nr *Canterbury* (Viscount Massereene and Ferrand)
Laid out by Capability Brown. Terraces, topiary, lake and trees.
Crittenden House, *Matfield* (B. T. Tompsett, Esq)
Spring shrubs, roses, lilies, foliage, waterside planting of ponds. Old
iron workshops.
Emmetts Garden, Nr *Brasted* (National Trust)
Shrub garden.

Great Comp, Nr *Borough Green* (Mr and Mrs R. Cameron)
Variety of trees, shrubs, heathers, herbaceous plants, lawns, paths and vistas.
Hall Place, *Leigh* (G. E. Hope-Morley, Esq)
Rhododendrons, specimen trees and shrubs, Dutch and rose garden. Lake.
Hole Park, *Rolvenden* (D. G. W. Barham, Esq)
Formal and natural gardens, rhododendrons and azaleas. Lawns, trees and yew hedges. Dell and water garden. Bluebells, spring bulbs. Autumn colours.
Ladham House, *Goudhurst* (Sir George and Lady Jessel)
Spring and summer flowering shrubs, mixed borders, roses, bog garden, spring and autumn heather garden.
St John's Jerusalem Garden, *Dartford* (National Trust)
Garden moated by River Darneth. Chapel open.
Scotney Castle Garden, *Lamberhurst* (National Trust)
Landscaped garden framing 14th-century and later moated castle.
Sissinghurst Court, *Cranbrook* (Mrs Darnton)
Ornamental cherries, azaleas, rhododendrons, herbaceous borders, yew hedges, rose garden and lily ponds.

HISTORIC MONUMENTS
Eynsford Castle, *Eynsford*
Remains of 12th-century castle including rectangular hall, walls and ditch.
Greyfriars Friary, *Canterbury*
Restored 13th-century remains of Franciscan friary.
Kit's Coty House and Little Kit's Coty House, *Aylesford*
Ruined burial chambers of 2 long barrows.
Lullingstone Roman Villa, *Lullingstone*
Excavated Roman farmstead.
Rochester Castle, *Rochester*
Commenced 1087. Storied keep of 1126–39.
Roman Fort and Anglo Saxon Church, *Reculver*
Remains of 3rd-century fort and of broad apsidal Saxon church.
Roman Fort and Town, *Richborough*
Roman 'Rutupiae' and fort on Saxon shore.
Roman Pavement, *Canterbury*
Foundations of Roman villa including 2 mosaic floors and hypocaust.
Temple Manor, *Strood*
Royal manor dating from c. 1158. A block of c. 1240 and the stone chambers over vaulted undercroft.
Tonbridge Castle, *Tonbridge*
Late 12th-century curtain walls, ruined shell keep and 14th-century gatehouse.

West Malling Tower, *West Malling*
Tower keep of 1100. Surviving part of fortified manor or castle.

MUSEUMS AND ART GALLERIES
Agricultural Museum, *Wye College* (University of London) Court
Lodge Farm, Brook, *Wye*
Agricultural implements, machinery, hand tools and other farming
equipment.
The Art Centre, New Metropole, The Leas, *Folkestone* (Kent County
Council Education Committee)
Art exhibitions, films, lectures, poetry and music.
The Buffs Regimental Museum, Poor Priests Hospital, Stour Street,
Canterbury (Canterbury City Council)
Medals, weapons, uniforms, pictures and trophies.
Dartford District Museum, Market Street, *Dartford*
Local geological and Roman, Saxon and natural history.
*****Deal Museum,** Town Hall, High Street, *Deal*
Local prehistoric and historic antiquities. Complete robes of a baron
of the Cinque Ports.
Dickens's House Museum, Victoria Parade, *Broadstairs* (Thanet
District Council)
Dickens's letters and personal belongings. Local Dickensian prints,
costume and Victoriana.
Dover Museum, Ladywell, *Dover*
Local history, Roman pottery, ceramics, lepidoptera, zoology,
horology, coins. Victoriana, geology, etc.
Eastgate House, High Street, *Rochester*
Local history, Dickens's relics, furniture, Victoriana, toys and dolls, etc.
Ellen Terry Museum, Smallhythe Place, *Tenterden* (National Trust)
Dame Ellen Terry's Tudor house containing relics of her Mrs
Siddons, etc.
Faversham Society Heritage Centre, *Faversham*
Displays history and heritage of 1,000 years.
Folkestone Museum and Art Gallery, Grace Hill, *Folkestone* (Kent
County Council)
Museum: local history, archaeology, and natural science.
Art Gallery: temporary loan exhibitions.
Guildhall Museum, *Sandwich* (Sandwich Town Council)
Ancient and interesting items.
Herne Bay Museum, High Street, *Herne Bay*
Exhibits of local or Kentish interest – Stone, Bronze and Early Iron
Age specimens. Roman material from Reculver. Pictures, maps and
bygones.
Howe Barracks, *Canterbury*
Exhibits of all former county regiments of Kent, Surrey, Sussex and
Middlesex from which Queen's Regiment formed.

286

Hythe Borough Museum, Oaklands, Stade Street, *Hythe* (Hythe Corporation)
Local antiquities.
Intelligence Corps Museum, Templer Barracks, *Ashford*
History of Corps from 1914 to present.
Maison Dieu, Ospringe, *Faversham* (Department of the Environment)
13th-century building containing finds from a Roman cemetery discovered at Ospringe.
Museum and Art Gallery, St Faith's Street, *Maidstone* (Maidstone Borough Council)
16th-century manor house containing archaeological, art and natural history collections for Kent. Pacific and Oriental section, William Hazlitt relics, costume gallery, bygones, ceramics and 17th-century Dutch and Italian oil paintings. Queen's Own Royal West Kent Regiment gallery.
Powell-Cotton Museum, Quex Park, *Birchington*
Zoological specimens. African and Indian jungle scenes, native arts, crafts, and household objects.
Rochester Public Museum, Eastgate House, *Rochester* (Medway Borough Council)
Charles Dickens's chalet and relics. Local history, archaeology, arms and armour, costumes, Victoriana, furniture, models of ships and aircraft.
Royal Engineers Museum, *Gillingham*
Includes relics of General Gordon.
Royal Museum, The Beaney, High Street, *Canterbury* (Canterbury City Council)
Local archaeological material, natural history collection, mineralogical exhibits, pottery and porcelain. Local and other prints, engravings and pictures.
Royal Tunbridge Wells Museum and Art Gallery, Civic Centre, *Tunbridge Wells* (Borough Council)
Prints of old Tunbridge Wells, domestic and agricultural bygones, dolls, toys, natural history, geology, Wealden prehistory, Tunbridge ware, Victorian paintings.
Tyrwhitt-Drake Museum of Carriages, Archbishop's Stables, Mill Street, *Maidstone* (Maidstone Borough Council)
Horse-drawn vehicles, including most types of state, official and private carriages and items such as models, dealing with history of horse transport and coach building.
Westgate, *Canterbury* (Canterbury City Council)
Museum of arms and armour housed in 14th-century city gatehouse.

LANCASHIRE
AREAS OF OUTSTANDING NATURAL BEAUTY
Arnside and Silverdale (part)
Forest of Bowland (part)

CASTLES AND HISTORIC HOUSES
Astley Hall, *Chorley* (Corporation of Chorley, 1922)
Elizabethan house reconstructed in 1666. Furniture, pottery, tapestries, pictures.
Chingle Hall, Goosnargh, Nr *Preston* (Mrs Margaret H. Howarth)
Small moated manor house built 1260. Birth place of Saint John Wall, 1620. Rose garden and lawns.
Gawthorpe Hall, *Padiham* (National Trust)
Early 17th-century manor house restored in 1860s. Fine panelling and moulded ceilings. Kay–Shuttleworth collection of lace and embroidery.
Leighton Hall, *Carnforth* (Major and Mrs Reynolds)
Early neo-Gothic façade. Fine pictures and furniture. Extensive grounds.
***Martholme Gatehouse,** *Great Harwood* (Mrs Rose McFarlane)
Tudor gatehouse, built 1561, restored 1969.
Rufford Old Hall, *Rufford* (National Trust)
Outstanding half-timbered hall with 15th-century screen. Philip Ashcroft Collection of relics of Lancashire folk life.

CATHEDRALS AND CHURCHES
Great Mitton (All Hallows)
Sherbourne chapel, 1594, and monuments. 15th-century rood screen; medieval roof; late 17th-century pulpit; 16th-century font cover.
Halsall (St Cuthbert)
15th-century perpendicular spire. Chancel, c. 1350, buttressed and pinnacled. Fine 14th-century tomb. Decorated doorway in north hall with original door. Effigies and brass of Halsall family. General restoration, 1886.
Hoole (St Michael)
1628, with tower of 1720 and chancel of 1859. Box pews; gallery; hatchment; 2-decker pulpit, 1695; Victorian glass.
Lancaster (St Mary)
1431. Tower, 1759. Fine stalls, Roubiliac, chapel restored.
Preston (St Peter)
By Rickman, 1822–5. Gothic with cusped interior. Fine east window.
Tarleton (St Mary)
1719. Turret and cupola, porch and vestry of 1824. Old benches, gallery, clear glass.
Whalley (St Mary)
13th century with 15th-century tower, clerestory and aisle windows.

Fine carved woodwork including 15th-century canopied stalls, 17th- and 18th-century screened pews and organ, 1729.

GARDENS
Cranford, *Aughton* (T. J. C. Taylor, Esq)
Modern half-acre garden, unusually planned.
Ravenhurst, *Bolton* (Mr and Mrs T. J. Arkwright)
Italian-style garden in wooded setting, sunken and water gardens, flowering shrubs and herbaceous borders.
Wildfowl Trust, Nr *Mere Brow*
Waterfowl garden, wild area and mere.
Windle Hall, *St Helen's* (Lord and Lady Pilkington)
3-acre walled garden, surrounded by lawns and woodland, herbceous borders, rockery, greenhouses and roses.

HISTORIC MONUMENTS
Roman Fort, *Ribchester*
Remains of fort of 'Bremetennacum'.
Roman Town, *Alderborough*
Remains of boundary wall, 2 tessellated pavements, museum.
Salley, *Salley*
Remains of small abbey.
Warton, *Warton*
Shell of small medieval manor house.
Whalley, *Whalley*
Medieval abbey gatehouse.

MUSEUMS AND GALLERIES
Bacup Natural History Society's Museum, 24 Yorkshire Street, *Bacup*
Natural history subjects; local geology and domestic bygones.
Blackburn Museum and Art Gallery, Library Street, *Blackburn*
Coins, local history, medieval manuscripts, Japanese prints, ceramics, ethnography and natural history; East Lancashire Regiment Collection.
British in India Museum, Sun Street, *Colne*
Paintings, photographs, coins, stamps, medals, diorama, model railway and other items.
Clitheroe Castle Museum, *Clitheroe*
Carboniferous fossils and items of local interest.
Grundy Art Gallery, Queen Street, *Blackpool* (Blackpool Corporation)
Collection of paintings and drawings by outstanding 19th- and 20th-century British artists.
Harris Museum and Art Gallery, Market Square, *Preston* (Preston Corporation)
Collections covering fine arts, decorative art, archaeology, natural

and social history, and includes work by Devis family, Newsham Bequest, and Cedric Houghton Bequest.

Haworth Art Gallery, Haworth Park, *Accrington* (Accrington Corporation)
Works of the early English watercolour period and collection of Tiffany glass. Special exhibitions.

Lancaster Museum, Old Town Hall, Market Square, *Lancaster* (Lancaster City)
Prehistory, Roman and medieval remains, bygones. Museum of King's Own Regiment.

Lewis Textile Museum, Exchange Street, *Blackburn*
Groups can be shown in action adventures of Kay, Hargreaves, Arkwright and Crompton, by a member of museum staff; art exhibitions.

*Mercer Museum and Art Gallery, Mercer Park, Rishton Road, *Clayton-le-Moors*
Relics of late John Mercer; collections of coal and coke products, sea-shells and fine arts.

The Ribchester Museum of Roman Antiquities, *Ribchester* (National Trust)
Remains from the Roman site of 'Bremetennacum'.

Rossendale Museum, Whitaker Park, *Rawtenstall* (Rossendale Borough Council)
Fine arts, natural history, Rossendale collection. Summer exhibitions.

Samlesbury Hall, *Samlesbury* (Samlesbury Hall Trust and Lancashire branch of Council for Protection of Rural England)
Changing exhibitions.

Towneley Hall Art Gallery and Museum, *Burnley* (Burnley Borough Council)
Oil paintings and early English watercolours, period furniture, ivories, 18th-century glassware and Chinese ceramics and natural history. Museum of Local Crafts and Industries, and East Lancashire Regiment Room.

Turton Tower, Turton, *Blackburn*
15th-century Pele tower with 16th-century farmhouse attached. Local history, weapons, period furniture.

LEICESTERSHIRE
CASTLES AND HISTORIC HOUSES

Belgrave Hall, *Leicester* (Leicestershire Museums, Art Galleries and Records Service)
Small Queen Anne house built 1709–13 with furniture of 18th and early 19th centuries. Garden.

Belvoir Castle, Nr *Grantham* (His Grace the Duke of Rutland)
Seat of Dukes of Rutland since Henry VIII's time, rebuilt by Wyatt 1816. Notable pictures, furniture, *objets d'art*.

Langton Hall, Nr *Market Harborough* (Mrs L. D. Cullings)
English country house dating from 15th and 16th centuries set in parkland. Gardens laid out in French style.

Manor House, *Donington-le-Heath* (Leicestershire Museums, Art Galleries and Records Service)
13th-century manor house with early English furniture.

Oakham Castle, *Oakham* (Leicestershire Museums, Art Galleries and Records Service)
Late 12th-century Norman hall with collection of horseshoes given by peers of realm.

Old Manor House, *Donington-le-Heath* (Leicestershire County Council)
Little altered medieval manor house, c. 1280.

Prestwold Hall, *Loughborough* (Mr and Mrs Packe-Drury-Lowe)
Early 19th-century house. Home of the Packe family for over 300 years.

Quenby Hall, *Hungarton* (The Squire de Lisle)
Jacobean hall built c. 1620. Fine panelling and ceilings, pictures and furniture. Lawns and majestic cedars.

Stanford Hall, *Lutterworth* (Lord and Lady Braye)
William and Mary house dating from 1690. Furniture, pictures, 1898 flying machine. Motor cycle and car museum. Antique kitchen utensils. Walled rose garden leading to old forge and crafts centre. Nature trail.

Stapleford Park, Nr *Melton Mowbray* (Lord Gretton, OBE)
House dates from 1500, restored 1633. Exterior decoration of exceptional interest. Thomas Balston collection of Victorian Staffordshire figures.

Whatton House, Nr *Kegworth*
House dates from 1800. Gardens with flowering shrubs, bulbs, roses, herbaceous border. Oriental gardens.

CATHEDRALS AND CHURCHES

Bottesford (St Mary)
15th-century nave and spire. Chancel rebuilt in 17th century to accommodate monuments of Earls of Rutland.

Breedon-on-the-Hill (St Mary and St Hardulph)
Norman and 13th century. 18th-century carved stones, monuments; Jacobean canopied pew of Shirley family.

Church Langton (St Peter)
15th century. Very fine tower and nave.

Claybrooke (St Peter)
Good perpendicular nave and 14th-century chancel.

291

Clipsham (St Mary)
14th-century with broach tower. Interior originally Norman with 14th-century rebuilding. Medieval glass.

Empingham (St Peter)
14th-century west tower and front and crocketed spire. Fine early English interior with double piscina and triple sedilia.

Exton (St Peter and St Paul)
Notable tower and spire. Very fine Noel and Harington monuments.

Gaddesby (St Luke)
1290–1340. Unique 14th-century ornamentation of exterior of south aisle, partly medieval seating and brick floors.

Great Casterton (St Peter and St Paul)
13th century, unrestored. Clear glass, Georgian pulpit, Ketton headstones.

Ketton (St Mary)
West front fine 12th-century work. Remainder mainly 13th century. Chancel practically rebuilt, 1863, with panelled roof, east window and altar by Comper, 1907. Notable carved headstones.

King's Norton (St John the Baptist)
1760–75. 18th-century fittings throughout.

Langham (St Peter and St Paul)
Mainly 14th century with 13th-century tower. Interior with plastered walls and clear glass. Some 15th-century enlargement. Good glass by Comper.

Leicester (St Martin)
(Now enjoys Cathedral status following post-1850 Diocesan re-organization.)
Medieval, drastically restored in 19th century. Fine spire and Swithland slate monuments.

Leicester (St Mary de Castro)
Good Norman work and sedilia with later additions. 15th-century spire.

Lyddington (St Andrew)
Mostly perpendicular. Medieval wall paintings, 17th-century arrangement of sanctuary with enclosed altar, medieval brasses.

Melton Mowbray (St Mary)
13th- and 15th-century tower. East and west aisles to transepts. Fine 18th-century chandeliers.

Oakham (All Saints)
14th-century tower and spire. 14th-century interior with notable sculptured capitals and arcades. 15th-century enlargement.

Ryhall (St John the Evangelist)
13th-century tower and spire. North arcading, c. 1200; south arcading slightly later. 15th-century chancel.

Stapleford (St Mary Magdalene)
1783. 'Gothick'. Original fittings. Monuments.

Staunton Harold (Holy Trinity)
1653–65. Unique as Cromwellian church preserving all fittings and painted ceilings.
Stoke Dry (St Andrew)
Mainly 13th–14th century with Norman work and 15th-century additions. Notable 15th–17th century Digby tombs. 15th-century chancel screen and wall paintings.
Stoke Golding (St Margaret)
1330–40. Fine decorated design and carving. Notable windows, particularly geometrical east windows of nave and aisle and north window.
Teigh (Holy Trinity)
14th-century tower. Remainder 18th century with pure 18th-century interior.
Whissendine (St Andrew)
14th–15th century. Notable 14th-century tower; north arcade 13th century. Roof with carved figures, 15th century. Early 16th-century screen.
Withcote (dedication uncertain)
Rich early 16th-century glass; 18th-century reredos and monuments.

GARDENS
Bradgate Park and Swithland Woods, Nr *Loughborough*
850-acre country park with Old John tower (1786) and ruins of 16th-century brick mansion.
University Botanic Gardens, *Leicester* (University of Leicester)
Rose, rock, water and sunken gardens, herbaceous borders and botanic border beds.

HISTORIC MONUMENTS
Ashby-de-la-Zouch Castle, *Ashby-de-la-Zouch*
Mainly 14th century with Hastings tower added in 1474.
Kirby Muxloe Castle, *Kirby Muxloe*
Ruined moated 15th-century fortified manor house.
Jewry Wall, *Leicester*
Huge Roman wall with arches. Built c. AD 130, and later incorporated into public baths.

MUSEUMS AND GALLERIES
Bosworth Field Exhibition, Ambion Farm, *Sutton Cheney*
Exhibition relating to Battle of Bosworth Field, 1485.
Jewry Wall Museum, St Nicholas Circle, *Leicester* (Leicestershire County Council)
Museum of archaeology from prehistoric times to 1500.
The Leicestershire Museum and Art Gallery, New Walk, *Leicester* (Leicestershire County Council)
Collections 18th-, 19th- and 20th-century English paintings, draw-

ings, and watercolours. Collection of German Expressionists, 19th-
and 20th-century French paintings and some old master paintings.
Old master and modern prints. English ceramics, from 17th to 20th
century, with some Oriental and Near Eastern specimens. English
silver including some civic plate, glass. British mammals, birds,
freshwater fish (aquarium). Leicestershire and general geology.
Egyptology.

Leicestershire Museum of Technology, Abbey Pumping Station,
Corporation Road, *Leicester*
Power gallery, knitting machines, transport items, steam shovel,
Beam engine 1891.

Leicestershire Record Office, 57 New Walk and New Walk Museum,
Leicester (Leicestershire County Council)
Official and private archives, rural and urban, relating to County.

Museum of Costume, Wygston's House, *Leicester* (Leicestershire
Museums, Art Galleries and Records Service)
House dates from 15th century. English costume 1760–1920. Re-
construction of draper's and shoe shop.

Museum of the Royal Leicestershire Regiment, The Magazine,
Oxford Street, *Leicester* (Leicestershire County Council)
Mementoes, battle trophies and relics.

Newarke Houses Museum, The Newarke, *Leicester* (Leicestershire
County Council)
Social history of city and county from 15th century to present. 19th-
century street scene, 17th-century room, local clocks, musical
instruments.

Rutland County Museum, Catmos Street, *Oakham* (Leicestershire
County Council)
Anglo-Saxon jewellery, Roman coins, craft tools, local history,
Victorian shop. Farm wagons and agricultural implements.

LINCOLNSHIRE

AREAS OF OUTSTANDING NATURAL BEAUTY
Lincolnshire Wolds (part)

CASTLES AND HISTORIC HOUSES
Auborn Hall, Nr *Lincoln* (H. N. Nevile, Esq)
16th-century house. Carved staircase and panelled rooms.

Belton House, *Grantham* (Lord Brownlow)
Built 1685 and attributed to Sir Christopher Wren. Fine furniture.
Grinling Gibbons carvings; paintings by old masters. Duke of
Windsor souvenirs. Park and formal gardens.

Doddington Hall, *Doddington* (A. G. Jarvis, Esq)
Elizabethan manor house, furniture. Rose gardens.

Fydell House, *Boston* (Boston Preservation Trust)
Built 1726 by William Fydell, three times Mayor of Boston. Now houses Pilgrim College.

Grantham House, *Grantham* (National Trust)
Dated from 14th and 15th centuries. Extensively altered in 18th century. Garden.

*Gunby Hall, *Burgh-le-Marsh* (National Trust)
Built by Sir William Massingberd, 1700. Walled gardens full of flowers and roses.

Marston Hall, *Grantham* (Rev. Henry Thorold, FSA)
16th-century manor house. Pictures and furniture. Held by Thorolds since 14th century. Ancient garden with notable trees. Gothic gazebo.

Old Hall, *Gainsborough* (Friends of the Old Hall Association)
15th-century black-and-white manor house.

Rectory, Market Deeping (Mrs K. Davies)
Dates from 13th–14th century with original hall, carved beams and monks' dormitory.

Woolsthorpe Manor, Nr *Grantham* (National Trust)
17th-century house, birthplace of Sir Isaac Newton.

CATHEDRALS AND CHURCHES

Addlethorpe (St Nicholas)
Late 15th century. Medieval stained glass; much original woodwork.

Algarkirk (St Peter and St Paul)
Cruciform with double aisles. Restored by R. C. Carpenter, 1850. Chancel and south transept windows by Hardman, remainder by Clayton and Bell.

Blyborough (St Alkmund)
Notable early 15th-century tomb. Rood screen from Thornton Abbey.

Boston (St Botolph)
One of England's largest and grandest parish churches. 14th-century late decorated. Magnificent south porch; 64 carved stalls; series of monuments, 13th–17th century.

Brant Broughton (St Helen)
Decorated tower and spire. 13th-century arcades and perpendicular clerestory. Much outside decoration. Restored by Bodley, 1876, with good carved wood, wrought iron, and rich stained glass.

Burgh-le-Marsh (St Peter and St Paul)
Late 15th century. Unusual parapet and fine windows in bell storey of tower. Unfortunate restoration of 1805. Leonard Palmer brass, 1610. Font and pulpit, 1623.

Croft (All Saints)
Good 15th-century woodwork. Pulpit, 1615. Pre-Reformation brass eagle lectern. Monuments.

Ewerby (St Andrew)
Decorated at its finest, spire one of best in England. Good woodwork; late 14th-century effigy; altar rails probably Laudian; good early 19th-century glass. Restored 1895.

Fleet (St Mary Magdalene)
14th century. Detached tower and spire. Decorated with early English arcades and perpendicular west windows. Chancel rebuilt, 1862.

Folkingham (St Andrew)
Noble Late Perpendicular tower. 14th-century arcades, early 15th-century windows. Early English chancel with traces of Norman work. Fine rood screen and south porch.

Freiston (dedication unknown)
Remains of priory. Clerestory windows above corbel table. Norman arcades, parclose screens and font cover.

Gainsborough (All Saints)
Late perpendicular tower. Remainder rebuilt, 1735.

Gedney (St Mary Magdalene)
Early English tower with unfinished perpendicular spire. 14th-century continental work in east windows. 14th- and 15th-century stained glass in north aisle. 13th–14th-century monuments.

Grantham (St Wulfram)
Fine 14th-century tower and spire. Late Norman pillars; late decorated north porch; late perpendicular chantry chapel; early 16th-century south porch; unusual font; vaulted 14th-century crypt.

Heckington (St Andrew)
Decorated with perfect exterior. Easter sepulchre and carved sedilia.

Kirkstead (St Leonard)
Part of abbey. Early English. Well restored, 1914.

Lincoln Cathedral
Mainly 13th century with 14th-century additions and Norman work in west towers and front. Angel choir, 1256–80. Note south-east porch and figure in bay to right of it; pair of doorways leading from transepts into choir aisles; carved decorated pulpitum; choir stalls, 1360–80; carved corbels, headstops and bosses; early 13th-century chapter house; north walk with library by Wren, 1674.

Long Sutton (St Mary)
Early English spire, finest in county. Notable 15th-century south porch; medieval brass eagle lectern.

Louth (St James)
1501–15. One of last great medieval Gothic masterpieces with magnificent spire. Restored by James Fowler, 1869.

Northorpe (St John the Baptist)
2 Norman arcades; fragments of medieval glass; brasses; early 14th-century south doorway.

Saltfleetby (All Saints)
Norman, rebuilt early 13th century. Note stone reredos; 13th-century font; 15th-century rood screen.
Scotter (St Peter)
Saxon to perpendicular work. Pre-Conquest tympanum and south door; early English nave and north aisle. 15th-century rood screen; memorials.
Silk Willoughby (St Denis)
14th-century tower with spire and flying buttresses. Mainly late 14th century. Notable south door; 14th-century pew ends; 15th-century rood screen; 17th-century pulpit.
Sleaford (St Denys)
Broach spire; double north aisle; late 14th-century windows; perpendicular clerestory and font.
Stainfield (St Andrew)
Queen Anne. 17th-century needlework; late medieval armour.
Stow (St Mary)
Finest Norman church in county. Notable Norman west door and font; remains of wall painting in north transept.
Tattershall (Holy Trinity)
Rebuilt mid-15th-century. Good 15th- and 16th-century Continental manufactured brasses. Very little stained glass.
Theddlethorpe (All Saints)
Mainly 14th and 15th century. Rood screen and stone reredos in south aisle both 15th century. 2 16th-century parclose screens; 18th-century monuments; brasses of 1424; fragments of medieval glass. Traces of early colour decoration on aisle walls.
Weston (St Mary)
Almost entirely early English. Note south porch and font.
Winthorpe (St Mary)
Late 15th century. Much glass and original woodwork; some early 16th-century brasses; restored churchyard cross.
Wrangle (St Mary the Virgin and St Nicholas)
Early English. Decorated and perpendicular with grand 14th-century east window and Elizabethan pulpit. Glass, 1345-1371. Altar tomb of Sir John Read, 1626. Ledger stone of 1705.

HISTORIC MONUMENTS
Bolingbroke Castle, *Bolingbroke*
Castle dates from 1230.
Bishop's Palace, *Lincoln*
Complex of medieval ruins.

MUSEUMS AND GALLERIES
Alford Manor House, *Alford*
Thatched Tudor manor housing folk museum.

Ayscoughfee Hall, Churchgate, *Spalding*
Ashly Maples collection of British Birds
Boston Museum, The Guildhall, South Street, *Boston* (Boston Corporation)
15th-century building associated with early Pilgrim Fathers. Items of local historical and archaeological interest; local prints and pictures.
Church Farm Museum, Church Road, *Skegness* (Lincolnshire County Council)
Bernard Best collection of agricultural and domestic equipment.
Lincoln Cathedral Library, The Cathedral, *Lincoln*
Medieval manuscripts, and early printed books. Wren library by appointment.
Lincoln Cathedral Treasury, The Cathedral, *Lincoln*
Gold and silver plate from the diocese; Magna Carta.
Lincoln City and County Museum, Broadgate, *Lincoln* (Lincolnshire County Council)
Local with emphasis on prehistoric, Roman and medieval antiquities, arms and armour, and natural history.
Museum, St Peter's Hill, *Grantham* (Lincolnshire County Council)
Local prehistoric, Roman and Saxon archaeology. Grantham local history, trades and industries, and collection devoted to Sir Isaac Newton.
Museum, High Street, *Stamford* (Lincolnshire County Council)
Local archaeology and history.
Museum of Lincolnshire Life, Burton Road, *Lincoln* (Lincolnshire County Council)
Life in Lincolnshire during the past 200 years.
Spalding Museum, Broad Street, *Spalding* (Spalding Gentlemen's Society)
Bygones, ceramics, glass, coins, metals and prehistoric relics.
Usher Gallery, Lindum Road, *Lincoln* (Lincolnshire County Council)
Collections include Usher collection of fine antique watches, miniature portraits and porcelain. Gallery of works by Peter de Wint. Tennyson Collection. Topographical collections relating to county and city.

(GREATER) LONDON
CASTLES AND HISTORIC HOUSES
Ashburnham House, *Westminster* (Westminster School)
Formerly home of Earls of Ashburnham.
Boston Manor House, *Brentford* (London Borough of Hounslow)
Tudor and Jacobean mansion with very fine examples of period ceilings. Park and gardens.
Charlton House, The Village, *Charlton* (Borough of Greenwich)
Early 17th-century mansion. Plasterwork ceilings, interesting

chimney pieces, original main stairway. Now educational and community centre.

Chiswick House, *Chiswick* (Department of the Environment)
Villa designed by Earl of Burlington 1725, derived from Palladio's Villa Capra. William Kent decorated the rooms.

Eastbury Manor House, *Barking* (National Trust, administered by London Borough of Barking)
Fine example of a medium-sized Elizabethan manor house.

Hall Place, *Bexley* (Bexley London Borough Council)
Historic mansion (1540). Rose, rock, water, herb, peat gardens. Conservatories. Parkland. Topiary designed in form of Queen's Beasts.

Hampton Court Palace (Department of the Environment)
Royal palace built in 1514 by Wolsey, additions by Henry VIII, and later by Wren for William III. State rooms, tapestries, pictures. Famous gardens are at their best in mid-May.

Kensington Palace, *Kensington* (Department of the Environment)
Bought by William III, 1689. Altered and added to by Wren; later alterations.

Kew Palace, *Kew* (Dutch House) (Department of the Environment)
Built 1631, Dutch style. Souvenirs of George III.

Lancaster House, Nr *St James's* (Department of the Environment)
Finest surviving example in London of great town mansion of early Victorian period.

Marble Hill House, *Twickenham* (Greater London Council)
Complete example of English Palladian villa. Early Georgian paintings and furniture.

*Marlborough House, *Pall Mall* (Foreign and Commonwealth Office)
Built by Wren for Sarah, Duchess of Marlborough, subsequently royal residence, now Commonwealth centre.

Old Palace, *Croydon* (Community of the Sisters of the Church)
Seat of Archbishops of Canterbury since 871. 15th-century banqueting hall and guardroom, Tudor chapel, Norman undercroft.

Osterley Park House, *Osterley* (National Trust, administered by the Victoria and Albert Museum)
Splendid state rooms furnished by Robert Adam, including Gobelins tapestry room. Garden houses and Tudor stable block.

Palace of Westminster, *Westminster*
Oldest remaining part of palace is Westminster Hall, 1097–99, with cantilever and hammer-beam roof. Palace designed by Barry in 19th century.

Palace of Whitehall, Banqueting House, *Whitehall*
Designed by Inigo Jones, 1619. Rubens paintings.

Queen's House, *Greenwich* (National Maritime Museum)
Designed by Inigo Jones for Anne of Denmark, wife of James I. Completed 1635 for Henrietta Maria, wife of Charles I.

Royal Naval College, *Greenwich* (The Admiralty)
Begun by Webb, finished by Wren, Hawksmoor and Vanbrugh. Painted hall and chapel.

Syon House, *Brentford* (His Grace the Duke of Northumberland, KG)
Magnificent Adam interior and furnishings, famous picture collections, and historical associations dating back to 1415. Capability Brown landscape.

*White Lodge, *Richmond Park* (Governors of the Royal Ballet School)
Former royal residence, built early 18th century.

CATHEDRALS AND CHURCHES
City (All Hallows, London Wall)
G. Dance, Junior, 1765–7. Barrel-vaulted ceiling with flower pattern in Adam style; broad frieze; semi-circular windows; coffered semi-dome.

City (St Bartholomew-the-Great, Smithfield)
Norman. 17th-century tower. Romanesque interior with triforium and apsidal end. East Lady chapel. Perpendicular tomb.

City (St Benet, Paul's Wharf)
Finished by Wren, 1683. Red brick exterior with stone dressings and swags, tower and dome. Interior with galleries, carved Renaissance altar piece pulpit and wainscoted walls.

City (St Bride, Fleet Street)
Wren, 1671–1703. Gutted, 1940, and restored. Wedding-cake steeple.

City (St James, Garlick Hythe)
Finished by Wren, 1683. Blitzed and restored. Portland stone steeple. Interior columned, wainscoted and plaster-vaulted with much Renaissance woodwork.

City (St Lawrence, Jewry)
Wren, 1671–7. Restored.

City (St Magnus the Martyr, London Bridge)
Portland stone tower and steeple. Interior with fine wood and ironwork.

City (St Margaret, Lothbury)
Wren. Tower and lead spire. Old woodwork from city churches destroyed by Victorians.

City (St Martin, Ludgate)
Wren. Rich interior with English Renaissance woodwork, and painted dome.

City (St Mary, Woolnoth)
Hawksmoor, 1716–27. Many original furnishings.

City (St Mary-at-Hill)
Plain exterior. Interior with very fine plaster, wood and ironwork.

300

City (St Mary-le-Bow)
Wren, 1670–80. Gutted, 1940, restored. Elaborate steeple. Roman Doric doorways. Norman crypt.

City (St Michael, Paternoster Royal)
Wren, 1686–1713. Octagonal and curved steeple.

City (St Nicholas, Cole Abbey)
Wren, 1671–7. Restored. Notable steeple.

City (St Peter, Cornhill)
Brick tower with leaded cupola and spire. Classical interior with fine woodwork, screen, organ gallery and pulpit.

City (St Stephen, Walbrook)
Tower with steeple. Fine interior with rich Renaissance woodwork and good plasterwork.

City (St Vedast, Foster Lane)
Wren, 1670–97. Gutted, 1940, and restored. Simple Baroque tower and steeple.

Chelsea (Holy Trinity, Sloane Street)
Sedding, 1888–90. Free and original perpendicular. Cathedral of Arts and Crafts movement.

Chelsea (St Luke, Sydney Street)
J. Savage, 1820–34. Ashlar faced. Tower and portico, sumptuous King's chapel style within. Galleries; stone vaulted chancel roof.

Deptford (St Paul)
Thomas Archer, 1712–30. Baroque. Steeple and 3 porticos. Interior rich and cruciform.

Greenwich (St Alfege)
Hawksmoor, 1711–14. Tower and spire added by John James, 1730.

Holborn (St Giles-in-the-Fields)
Flintcroft, 1731–3. Well restored Georgian interior. Last judgment carving, 1687, in churchyard gate.

Paddington (All Saints, Talbot Road)
William White, 1850–61. Dramatic tower. Furnished by Comper, Travers and Hare.

Rainham (St Helen and St Giles)
Norman, 1170. Note nave piers with attached shafts and scalloped capitals.

St Marylebone (All Souls, Langham Place)
Nash, 1822–4. Corinthian hall with flat ceiling. Well restored.

St Marylebone (St Cyprian's, Clarence Gate)
Comper, 1903. Sumptuous interior. Altars, hangings, statues, light fittings, font cover and stained glass.

St Marylebone (St Peter, Vere Street)
Gibbs, 1724. Tuscan portico and bell turret. Fine ceiling, carved with plasterwork. Stained glass and painted altar piece by Burne-Jones.

St Paul's Cathedral
England's only major cathedral in classical style and Wren's masterpiece. Great dome of 102-ft diameter, one of finest in world. Dome
surmounted by lantern with fine pair of Baroque towers at west end.
Grinling Gibbons carving on exterior. Interior wood carving and
elaborate wrought-iron work.

Southwark Cathedral
Eastern half is medieval, nave dates from 1889–97. Pure early
English choir. Tudor reredos and early English retrochoir.

Stepney (Christ Church, Spitalfields)
Hawksmoor, 1723–9. Massive aisled and columned interior.

Stepney (St Anne, Limehouse)
Hawksmoor, 1712–14. Majestic exterior. West end is pilastered apse
with semi-dome. Interior restored after fire 1850; galleried with great
oval ceiling. East window by Clutterbuck.

Stepney (St George's-in-the-East)
Hawksmoor, 1715–23. Complex ground plan and castellated tower.
Restoration by Ansell and Baily: combination of modern forms with
surviving Georgian and Victorian decoration.

Wanstead (St Mary the Virgin)
18th century. Corinthian interior. Magnificent monument to Sir
Josiah Child, 1699.

Westminster Abbey
Founded 1065. Norman undercroft. Henry III's 13th-century church
now forms east end transepts and choir. Nave, 1376–1500. Fine fan
vaulting in early 16th-century King Henry VII's chapel. Stained
glass. Royal tombs. Statesmen's Aisle. Poet's Corner.

Westminster (St James, Piccadilly)
Wren, 1632–4. Modest exterior. Outdoor pulpit. Galleried interior,
de-Victorianized. Organ case from Chapel Royal, Whitehall.
Grinling Gibbons carving.

Westminster (St Martin-in-the-Fields)
Gibbs, 1722–6. Porticoed body and elegant steeple. Interior with
galleries and vaulted nave ceiling with fine plasterwork.

Westminster (St Mary-le-Strand)
Gibbs, 1714–17. Exterior with 2-storied effect and strong cornices.
No galleries; rich vaulted ceiling.

Whitchurch (St Lawrence, Little Stanmore)
1715. Built for Duke of Chandos. Interior frescoed with panels and
grisaille, probably by Laguerre and Bellucci, c. 1720. Many original
fittings. Chandos chapel. Organ by Jordan, c. 1720.

GARDENS
Arkley Manor, Nr *Barnet* (Dr W. E. Shewell-Cooper, MBE)
Organic garden. Fruit, flowers and vegetables, weeping garden.

Danson Park, Nr *Welling*
Lake-watered park originally designed by Capability Brown.
Kew Gardens, *Kew* (Royal Botanic Gardens)
300 acres containing living collection of 25,000 different plant species
and varieties. Greenhouses, herbarium, museums.
Syon Park Gardens, *Brentford* (His Grace the Duke of Northumber-
land, KG)
Includes Great Conservatory by Dr Fowler, containing aviary and
aquarium.
Winter Gardens, *Eltham*
Tropical and temperate plants in cool houses.

HISTORIC MONUMENTS
Eltham Palace, *Eltham*
14th-century Royal Palace with great hall of 1470s. Excavation has
begun to reveal other rooms.
Tower of London, *Tower Bridge*
Dates from Norman times. Historical relics, armouries, dungeons.

MUSEUMS AND GALLERIES
Artillery Museum, The Rotunda, *Woolwich*
Rotunda was tent erected in St James's Park for the visit of the Allied
Sovereigns in 1814. Collection of guns, muskets, rifles, etc.
Baden-Powell House, Queen's Gate, *Kensington* (The Scout Associa-
tion)
Mementoes of Baden-Powell and historical records.
Barnet Museum, 31 Wood Street, *Barnet* (Barnet and District Local
History Society)
Archaeological and historical exhibits relating to area. Bygones and
miscellaneous. Reference library.
Bethnal Green Museum, Museum of Childhood, *Bethnal Green*
(Victoria and Albert Museum)
Museum is being developed as a Museum of Childhood and is
notable for its collections of toys, games, dolls and dolls' houses.
Also Spitalfields silks (once a local industry); sculptures by Rodin;
wedding dresses; 19th-century continental decorative arts.
Bexley London Borough Museum, Hall Place, Bourne Road, *Bexley*
Temporary exhibitions, general and local. Local studies centre.
Beautiful gardens. Erith Museum Study Centre.
British Museum, Great Russell Street, *Bloomsbury*, W1
National Museum of Antiquities, Ethnography, and Prints and
Drawings. Museum departments are: coins and medals; Egyptian
antiquities; Western Asiatic antiquities; Greek and Roman antiqui-
ties; prehistoric and Romano–British antiquities; medieval and later
antiquities; Oriental antiquities and prints and drawings.
British Museum (Natural History), Cromwell Road, *South Kensing-
ton*, SW7

National collections of animals and plants, extinct as well as existing, and of the rocks and minerals which make up earth's crust. Galleries have special exhibits illustrating evolution and other biological topics.

Broomfield Museum, Broomfield Park, *Palmers Green*, N13 (London Borough of Enfield)
Ancient mansion situated in beautiful park. Collections of local antiquities and bygones, natural history, pottery and paintings.

Bruce Castle Museum, Lordship Lane, *Tottenham*, N17
Local history. Postal history. Museum of the Middlesex Regiment.

Buckingham Palace, The Queen's Gallery, Buckingham Palace Road, *Victoria*, SW1
Exhibitions from Royal collection of paintings, furniture and other works of art.

Butler Museum, Harrow School, *Harrow-on-the-Hill*
Natural history, herbarium, British and tropical lepidoptera, British birds.

Carlyle's House, 24 Cheyne Row, *Chelsea*, SW3 (National Trust)
Portraits, letters, furniture, prints, manuscripts and small library of books belonging to Thomas Carlyle.

Chartered Insurance Institute's Museum, 20 Aldermanbury, *Cheapside*, EC2
Collection of insurance companies' fire marks, fire-fighting equipment, helmets, medals indicating part played by insurance companies in lessening dangers of fire.

The Church Farm House Museum, Greyhound Hill, *Hendon*, NW4 (London Borough of Barnet)
Local history, furnished rooms in period style.

Commonwealth Institute, Kensington High Street, *Kensington*, W8
National centre for spreading knowledge and understanding of the Commonwealth.

Courtauld Institute Galleries, Woburn Square, WC1
Galleries of University of London; including Lee collection, Gambier-Parry collection, important Courtauld collection of Impressionist and Post-Impressionist paintings, and Fry collection.

The Cricket Memorial Gallery, Lord's Ground, *St John's Wood*, NW8 (Marylebone Cricket Club)
Unique collection of pictures, *objets d'art*, trophies and bygones illustrating history of cricket (including the Ashes).

Cuming Museum, Walworth Road, *Southwark*, SE17 (London Borough of Southwark)
History of Southwark and district.

Dickens House, 48 Doughty Street, WC1
House occupied by Dickens and his family 1837–9. Relics displayed include manuscripts, furniture, autographs, portraits, letters and first editions.

Dulwich College Picture Gallery, College Road, *Dulwich*, SE21
Excellent examples of Rembrandt, Rubens, Claude, Poussin, Gainsborough, Watteau, Lancret, etc. Collection includes Spanish paintings and some small Dutch paintings.

Epping Forest Museum, Queen Elizabeth's Hunting Lodge, *Chingford*, E4 (Corporation of London – Conservators of Epping Forest)
Exhibits illustrative of animals, birds and plant life in Epping Forest and man's association therewith.

Federation of British Artists, The Mall Galleries, *The Mall*, SW1
Changing exhibitions.

Fenton House, Hampstead Grove, *Hampstead*, NW3 (National Trust)
Benton-Fletcher collection of early musical instruments and Binning collection of porcelain and furniture in William and Mary House.

Forty Hall Museum, Forty Hall, *Enfield* (London Borough of Enfield)
Built in 1629 by Sir Nicholas Baynton, Lord Mayor of London. 17th- and 18th-century furniture and pictures. Local history. Exhibitions.

Geffrye Museum, Kingsland Road, *Shoreditch*, E2 (Greater London Council, administered by the Inner London Education Authority)
Period rooms show development of middle-class English home from about 1600. Reference library of books and periodicals on decorative arts. Temporary exhibitions, art film shows.

Geological Museum, Exhibition Road, *South Kensington*, SW7
Illustrates earth history and general principles of geological science; regional geology of Great Britain and economic geology and mineralogy of world. Collection of gemstones. Special exhibits arranged at intervals.

*Goldsmiths' Hall, Foster Lane, *Cheapside*, EC2 (Worshipful Company of Goldsmiths)
Collection of antique plate, including some pieces with interesting historical associations. The largest collection of modern silver and jewellery in country.

Greenwich Borough Museum, 232 Plumstead High Street, *Greenwich*, SE18 (London Borough of Greenwich)
Prehistory, history and natural history relating to environment of Greenwich.

Guildhall Art Gallery, King Street, *Cheapside*, EC2 (Corporation of London)
Exhibitions, at intervals, of selections from permanent collection, Corporation sponsored exhibitions, loans cf master paintings, and work of art societies.

Gunnersbury Park Museum, Gunnersbury Park, *Ealing*, W3 (London Boroughs of Ealing and Hounslow)
Local archaeology, history, social history and topography, some transport items, in Rothschilds' early 19th-century mansion.

Ham House, Petersham, *Richmond* (National Trust administered by the Victoria and Albert Museum)
Built in 1610 and altered at various times in 17th century. Collection of late Stuart furniture.

Hayes and Harlington Museum, Gold Crescent, *Hayes* (Hayes and Harlington Local History Society and London Borough of Hillingdon)
Small museum of local history.

Hayward Gallery, Belvedere Road, *South Bank*, SE1 (Arts Council)
Temporary exhibitions of British and foreign art.

HMS 'Belfast', Symons Wharf, Vine Lane, *Southwark*, SE1
Largest cruiser ever constructed for Royal Navy. On exhibition as a museum.

Hogarth's House, Hogarth Lane, *Chiswick*, W4
Artist's country house for 15 years. Copies of Hogarth's paintings, impressions from engravings and relics.

Horniman Museum, London Road, *Forest Hill*, SE23 (Greater London Council, administered by the Inner London Education Authority)
Ethnographical museum dealing with study of man and his environment. Natural history collections and aquarium. Musical instruments from all parts of world. Extensive library. Education centre for schools and children's leisure activities.

Imperial War Museum, Lambeth Road, *Lambeth*, SE1
All aspects of two world wars and other operations involving Britain and the Commonwealth since 1914.

The Iveagh Bequest, Kenwood, *Hampstead*, NW3 (Greater London Council)
Works by Rembrandt, Vermeer, Van Dyck, Reynolds, Gainsborough etc.

The Jewish Museum, Woburn House, *Upper Woburn Place*, WC1 (Jewish Memorial Council)
Comprehensive collection of Jewish antiquities illustrating public and private worship of Jews.

John Evelyn Society's Museum, Village Club, Ridgway, *Wimbledon*, SW19
Watercolours, prints and photographs of Wimbledon's historic buildings and worthies.

Dr Johnson's House, 17 Gough Square, *Holborn*, EC4
Where he lived from 1748–59. Relics and small library.

Keats's House (Wentworth Place), Keats Grove, *Hampstead*, NW3 (Camden Borough Council)
Keats's Regency home where he spent the greater part of his 5 creative years. Relics and manuscripts.

Kingston-upon-Thames Museum and Art Gallery, Fairfield West, *Kingston-upon-Thames*
Local archaeology (especially Bronze Age and Anglo Saxon),

306

history and natural history. Also 'Zoopraxiscope' of Eadweard Muybridge. Art Gallery; circulating and local artists' exhibitions.

Leighton House Art Gallery and Museum, 12 Holland Park Road, *Holland Park*, W14 (Kensington and Chelsea Borough Council)
Designed by George Aitchison RA, in collaboration with Frederic, Lord Leighton, PRA. Contains Arab Hall with applied tiles from Rhodes, Damascus, Cairo and elsewhere. Exhibition of high Victorian art includes paintings, drawings and sculpture by Leighton, Burne-Jones, Alma-Tadema, Millais, Poynter, Stevens, Watts and other contemporaries and friends. Rooms in period decoration, also Victorian furniture. Includes loan collections from Tate Gallery, Victoria and Albert Museum and York Art Gallery.

Livesey Museum, 682 Old Kent Road, *Southwark*, SE15 (London Borough of Southwark)
Changing exhibitions of local interest.

London Dungeon, Tooley Street, SE1
Exhibitions depicting horror in British history.

London Transport Collection, Syon Park, *Brentford* (London Transport Executive)
Transport relics, buses, trains, trolleybuses, tramcars, horse-drawn vehicles, posters, signs and models.

Martinware Pottery Collection, Public Library, Osterley Park Road, *Southall* (London Borough of Ealing)
Collection of Martinware, including birds, face mugs, grotesques and other delightful pieces.

Museum of London, *London Wall*, EC2
Formed from collections of former London and Guildhall museums. New permanent exhibition illustrates social history of London, in chronological sequence, from prehistoric times to present day.

Museum of Mankind, 6 Burlington Gardens, *Piccadilly*, W1
Ethnology Department of the British Museum.

The Musical Museum, by the gasholder, Kew Bridge, *Chiswick*
Automatic pianos, organs, orchestrations and music boxes that all work.

National Army Museum, Royal Hospital Road, *Chelsea*, SW3
Paintings, uniforms, weapons, equipment, regimental and personal mementoes and colours illustrating history of British, Indian and Colonial forces from 1485 to 1914.

National Film Archive, 81 Dean Street, W1 (British Film Institute)
Collection of cinematograph films and recorded television programmes, both fiction and non-fiction, illustrating history of cinema and television as art and entertainment, and contemporary life and people, ethnography, transport, exploration, etc. Also a large collection of film stills and posters.

National Gallery, *Trafalgar Square*, WC2
Founded 1824 as National Collection of European Painting.

Representative collection of Italian, Dutch, Flemish, Spanish, German schools; French painting up to 1900; selection of British painters from Hogarth to Turner.

National Maritime Museum, Romney Road, *Greenwich*, SE10
Galleries here and in Old Royal Observatory in Greenwich Park show many aspects of maritime history in paintings and prints, ship models, relics of distinguished sailors and events, navigational instruments and charts, history of astronomy, medals, library with a reference section and information service, and manuscripts. New Neptune Hall with paddle tug. *Reliant*, boat-building shed, Barge House and collection of boats. Also east wing new galleries and Convoy Room. Planetarium.

National Monuments Record, Fortress House, 23 *Savile Row*, W1 (Royal Commission on Historical Monuments)
Includes National Buildings Record. Library of over 800,000 photographs, measured drawings of historic architecture of England.

National Museum of Labour History, Commercial Road, *Tower Hamlets*
Portrays development of democracy over last 200 years.

National Portrait Gallery, St Martin's Place, *Trafalgar Square*, WC2
Portraits of famous and infamous in British history, including paintings, sculpture, miniatures, engravings and photographs. Exhibition annexe at 15 Carlton House Terrace, SW1.

National Postal Museum, King Edward Building, King Edward Street, *Cheapside*, EC1
Reginald M. Phillips and Post Office collections of British postage stamps. UPU Collection of whole world since 1878. Philatelic archives of Thos De La Rue and Co, covering postage stamps of 200 countries 1855–1965.

Orleans House Gallery, Riverside, *Twickenham* (London Borough of Richmond-upon-Thames)
James Gibbs's baroque Octagon Room, 1720. Ionides collection of 18th- and 19th-century paintings, watercolours and engravings of Richmond and Twickenham. Some special exhibitions.

Passmore Edwards Museum, Romford Road, *Stratford*, E15 (London Borough of Newham)
Collection of Essex archaeology, local history, geology, and natural history.

Percival David Foundation of Chinese Art, 53 *Gordon Square*, WC1 (University of London School of Oriental and African Studies)
Chinese ceramics and library of Chinese and other books dealing with Chinese art and culture presented by Sir Percival David.

*****Pharmaceutical Society's Museum,** 17 Bloomsbury Square, *Bloomsbury*, WC1
Collection of crude drugs of vegetable and animal origin used in

17th century; early printed works, manuscripts and prints relating to pharmacy; English delft drug jars, leech jars, bell-metal mortars, medicine chests, dispensing apparatus, etc.

Priory Museum, *Orpington*
Small local museum in 13th–14th-century house with addition of 15th-century manor house.

Public Record Office and Museum, Chancery Lane, *Holborn*, WC2
National archives. Museum is rich in fascinating possessions. William the Conqueror's Domesday Book. Signatures of Kings and Queens of England, Shakespeare, Milton and Guy Fawkes; Wellington's despatch from Waterloo. Log of Nelson's *Victory* and several Churchill documents.

Ranger's House, Chesterfield Walk, *Blackheath*, SE10 (Greater London Council)
New gallery of English portraits from Elizabethan to Georgian period in 4th Earl of Chesterfield's house at Blackheath.

RIBA Heinz Gallery, RIBA Drawings Collection, 21 *Portman Square*, W1
Regular exhibitions of architectural drawings.

Royal Academy of Arts, *Piccadilly*, W1
Annual summer exhibition of painting, sculpture, architecture and engraving by living artists (May to July). Major loan exhibitions and other special exhibitions.

Royal Air Force Museum, Aerodrome Road, *Hendon*, NW9
National museum devoted solely to aviation and to telling story of a service, including its predecessors, from its start to present.

Royal Artillery Regimental Museum, Royal Military Academy, Academy Road, *Woolwich*

Royal College of Music, Prince Consort Road, *South Kensington*, SW7
Museum of historical musical instruments.

*Royal College of Surgeons' Museum, *Lincoln's Inn Fields*, WC2
Hunterian collection and other items of interest in medical history.

Royal Hospital Museum, Royal Hospital, Royal Hospital Road, *Chelsea*, SW3 (Commissioners Royal Hospital)
Pictures, plans and maps, medals and uniforms, connected with Royal Hospital.

Royal Mews, Buckingham Palace Road, *Victoria*, SW1 (Her Majesty the Queen)
Royal horses and equipages.

Royal Society of Painter-Etchers, 26 *Conduit Street*, W1
Contemporary print exhibition.

St Bride's Crypt Museum, St Bride's Church, *Fleet Street*, EC4 (Rector and Churchwardens of St Bride's Church)
Roman pavement and remains of 7 previous churches (dating from 6th century) on site can be seen together with permanent display of history of print, etc.

*St John's Gate, St John's Square, *Clerkenwell*, EC1
The headquarters of Most Venerable Order of St John of Jerusalem. Early 16th-century gatehouse containing silver, furniture, pictures and other treasures of the Knights of St John.

Science Museum, Exhibition Road, *South Kensington*, SW7 (Department of Education and Science)
Historical collection portraying the sciences of mathematics, physics and chemistry and their applications, and development of engineering, transport and communications, mining and industries generally from early times to present day.

Serpentine Gallery, South Carriageway, Kensington Gardens, *Kensington*, W2 (Arts Council)
Exhibitions of contemporary art.

Sir John Soane's Museum, 13 *Lincoln's Inn Fields*, WC2
Built by Sir John Soane, RA, in 1812–13 as his private residence and contains his collection of antiquities and works of art.

South London Art Gallery, Peckham Road, *Peckham*, SE5 (London Borough of Southwark)
Reference collection of original 20th-century prints. Changing exhibitions.

Tate Gallery, *Millbank*, SW1
National collections of British painting up to about 1900 and modern painting and sculpture, British and foreign, from Impressionism to present day. Special collections of Turner, Blake and the Pre-Raphaelites.

Thomas Coram Foundation for Children, 40 Brunswick Square, *Bloomsbury*, WC1
Pictures by Hogarth, Gainsborough, Reynolds, sculpture by Roubiliac and Rysbrack. Relics of Handel. Mementoes of Foundling Hospital.

Tudor Barn Art Gallery, Well Hall Pleasaunce, *Greenwich*, SE9 (London Borough of Greenwich)
Restored 16th-century building housing art gallery on first floor. Temporary exhibitions, mostly by local amateur societies.

*University College Department of Egyptology Museum, Gower Street, *Bloomsbury*, WC1
Contains collections of late Miss Amelia Edwards and of late Professor Sir Flanders Petrie.

Valence House Museum, Becontree Avenue, *Dagenham*, Essex (London Borough of Barking)
A 17th-century manor house still partly moated, devoted exclusively to local history, including Fanshawe portraits.

Victoria and Albert Museum, Cromwell Road, *South Kensington*, SW7 (Department of Education and Science)
Collections of fine and applied arts of all countries, periods and styles. The European collections are mostly of art from early Christian

times to the 19th century. Series of special rooms displays master-pieces from all periods.

Wallace Collection, Hertford House, *Manchester Square*, W1
Paintings of French, Spanish, Italian, Flemish, Dutch and British schools. Miniatures, sculpture, furniture, armour, goldsmiths' work, ceramics, and other works of art bequeathed to nation by late Lady Wallace in 1897.

Walthamstow Museum, Old Vestry House, Vestry Road, *Waltham-stow*, E1 (London Borough of Waltham Forest)
Early 18th-century workhouse containing local relics and objects of historical interest. Local archives.

Wellcome Institute for the History of Medicine, The Wellcome Building, *Euston Road*, NW1 (The Wellcome Trustees)
History of medicine and allied sciences from earliest times to the present century.

Wellington Museum (Apsley House), *Hyde Park Corner*, W1 (Victoria and Albert Museum)
Duke of Wellington's London home, containing many of his trophies, uniforms, decorations, batons and presentations made by grateful royalty; also fine paintings from Duke's collection.

Wesley's House and Museum, 47 *City Road*, EC1
House in which John Wesley lived and died. Contains collection of his personal possessions, etc.

Whitechapel Art Gallery, Whitechapel High Street, *Whitechapel*, E1
Exhibition gallery principally for modern and contemporary art. No permanent collection.

William Morris Gallery, Water House, Lloyd Park, Forest Road, *Walthamstow*, E17 (London Borough of Waltham Forest)
18th-century house, boyhood home of William Morris. Collections include textiles, wallpapers, designs, etc., by Morris, the Pre-Raphaelites and contemporaries. Frank Brangwyn collection of pictures and sculptures by 19th-century and other artists and by donor.

'Woodlands' Local History Centre and Art Gallery, 90 Mycenae Road, *Greenwich*, SE3 (London Borough of Greenwich)
Built in 1774 for John Julius Angerstein, founder of Lloyd's and patron of arts. Permanent collection of material relating to Green-wich. Temporary exhibitions.

MERSEYSIDE
CASTLES AND HISTORIC HOUSES
Speke Hall, *Liverpool* (National Trust, administered by Merseyside County Museums Department)
Richly half-timbered house, c. 1490–1612. Great hall. Elaborate plasterwork.

CATHEDRALS AND CHURCHES
Billinge (St Aidan)
1717. Clock turret. Unusual 'Gothick' tracery in rounded windows and Gothic flavour in transepts. Otherwise classic. Chandelier; glass.
Formby (St Peter)
1736. Bell turret. Gothic chancel and side chapel, 1873. Glass.
Liverpool (All Saints, Childwall)
Medieval with tower and spire of 1810. Hatchments; Royal Arms, 1664; monuments and brasses; 19th-century glass; pews with doors, 1853; ancient font.
Liverpool (Holy Trinity, Wavertree)
Hope, 1794. Classic with flat ceiling; marble wall tablets; glass.
Sefton (St Helen)
Late perpendicular with 14th-century spire. Fine early 16th-century carving. Notable Molyneux monuments.

GARDENS
Wirral Country Park, *Thurstaston*
Wirral Way and associated public footpaths. Visitor centre.

HISTORIC MONUMENTS
Birkenhead Priory, *Birkenhead*
Remains of Benedictine monastery, founded 1150. Site museum.

MUSEUMS AND GALLERIES
Atkinson Art Gallery, Lord Street, *Southport*
Paintings, watercolours and sculpture. Exhibitions of art.
Botanic Gardens Museum, Churchtown, *Southport* (Merseyside-Sefton Borough)
Local and natural history. Victorian period room.
Bootle Museum and Art Gallery, Oriel Road, *Bootle* (Sefton Metropolitan Borough)
Lancaster collection of English figure pottery and Bishop collection of Liverpool pottery. Art exhibitions changed monthly.
Hornby Library, William Brown Street, *Liverpool* (Merseyside County Council)
Prints, manuscripts, fine bindings, illustrated and rare books illustrating the art of the print, manuscript and book through ages.
Lady Lever Art Gallery, *Port Sunlight*
Paintings, watercolours, engravings and miniatures, mainly of the British school; antique, Renaissance and British sculpture; Chinese pottery and porcelain; Wedgwood wares; English furniture.
Merseyside County Museums, William Brown Street, *Liverpool* (Merseyside County Council)
Selection from Joseph Mayer collections. Rushworth and Dreaper collection of historic musical instruments. Land transport, natural history, shipping, history of King's Regiment. Also Planetarium.

Museum and Art Gallery, Gamble Institute, *St Helens* (St Helens Borough Council)
Local history and industries, clay pipe-making, glass containers. Natural history, geology, archaeology, Egyptology, ceramics. Pilkington collection of watercolours. Local society exhibitions.
Pilkington Glass Museum, Prescot Road, *St Helens* (Pilkington Brothers Limited)
Evolution of glass-making techniques.
Sudley Art Gallery, Mossley Hill Road, *Liverpool* (Merseyside County Council)
Emma Holt Bequest of 18th- and 19th-century paintings, mainly English.
Walker Art Gallery, William Brown Street, *Liverpool* (Merseyside County Council)
European paintings, famous for early Italian and Flemish pictures. Later Italians, Dutch and Germans and the English schools from Holbein onwards are well represented. Also paintings by Liverpool school, Pre-Raphaelites, late Victorian academic paintings, and 20th-century paintings and sculpture.
Williamson Art Gallery and Museum, Slatey Road, *Birkenhead* (Wirral Metropolitan Borough Council)
Art collection including comprehensive watercolour section. Applied arts include Della Robbia (Birkenhead) pottery and collection of Liverpool porcelain. Shipping gallery. Local exhibits. Art exhibitions.

NORFOLK
AREAS OF OUTSTANDING NATURAL BEAUTY
Norfolk Coast (part)

CASTLES AND HISTORIC HOUSES
Anna Sewell House, Church Plain, *Great Yarmouth*
17th-century Tudor-fronted building. Birthplace of authoress Anna Sewell.
Blickling Hall, *Aylsham* (National Trust)
Great Jacobean house, altered 1765–70. State rooms include Peter the Great Room with fine Russian tapestry. Long gallery with exceptional ceiling and state bedroom. The formal garden design dates from 1729. Temple and orangery, park and lake.
Felbrigg Hall, Nr *Cromer* (National Trust) ·
17th-century country house with Georgian interiors set in a fine wooded park. Important 18th-century library and orangery. Traditional walled garden. Woodland walk.
Holkham Hall, *Wells* (The Earl of Leicester, MVO, DL)
Fine Palladian mansion (1734). Pictures, tapestries, statuary, furnishings. Sir Charles Berry laid out formal garden.

313

Houghton Hall, *King's Lynn* (Marquess of Cholmondeley)
18th-century mansion built for Sir Robert Walpole. State rooms, pictures and china. Pleasure grounds.

Oxburgh Hall, *Swaffham* (National Trust)
Late 15th-century moated house. Outstanding gatehouse tower. Needlework by Mary Queen of Scots. French parterre laid out c. 1845.

Wolterton Hall, Nr *Norwich* (Lord and Lady Walpole)
Built by Horatio Walpole (1727–41). Tapestries, porcelain, furniture.

CATHEDRALS AND CHURCHES

Attleborough (St Mary)
Norman and late 14th century. Notable rood screen and frescoes above it.

Bale (All Saints)
Very fine 15th-century glass, also fragments of 14th-century glass.

Barton Turf (St Michael and All Angels)
Magnificent screen with paintings of Nine Orders of Angels.

Beeston-next-Mileham (St Mary)
14th-century. Fine tracery in nave and chancel windows. Perpendicular clerestory tower and spire. Hammer beam roof, fine parclose screens, benches, font cover, Hanoverian arms.

Binham (St Mary)
Fragment of Benedictine priory. Norman and early English arcading. Fine 13th-century west front and bellcote. Interior with Norman moulding, remains of screen, good stalls and bench-ends. 7-sacrament font.

Cawston (St Agnes)
Tower faced with freestone. Fine 15th-century angel roof. Painted screen, wall paintings, tower screen and gallery.

Cley-next-the-Sea (St Margaret)
Unusual 14th-century clerestory. Fine perpendicular south porch. Richly carved arcades. Some medieval glass. Brasses and fine ledger slabs.

East Hardling (St Peter and St Paul)
Mainly 14th century with 15th-century alterations. Fine medieval glass. 15th–17th-century monuments.

Erpingham (St Mary)
Notable tower. 16th-century Rhenish glass, military brass to Sir John de Erpingham, 1370.

Gooderstone (St George)
Norman west tower. Porch with trefoiled windows. Screen with painted panels. 14th-century glass.

Great Walsingham (St Peter)
Decorated. Fine window tracery. Some 14th-century glass, old benches with poppy-heads and carved backs.

Gunton (St Andrew)
Robert Adam, 1769. Classical interior in dark wood with much gilding.
Hales (St Margaret)
Norman with broad tower, apse and good doorways. Early 15th-century paintings. Remains of screen and Jacobean font cover.
King's Lynn (St Margaret)
Norman foundation with some Norman work at west end. Two great 14th-century Flemish brasses. Fine 14th-century screens; Georgian pulpit with sounding board; Snetzler organ; reredos by Bodley.
King's Lynn (St Nicholas)
Chapel of ease to St Margaret's. 1419 with fine early English tower. East window, south porch, angel roof, important monuments.
Knapton (St Peter and St Paul)
Magnificent angel roof.
North Runcton (All Saints)
1713. Classical. Tower and steeple. Painted reredos, candelabra, monuments.
Norwich (St Helen)
1249. Chancel with painted ceiling in honour of Anne of Bohemia, 1393. Vaulted ceiling of south transept, Georgian reredos.
Norwich (St Peter Mancroft)
15th century. Tall arches and fine hammer-beam roof. Medieval glass and glass by H. Hendrie, 1921. Perpendicular font canopy. Monuments and brasses. Reredos by Seddon and Comper.
Norwich Cathedral
Romanesque and late Gothic. Late 15th-century spire. Perpendicular lierne vaults in nave, transepts and presbytery. Splendid presbytery with apsidal east end.
Oxborough (St John the Evangelist)
Medieval glass, fine roof to chancel, piscina and sedilia. Bedingfeld chantry and tombs.
Ranworth (St Helen)
15th-century screen, best in Norfolk. Sarum Antiphoner, 14th-century illuminated manuscript of East Anglian workmanship.
Ringland (St Peter)
Very fine medieval glass, hammer-beam roof and vaulting over clerestory.
Salle (St Peter and St Paul)
15th century. Richly decorated west tower and porches. Fine roofs; medieval glass; base of screen with painting. Pulpit with 15th-century panels and Jacobean tester. Good stalls, misericords and bench-ends. Brasses and monuments. Perpendicular font cover, beam and pulley. 7-sacrament font.
Salthouse (St Nicholas)
Late 15th century. Perpendicular east windows, remains of screen, medieval glass.

Sandringham (St Mary Magdalene)
Home church of Royal family since 1861. Family monuments and glass.

Saxlingham Nethergate (St Mary the Virgin)
Perpendicular. Some of county's best glass.

Shelton (St Mary)
1480s. Perpendicular except for earlier tower. 15th-century glass; monument to Sir Robert Houghton, 1623; carved Royal Arms, William III. 18th-century commandment boards as reredos. Old brick floor.

Snettisham (St Mary)
Fine spire. West front with tripartite porch and 6-light decorated window. Good brasses.

South Creake (St Mary)
Decorated tower and chancel, perpendicular nave and aisles. Nave with hammer-beam roof, 7-sacrament font, fine perpendicular screen, some medieval glass.

Sparham (St Mary)
Mainly perpendicular with tall tower. Very fine panels of old screen.

Terrington (St Clement)
Perpendicular detached tower. West front with fire-light window and canopied niches. Chancel screen; Georgian panelling west of nave; painted 17th-century font cover; Jacobean commandment boards.

Tilney (All Saints)
12th-century arcades; 13th-century tower; 15th-century aisles and clerestory. Double hammer-beam roof and good screen of 1618. Arms of Queen Anne.

Trunch (St Botolph)
Screen with painted panels, 1502; medieval glass; Elizabethan monument; 15th-century roof; ringer's gallery with some original colour. Famous font canopy, 15th century, with fine carving and painting.

Walpole (St Peter)
Very fine exterior; processional way under east end, battlements, perpendicular windows, porches. Jacobean interior.

Walsoken (All Saints)
Late Norman and early English with much early decoration. Elaborate roof, 2 screens, carved stalls and few benches. Paintings over tower and chancel arches.

West Walton (St Mary)
Early English. Detached tower. Fine arcades and wall paintings.

Wiggenhall (St Germans)
Fine 15th-century bench-ends, 17th-century pulpit, table, clerk's desk and chair.

316

Wiggenhall (St Mary Magdalene)
Box pews, 17th-century panelling and remains of screen. Very fine 15th-century glass.
Wiggenhall (St Mary the Virgin)
Fine 15th-century carved benches. Remains of screen and brass lectern, 1518. Alabaster monuments, 1625.
Worstead (St Mary)
14th century, with 2 side chapels and contemporary screens. Box pews, ringing gallery, font cover, tower screen, 1501. Brasses, remains of wall paintings.
Wymondham (St Mary and St Thomas of Canterbury)
Much Norman work, including arcades and triforium windows, 15th-century clerestory and roof. Fragments of 13th-century font and whole 15th-century font. Terracotta Ferrers monument, 1525, Comper reredos, famous Corporas Case, rare example of 13th-century Opus Anglicanum.

GARDENS
Fritton Lake and Gardens, Nr *Great Yarmouth* (Lord and Lady Somerleyton)
2-mile-long lake. Spring bulbs, herbaceous borders, and ornamental trees.
Sandringham Grounds, *Sandringham* (Her Majesty the Queen)
Grounds and museum only open.
Wildfowl Trust Welney Refuge, Nr. *Downham Market*
Wildfowl refuge on Ouse Washes. Observatory. Floodlit lagoon.

HISTORIC MONUMENTS
Baconsthorpe Castle, Nr *Holt*
Late 15th-century moated semi-fortified house. Gatehouse and remains of curtain walls.
Binham Priory and Cross, *Binham*
Ruins of 12th-century Benedictine foundation.
Caister Castle, *Great Yarmouth*
Ruins of moated castle, c. 1432. Motor museum.
Carmelite Friary, *Burnham Market*
Gatehouse and remains of friary, founded in 1241.
The Castle, *Burgh Castle*
Walls from former 3rd-century Saxon fort.
Castle Acre Priory and Castle Gate, Nr *Swaffham*
Remains of 11th-century priory, including 12th-century church. Earthworks of former castle, slight remains of keep and 13th-century bailey gate from fortified borough.
Castle Rising, *Castle Rising*
Fine Norman keep and earthworks.

Creake Abbey, *North Creake*
Ruins of crossing and eastern arm of church of house of Augustinian canons, founded in 1206.
Greyfriars, *Great Yarmouth*
West cloister walk survives.
Grime's Graves, *Weeting*
Neolithic flint mines. One of hundreds of shafts dug in chalk can be inspected.
Kent Village, *Cockley Cley*
Full-scale site reconstruction of Kent encampment. Museums.
Roman Town, *Caister-on-Sea*
Remains of gate and wall.
Saxon Cathedral, *North Elmham*
Remains of walk, c. 1020–50.
Thetford Castle, *Thetford*
Motte and bailey castle.
Thetford Priory, *Thetford*
Remains of Cluniac monastery founded early 12th century.
Walsingham Abbey, *Walsingham*
Ruins of Augustinian priory, gatehouse and number of wells.
Warren Lodge, *Thetford*
Remains of hunting lodge in 15th century. Flint with stone dressings.
Weeting Castle, Nr *Brandon*
Ruined 11th-century fortified manor house.

MUSEUMS AND GALLERIES

Ancient House Museum, White Hart Street, *Thetford* (Norfolk Museums Service)
15th-century timbered house with collections illustrating Thetford and Breckland life, history and natural history.
Bishop Bonner's Cottages, *Dereham*
Row of restored cottages, with coloured East Anglian pargetting (1502), now museum with archaeological discoveries and exhibitions of rural crafts.
Bridewell Museum of Local Industries and Rural Crafts, Bridewell Alley, *Norwich* (Norfolk Museums Service)
Industries and rural crafts of Norwich, Norfolk and North Suffolk.
Duleep Singh Collection, The Guildhall, *Thetford* (Thetford Town Council)
Norfolk and Suffolk portraits.
Elizabethan House Museum, South Quay, *Great Yarmouth*
Merchant's house displaying Victorian domestic life.
Exhibition Galleries, Central Library, *Great Yarmouth*
Travelling and local art exhibitions.

Lynn Museum, on Bus Station, *King's Lynn* (Norfolk Museum Service)
Natural history, archaeology, local history, folk history relating to north-west Norfolk.
Maritine Museum for East Anglia (Norfolk Museums Service)
Maritime history of East Anglia including herring fishery, the Wherry, life-saving and oil and gas industry.
Museum of Social History, 27 King Street, *King's Lynn*
Domestic life and dress, toys, dolls, notable local glass collection.
Norfolk Rural Life Museum, Beech House, *Gressenhall*
County history over past 200 years emphasizing agriculture.
Norwich Castle Museum, *Norwich* (Norfolk Museums Service)
Collections of art (particularly of the Norwich school), local archaeology and natural history (Norfolk room dioramas) and social history. Loan exhibitions.
Old Merchant's House, Row 117, *Great Yarmouth* (Department of the Environment)
Domestic ironwork from 17th to 19th century in early 17th-century house.
Royal Norfolk Regiment Museum, Britannia Barracks, *Norwich*
Regimental collection from 1685–1959
St Peter Hungate Church Museum, Princes Street, *Norwich* (Norfolk Museums Service)
15th-century church used for display of ecclesiastical art and East Anglian antiquities.
Shirehall Museum, *Walsingham* (Norfolk Museums Service)
18th-century court room with original fittings and items illustrating life of Walsingham.
Stranger's Hall, Charing Cross, *Norwich* (Norfolk Museums Service)
Late medieval mansion furnished as museum of urban domestic life 16th-19th centuries.
Tolhouse, Tolhouse Street, *Great Yarmouth*
Medieval building housing local history museum.

NORTHAMPTONSHIRE
CASTLES AND HISTORIC HOUSES
Althorp, *Northampton* (The Earl Spencer)
Dates from 16th century, with alterations 1670, 1790 and 1877. Splendid interior containing pictures of many European schools: historic portraits; porcelain, Oriental and European, and 18th-century furniture.
Aynhoe Park, *Aynhoe* (Mutual Households Association Limited)
17th-century mansion. Alterations by Soane.
Boughton House, *Kettering* (Buccleuch Estates)
15th-century monastery added to, 1530–1695. Early French and English furniture, tapestries, carpets, porcelain. Parkland with lakes.

Burghley House, Stamford (The Marquess of Exeter, KCMG, LLD)
Finest example of later Elizabethan architecture. State apartments, pictures, furniture, silver fireplaces, painted ceilings, tapestries.

Castle Ashby, *Northampton* (The Earl of Compton)
Elizabethan with Inigo Jones (1635) front. 17th-century ceilings, staircases and panelling. Pictures, garden.

*Cotterstock Hall, Nr *Peterborough* (Mr and Mrs Lewis F. Sturge)
17th-century grey stone manor house having associations with the poet Dryden. Herbaceous borders, yews and shrubs.

Deene Park, Nr *Corby* (Edmund Brudenell, Esq)
Home of the Brudenells since 1514. House of great architectural importance and historical interest. Large lake and well-wooded park. Long border. Rare trees and shrubs.

Delapre Abbey, Nr *Northampton* (Northamptonshire County Council)
House rebuilt or added to 16th–19th centuries. Converted for use as offices and storerooms.

Hinwick House, Nr *Wellingborough* (Capt. R. A. B. Orlebar)
Queen Anne house. Pictures by Van Dyck, Lely, Kneller, etc. Tapestries and needlework. Furniture.

Lamport Hall, *Northampton* (Sir Gyles Isham, Bt)
Home of Isham family since 1560. Present house dates mainly from 17th and 18th centuries.

*Priest's House, *Easton-on-the-Hill* (National Trust)
Pre-Reformation priest's house.

Rockingham Castle, Nr *Corby* (Cdr Michael Watson)
Royal castle till 1530, since then home of Watson family. Spans 900 years of English life and culture set amid lovely gardens and fine views.

Southwick Hall, Nr *Oundle* (G. C. Capron, Esq)
Manor house, retaining medieval building, dating from 1300, with Tudor rebuilding and 18th-century additions. Exhibition of Victorian dresses, etc.

Stoke Park Pavilions, *Towcester* (R. D. Chancellor, Esq)
Two pavilions and colonnade. Built 1630 by Inigo Jones.

Sulgrave Manor, *Banbury* (Sulgrave Manor Board)
Early English home of ancestors of George Washington. Good example of a small manor house and garden of Shakespeare's time.

CATHEDRALS AND CHURCHES
Brixworth (All Saints)
Early Saxon, mainly late 7th century. Roman tiles used for abaci and arches.

Earls Barton (All Saints)
Saxon tower with fine surface decoration. Good Norman entrance door; 15th-century screen, mid-17th-century tower clock.

Finedon (St Mary)
Curious relieving arch across nave in front of chancel. 18th-century theological library, rich organ case by Shrider.

Fotheringhay (St Mary and All Saints)
Fragments of great 15th-century collegiate church. 18th-century fittings include reredos with decalogue, creed etc., pulpit, gift from Edward IV, perpendicular font.

Higham Ferrers (St Mary)
Steeple with flying buttresses and early English mouldings. 13th-century west tower with finely carved doorway. 13th- and 14th-century interior. Good carved woodwork.

Kettering (St Peter and St Paul)
Fine steeple.

King's Sutton (St Peter)
Famous spire, richly ornamented. Interesting 19th-century work in chancel and screen by Scott.

Lowick (St Peter)
15th-century pinnacled lantern tower. Fragments of 14th-century glass, 14th-century effigies. Westmacott sculpture commemorating 5th Duke of Dorset, 1843.

Middleton Cheney (All Saints)
Decorated with perpendicular spire. 15th-century painted ceiling and pulpit. Restored, 1865. Pre-Raphaelite glass.

Northampton (All Saints)
Rebuilt, 1675. Domed classical interior.

Northampton (Holy Sepulchre)
One of 5 surviving round churches in England. Dates from 12th century. Clerestory rebuilt in 15th century. Chancel and all outer walls except round part and south aisle are 19th century.

Oundle (St Peter)
Fine steeple. Interior spoilt by scraping and repainting masonry.

Passenham (St Guthlac)
Decorated. 17th-century woodcarving of stalls and paintings above them. Jacobean pulpit and west gallery. Box pews.

Rushden (St Mary)
Sister church to Finedon with similar relieving arch across nave.

Stanford-on-Avon (St Nicholas)
17th-century organ case, expelled from Whitehall by Cromwell. Monuments, 14th–16th-century stained glass, linenfold panelling, Jacobean embroidery.

Titchmarsh (St Mary the Virgin)
Noble perpendicular tower. 17th-century Pickering family pew.

Warmington (St Mary)
Early English fine broach spire. Ribbed-vaulted nave. Good 14th-century woodwork and Jacobean screen.

Wellingborough (St Mary)
1908. Comper's blend of Gothic and Classic with sumptuous fittings.
Whiston (St Mary the Virgin)
Early 16th-century tower. Fittings include some original benches and classical monuments by Nollekens.

GARDENS
Coton Manor Wildlife Garden, Nr *Northampton* (Cdr and Mrs H. Pasley-Tyler)
Old English garden. Wildlife.
Guilsborough Grange Bird and Pet Park, *Guilsborough* (Major and Mrs S. J. Symington)
Birds and wildlife in country house and garden setting in beautiful natural surroundings with fine views.

HISTORIC MONUMENTS
Chichele College, *Higham Ferrers*
Remains of college of 1422 established by founders of All Souls College, Oxford.
Kirby Hall, *Gretton*
Fine half-ruined mansion, 1570–1640, with skeletal garden layout of 1686.

MUSEUMS AND GALLERIES
Abington Museum, Abington Park, *Northampton* (Northampton Borough Council)
15th-century manor house, rebuilt in part in 1745. Period rooms, folk material, Chinese ceramics. Ethnographic and natural history material.
Alfred East Art Gallery, Sheep Street, *Kettering*
Permanent collection including oils, watercolours and etchings by Sir Alfred East, RA. Loan exhibitions.
Central Museum and Art Gallery, Guildhall Road, *Northampton* (Northampton Borough Council)
Collections of footwear through the ages; cobbler's shop. Local archaeology and English ceramics. Old master and modern oil and watercolour paintings.
Waterways Museum, *Stoke Bruerne*
Former corn mill. Items recording 2 centuries of canal history.
Westfield Museum, West Street, *Kettering*
Archaeological and social history material from area. Collections of footwear, shoe-making tools and machinery. Geology of North Northamptonshire.

NORTHUMBERLAND
AREAS OF OUTSTANDING NATURAL BEAUTY
Northumberland Coast

CASTLES AND HISTORIC HOUSES

Alnwick Castle, *Alnwick* (His Grace the Duke of Northumberland, KG)
Important example of medieval fortification restored by Salvin, dating to 12th century.

Bamburgh Castle, *Bamburgh* (Lord Armstrong)
Fine 12th-century Norman keep. Remainder of castle considerably restored.

Callaly Castle, *Whittingham* (Major A. S. C. Browne, DL)
17th-century mansion incorporating 13th-century Pele tower with Georgian and Victorian additions.

Lindisfarne Castle, *Holy Island* (National Trust)
Built about 1550. Made habitable by Lutyens.

Seaton Delaval Hall, Nr *Newcastle-upon-Tyne* (Lord Hastings)
Masterpiece of Sir John Vanbrugh.

Wallington Hall, *Cambo* (National Trust)
Built 1688, altered 18th century. Central hall added in 19th century and decorated by Ruskin and others.

CATHEDRALS AND CHURCHES

Alnwick (St Michael and All Angels)
15th century. 14th-century effigies, 15th-century fragments of glass, Hanoverian Arms.

Hexham (St Andrew)
Foundations of Wilfrid's 7th-century church. Roman dressed stones. Unique survival of night staircase. Pre-Conquest Frith stool. 15th-century wooden pulpit. Painted screen, 1491–1524. Effigies. Royal Arms, George I.

Norham (St Cuthburt)
Norman chancel arch and south arcade. 14th-century effigy. Stuart Royal Arms, carved unpainted.

Morpeth (St Mary the Virgin)
14th century. Note medieval glass in east window.

GARDENS

Chillingham Wild Cattle, *Chillingham*
Park containing herd of wild white cattle.

Howick Gardens, *Alnwick* (Lord Howick of Glendale)
Flower, shrub and rhododendron gardens.

HISTORIC MONUMENTS

Brinkburn Priory, *Brinkburn*
Remains of 13th-century Augustinian priory. Church complete.

Castle and Town Walls, *Berwick-upon-Tweed*
Remains of 12th-century stronghold. Medieval town walls reconstructed in Elizabethan period.

323

Dunstanburgh Castle, Nr *Alnwick*
Remains of 14th-century stronghold.
Hadrian's Wall: Housesteads Museum and Fort, *Housesteads*
3½ miles of wall itself, several castles. Housesteads, best preserved of forts. Site museum.
Lindisfarne Priory, *Holy Island*
Ruins of priory church of 12th century. Site museum.
Mithraic Temple, *Carrawbrough*
Remains of Mithraic temple dating from 3rd century, on line of Roman wall near fort of 'Brocolitia'.
Norham Castle, *Norham*
Ruins of much besieged castle dating from 12th century.
Prudhoe Castle, *Prudhoe*
12th–14th-century stronghold. Keep in inner bailey and notable gatehouse.
Roman Fort, *Chesters*
Fort with extensive remains of bath house.
Roman Station, *Corbridge*
Remains of Roman 'Corstopitum', c. AD 210. Site museum.
Vindolanda, Nr *Barton Mill*
Remains of 3rd–4th-century Roman fort and frontier town.
Warkworth Castle, *Warkworth*
11th–14th century with great keep and gatehouse.
Warkworth Hermitage, *Warkworth*
14th-century hermitage with small chapel cut in solid rock.

MUSEUMS AND GALLERIES
Berwick-on-Tweed Museum and Art Gallery, Marygate, *Berwick-upon-Tweed* (Borough of Berwick-upon-Tweed)
Museum: general collection including ceramics and brassware. Special exhibition of local antiquities.
Art Gallery: artists include Degas, Daubigny, Boudin and Opie.
Clayton Collection, Hadrian's Wall, Nr *Chollerford,* Chesters (Department of the Environment)
Roman inscriptions, sculpture, weapons, tools and ornaments from the forts at Chesters, Carrawburgh, Housesteads, Greatchesters and Carvoran.
Corbridge Roman Station, *Corbridge* (Department of the Environment)
Roman pottery, sculpture, inscribed stones, and small objects.
Grace Darling Museum, *Bamburgh* (Royal National Lifeboat Institution)
Grace Darling relics.
Museum of King's Own Scottish Borderers, The Barracks, Roversdown, *Berwick-upon-Tweed*
Designed by Vanbrugh, 1717.

NORTH YORKSHIRE
AREAS OF OUTSTANDING NATURAL BEAUTY
Forest of Bowland (part)

CASTLES AND HISTORIC HOUSES
Bedale Hall, *Bedale* (Hambleton District Council)
Georgian mansion with fine ballroom wing and museum room.
Domestic and craft exhibits.
Beningbrough Hall, Nr *Shipton* (National Trust)
Early 18th-century house, possibly by Thomas Archer. Fine hall,
staircase, friezes and panelling.
***Braithwaite Hall,** Nr *Middleham* (National Trust)
17th-century hall, now a working farmhouse.
Brandsby Hall, *York* (Mr and Mrs G. Little)
Built 1743. Cortese ceilings. Stable block by John Carr.
***Broughton Hall,** *Skipton* (H. R. Tempest, Esq)
Georgian front. Built 1598 and altered in 1810 and 1840. Private
Chapel. Extensive grounds with Italian garden by W. A. Nesfield.
Carlton Towers, *Carlton* (Duke of Norfolk)
Dates from 1614, remodelled in 18th–19th century. State rooms by
John Francis Bentley, architect of Westminster Cathedral. Paintings,
furniture, silver.
Castle Howard, *York* (George Howard, Esq)
Designed by Vanbrugh 1699–1726 for the 3rd Earl of Carlisle,
assisted by Hawksmoor, who designed mausoleum. Fine collection
of pictures, statuary and furniture. Beautiful park and grounds.
Costume Galleries covering 18th to 20th centuries. Displays changed
every year.
Ebberston Manor, *Ebberston* (Mr and Mrs de Wend-Fenton)
Small Palladian-style house designed by Colin Campbell, 1718.
Gilling Castle, *Helmsley* (Ampleforth Abbey Trustees)
Original Norman keep with 16th- and 18th-century additions.
Markenfield Hall, *Ripon* (The Lord Grantley, MC)
Fine example of English manor house. 14th-, 15th- and 16th-century
buildings surrounded by moat.
***Moulton Hall,** Nr *Richmond* (National Trust)
Built about 1650 with fine carved wood staircase.
Newburgh Priory, *Coxwold* (Capt. V. M. Wombwell)
Originally 12th-century Augustinian priory with 16th-, 17th- and
18th-century alterations and additions. Wild water garden and
collection of rock plants. Walled garden.

325

Newby Hall, *Ripon* (R. E. J. Compton)
Famous Adam house, tapestries and fine collection of sculpture. 25 acres of gardens.
Norton Conyers, *Ripon* (Sir R. Graham, Bt)
Jacobean house and walled garden.
Nunnington Hall, *Ryedale* (National Trust)
Large manor house, mainly of late 17th century.
*Old Rectory – Foston, *Thornton-le-Clay* (Major R. F. Wormald)
Designed and built by Sydney Smith, 1813–14. Pink brick, largely in Flemish Bond. Walled garden, roses.
Parcevall Hall, Nr *Burnsall*
Elizabethan house, now conference centre.
Ripley Castle, *Ripley* (Sir Thomas Ingilby, Bt)
Home of the Ingilby family since early 14th century. Main gateway dates from reign of Edward IV. Extensive gardens.
Shandy Hall, *Coxwold* (Laurence Sterne Trust)
Unusual medieval house. Altered in 17th and 18th centuries.
Sutton Park, *Sutton-on-the-Forest* (Major E. C. R. Sheffield, DL, TD, JP and Mrs Sheffield)
Early 18th-century house. Landscaped by Capability Brown. 18th-century furniture, pictures and porcelain. Terraced gardens, herbaceous borders and woodland walks.
Treasurer's House, *York* (National Trust)
Large 17th-century house. Fine furniture and paintings.

CATHEDRALS AND CHURCHES

Alne (St Mary)
Notable medieval and Renaissance tower. Good Norman work, Jacobean pulpit. 19th-century tiles and Kempe glass.
Bolton Percy (All Saints)
1424. Original glass in east window, fine sedilia and piscina, gabled cross with Crucifixion and Mother and Child. 15th-century roofs, base of rood screen and return stalls, nave pews, 1631. Jacobean font cover and reader's desk. Georgian pulpit, 1715; 17th–19th century monuments.
Brayton (St Wilfrid)
Notable Norman tower with perpendicular spire and lantern. Norman south door and chancel arch. Decorated chancel with Darcy monument, 1558; ledger stones.
Coxwold (St Michael)
15th-century exterior with chancel rebuilt in 1777. 17th- and 18th-century interior, west gallery, plasterwork, box pews, pulpit and monuments. Fauconberg tombs. Much fragmentary 15th-century glass.
Croft (St Peter)
14th-century chancel with good buttresses and tracery. Piece of

Romano–British sculpture built into south wall. Elevated pew. 14th-century piscina and sedilia, monument of Sir Richard Clervaulx, Milbanke tomb.

Danby-in-Cleveland (St Hilda)
Detached 15th-century tower. Nave classicized, then medievalized, 1903. 18th-century gallery. Royal Arms of George IV, 17th- and 18th-century monuments.

Easby (St Agatha)
Norman font; 19th-century nave, roof and pews; hatchments; wall paintings; glass of east window.

Lastingham (St Mary)
Mainly 11th-century monastic, 18th-century Calvary. Abbot Stephen's crypt. Interior crowned with ribless groined vaults in stone by J. L. Pearson, 1879.

Nun Monkton (St Mary)
Late 12th–early 13th-century nave of Benedictine nunnery. Front with good Transitional door and niches with fragmentary sculpture. Internal walls with lancets separated by tall, open arcading. Superb stained glass by Morris.

Old Malton (St Mary)
Fragment of Gilbertine priory church. Early Gothic revival head-stones. Impressive west front. Tester at east end, stalls and organ case by Temple Moore, 1887–8. 19th-century font. Good 11th-century work at base of south-west tower and in triforium.

Pickering (St Peter and St Paul)
12th-14th century but suffers from 19th-century restoration. Originally 15th-century wall paintings, 20th-century Jacobean-type screen to tower arch, font cover by G. G. Pace, 18th-century brass chandeliers and pulpit, 20th-century chancel screen, banner in Bruce chapel.

Ripon Cathedral
Small cathedral in mix of architectural styles including Saxon. Notable west front, east end and gabled buttresses flanking nave. Sedilia, rich decorated choir stalls, 1490, fine though much restored.

Scarborough (St Mary)
12th–13th-century piers, arcades, clerestory and nave wall shafts. Ribbed barrel vaults to chapels. Monuments, 17th–19th-century tombs.

Selby (St Mary and St Germaine)
Monastic church. Nave, Norman to Transitional. Unusual triforium. Early English clerestory, excellent west door and north porch. Decorated choir with restored original glass in east windows. Perpendicular font cover. Monuments.

Stainburn (St Mary the Virgin)
Norman. 17th-century pews, pulpit and south window. Norman font.

Thirsk (St Mary the Virgin)
Perpendicular exterior. Font cover partly 15th century. Some medieval glass, traces of 17th-century paintings, magnificent altar table.

Wensley (Holy Trinity)
Early benches and box pews, 15th-century screen with Jacobean extras and great banner and hangings forming Bolton family pew. Oval frame hanging within chancel arch and charged with coats of arms. Font and cover, 1662; wall paintings; incised slab in north aisle wall; Jacobean pulpit; 13th-century sedilia; 17th-century altar and rails; 15th-century stall ends; Flemish brass, 1395.

Whitby (St Mary)
12th-century tower and south doorway. Interior remodelling in 18th century, box pews and galleries, high pulpit and reading desk. 12th-century chancel. Screen at entrance to chancel with Corinthian columns. Chippendale–Gothic table tombs.

York (All Saints, North Street)
15th-century roofs in chancel and south aisle. Outstanding medieval painting and glass, many incised stones, 18th-century pulpit.

York (Holy Trinity, Goodramgate)
2-deck pulpit, 1785. 18th-century font and cover, altar-piece, 1721, with Holy Table covered by 18th-century frontal. Much 15th-century stained glass. Fine west window.

York Cathedral
Rich west front. Lancet style in 'Five Sisters' of north front. Late 15th-century pulpitum. Medieval stained glass. Octagonal chapter house roof with fine naturalistic carvings.

GARDENS

Duncombe Park, *Helmsley* (Trustees of Duncombe Park)
Two 18th-century temples. Formal gardens.

Rievaulx Terrace, Nr *Helmsley* (National Trust)
Two 18th-century temples. Grass terrace with views of abbey.

Rudding Park Gardens, *Harrogate* (Mackaness Organisation)
Rose garden, rhododendron walks, parkland and woods.

HISTORIC MONUMENTS

Bylands Abbey, Nr *Kilburn*
12th–13th-century remains of church and monastic building.

Devil's Arrows, *Boroughbridge*
Three Bronze Age monoliths.

Easby Abbey, Nr *Richmond*
Premonstratensian abbey, founded 1155. Considerable remains of monastic buildings.

Fountain's Abbey, *Ripon*
Ruined Cistercian abbey in ornamental gardens laid out by John Aislabie, 1720.

Helmsley Castle, *Helmsley*
Ruined 12th–13th-century stronghold with domestic buildings added in 14th century.

Jervaulx Abbey, Nr *Helmsley*
Ruins of 11th-century Cistercian monastery in gardens.

Kirkham Priory, Nr *Norton*
Fine sculptured 13th-century gatehouse.

Knaresborough Castle, *Knaresborough*
Remains of 14th-century stronghold including keep, 2 baileys and gatehouse.

Middleham Castle, *Middleham*
Keep standing within 13th-century curtain wall.

Mount Grace Priory, Nr *Northallerton*
Ruined 14th-century Carthusian priory.

Pickering Castle, *Pickering*
12th-century keep on mound between 2 baileys.

Richmond Castle, *Richmond*
Dates from 11th and 12th century. Keep and curtain wall.

Rievaulx Abbey, Nr *Harome*
Extensive well-preserved monastic buildings dating from 1132.

Roman Town, *Aldborough*
Portion of boundary walls, 2 tessellated pavements.

Scarborough Castle, *Scarborough*
12th-century castle damaged in Civil War and First World War.

Spofforth Castle, *Spofforth*
Remains of 14th-century fortified manor house.

Stanwick Oppidum, *Stanwick*
Short length of defences of Brigantian capital of 1st century AD.

Wheeldale Moor Roman Road, Nr *Cawthorn*
Almost a mile of road of 1st century AD near Roman camps at Cawthorn.

Whitby Abbey, *Whitby*
Remains of fine church dating from 13th century.

York Castle, *York*
13th-century keep on 11th-century motte.

MUSEUMS AND GALLERIES

Aldborough Roman Museum, Boroughbridge, *Aldborough* (Department of the Environment)
Roman finds, including pottery, glass, metalwork and coins, from Roman town.

Ark Museum, *Tadcaster* (Mrs Brewster)
Restored old timbered house. Museum of pubs and brewing.

Art Gallery, Library Buildings, Victoria Avenue, *Harrogate*
Oils and watercolours. Temporary exhibitions

Beck Island Museum of Rural Life, *Pickering*
Georgian house containing local folk museum.

Borthwick Institute of Historical Research, St Anthony's Hill, *York*
(York University)
Originally late 15th-century guildhall. Collection of ecclesiastical
archives.

Captain Cook School-room Museum, *Great Ayton*
Exhibits relating to explorer. Maps, books, pictures, etc.

City of York Art Gallery, Exhibition Square, *York* (York District
Council)
Old master, modern English and European paintings; ceramics,
topographical watercolours and prints.

Craven Museum, Town Hall, High Street, *Skipton*
Craven antiquities, social history, geological specimens.

Crescent Art Gallery, The Crescent, *Scarborough* (Scarborough
Corporation)
Local artists. Laughton collection (English school). Frequent loan
exhibitions.

George Leatt Industrial and Folk Museum, Corn Mill, *Skipton*
Old mill containing 2 watermills. 1912 turbine and 1884 winnower.

Green Howards Museum, Trinity Church Square, *Richmond*
Uniforms, medals, campaign relics, contemporary manuscripts,
pictures and prints, head-dresses, buttons, badges and embellishments from 17th century onwards.

Londesborough Lodge, *Scarborough*
Scarborough history.

Lotherton Hall, Nr *Aberford* (City of Leeds)
Built round early 18th-century house with 1896–1903 extensions.
Country museum with furniture, pictures, silver, ceramics; gas
engine collection and works of art from Leeds collection. Gallery of
oriental art.

Museum of Horse Drawn Transport, *Aysgarth*
Old corn mill housing 60 horse-drawn vehicles.

National Railway Museum, Leeman Road, *York* (Department of
Education and Science)
History and development of British railway engineering including
the social and economic aspects.

Roman Malton Museum, Milton Rooms, Market Place, *Malton*
Romano–British collections from Malton District and the Roman
Derventio Fortress. Also prehistoric and medieval material.

Rotunda Museum, Vernon Road, *Scarborough* (Scarborough
Corporation)
Archaeological collections of all periods represented in north-east
Yorkshire. Scarborough bygones.

Royal Pump Room Museum, opp. Valley Gardens, *Harrogate*
Original sulphur well of the Victorian spa. Costume, pottery, local
history and prehistory.
Ryedale Fold Museum, *Hutton-le-hole* (Crossland Foundation)
Prehistoric and Roman antiquities; tools of many 19th-century crafts.
Furniture and domestic equipment covering 300 years of history.
Blacksmith's shop, wagon park, unique Elizabethan glass furnace,
16th-century manor house and medieval longhouse.
St Mary's Heritage Centre, Castle Gate, *York* (York City Council)
Interprets city's social and archaeological heritage.
Wakeman's House Museum, Market Place, *Ripon* (Ripon Corpora-
tion)
Small folk museum.
Whitby Art Gallery, Pannett Park, *Whitby* (Whitby Urban District
Council)
Early and contemporary English watercolours and oil paintings.
Whitby Museum of Whitby Literary and Philosophical Society,
Whitby
Fossils, relics of prehistoric man and of Roman occupation. Local
history and bygones. Shipping gallery. Captain Cook relics. Natural
history.
Woodend Museum, The Crescent, *Scarborough* (Scarborough
Corporation)
Formerly home of Sitwell family. Paintings and first editions of this
famous literary family. British and foreign natural history. York-
shire geological material and an aquarium.
York Castle Museum, Tower Street, *York* (York City Council)
Folk museum of Yorkshire life based on the Kirk collection of
bygones and including period rooms, cobbled street, domestic and
agricultural equipment, early crafts, costumes, toys. Yorkshire
militaria, an Edwardian street and a water-driven corn mill.
The Yorkshire Museum, Museum Gardens, *York* (North Yorkshire
County Council)
Natural history, archaeological galleries, geology, pottery and coins
and the Medieval Architectural Museum. Gardens contain Roman
and medieval ruins and Hospitium housing large Roman collection.

NATIONAL PARKS
North Yorkshire Moors (part)
Yorkshire Dales (part)

NOTTINGHAMSHIRE
CASTLES AND HISTORIC HOUSES
Holme Pierrepont Hall, Nr *Nottingham* (Mr and Mrs R. Brackenbury)
Medieval brick manor house. Formal 19th-century courtyard
garden. Oak furniture.

Newstead Abbey, *Linby* (Nottingham City Council)
Part of original priory survives, bought by Sir John Byron, 1540, and converted to house. Byron relics, pictures, furniture.
Thoresby Hall, *Ollerton* (Countess Manvers)
Built by Salvin, 1864. State apartments. Great hall. Frank Bradley exhibition of toy and model theatres.
Thrumpton Hall, *Nottingham* (George FitzRoy Seymour, Esq)
Jacobean. Magnificent carved staircase. Fine pictures and furniture.

CATHEDRALS AND CHURCHES

Blyth (St Mary and St Martin)
Priory fragment with late 11th-century nave. Fine altar with medieval screen as reredos, medieval paintings.
East Markham (St John the Baptist)
Perpendicular. Comper east window. Baseless Jacobean pulpit, altar mensa.
Egmanton (St Mary)
Magnificent interior by Comper, canopied rood screen. Norman doorway and font, 17th-century altar, fragments of old glass.
Hawton (All Saints)
15th-century tower with fine carved and inscribed door. Chancel with curvilinear east window and 14th-century stonework. Easter sepulchre is best in England.
Newark (St Mary Magdalene)
15th century. Gilded reredos by Comper, 1907, 2 painted panels of 'Dance of Death'. Medieval glass.
Nottingham (St Mary)
Perpendicular. Bronze doors by Wilson, 1904. Good Victorian furnishing and stained glass. Fragments of old glass and alabaster in Temple Moore south choir aisle. Note medieval vestry, wall monuments, incomplete rood screen, woodcarved Lion and Unicorn, 1710.
Papplewick (St James)
Georgian Gothic. 14th-century tower, 18th-century furnishings.
Southwell Cathedral
Unvaulted Norman nave with unusual windows in clerestory. Fine, small early English choir. Decorated pulpitum. 6 canopied stalls with fine misericords. Small octagonal chapter house and vestibule are supreme example of middle-Gothic nature worship.
Teversal (St Catherine)
12th–13th century with unrestored 17th–18th-century interior.
Willoughby-on-the-Wolds (St Mary and All Saints)
13th–15th-century Willoughby monuments.
Worksop (St Mary and St Cuthbert)
Twin-towered west front with fine doorway. Drastic and continuous rebuilding. Paintings. Rebuilt Lady chapel, 1922. Small Calvary and 'Baroque' Madonna.

Wysall (Holy Trinity)
12th-century core, 14th-century chancel with 15th-century roof, 15th-century pulpit, screens and stalls.

HISTORIC MONUMENTS
Rufford Abbey, *Rufford*
West cloister range of Cistercian abbey, begun in 1146.

MUSEUMS AND GALLERIES
Brewhouse Yard Museum, *Nottingham* (Nottingham City Council)
Domestic life in Nottingham.
Castlegate Museum, *Nottingham* (Nottingham City Council)
Row of Georgian terraced houses containing the City's costume and textile collections. Women's costume from 17th century to present day. Smaller collections of men's and children's wear. Middleton collection of 17th-century and later embroideries. Foreign textiles. Dolls in fashionable dress. Collection of lace, especially machine made. Lace-making equipment.
Framework Knitter's Museum, Chapel Street, *Ruddington*
Unique complex of frameshops and cottages: reconstructed stockingers' shop, handframes, etc.
Industrial Museum, Wollaton Park, *Nottingham* (Nottingham City Council)
18th-century stables presenting history of Nottingham's industry: printing, pharmacy, hosiery and lace-making. Victorian beam engine, horse gin, agricultural machinery, transport and craft workshops.
Mansfield Museum and Art Gallery, Leeming Street, *Mansfield* (Mansfield District Council)
Zoological specimens, Wedgwood, Rockingham, Derby, Pinxton and lustre ware, watercolours of Old Mansfield, bygones. Regular loan exhibitions.
Museum and Art Gallery, Appleton Gate, *Newark-on-Trent* (Newark District Council)
Local archaeology and history, natural history and art, and temporary exhibitions.
Natural History Museum, Wollaton Hall, *Nottingham* (City of Nottingham)
Fine example of Elizabethan Renaissance architecture. Botany, zoology, geology, British and foreign herbaria. Insect gallery.
Nottingham Castle Museum, *Nottingham* (Nottingham City Council)
17th-century residence built by dukes of Newcastle. Fine collections of ceramics, silver and glass, medieval Nottingham alabaster carvings, local historical and archaeological displays, classical, oriental and ethnographical antiquities. Art gallery including works by Nottingham born artists R. P. Bonington and Thomas and Paul Sandby. Tem-

porary exhibition galleries. Sherwood Foresters' Regimental Museum is also in the Castle.

University Art Gallery, Portland Building, University Park, *Nottingham*
Exhibitions changed 3 to 4 times each term.

Village Museum, *Ruddington* (Ruddington and District History Society)
Local archaeological and folk material.

Worksop Museum, Memorial Avenue, *Worksop* (Bassetlaw District Council)
Local archaeological and historical display. Bygones and Victoriana. Local birds, butterflies and moths.

OXFORDSHIRE

AREAS OF OUTSTANDING NATURAL BEAUTY
Chilterns (part)
Cotswolds (part)
North Wessex Downs (part)

CASTLES AND HISTORIC HOUSES
Ashdown House, Nr *Lambourn* (National Trust)
Built late 17th century by first Lord Craven for Elizabeth of Bohemia. Mansard roof crowned by cupola with golden ball. Contains Craven family portraits associated with Elizabeth of Bohemia. Box parterre.

Blenheim Palace, *Woodstock* (His Grace the Duke of Marlborough)
Masterpiece of Sir John Vanbrugh in classical style. Pictures and tapestries. Gardens and park designed by Vanbrugh and Henry Wise. Later construction by Capability Brown, who created Blenheim lake.

Broughton Castle, *Banbury* (Lord Saye and Sele)
Moated Elizabethan mansion with early 14th-century nucleus. Fine fireplaces, ceilings and panelling.

Buscot Old Parsonage, Nr *Lechlade* (National Trust)
Built 1703 of Cotswold stone and stone tiles. On banks of the Thames.

Buscot Park, Nr *Faringdon* (National Trust)
Built 1780. Fine paintings and furniture. Briar Rose room. Attractive garden walks, lake.

Chasleton House, *Moreton-in-Marsh* (Alan Clutton Brock, Esq)
Built 1603. Fine plasterwork and panelling. Original furniture and tapestries. Topiary garden designed 1700.

Ditchley Park, *Enstone* (Ditchley Foundation)
Great 18th-century mansion. Designed by Gibbs, decoration of great hall by Kent.

Edgcote, *Chipping Warden* (E. R. Courage, Esq)
Stone-built mid-18th-century house. Good Palladian and rococo interior features.

Greys Court, *Henley-on-Thames* (National Trust)
Gardens, medieval ruins, a Tudor donkey wheel for raising well water and 16th-century house containing interesting 18th-century plasterwork and furniture.

Hinton Manor, *Hinton Waldrist* (N. Davenport, Esq)
Regicide's house. (Elizabethan with 1700 and 1830 additions.) Norman motte and bailey earthworks.

Mapledurham House, *Mapledurham* (J. J. Eyston, Esq)
Late 16th-century Elizabethan home of the Blount family. Original moulded ceilings; great oak staircase; paintings and private chapel.

Milton Manor House, Nr *Abingdon* (Surgeon Capt. and Mrs E. J. Mockler)
17th-century house with Georgian wings. Traditionally designed by Inigo Jones. Walled garden and pleasure grounds.

Nuneham, Nr *Oxford* (University of Oxford, leased to Culham College of Education)
Thames-side Palladian villa (additions by Brown and Smirke) in setting created by William Mason and Capability Brown. Temple church by 'Athenian' Stuart. No contents.

Priory Cottages, *Steventon* (National Trust)
Formerly monastic buildings, converted into three houses, one containing great hall of original priory.

Rousham House, Steeple Ashton (C. Cottrell-Dormer, Esq)
17th century house. Portraits and miniatures. Garden by William Kent.

University of Oxford (in most Colleges, only chapels and halls are open)

All Soul's College, High Street (1438)
Balliol College, Broad Street (1263)
Brasenose College, Radcliffe Square (1509)
Christ Church, St Aldate's (1546)
Corpus Christi College, Merton Street (1516)
Exeter College, Turl Street (1314)
Hertford College, Catte Street (1284, 1740 and 1874)
Jesus College, Turl Street (1571)
Keble College, Parks Road (1868)
Lincoln College, Turl Street (1427)
Magdalen College, High Street (1458)
Merton College, Merton Street (1264)
New College (admission at New College Lane and Holywell Street) (1379)
Nuffield College, New Road (1937)
Oriel College, Oriel Square (1326)
Pembroke College, St Aldate's (1624)
The Queen's College, High Street (1340)
St Edmund Hall, Queen's Lane (1270)

335

St John's College, St Giles' (1555)
Trinity College, Broad Street (1554)
University College, High Street (1249)
Wadham College, Parks Road (1610)
Worcester College, Worcester Street (1714)

CATHEDRALS AND CHURCHES

Abingdon (St Helen)
Mostly 14th–16th-century perpendicular. Late 14th-century painted roof; Hawkins monument, 1780; late Georgian stained and enamelled glass. Bodley reredos, 1897.

Adderbury (St Mary the Virgin)
Decorated and perpendicular. Note corbel table on north wall, late perpendicular chancel in style of Divinity schools at Oxford. Tower, spire and windows, screen, brasses.

Bloxham (Our Lady of Bloxham)
14th-century spire. Fine north and south porches, 15th-century south chancel, painted panels in screen, Thornycroft monument, 1725.

Burford (St John the Baptist)
Largely 15th century. Tombs, some old glass. Churchyard rich in sculptured table tombs, Georgian and earlier.

Chislehampton (St Katherine)
1763. Bellcote and rare and clear glass, round headed windows. Unspoilt Georgian interior.

Church Handborough (St Peter and St Paul)
Norman and later. Spire, 12th-century south door carvings, font, 15th-century nave arcades, pulpit and screens across chancel, aisles with coloured rood-loft, tomb recesses.

Compton Beauchamp (St Swithin)
Painted tomb stones, gilded altar, classic font cover, gilded monuments, rich rood and other furnishings, mostly 20th century by Travers.

Dorchester (St Peter and St Paul)
Mainly decorated with Butterfield lych-gate. Jesse window with some original figures in glass and stone, old glass, tombs including stone effigy of late 13th-century knight.

East Hagbourne (St Andrew)
Mostly 14th–15th century. Fine 18th-century tombs. Old wooden roofs, some 14th-century glass, remains of 15th-century screen, Royal Arms of Charles II.

Ewelme (St Mary the Virgin)
Castellated 15th century, all late perpendicular. Screen, spired font cover, old roofs. Chaucer and Suffolk tombs, old floors, brasses, early 19th-century poppy-head pews.

Iffley (St Mary the Virgin)
Late Norman, 1170. Richly carved west front. Interior with 2

336

elaborate Norman arches with vaulting between, leading to contrasting light early English vaulted west end.

Langford (St Matthew)
Early Norman with early English chancel and west end. Fine Norman tower and carving on south porch.

North Moreton (All Saints)
Late 13th century. Very fine 14th-century chantry chapel of Stapleton family with notable glass and tracery.

Oxford (St Mary the Virgin)
14th century, 15th-century windows and Baroque porch, 18th-century iron-work gates. Chancel, 1467, with clear old glass; 17th-century communion rails and niched east wall.

Oxford Cathedral
Smallest of English cathedrals, only 4 out of 8 bays of nave remain. Stone spire, 1230, among oldest in country. Interior: double arches of Norman arcade, 14th-century glass in south transept and Latin Chapel, choir vault.

Rycote (St Michael and All Angels)
15th century. Note 15th-century benches and screen base, 17th-century family and royal pews, late 17th-century altar-piece and communion rails, clear old glass, fine ceiling.

Stanton Harcourt (St Michael)
Early English and perpendicular detail. Old stone and marble floor. Early English screen with painting, old glass, Harcourt monuments, 17th–19th century.

Thame (St Mary the Virgin)
Norman with much later building. Note south porch, window tracery. Decorated screen, brasses, monuments.

Uffington (St Mary the Virgin)
Mostly 13th-century early English. Restored by G. E. Street, 1850. Clear glass, 17th-century monument.

Wheatfield (St Andrew)
Medieval with classical embellishments, 1750. Hatchments, tombs, 2-decker pulpit, clear glass, classical altar and rails, old pews. Scheemakers tomb, 1739.

Yarnton (St Bartholemew)
13th century with late perpendicular additions. Old woodwork, Jacobean screen, 15th-century alabaster reredos, fragments of old English and Flemish glass.

GARDENS
Botanic Gardens, *Oxford* (University of Oxford)
Oldest botanic garden in Britain, founded 1621.
Pusey House Gardens, Nr *Faringdon* (Michael Hornby, Esq)
Herbaceous borders, walled gardens, water garden, shrubs and roses. Fine trees.

HISTORIC MONUMENTS
Deddington Castle, *Deddington*
Portions of 13th-century chapel. Earthworks of outer bailey and inner ward.
Minster Lovell House, *Minster Lovell*
Ruined 15th-century establishment of medieval lord.
North Leigh Roman Villa, Nr *Witney*
Excavations of villa occupied 2nd–4th century. Tessellated pavement.
Rollright Stones, Nr *Chipping Norton*
Circle of 77 stones. Also in vicinity – ancient burial chamber and isolated King's stone.
Uffington Castle and White Horse, *Uffington*
Iron Age hill fort and white horse cut in chalk.
Wayland's Smithy, *Ashbury*
Gallery grave chamber.

MUSEUMS AND GALLERIES
Ashmolean Museum of Art and Archaeology, Beaumont Street, *Oxford*
British, European, Mediterranean, Egyptian and Near-Eastern archaeology. European oil paintings, old masters and modern drawings, watercolours, and prints; miniatures; European ceramics; sculpture and bronzes; English silver; objects of applied art. Hope collection of engraved portraits. Chinese, Japanese, Tibetan and Islamic collections.
Banbury Museum, Marlborough Road, *Banbury* (Oxfordshire County Council with Cherwell District Council)
'Scrapbook of Victorian Banbury' exhibition. Items and displays of local interest. Globe Room: fine 17th-century panelling from local inn. Temporary exhibitions.
Christ Church Library, Peckwater Quadrangle, *Oxford*
Statuary, music, Carrolliana, manuscripts and printed books.
Christ Church Picture Gallery, Canterbury Quadrangle, *Oxford*
Old master paintings and drawings.
Museum of the History of Science, Broad Street, *Oxford*
Early scientific instruments, photographic apparatus, clocks and watches. Also library, manuscripts and photographic records.
Museum of Modern Art, Pembroke Street, *Oxford*
Temporary exhibitions of contemporary British and international art.
Museum of Oxford, St Aldate's, *Oxford* (Oxfordshire County Council)
Exhibition of 'The Story of Oxford' including many treasures on loan from colleges, etc. Temporary exhibitions.
Oxford University Museum, Parks Road, *Oxford*
Zoological, entomological, geological and mineralogical collections of University.

Oxfordshire County Museum, Fletcher's House, *Woodstock* (Oxford-shire County Council, Department of Museum Services)
Archaeology, crafts, industry and domestic life of region. Temporary exhibitions.

Pendon, Museum of Miniature Landscape and Transport, Long Wittenham, *Abingdon*
Scenes in miniature showing countryside and its transport in thirties, including historically accurate trains and parts of thatched village in fine detail. Railway relics from 1812 to present day.

The Pitt Rivers Museum, Parks Road, *Oxford*
Ethnology and prehistoric archaeology of the peoples of the world. Musical instruments.

The Rotunda, Grove House, 44 Iffley Turn, *Oxford*
Early dolls' houses, 1700–1885, and contents.

Tolsey Museum, High Street, *Burford* (Tolsey Museum Committee)
Charters, maces, seals, bygones and Burford craftsmen's dolls' house in a replica Regency room with period furnishings and costumes.

Town Museum, The County Hall, *Abingdon* (Abingdon Town Council)
Fine 17th-century building containing local fossil remains, archaeological material (including finds from Anglo-Saxon cemetery) and history. Collection, prints, charters and documents.

Wantage Museum, Civic Hall, *Wantage*
History of Wantage and neighbouring area.

SALOP (SHROPSHIRE)
AREAS OF OUTSTANDING NATURAL BEAUTY
Shropshire Hills

CASTLES AND HISTORIC HOUSES

Action Round Hall, *Bridgnorth* (H. L. Kennedy)
Built c. 1695 as dower house for Aldenham Park. Retains much original panelling.

Albright Hussey, Nr *Albrighton* (K. J. Micah)
Half-timbered portion of moated manor house dates from 1524, brick portion from 1560.

Attingham Park, Nr *Shrewsbury* (National Trust)
Designed, 1785, by George Stuart for 1st Lord Berwick. Remarkable interior decorations. Famous painted boudoir.

Benthall Hall, *Much Wenlock* (National Trust)
16th-century stone house with mullion windows, interior improved in 17th century. Fine oak staircase and plaster ceilings. Interesting small garden.

Bishop Percy's House, *Bridgnorth*
Half-timbered house, 1580. Birthplace of Bishop Percy of Dromore.
Now boys' club.
Boscobel House, *Shifnal* (Department of the Environment)
17th-century house.
Condover Hall, *Condover*
Late 16th-century mansion. Now school for blind children.
*Mawley Hall, *Cleobury Mortimer* (A. M. G. Galliers-Pratt, Esq)
18th-century house attributed to Smith of Warwick. Notable
contemporary plasterwork and panelling.
*Morville Hall, Nr *Bridgnorth* (National Trust)
Modest Elizabethan house converted in 18th century.
Shipton Hall, *Much Wenlock* (C. R. N. Bishop, Esq)
Elizabethan manor house, with interior designs and stable block by
Pritchard. Stone walled garden, medieval dovecote.
Stokesay Castle, *Stokesay* (Sir Philip and Lady Magnus-Allcroft)
13th-century fortified manor house with half-timbered north tower
and fine Elizabethan timbered gatehouse.
*Tyn-y-Rhos Hall, Nr *Oswestry* (Chevalier M. Thompson-Butler-
Lloyd)
Small ancient seat of Phillips family. Contains fine oak staircase, 2
carved oak fireplaces with early Delph tiles. Furnished in Victorian
style.
Upton Cressett Hall, *Bridgnorth* (William Cash, Esq)
Elizabethan manor house with fine brick and plasterwork and 14th-
century aisled hall and gate-house.
Weston Park, Nr *Shifnal* (Earl of Bradford)
Built 1671 by Lady Wilbraham, fine example of Restoration period.
Gardens and parklands by Capability Brown.
White House, *Aston Munslow* (Miss J. C. Purser)
Medieval site comprising Norman dovecote, 13th-century. Under-
croft, 14th-century. Cruck hall, 1570 half-timbered cross-wing,
18th-century addition. Implements and tools, domestic and dairy
utensils in their natural environment.
Wilderhope Manor, *Wenlock Edge* (National Trust)
Built in 1586. 17th-century plaster ceilings.

CATHEDRALS AND CHURCHES
Cheswardine (St Swithun)
1880–9. Early English with 13th-century chapel. Notable sculpture;
19th-century glass; old brasses.
Langley Chapel (dedication unknown)
17th century, unrestored. Old floors; plastered walls; woodwork.
Longor (St Mary the Virgin)
13th century. Outside staircase to west gallery. Not suffered Victorian restoration.

Ludlow (St Lawrence)
15th century with pinnacled tower. 14th-century nave and transepts.
Expensive restoration in 19th century. Note carved choir stalls, 1447;
reredos and screens in perpendicular chancel with original glass.
Monuments.
Lydbury North (St Michael)
Norman of two periods with 14th-century transept and 17th-century
south transept. Fine 15th-century nave roof; 17th-century box pews;
Norman font with 17th-century cover; late 17th-century altar rails;
rood screen with plastered tympanum above.
Onibury (St Michael)
Norman, well restored, 1902. Simple oak woodwork.
Shrewsbury (St Chad)
1790–2. Interior plaster and original woodwork in low relief.
Shrewsbury (St Mary)
Norman to 15th century. Note 14th- and 15th–16th-century English
glass.
Stottesdon (St Mary)
Fine Norman font; 12th-century carvings; nobly decorated; tracery
and columns.
Tong (St Mary the Virgin with St Bartholomew)
Mainly 1410. Inside scraped but some of best monuments in England.
Screens with remains of paintings; brasses; Golden chapel, 1515,
with old stencilled walls, gilt fan vaulted ceiling and effigies.
Whitchurch (St Alkmund)
1712–13. Fine red sandstone tower. Drastically restored interior but
still some good woodwork; Tuscan arcades to nave; tombs.

GARDENS
Burford House Gardens, Nr *Tenbury Wells* (J. Treasure, Esq)
Many interesting trees, shrubs, clematis and plants, ornamental pools
and streams by River Teme.
Hodnet Hall Gardens, Nr *Market Drayton* (Mr and the Hon. Mrs
Heber Percy)
Garden extends over 60 acres.

HISTORIC MONUMENTS
Acton Burnell Castle, Nr *Longnor*
Ruined 13th-century fortified manor.
Bridgnorth Castle, *Bridgnorth*
Only leaning tower remains from Norman castle (1101).
Buildwas Abbey, Nr *Telford*
Ruined Savignac Abbey, founded in 1135.
Haughmond Abbey, Nr *Shrewsbury*
Extensive remains of house of Augustinian canons, founded c. 1135.

341

Lilleshall Abbey, Nr *Newport*
Considerable remains of abbey of Augustinian canons, established c. 1150.
Mitchell's Fold Stone Circle, *Chirbury*
Prehistoric stone circle.
Moreton Corbet Castle, *Moreton Corbet*
Keep c. 1200, gatehouse altered in 1519 and notable Elizabethan features all damaged in Civil War.
Old Oswestry, Nr *Oswestry*
Iron Age hill fort.
Roman Town, *Wroxeter*
Remains of town of 'Viroconium' dating from AD 140–50, including public baths and colonnade.
Wenlock Priory, *Much Wenlock*
Ruins of 13th-century abbey adjacent to chapter house, lavabo, and transepts.
White Ladies Priory, *Shifnal*
Remains of Augustinian nunnery dating from 1158.

MUSEUMS AND GALLERIES
Acton Scott Working Farm Museum, Nr *Church Stretton*
Site museum demonstrating agricultural practice as it was at turn of century prior to advent of electricity and petrol engine.
Clive House, College Hill, *Shrewsbury*
Georgian house containing outstanding collection of Shropshire ceramics, art, furniture and Regimental Museum of 1st Queen's Dragoon Guards.
Clun Town Trust Museum, *Clun*
Local geology, pre-history earthworks, footpaths, commons, rights of way, etc, local history, early photographs, etc.
Coleham Pumping Station, Old Coleham, *Shrewsbury*
Preserved beam engines.
Ironbridge Gorge Museum, *Telford* (Ironbridge Gorge Museum Trust)
Open-air museum based on series of industrial monuments in Severn Gorge:
> **Blists Hill Open-Air Museum**
> 42-acre woodland site with steam blowing engines, pitheads, restored canal and Hay Inclined Plane. Telford road and working potter.
> **Coalbrookdale Museum and Furnace Site**
> Abraham Darby's blast furnace history of Coalbrookdale Company and collection of art castings.
> **Iron Bridge Information Centre**
> In the tollhouse, next to world's first iron bridge.

Ludlow Museum, Butter Cross, *Ludlow*
Fossils; local prehistoric, Roman and medieval material, including local arms and armour.
Mortimer Forest Museum, Nr *Ludlow*
Past and present forest industries. Ecology of forest and fallow deer.
Much Wenlock Museum, *Much Wenlock*
Local history, geology and natural history. Town relics.
Reader's House, *Ludlow* (King Edward VI Ludlow Charities)
Fine 16th-century town house.
Rowley's House Museum, Barker Street, *Shrewsbury* (Borough of Shrewsbury and Atcham)
Roman material from Viroconium (Wroxeter), medieval, prehistoric.
Shrewsbury Art Gallery, Castle Gates, *Shrewsbury* (Borough of Shrewsbury and Atcham)
Viroconium Museum, *Wroxeter* (Department of the Environment)
Objects found during the excavation of site, Roman inscription, pottery, coins and other small objects.
Whitehouse Museum of Buildings and Country Life, *Aston Munslow*
Stedman Homestead, 4 houses in one, 13th, 14th, 16th and 18th century, dovecote 13th century; another 16th-century house; cider house 17th century; stable 1680; other buildings of 17th, 18th century in original positions in functional relation to each other. Farming implements, tools, domestic utensils, dairy equipment in functional positions. Horse-drawn wagons, carts, etc.

SOMERSET
AREAS OF OUTSTANDING NATURAL BEAUTY
Mendip Hills (part)
Quantock Hills

CASTLES AND HISTORIC HOUSES
Abbot's Fish House, *Meare* (Mrs C. J. Look)
14th-century house of former abbey official in charge of fish ponds.
Barford Park, *Enmore* (Mr and Mrs Michael Stancomb)
Georgian mansion in miniature.
Barrington Court, *Ilminster* (National Trust)
16th-century house and extensive garden.
Brympton D'Evercy, Nr *Yeovil* (Charles E. B. Clive-Ponsonby-Fane, Esq)
Mansion house with late 17th-century south front and Tudor west front. 13th-century priest house and church adjacent. Longest straight staircase in England. Vineyard and formal gardens. Agricultural museum.
Coleridge Cottage, *Nether Stowey* (National Trust)
Home of S. T. Coleridge, 1797–1800.

Dodington Hall, *Nether Stowey* (Lady Michael Gass)
Hall dating from 14th and 15th centuries. Timbered minstrels' gallery.
Dunster Castle, *Dunster* (National Trust)
Castle dating from 13th century, remodelled by Anthony Salvin in
19th century. Fine 17th-century staircase and plaster ceilings.
East Lambrook Manor, *South Pether* (Mr and Mrs F. H. Boyd-
Carpenter)
15th-century house with 16th-century additions and panelling.
Cottage-style garden with rare plants. Memorial to late Margery
Fish.
Gaulden Manor, Tolland, Nr *Taunton* (Mr and Mrs James LeGendre
Starkie)
Small manor originating from 12th century. Past home of the
Turberville family. Great hall has unique plaster ceiling and oak
screen to former chapel. Fine antique furniture. Grounds include bog
garden with many varieties of primula. Herb garden.
Halsway Manor, Nr *Crowcombe* (Halsway Manor Society Ltd)
Begun in 14th century. Red sandstone. Panelling in old hall, lounge
and library. Residential folk centre.
Hatch Court, *Hatch Beauchamp* (Commander and Mrs Barry
Nation)
Palladian style Georgian house. Small Canadian military museum.
China room. Deer park.
King John's Hunting Lodge, *Axbridge* (National Trust)
Early Tudor merchant's house extensively restored in 1971. Museum
of local history.
Lytes Cary, *Somerton* (National Trust)
14th- and 15th-century manor house with chapel; formal garden.
Montacute House, *Yeovil* (National Trust)
Elizabethan house of Ham Hill stone begun in 1588 by Edward
Phelips. Fine heraldic glass, tapestries, panelling and furniture.
National Portrait Gallery exhibitions of Elizabethan and Jacobean
portraits. Formal garden and topiary.
***Priest's House,** *Muchelney* (National Trust)
Late medieval house, originally residence of secular priests who
served parish church.
Treasurer's House, *Mortlock* (National Trust)
Small house dating from 13th and 14th centuries with medieval
kitchen and hall.
Stoke-Sub-Hamdon Priory, *Montacute* (National Trust)
Complex of buildings begun in 14th century for priests of chantry
chapel of St Nicholas (destroyed). Only great hall is left open to
public.
Tintinhull House, *Yeovil* (National Trust)
17th-century house with beautiful garden.

CATHEDRALS AND CHURCHES

Axbridge (St John the Baptist)
Fine plaster ceiling, 1636, in nave. Good panelled roofs in aisles. Prowse monument, 1670. Embroidered 18th-century frontal.

Babington (St Margaret)
Mid-18th century, unaltered. Apsidal sanctuary and tower with cupola. Moulded plasterwork, clear glass, woodwork, pedestal font.

Batcombe (St Mary)
Mainly 15th-century fabric with outstanding tower. Pierced parapets, notable aisle roofs, fan vault to tower, 17th-century altar rails and brass, altar and hangings by W. H. Randoll Blacking.

Bishop's Lydeard (St Mary)
Rebuilt in 15th century with noble tower. Notable rood screen, Comper altars and glass in chancel and chapel, carved bench-ends, and finely carved churchyard cross.

Brent Knoll (St Michael)
Largely 15th century. Notable for woodwork in roofs, pulpit and bench-ends.

Bruton (St Mary)
Notable 2-towered church, rebuilt in 15th and 16th centuries. Chancel is fine Georgian. Fine tie-beam roof in nave, Georgian reredos, Jacobean screen in tower arch, 15th-century embroidery and 17th-century monuments.

Chewton Mendip (St Mary Magdalene)
12th century with later additions. Magnificent 16th-century tower. Notable 12th-century north doorway, late 15th-century bench-ends, 17th-century lectern and holy table, medieval churchyard cross.

Crewkerne (St Bartholomew)
Perpendicular with magnificent west front. Roofs.

Croscombe (St Mary)
15th–16th century, with 17th-century interior. Notable chancel roof; 2-storied vestry; 13th-century south doorway; 15th-century painted glass; 18th-century chandeliers.

East Brent (St Mary)
Mainly 15th century with spire; plaster ceiling to nave, 1637; late 15th-century bench-ends, painted glass and wooden lectern; 17th-century pulpit and gallery.

Evercreech (St Peter)
14th–15th-century tower and nave roof.

Glastonbury (St John the Baptist)
One of country's finest perpendicular towers. Tie-beam roof in nave; tower vaulting; late medieval painted glass; portion of medieval vestment; early 16th-century altar tomb.

High Ham (St Andrew)
Perpendicular. Clerestoried nave, sumptuous roofs and vaulted rood

screen. Carved bench-ends, Norman font, Jacobean lectern and some medieval painted glass.

Ilminster (St Mary)
Mainly 15th century with noble centre tower. Fine Wadham monuments, 15th–17th century. Note fan vault of tower, 17th-century pulpit and screen, and 18th-century chandelier.

Isle Abbotts (St Mary)
Perpendicular tower. Decorated chancel. Remainder 15th and early 16th century. Notable panelled roof of aisle. Norman font and 15th- and 17th-century screens.

Kingsbury Episcopi (St Martin)
14th–15th century with notable tower. Note fan vaulting of tower; 15th-century screen; late medieval painted glass.

Long Sutton (Holy Trinity)
Late 15th century with noble tower. Clerestoried nave, magnificent tie-beam roof; 15th-century pulpit and rood screen; 15th-century tower vaulting; 17th-century lectern.

Martock (All Saints)
Perpendicular with 13th-century chancel. Tie-beam roof of nave is one of finest of its kind. Canopied niches in clerestory with 17th-century paintings of Apostles.

Mells (St Andrew)
Rebuilt in 15th century with noble tower and carved detail. Notable nave and chapel roofs, Norman font, fragments of medieval painted glass, and monuments.

North Cadbury (St Michael)
Perpendicular. Fine chancel. Roofs; early 16th-century seating; 15th-century painted glass.

North Petherton (St Mary)
Mainly 15th century with superb tower and sacristy. Notable roofs of nave and aisles, 15th-century font and pulpit and 17th-century manorial pew.

Pawlett (St John the Baptist)
12th century later refashioned. 12th-century font; 15th-century screen; 17th-century fittings.

Pilton (St John the Baptist)
12th century refashioned in 15th century. Clerestoried nave and chancel. 12th-century arcades; 15th-century roofs, paraclose and portion of cope; fragments of late medieval painted glass; chandelier, 1749.

Stoke-Sub-Hamdon (St Mary)
Notable Norman fabric. Norman and early English detail; 15th-century roof to nave; 17th-century pulpit.

Taunton (St Mary Magdalene)
Highest and most elaborate of county's towers. Fine nave roof, niches over arcades, fragments of late medieval painted glass. Extensive restoration.

346

Trull (All Saints)
15th century with many late medieval art treasures: rood screen, pulpit, carved bench-ends and late 15th-century glass.
Watchet (St Decuman)
Mostly 15th century. Tower; 15th-century roofs; 17th-century gated altar rails; 16th- and 17th-century monuments; 17th-century pulpit with tester; late 15th-century screens.
Wedmore (St Mary)
12th-century core with additions. Notable chapel roofs; 16th-century wall painting; Jacobean pulpit; ironwork on south door; 18th-century chandeliers.
Wells (St Cuthbert)
15th-century tower among finest in county. Good roofs. Rich Carolean pulpit. Remains of medieval painted glass; early 17th-century monument; medieval font cover.
Wells Cathedral
Fine west front, much original sculpture, and elevated octagonal chapter house. Splendid central tower. Early English arcade of nave and transepts. Vault under tower. Set of 60 fine misericords, c. 1330. Late decorated stone panelled presbytery with Golden window. Retrochoir with cross-vistas. Lady chapel with rich glass and star vault. Good 15th-century cloisters.
Weston Zoyland (St Mary)
Perpendicular, carefully restored by Caroe. Note tie-beam roof of nave; 15th-century bench-ends; 16th-century heraldic glass and Jacobean pulpit.

GARDENS
Ambleside Water Gardens and Aviaries, *Axbridge*
Shrubs, waterfowl, birds, guinea pigs.
Brean Down Bird Gardens, *Brean Down* (National Trust)
Garden built in 1972. Bird sanctuary.
Hadspen House, *Castle Cary* (Trustees of late Sir Arthur Hobhouse)
6-acre garden. New planting of trees for bark and foliage interest, shrubs, hostas, roses, tender wall shrubs.
Hestercombe, Nr *Cheddon Fitzpaine* (Somerset Fire Brigade)
Gardens originally planted by Sir Edwin Lutyens, 1905.
Stowell Hill, *Templecombe* (Lady McCreefy)
Spring bulbs; collection of flowering shrubs, including rhododendrons, azaleas, magnolias, and Japanese cherries.
Widcombe Bird Gardens, *Blagdon Hill*
20 acres of garden with aviaries, paddocks, fine trees and shrubs.

HISTORIC MONUMENTS
Cleeve Abbey, *Cleeve*
Ruined 13th-century Cistercian house. Noted for gatehouse,

dormitory and refectory with traceried windows, timber roof and wall paintings.
Farleigh Castle, *Farleigh Hungerford*
14th-century remains. Museum in chapel.
Glastonbury Abbey, *Glastonbury*
Well-preserved 12th–13th-century ruins. St Joseph's chapel. Abbot's kitchen.
Muchelney Abbey, *Muchelney*
15th–16th-century remains of Benedictine abbey.
Nunnery Castle, *Nunnery*
Ruins of 14th-century tower house.
Stanton Drew Stone Circles, *Stanton Drew*
Religious centre of Neolithic or Bronze Age periods.

MUSEUMS AND GALLERIES
Admiral Blake Museum, Blake Street, *Bridgwater* (Sedgemoor District Council)
Reputed birthplace of Admiral Blake, containing Blake relics, exhibits relating to Battle of Sedgemoor. Archaeology and local history.
Axbridge Caving Group and Archaeology, The Museum, Town Hall, *Axbridge*
History and prehistory of Axbridge–Banwell–Cheddar area.
Bardon Manor, Nr *Washford*
14th-century manor house with Saxon fireplace and cockpit. Exhibition of paintings and handicrafts by West Country artists.
Borough Museum, Hendford Manor Hall, *Yeovil* (Yeovil Corporation)
Local history and archaeology, Henry Stiby Firearm Collection and Bailward Costume Collection.
Cheddar Motor and Transport Museum, The Cliffs, *Cheddar* (Cheddar Veteran and Vintage Car Museum Limited)
Cars, motor cycles, cycles and motoring accessories and Cheddar section on discovery of caves, etc.
Fleet Air Arm Museum, Royal Naval Air Station, *Yeovilton*
Development of Naval aviation from origins in 1910, through Royal Naval Air Service of First World War, to Fleet Air Arm of today.
Glastonbury Lake Village Museum, The Tribunal, High Street, *Glastonbury*
Late prehistoric antiquities from Glastonbury Lake Village and items of local interest.
Gough's Cave Museum, *Cheddar*
Upper Paleolithic remains: almost complete skeleton, flints, amber and engraved stones.
Military Museum, *Taunton*
Relics of Somerset Light Infantry, 1685–1959.

Somerset County Museum, Taunton Castle, *Taunton*
Collections relevant to County of Somerset, including archaeology, geology and palaeontology, natural history, ceramics, folk-life, costume and military gallery.
Street Shoe Museum, High Street, *Street* (C. and J. Clark Limited)
Shoes from Roman times to present; shoe machinery from 1860s to 1920; 19th-century documents and photographs illustrating early history of C. and J. Clark.
Wells Museum, Cathedral Green, *Wells*
Local bygones, prehistoric cave finds, coins, natural history, Mendip rocks, fossils and minerals.
Wookey Hole, The Caves, *Wookey Hole*
Caves Museum – animal remains of newer Pliocene period. Relics of late Celtic and Romano–British civilization. Madame Tussaud's store room. Lady Bangor's collection of fairground carvings. Paper mill – exhibition about handmade paper-making.

NATIONAL PARKS
Exmoor (part)

SOUTH YORKSHIRE
CASTLES AND HISTORIC HOUSES
Bishop's House, Meersbrook Park, *Sheffield* (Sheffield Corporation)
Late 15th-century timbered building with 16th- and 17th-century additions.
Oakes Park, Nr *Sheffield* (Major and Mrs T. Bagshawe)
Georgian house with old oak furniture, tapestries, paintings and collection of dolls, etc. Gardens with long lake.

CATHEDRALS AND CHURCHES
Arksey (All Saints)
Excellent Norman, early English and perpendicular work. East wall of chancel by Sir G. G. Scott, 1869. Notable font cover, 1602; pulpit, 1634; coeval pews; monuments; scraps of medieval glass.
Campsall (St Mary Magdalene)
Notable Norman tower; magnificent 15th-century rood screen; Pugin carved and painted stone altar.
Ecclesfield (St Mary)
Rebuilt late 15th century. Excellent timber roofs in north and south chapels; perpendicular screens; 16th-century benches; font, 1662; some medieval stained glass; hatchments and monuments.
Fishlake (St Cuthbert)
Richly carved Norman doorway; 13th-century arcades with handsome west responds; fine decorated work in chancel, especially east window. Late 14th-century font with statuettes in niches and Jacobean cover.

Hatfield (St Lawrence)
Norman work in west front, north aisle and south door; 13th-century nave arcades; east part of church largely perpendicular; original roofs with carved bosses to north and south chapels; fine 15th-century screen; old pews in south chapel; monuments.

Rotherham (All Saints)
Perpendicular with central tower and spire and battlemented and pinnacled parapets. Fan-vaulted crossing; pulpit, 1604, with Georgian tester; 15th-century stalls; Snetzler organ with fine 18th-century case; brasses; monuments. Late 18th- and 19th-century restoration.

Silkstone (All Saints)
Perpendicular; tall tower; early 13th-century work in chancel arch and arcade; screens; Wentworth monument; effigies.

HISTORIC MONUMENTS
Conisbrough Castle, *Conisbrough*
12th-century circular 6-buttressed keep. Curtain walls with solid round towers.

Monk Bretton Priory, Nr *Barnsley*
Considerable remains of church and cloistered buildings of Cluniac house.

Roche Abbey, Nr *Maltby*
Cistercian abbey, founded 1147, with walls of north and south transepts still standing to full height.

MUSEUMS AND GALLERIES
Abbeydale Industrial Hamlet, Abbeydale Road South, *Sheffield* (Sheffield Corporation)
18th-century scytheworks comprising Huntsman's type crucible steel furnace, tilt-hammers, grinding hull, hand-forges and workman's cottage.

Art Gallery, Frederick Street, *Rotherham* (Rotherham Metropolitan Borough Council)
Small permanent collection. Temporary exhibitions.

Bentley Museum, Bentley Public Library, *Doncaster*
Local historical and environmental exhibits.

Cannon Hall Art Gallery, *Barnsley* (Barnsley Metropolitan Borough Council)
18th-century house by John Carr of York. Fine furniture, paintings, and glassware. William Harvey bequest of Flemish and Dutch paintings. Regimental museum of 13th/18th Royal Hussars.

Cooper Art Gallery, Church Street, *Barnsley* (Trustees)
17th-, 18th- and 19th-century paintings; English drawings, Sir Michael Sadler collection; temporary loan exhibitions.

Cusworth Hall Museum, Cusworth Lane, *Doncaster*
Fok-life exhibits, particularly relating to South Yorkshire.

Doncaster Museum and Art Gallery, Chequer Road, *Doncaster*
Natural history, prehistoric and Romano–British exhibits, local
history and costumes. Art collection and temporary loans.
Graves Art Gallery, Surrey Street, *Sheffield* (Sheffield Corporation)
Introduction to British portraiture and important examples of
European painting. Chinese, Indian, Islamic and African art.
Frequent loan exhibitions.
Industrial Store, Kelham Island, *Sheffield* (Sheffield Corporation)
Palletized warehouse where material for projected industrial museum
is being collected.
Mappin Art Gallery, Weston Park, *Sheffield* (Sheffield Corporation)
Paintings and sculpture mainly representative of British School of
18th, 19th and 20th centuries. Frequent loan exhibitions of contem-
porary painting, sculpture and graphic art.
Rotherham Museum and Art Gallery, Clifton Park, *Rotherham*
(Rotherham Metropolitan Borough Council)
Antiquities from Roman forts at Templebrough; gem stones and
jewellery; English glass, church silver. Rockingham porcelain and
natural history.
Saddleworth Museum, *Saddleworth*
Part of old wool mill. Items of local domestic and industrial interest.
Sheffield City Museum, Weston Park, *Sheffield* (Sheffield Corpora-
tion)
Natural history, geology, ceramics, coins and bygones; cutlery. Old
Sheffield plate, local archaeology and local history. Temporary exhibi-
tion gallery.
Shepherd Wheel, Whiteley Wood, Hangingwater Road, *Sheffield*
(Sheffield Corporation)
Sheffield 'Little Mesters' water-powered grinding shop.
Victoria Jubilee Museum, *Cawthorne*
Natural history, geology and objects of local interest.

NATIONAL PARKS
Peak District (part)

STAFFORDSHIRE
AREAS OF OUTSTANDING NATURAL BEAUTY
Cannock Chase

CASTLES AND HISTORIC HOUSES
Blithfield Hall, Nr *Rugeley* (Lady Bagot)
Elizabethan house with Georgian and Regency Gothic additions.
Landscape gardens, orangery and formal rose garden. 14th-century
church. Children's toy museum.
Chillington Hall, Nr *Wolverhampton* (P. R. de L. Giffard)
Georgian house, part 1724 (Francis Smith), part 1785 (Sir John
Soane). Fine saloon. Grounds by Capability Brown.

Hoar Cross Hall, Nr *Burton-upon-Trent* (W. A. Bickerton-Jones, Esq)
Elizabethan-style mansion. Varied collection of arms and armour.
17th-, 18th- and 19th-century furniture and paintings. Plasterwork
in hall and chapel by G. F. Bodley. Landscaped and terraced gardens,
yew tree walks and lily ponds.

CATHEDRALS AND CHURCHES

Bradley (All Saints)
15th-century tower; fine nave arcade, c. 1260. Carved Norman tub-
font; rood stair; glass fragments; 16th-century alabaster effigies.

Brewood (St Mary)
Perpendicular nave; mid-13th-century chancel. Magnificent 16th–
17th-century Gifford tombs.

Broughton (St Peter)
Late Gothic, 1630. Box pews; font; memorials; 14th–15th-century
glass.

Checkley (St Mary and All Saints)
Notable medieval church. Saxon cross-shafts; fine 14th-century
chancel; tracery; 14th-century glass; sedilia; 16th-century stalls and
tomb effigies; parclose screen, glass and altar by Comper.

Clifton Campville (St Andrew)
13th–14th century. Queen post roof; carved stone heads; wall
paintings; some old glass; memorials; screens; misericords.

Elford (St Peter)
Tower, 1598; remainder mostly by Street, 1870. Notable tombs; fine
roof; altar rail, ironwork on door.

Gnosall (Collegiate Church of St Lawrence)
Mainly 14th–15th century. Flamboyant east window with 20th-
century memorial glass. Norman detail.

Hamstall Ridware (St Michael)
Mainly 14th–15th century. Old glass; parclose screens; tombs;
memorials; medieval painted panels.

Hoar Cross (Church of the Holy Angels)
Bodley, 1876. Glass; stations of the Cross; tombs; woodwork; stone
vaulting.

Ingestre (St Mary)
Sir Christopher Wren, 1676. Once private chapel. Most elaborate
country church of its time.

Lichfield Cathedral
Restoration necessary after Civil War and due to frailty of local red
sandstone. Only English cathedral to have 3 stone spires: Ladies of
the Vale. Elaborate font with Victorian sculpture. Fine Lady chapel
with 16th-century Flemish glass.

Norbury (St Peter)
Fine 14th-century nave and chancel with original roof. Brick

Georgian Gothic. Four sedilia; founder's tomb; Scrymsher tomb, 1708; font, 1733.

Penkridge (St Michael and All Angels)
Mainly 16th-century perpendicular. 13th-century arcades. 16th–17th-century Littleton tombs; 15th–16th-century incised slabs with figures; 18th-century Dutch wrought-iron screen.

Sandon (All Saints)
Mainly 14th century. 17th-century pulpit; screen supporting family pew of Harrowbys; tombs; wall paintings.

Tamworth (Collegiate Church of St Editha)
Mostly late 14th century. Baroque monument, c. 1680; open stone screen at east end of tower; 18th-century wrought-iron screen; effigies; some pre-Raphaelite glass; double spiral staircase in tower.

Tutbury (Priory Church of St Mary)
Norman. Rich west front and fine doorway of 7 orders including earliest English alabaster work. Good west wall; fine ironwork on doors.

GARDENS

Elds Wood, *Willoughbridge* (Willoughbridge Garden Trust)
200-year-old gravel quarry converted into woodland garden.

Himley Hall, *Himley* (Dudley and Wolverhampton Corporation)
Extensive parkland. Grounds only open.

Trentham Gardens, *Trentham* (Countess of Sutherland)
Some 600 acres of formal gardens, woodland and parkland.

HISTORIC MONUMENTS

Alton Towers, *Alton*
Ruined early 19th-century mansion. Former home of Earl of Shrewsbury.

Croxden Abbey, *Croxden*
Ruins of small Cistercian abbey, started in 1176.

Roman Baths, *Wall*
Excavated remains of town baths.

Tutbury Castle, Nr *Burton-upon-Trent*
Ruined 14th-century stronghold.

MUSEUMS AND GALLERIES

Arnold Bennett Museum, 205 Waterloo Road, Cobridge, *Stoke-on-Trent* (Stoke District Council)
Arnold Bennett's early home. Drawings and personal relics.

Borough Museum and Hobbergate Art Gallery, Brampton Park, *Newcastle-under-Lyme*
Museum: ceramics, weapons, clocks, textiles, natural and local history. Art Gallery: English oil and watercolour paintings, 17th to 20th centuries; changing exhibitions of contemporary art and sculpture.

353

Cheddleton Flint Mill, Nr *Leek* (Cheddleton Flint Mill Industrial Heritage Trust)
Twin water wheels on River Churnet operate flint grinding pans. Museum collection of machinery used in pottery milling. Narrow boat *Vienna* moored on Caldon Canal.
City Museum and Art Gallery, Broad Street, Hanley, *Stoke-on-Trent* (Stoke District Council)
Local ceramics.
Dr Johnson's Birthplace, Breadmarket Street, *Lichfield*
Relics and pictures of Dr Johnson and his contemporaries.
Ford Green Hall, Smallthorne, *Stoke-on-Trent* (Stoke District Council)
16th-century timbered-frame manor house containing furniture and utensils. Associations with Izaak Walton and early Quakers.
Gladstone Pottery Museum, Uttoxeter Road, Longton, *Stoke-on-Trent* (Staffordshire Pottery Industry Preservation Trust)
Working museum of British pottery. Early Victorian 'potbank' complete with original bottle ovens and restored old workshops in which pottery is seen being made. Galleries relate the development of Staffordshire potteries, ceramic tiles, sanitary ware and decorating techniques.
Izaak Walton Cottage, Shallowfield, *Stafford* (Staffordshire County Council)
Angler Izaak Walton's restored country cottage.
Leek Art Gallery, Nicholson Institute, *Leek*
Small permanent collection supplemented by travelling exhibitions.
Letocetum Museum, *Wall* (Department of the Environment)
Finds from excavated Roman Station Letocetum.
Lichfield Art Gallery and Museum, Bird Street, *Lichfield* (Lichfield Corporation)
Local history museum. Art Gallery shows loan and local exhibitions and has picture loan service.
Museum and Art Gallery, Guild Street, *Burton-upon-Trent*
Museum of local history and British birds. Art Gallery sponsors travelling art exhibitions.
Spitfire Museum, Bethesda Street, Hanley, *Stoke-on-Trent*
Houses a Spitfire RW388 Mk LF 16E built in 1944, together with a number of other items of aeronautical interest.
Spode Museum and Factory, Church Street, *Stoke-on-Trent*
Working museum. Examples of 18th–20th-century Spode pottery.
Stafford Museum and Art Gallery, The Green, *Stafford* (Staffordshire County Council)
History, social life, art and industry of the locality. Art Gallery shows loan and local art exhibitions.
Staffordshire County Museum and Mansion House, *Shugborough*

(National Trust, administered by Staffordshire County Council)
Estate buildings, brewhouse, laundry, stables, coach houses, farm
equipment, crafts, domestic life, costume, geology and natural
history. Ancestral home of Earls of Lichfield, fine neo-classical
park monuments. House with 18th-century French furniture,
paintings, porcelain, silver, etc.
Tamworth Castle Museum, The Holloway, *Tamworth*
Norman castle with medieval banqueting hall and Jacobean state
apartments; houses local history museum.
Wedgwood Museum, Barlaston, *Stoke-on-Trent* (Josiah Wedgwood
and Sons Ltd)
Extensive collection of early Wedgwood ware.
William Salt Library, *Stafford*
18th-century town house. Books and manuscripts dealing with county.

NATIONAL PARKS
Peak District (part)

SUFFOLK
AREAS OF OUTSTANDING NATURAL BEAUTY
Dedham Vale (part)
Suffolk Coast and Heaths

CASTLES AND HISTORIC HOUSES
Christchurch Mansion, *Ipswich* (Borough of Ipswich)
Tudor house, furnished as period house.
Euston Hall, *Thetford* (Duke of Grafton)
18th-century house. Fine collection of paintings. Pleasure grounds by
John Evelyn and William Kent. Gardens and 17th-century parish
church in Wren style.
Gainsborough's House, *Sudbury* (Gainsborough's House Society)
Gainsborough's birthplace. Pictures, etc.
Glemham Hall, Nr *Woodbridge* (Lady Blanche Cobbold)
Red brick Elizabethan house. Altered early 1700. Panelled rooms,
fine staircase, Queen Anne furniture. Red brick-walled garden.
Haughley Park, Nr *Stowmarket* (Mr and Mrs A. J. Williams)
Jacobean manor house. Gardens and park.
Heveningham Hall, Nr *Halesworth* (Department of the Environment)
Georgian mansion in English Palladian tradition. Interior design and
decoration by James Wyatt in neo-classical style. Park and gardens
by Capability Brown.
Ickworth, Nr *Bury St Edmunds* (National Trust)
The house, begun c. 1794, not completed until 1830. Contents
include late Regency and 18th-century French furniture, silver,
pictures. Formal gardens, herbaceous borders, orangery. Albana
woodland walk.

355

Ixworth Abbey, Ixworth, *Bury St Edmunds* (Mrs Alan Rose)
House contains 12th-century monastic buildings with 15th- and 19th-century additions.

Kentwell Hall, *Long Melford* (J. Patrick Phillips, Esq)
Red brick Elizabethan E-plan mansion surrounded by broad moat. Exterior little altered. Interior recently refurbished. Inter-connecting gardens with specimen trees and magnificent avenue of ancient limes.

Little Hall, *Lavenham* (Suffolk Preservation Society)
15th-century high hall house. Gayer Anderson collection of furniture, pictures, china, books, etc.

Melford Hall, Nr *Sudbury* (National Trust)
Built between 1554 and 1578 by Sir William Cordell. Fine pictures, furniture and Chinese porcelain. Garden and gazebo.

Somerleyton Hall, Nr *Lowestoft* (Lord and Lady Somerleyton)
Dates from 16th century, added to in 1844. Grinling Gibbons carving, library, tapestries, pictures. Beautiful garden. Children's farm. Heritage display.

CATHEDRALS AND CHURCHES

Bacton (St Mary)
East Anglian stone and flint work. 15th-century timber roofs.

Blythburgh (Holy Trinity)
15th century. Fine cambered tie-beam roof; 15th-century bench-ends and carved stalls.

Bramfield (St Andrew)
Very early circular tower. Fine screen with vaulting. Nicholas Stone's Renaissance effigy of Mrs Arthur Coke, 1634.

Bury St Edmunds (St Mary)
15th-century hammer-beam roof in nave and wagon roof in chancel. North chapel furnished by Comper. South chapel with Boret monument, 1467.

Dennington (St Mary)
Aisle and parclose screens complete with lofts and parapets. 17th- and 18th-century pulpit and box-pews, 15th-century bench-ends, 15th-century alabaster monument.

Denston (St Nicholas)
Late 15th century. Fine arch braced roof with cambered tie-beam; good choir stalls; 7-sacrament font.

Earl Stonhay (St Mary)
Rebuilt in 14th century. Fine hammer-beam roof. 17th-century pulpit with 4 hour-glasses.

Euston (St Genevieve)
17th century. Note panelling; reredos possibly by Grinling Gibbons; plaster ceiling in south aisle.

Framlingham (St Michael)
Chancel rebuilt in 16th century to house tombs of Howard family;

treasures of monumental art. Chancel itself furnished with altar and reredos by Sir Thomas Jackson, RA and organ by Thamar, 1674. 15th-century nave and west tower with hammer-beam roof enclosed in false vaulting.

Fressingfield (St Peter and St Paul)
Very fine 15th-century woodwork.

Hessett (St Ethelbert)
15th-century tower. Late medieval wall paintings.

Kedington (St Peter and St Paul)
Medeival fabric. 16th-century hammer-beam roof. Fine 17th–18th-century woodwork. Barnardiston monuments.

Lavenham (St Peter and St Paul)
Late 15th century. Perpendicular with fine towers. Chantry chapel. Some original stalls and return stalls; 14th-century chancel screen. 17th-century alabaster monument.

Long Melford (Holy Trinity)
Cathedral-like proportions. Notable 15th-century glass. Cornelius Cure's monument to Sir William Cordell, 1530. Fine brasses. Clopton chantry chapel with fine roof. 15th-century Lady chapel surrounded by ambulatory with cambered tie-beam roof.

Mildenhall (St Mary)
Magnificent cambered tie-beam roof with arch-braced hammer-beams. 13th-century fabric with 15th-century rebuilding.

Needham Market (St John the Baptist)
Very fine cambered tie-beam and hammer-beam roof to nave.

Rougham (St Mary)
14th–15th century with early 16th-century north aisle. 15th-century hammer-beam roof to nave.

Southwold (St Edmund)
15th century with many contemporary fittings including notable stalls, return stalls, screen and pulpit. Hammer-beam roof.

Stoke-by-Nayland (St Mary)
Noble tower. 16th–17th-century library. Fine nave and arcades. Monuments and brasses.

Sudbury (St Gregory)
Fine font cover; 15th-century roof with canopy of honour for rood; 14th-century chancel. One original screen painting survives.

Ufford (St Mary)
Magnificent medieval font cover.

GARDENS
Helmingham Hall Gardens, *Ipswich* (Lord and Lady Tollemache)
Moated gardens in ancient deer park, ornamental waterfowl, safari rides.

HISTORIC MONUMENTS
Bungay Castle, *Bungay*
Dates from 12th century. Restored 13th-century gatehouse and drawbridge.
Burgh Castle Roman Fort, *Burgh*
3rd-century coastal defence.
Bury St Edmund's Abbey, *Bury St Edmunds*
Only west end of abbey stands above ground.
Framlingham Castle, *Framlingham*
12th–13th century with Tudor almshouses and chimneys.
Herringfleet Priory, *Herringfleet*
Remains of small Augustinian priory started in 1216.
Leiston Abbey, *Leiston*
14th-century remains including choir and transepts of church and range of cloisters.
Orford Castle, *Orford*
3 towers. 18-sided keep, c. 1165.

MUSEUMS AND GALLERIES
Abbot's Hall Museum of Rural Life of East Anglia, *Stowmarket*
Rural life of the area, agriculture, crafts, and domestic utensils. 70-acre open-air museum.
Dunwich Museum, *Dunwich*
Local history, flora and fauna.
Gershom-Parkington Memorial Collection of Clocks and Watches, 8 Angel Hill, *Bury St Edmunds* (National Trust and Bury St Edmunds Borough Council)
A collection of clocks and watches in a Queen Anne House.
Ipswich Museum, High Street, *Ipswich*
Geology, prehistory, archaeology of Suffolk from earliest times to medieval period; natural history; ethnography.
Laxfield and District Museum, *Laxfield*
Local geography and history in 14th-century guildhall.
Moyse's Hall Museum, Buttermarket, *Bury St Edmunds* (Bury St Edmunds Borough Council)
12th-century dwellinghouse containing local antiquities and natural history.
Southwold Museum, St Bartholomew's Green, *Southwold*
Local archaeology, natural history and bygones.

SURREY
AREAS OF OUTSTANDING NATURAL BEAUTY
Surrey Hills

CASTLES AND HISTORIC HOUSES
Albury Park, Albury, *Guildford* (Mutual Households Association Ltd)
Country mansion by Pugin.

Clandon Park, Nr *Guildford* (National Trust)
Palladian house built 1731–5 by Giacomo Leoni. Fine plasterwork. Furniture and pictures.

Claremont, *Esher* (Claremont School Trust Ltd)
Excellent example of Palladian style, built 1772 by Capability Brown for Clive of India. Henry Holland and John Soane responsible for interior. Now girls' school.

Detillens, *Limpsfield* (D. G. Neville)
Mid-15th-century Wealden house. Fine inglenooks and firebacks, medieval furniture. 1½ acres of mixed garden.

Greathed Manor, *Lingfield* (Mutual Households Association Ltd)
Victorian manor house.

Hatchlands, *East Clandon* (National Trust)
Built by Admiral Boscawen in 18th century. Interior by Robert Adam with later modifications.

Loseley House, *Guildford* (J. R. More-Molyneux, Esq)
Elizabethan mansion built 1562. Panelling, furniture, paintings, ceilings.

Polesden Lacy, Nr *Dorking* (National Trust, 1946)
Regency villa altered in Edwardian period. Greville collection of pictures, tapestries, furniture. 18th-century garden extended 1906, with herbaceous borders, rose garden, clipped hedges, lawns, beeches. Views.

CATHEDRALS AND CHURCHES

Compton (St Nicholas)
Only 2-storied sanctuary in England. 17th-century pulpit, rails and screen.

Esher (St George)
Brick transept with gallery pew, 1725–6. Altar-piece by Sir Robert Ker Porter. Picture of 'Apotheosis of Princess Charlotte' by A. W. Devis and marble monument to her by F. J. Williamson.

Gatton (St Andrew)
Modernized, 1834 and fitted with glass and woodwork from Europe.

Guildford Cathedral
Sir Edward Maufe, 1956–62. 'Simplified Gothic' interior with plaster rendering and Doulton limestone dressing.

Hascombe (St Peter)
H. Woodyer, 1864. Rich interior with gilded and painted reredos and roofs and moulded arches of windows.

Lingfield (St Peter and St Paul)
15th century. Stalls, screen and lectern with chained bible. Fine monuments.

Lowfield Heath (St Michael)
W. Burges, 1867. French–Gothic style. Fine sculpture.

Ockham (St Mary and All Saints)
13th-century work including east window of 7 lancets. 14th-century south side of nave; 15th-century tower. Monuments by Rysbrack; bust of Peter, 7th Baron King, 1783; Voysey casket.

Petersham (St Peter)
17th century unrestored. Pulpit, 1797. Pews and gallery.

Shere (St James)
12th century. South aisle and top of tower good 13th-century work; some work of 14th and 15th century. Carefully restored by S. Weatherley, 1895.

Stoke D'Abernon (St Mary)
Pre-Conquest south wall; north aisle late 12th century, chancel remodelled in 13th century. Norbury chapel, 15th century. Destructive restoration by Ford and Hesketh, 1866. Earliest brasses in England, 1277; remains of 13th-century painting in chancel; monuments; early 17th-century pulpit with tester, hour-glass.

GARDENS
Chilworth Manor, Nr *Guildford* (Sir Lionel Heald, QC)
Garden laid out in 17th century on site of 11th-century monastery: 18th-century walled garden; spring flowers, flowering shrubs, herbaceous border; 11th-century stewponds.

Feathercombe Gardens, *Hambledon* (Mrs Wieler and Miss Parker)
Wide views, flowering shrubs, heathers.

Hascombe Court, Nr *Godalming* (Mrs C. C. Jacobs)
Massed spring bulbs, rhododendrons, azaleas, camellias, magnolias; herbaceous borders.

Pyrford Court, *Pyrford* (Burnhill Estates Co. Ltd)
Shrubs, rhododendrons, wild garden, grey and golden borders, wistarias.

Ramster, *Chiddingfold* (Sir Aubrey and Lady Burke)
Large woodland garden, fine rhododendrons, azaleas, camellias, magnolias, trees and shrubs.

Winkworth Arboretum, Nr *Godalming* (National Trust)
95 acres of trees and shrubs planted mainly for autumn colour.

Wisley Garden, *Wisley* (Royal Horticultural Society)
British gardening at its best in all aspects.

HISTORIC MONUMENTS
Guildford Castle, *Guildford*
Ruined 12th-century keep.

Waverley Abbey, Nr *Farnham*
First Cistercian abbey in England, 1128. Excavation and clearance proceeding.

MUSEUMS AND GALLERIES

Camberley Museum, Knoll Road, *Camberley* (Surrey Heath Borough Council)
Local natural history, history and archaeology.

Charterhouse School Museum, *Godalming*
Carthusiana, archaeology. Greek pottery, medals, old English household equipment, ethnography, natural history. Peruvian pottery.

Chertsey Museum, The Cedars, Windsor Street, *Chertsey* (Runnymede District Council)
18th- and 19th-century costume and furniture, ceramics, local history and archaeology.

The Egham Museum, The Literary Institute, *Egham* (Runnymede Historical Society)
Archaeology and local history.

Farnham Museum, Willmer House, 38 West Street, *Farnham* (Waverley District Council)
Early Georgian front of cut and moulded brick; fine carving and panelling; walled garden.

Guildford House, 155 High Street, *Guildford* (Guildford Borough Council)
Monthly art exhibitions and picture loan service. 17th-century house of architectural interest.

Guildford Museum, Castle Arch, *Guildford* (Guildford Borough Council)
Archaeological and historical museum for the county, especially West Surrey and Guildford Borough. Needlework collection.

Haslemere Educational Museum, High Street, *Haslemere*
British birds, geology, zoology, botany, local industries, etc.

National Army Museum Detachment RMA, Sandhurst, Camberley
Indian Army Memorial Room. Blenheim Basement includes museums of the six Irish regiments disbanded in 1922.

Old Kiln Agricultural Museum, *Tilford*
Old farm implements. Examples of crafts and trades allied to farming.

*The Picture Gallery, Royal Holloway College, *Egham* (University of London)
Pictures mainly by British artists of late 18th and early 19th centuries.

Priory Museum, *Reigate*
Dates from 1235. Tudor manor with Palladian stucco embellishments. Local history.

*Royal Earlswood Hospital Museum, *Redhill*
Sections dealing with finance, medical and nursing matters, elections, early history and development, education, training and occupation, entertainment, building, farming and engineering.

361

Watermill Museum, *Haxted*
17th–18th-century mill. Mill machinery and 2 working water wheels.
Watts Gallery, Compton, *Guildford*
Paintings by G. F. Watts, OM, RA.
Weybridge Museum, Church Street, *Weybridge*
Local exhibits of archaeology, costume and local history.

TYNE AND WEAR
CASTLES AND HISTORIC HOUSES
Washington Old Hall, *Washington* (National Trust, administered by Washington Urban District Council)
Jacobean manor house incorporating portions of 12th-century house of the Washington family.

CATHEDRALS AND CHURCHES
Jarrow (St Paul)
Church where Bede worshipped. 2 churches joined in late 11th century. Carved stones, medieval chair.
Newcastle (St Andrew)
12th-century chancel arch and nave arcading 15th-century font cover. Hanoverian Royal Arms.
Newcastle (St Nicholas)
(Now enjoys Cathedral status following post-1850 Diocesan re-organisation.) 14th century with fine 15th-century lantern tower. 15th-century heraldic font and cover. 17th-century monuments. Roundel of 14th-century glass. Charles II Royal Arms.

GARDENS
Wildlife Trust Refuge, Nr *Sunderland*
103 acres with waterfowl in landscaped surroundings.

HISTORIC MONUMENTS
Arbiea Roman Fort, *South Shields*
Remains include gateways, headquarters and granaries.
Tynemouth Priory and Castle, *Tynemouth*
16th-century ruin with towers, gatehouse and keep erected to defend nearby 11th–13th-century priory.

MUSEUMS AND GALLERIES
Arbiea Roman Fort Museum, Baring Street, *South Shields* (Tyne and Wear County Council)
Memorial stones and small objects found on site.
Bagpipe Museum, The Black Gate, St Nicholas Street, *Newcastle-upon-Tyne*
Gate-house added to 'New Castle' in 1247 now contains collection of bagpipes.

Grindon Museum of Local History, Grindon Lane, *Sunderland* (Tyne and Wear County Council)
Period rooms and shop interiors.

Jarrow Hall, Church Bank, *Jarrow* (St Paul's Jarrow Development Trust)
Archaeological finds from excavations of Saxon and medieval monastery of St Paul's, Jarrow. Information room of early Christian sites in north. Temporary exhibitions of photographs and artists' work. Period furniture.

John G. Joicey Museum of Local History, City Road, *Newcastle-upon-Tyne* (Tyne and Wear County Council)
Local historical exhibits, furniture and armour.

Keep Museum, St Nicholas Street, *Newcastle-upon-Tyne*
Collections of medieval material.

Laing Art Gallery, Higham Place, *Newcastle-upon-Tyne* (Tyne and Wear County Council)
British art in oils and watercolours from 17th century onwards. Pottery and porcelain, glass, silver and metal work.

Monkwearmouth Museum of Land Transport, North Bridge Street, *Sunderland* (Tyne and Wear County Council)
Neo-classical station of 1848. Restored North Eastern Railway booking office. Exhibits show history of local land transport and of St Peter's Church.

Museum and Art Gallery, Borough Road, *Sunderland* (Tyne and Wear County Council)
Zoology, botany, geology, archaeology, local history, ship models, pottery and English silver. Period rooms. Collection of paintings by British artists in the Art Gallery. Frequent loan exhibitions.

National Music Hall Museum, 2 Garden Row, *Sunderland* (Tyne and Wear County Council)
History and developments of music hall in England. Late 19th- and 20th-century collection of costume and associated artefacts.

Plummer Tower, Croft Street, *Newcastle-upon-Tyne* (Tyne and Wear County Council)
18th-century period rooms, also Thomas Bewick Room, principally collection of his prints and drawings.

Ryhope Engines Museum, *Sunderland*
Victorian water pumping station with pair of restored beam engines and small museum.

Science Museum, Exhibition Park, Great North Road, *Newcastle-upon-Tyne* (Tyne and Wear County Council)
Engineering, shipbuilding, mining, transport, electrical and other industries, with special reference to north-east.

Shipley Art Gallery, Prince Consort Road South, *Gateshead* (Tyne and Wear County Council)

Collection of Dutch and Flemish schools of painting. Modern crafts. Loan exhibitions.

The University of Newcastle-upon-Tyne

The Greek Museum, Percy Building, The Quadrangle
Greek and Etruscan art ranging from Minoan to Hellenistic times; vases, terracottas, bronzes, gems and armour.

Hancock Museum, Barras Bridge (Jointly with the Natural History Society of Northumbria)
Natural history. Ethnographical section. Original drawings by Thomas Bewick, Tyneside engraver. Recently completed displays of British Mammals and 'A Picture of Northumberland'. Also Border Forest Museum at Lewisburn, Kielder, Northumberland, dealing with all aspects of natural history, geology and human history in the area.

The Hatton Gallery, The Quadrangle
Collection of Italian and other paintings. Regular loan exhibitions.

Museum of Antiquities, The Quadrangle (Jointly with the Society of Antiquaries)
Prehistoric, Roman and Anglo-Saxon antiquities, chiefly from Northumberland. Scale models of Hadrian's Wall and reconstructions of Roman arms and armour and a temple of Mithras.

Museum of the Department of Mining Engineering, Queen Victoria Road
Mine safety lamps and other exhibits illustrating history of mining. Watercolours of Northumberland and Durham mines, 1838–42, by T. H. Hair.

WARWICKSHIRE

CASTLES AND HISTORIC HOUSES

Arbury Hall, *Nuneaton* (F. H. FitzRoy Newdegate, Esq)
George Eliot's 'Cheverel Manor'. 18th-century Gothic mansion, pictures, period furniture, etc. Park and landscaped gardens.

Charlecote Park, *Warwick* (National Trust)
Originally built by Lucy family 1558. Deer park.

Compton Wynyates, *Tysoe* (Earl Compton)
Dates from 1480, a picturesque example of Tudor domestic architecture. Topiary garden.

Coughton Court, *Alcester* (National Trust)
Central gatehouse, 1509. 2 mid-Elizabethan half-timbered wings. Jacobite relics. Home of Throckmorton family since 1409.

Farnborough Hall, Nr *Banbury* (National Trust)
Dates from 17th and 18th centuries. Terrace walk with garden temples and splendid views.

Harvard House, *Stratford-upon-Avon* (Harvard House Memorial Trust)
Built 1596. Home of mother of John Harvard, founder of American University.

Packwood House, *Hockley Heath* (National Trust)
Timber-framed Tudor house with mid-17th century additions. Tapestry, needlework, Carolean formal garden, and yew garden of c. 1650 representing the Sermon on the Mount.

Ragley Hall, *Alcester* (Marquess of Hertford)
Built in 1680. Fine paintings, china and furniture and works of art, and a valuable library. Gardens, park and lake.

Shakespeare's Birthplace Trust Properties, *Stratford-upon-Avon*

Anne Hathaway's Cottage, Shottery
Thatched home of Anne Hathaway before her marriage to Shakespeare.

Hall's Croft, in Old Town
Fine Tudor house, period furniture and walled garden where Shakespeare's daughter Susanna and Dr John Hall lived.

Mary Arden's House, Wilmcote
Tudor farmhouse where Shakespeare's mother lived, with a farming museum in the barns. Dovecote.

New Place, Chapel Street
Foundations of Shakespeare's last home, preserved in Elizabethan garden setting with Nash's House adjoining.

Shakespeare's Birthplace, Henley Street
Half-timbered house where Shakespeare was born, containing many rare Shakespearian exhibits.

Upton House, *Edgehill* (National Trust)
Tapestries. Fine collection paintings, porcelain. Terraced gardens.

Warwick Castle, *Warwick* (Lord Brooke)
Fine inhabited medieval castle. Present castle is example of 14th-century fortification. State apartments. Grounds and gardens by Capability Brown.

CATHEDRALS AND CHURCHES

Astley (St Mary the Virgin)
1608. Remains of 14th-century chancel of ruined collegiate church. Notable 15th-century painted choir stalls.

Beaudesert (St Nicholas)
Norman. Note chancel arches. Norman style vault to chancel, 1865.

Brailes (St George)
15th-century steeple; good decorated nave and aisles; 14th-century font; famous 15th-century carved chest.

Coleshill (St Peter and St Paul)
14th–15th-century; fine steeple; Digby memorials; Norman font.

Compton Wynyates (no dedication)
Restoration church. 2 ceiling paintings.
Great Packington (St James)
Classic 'Mausoleum' by Bonomi, 1790. Made to appear hollowed as from solid rock.
Hampton Lucy (St Peter and Vincula)
19th-century Gothic. Fine vaulted nave. Window tracery.
Lapworth (St Mary)
Largely 13th–14th-century. Steeple connected by passage with north aisle; square headed clerestory; double-storey annexe at west end.
Preston-on-Stour (The Blessed Virgin Mary)
Mainly 18th century. Gothic gilded ceiling; monuments; 17th–18th-century glass.
Stratford-upon-Avon (Holy Trinity)
15th century. Steeple is Georgian pastiche by Hiorn of Warwick, 1763.
Tredington (St Gregory)
Saxon nave walls pierced by later arcades, otherwise 14th century. Fine spire; 14th-century benches; 17th-century screen and pulpit.
Warwick (St Mary)
15th-century Beauchamp Chapel; fine vaulted choir; remainder late 17th-century Gothic Revival by Wilson and Wren.
Wootton Wawen (St Peter)
Saxon. Fragments of medieval wall paintings; small 17th-century chained library; 15th-century pulpit and screens; monuments from 15th century onwards.

GARDENS
Pleck Gardens, *Alcester* (Miss E. C. Chapman)
Roses, heather, rhododendrons, etc. Formal garden and ponds.

MUSEUMS AND GALLERIES
Doll Museum, Oken's House, Castle Street, *Warwick*
Joy Robinson collection of antique and period dolls and toys.
Leamington Spa Art Gallery and Museum, Avenue Road, *Leamington Spa* (Warwick District Council)
Paintings by Dutch and Flemish masters; mainly English 20th-century oils and watercolours. 16th–19th-century pottery and porcelain. 18th-century and modern English glass.
Nuneaton Museum and Art Gallery, Riversley Park, *Nuneaton*
Prehistory, archaeology, geology, mining, ethnography and anthropology, paintings and engravings, coins and medals. George Eliot personalia, artistic exhibitions, etc.
The Royal Shakespeare Theatre Picture Gallery, *Stratford-upon-Avon*
Original paintings and designs, portraits of famous actors and actresses. Exhibition of Shakespeare portraits, and X-ray radiographs of 'Flower' and 'Venice' portraits.

Rugby Library, Exhibition Gallery and Museum, St Matthew Street, *Rugby*
Loan exhibitions by local societies.
St John's House, Coten End, *Warwick* (Warwickshire County Council)
Warwickshire bygones, period costume and furniture. Changing exhibitions. Museum of the Royal Warwickshire Regiment. The Museum Education Service.
Warwickshire Museum, Market Place, *Warwick* (Warwickshire County Council)
Headquarters of Museum Service. Wild life, geology, archaeology and history of Warwickshire. Changing exhibitions.

WEST MIDLANDS

CASTLES AND HISTORIC HOUSES

Aston Hall, Trinity Road, *Birmingham* (Corporation of Birmingham)
Fine Jacobean house built 1618–35. Many rooms furnished as period settings
Moseley Old Hall, *Wolverhampton* (National Trust)
Elizabethan house, formerly half-timbered. Reproduction 17th-century box parterre; period plants.
Oak House, *West Bromwich* (Metropolitan Borough of Sandwell)
Example of Tudor domestic architecture with Jacobean additions, fine oak panelling and carving, period furniture and furnishings. Public park with Elizabethan-style garden at the front.
Selly Manor House and Minworth Greaves, Bournville, *Birmingham*
Two 13th-century and early 14th-century timbered houses. Old furniture and domestic equipment.
Wightwick Manor, *Wolverhampton* (National Trust)
William Morris period house. Garden of varied interest.

CATHEDRALS AND CHURCHES

Berkswell (St John the Baptist)
Rich Norman work. Vaulted crypt. Black-and-white 2-storey timber porch.
Binley (St Bartholomew)
Probably by Robert Adam, 1773. Classical coloured windows painted naturalistically. Interior with Adamesque plaster to resemble salon of period.
Birmingham (St Peter and St Paul, Aston)
15th-century tower and spire. Notable 15th-century monuments.
Birmingham (St Philip)
(Now enjoys cathedral status following post-1850 Diocesan reorganization.) Designed by T. Archer. Notable Baroque tower.

Castle Bromwich (St Mary and St Margaret)
Brick box of 1732 enclosing medieval timber-framed chapel. 18th-century fittings; box pews, 2-decker pulpit, wrought-iron altar rails.
Coventry Cathedral
Sir Basil Spence, 1956–62. Sutherland altar tapestry; west screen, a wall of glass etched by John Hutton; stained glass; Epstein's 'St Michael and Lucifer'.
Warburton (St Werburgh)
Mainly timber building. Jacobean pulpit altar and rails.
Wolverhampton (Collegiate Church of St Peter)
Mostly 1480 with Victorian chancel. Fine stone pulpit; woodwork; monuments.

GARDENS
Botanical Gardens, Edgbaston, *Birmingham*
Wide range of trees, flowering shrubs, plants and glasshouses, alpine garden, rose and rhododendron gardens, lily ponds, aviaries.

HISTORIC MONUMENTS
Dudley Castle, *Dudley*
14th-century ruins.
Lune Roman Fort, Baginton, *Coventry*
Reconstruction of Roman fort which stood on site AD 71–5.
Weoley Castle, Selly Oak, *Birmingham*
Ruins of fortified manor house dating from late 13th century. Small museum.

MUSEUMS AND GALLERIES
Art Gallery and Museum, Holyhead Road, *Wednesbury* (Sandwell Corporation)
Edwin Richards collection of Victorian paintings and watercolours, local history, frequent temporary exhibitions.
*The Assay Office, Newhall Street, *Birmingham*
Old Birmingham and other silverware, coins, tokens and medals. Library dealing with all aspects of gold and silversmithing. Collection of correspondence of Matthew Boulton comprising some thousands of letters, c. 1760–1810.
Bantock House, Bantock Park, *Wolverhampton* (Wolverhampton Corporation)
English painted enamels and Japanned ware. Worcester porcelain and Staffordshire and Wedgwood pottery. Dolls and local collections.
Barber Institute of Fine Arts, The University, *Birmingham*
Art collection belonging to the Trustees.
Bilston Museum and Art Gallery, Mount Pleasant, *Wolverhampton* (Wolverhampton Corporation)
English painted enamels and 18th- and 19th-century local trades.

368

Birmingham City Museum and Art Gallery, Congreve Street, *Birmingham*
Department of Archaeology, Ethnology, and Birmingham History
Archaeological objects from West Midlands and other parts of Britain, Near East, Mediterranean area, India, South and Central America. Ethnographic material from North America and Pacific. Also Pinto collection of wooden bygones, collection of Birmingham-made coins and medals and other items of local interest.
Department of Art
Old master paintings, Italian 17th-century paintings and English watercolours. Sculpture, costume and silver.
The Department of Natural History
Collections include Beale, Chase and Lysaght collections of British birds; Bagnall and Whitwell herbaria; Kenrick lepidoptera and Bragge and Ansell collections of gemstones.
Museum Education Department
Assists teachers wishing to use Museum collections in their work.
Museum of Science and Industry, Newhall Street
Items of general and scientific interest. Also temporary exhibitions, films and lectures.
Blakesley Hall, Blakesley Road, Yardley, *Birmingham*
Timber-framed yeoman's farmhouse of about 1600 partly furnished as period house with displays of history and crafts of Yardley.
Brierley Hill Glass Museum and Art Gallery, Moor Street, *Dudley*
Collection of international glass, reference library. Occasional temporary exhibitions of glass and fine art.
Cannon Hill Nature Centre and Museum, south-west entrance to Cannon Hill Park, *Birmingham*
6 acres showing variety of natural history and conservation subjects, including animals and plants. Designed primarily to satisfy needs of children.
Central Art Gallery, Lichfield Street, *Wolverhampton* (Wolverhampton Corporation)
18th- and 19th-century English watercolours and oil paintings including works by Bonington, Fuseli, Gainsborough and Wilson. Modern prints, paintings and drawings. Oriental collections.
Dudley Museum and Art Gallery, St James's Road, *Dudley*
Fine art; temporary exhibitions. Geological gallery; reconstructed Black Country nail forge. Adjacent Brooke Robinson museum shows benefactor's personal collection of fine art, Greek pottery, Japanese inro and netsuke and English enamels. Black Country Museum.
*Geological Department Museum, The University, Edgbaston, *Birmingham*
Collections in palaeontology, stratigraphy, petrology, mineralogy

and physical geology, including Holcroft collection of fossils and the Lapworth collection of graptolites.

Herbert Art Gallery and Museum, Jordan Well, *Coventry*
Collections are primarily local. Natural history and industry. Art Gallery displays frequent loan exhibitions and has built up collections of British landscape watercolours, watercolours of Warwickshire, topography, British domestic life, figure drawings by British artists of the twentieth century and it also houses Iliffe collection of Sutherland sketches for great Cathedral tapestry.

Museum and Art Gallery, Lichfield Street, *Walsall* (Walsall Metropolitan Borough Council)
Garman-Ryan collection of fine art, antiquities and ethnographical material. Local history material including Sister Dora, Loriners and Jerome K. Jerome collections. Museum of Leathercraft. Lock collections (at Willenhall). Regular loan exhibitions from national, regional and local sources.

The Museum of Leathercraft, Central Library and Art Gallery, Lichfield Street, *Walsall*
'Leather in Life' permanent exhibition.

Stourbridge Glass Collection, Mary Stevens Park, *Stourbridge*
Local glass. John Northwood II and Benjamin Richardson II collections.

Whitefriars Museum, Whitefriars Street, *Coventry*
Mainly medieval archaeological exhibits in dormitory of medieval white friary.

WEST SUSSEX
AREAS OF OUTSTANDING NATURAL BEAUTY
Chichester Harbour (part)
Sussex Downs (part)

CASTLES AND HISTORIC HOUSES
Arundel Castle, *Arundel* (His Grace the Duke of Norfolk)
Ancient castle rebuilt 18th century and altered 1890. Fine portraits and furniture dating from 15th century.

Cuckfield Park, *Cuckfield* (M. J. Holt, Esq)
Elizabethan manor house and gatehouse, outstanding screen, fine panelling and ceilings. Large garden, shrubs, rhododendrons.

Danny, *Hurstpierpoint* (Mutual Households Association Ltd)
Elizabethan E-shaped house, dating from 1593.

Goodwood House, *Chichester* (1780–1800) (Goodwood Estate Company Limited)
Jacobean House added to by Chambers and Wyatt; stables by Chambers. Excellent Sussex flintwork. Pictures, tapestries, French and English furniture and porcelain. Specimen trees in park and 'High Wood'.

Newtimber Place, Newtimber, Nr *Hassocks* (Mr and Mrs John Clay)
Moated house. Etruscan wall paintings.
Parham, *Pulborough* (Mr and Mrs P. A. Tritton)
Elizabethan house. Elizabethan, Jacobean and Georgian portraits.
Fine furniture and needlework.
Petworth House, *Petworth* (National Trust)
Rebuilt 1688–96 by 6th Duke of Somerset. Later reconstruction by
Salvin. Deer park by Capability Brown. 13th-century chapel.
Paintings.
St Mary's, *Bramber* (Miss D. H. Ellis)
15th-century timber-framed house. Rare panelling. Collection of
handicrafts.
Tanyard, *Sharpthorne* (M. R. Lewinsohn, Esq)
Medieval tannery with 16th- and 17th-century additions. Greak oak
beams with open fireplaces with bric-a-brac typical of the period.
Walled garden.
*'The Thatched Cottage', *Lindfield* (Mrs Margaret G. Aldridge)
Close-studded Wealden house. Reputed Henry VII shooting lodge.
Small cottage garden.
Uppark, South Harting, Nr *Petersfield* (National Trust)
Built by Lord Tankerville 1690. Interior decoration and furnishings
unaltered since 18th century. Victorian kitchen with original fittings.
Small garden by Humphrey Repton.

CATHEDRALS AND CHURCHES
Arundel (St Nicholas)
Late 14th century. Wall paintings; wrought-iron grille; Fitzalan
chapel with monuments is property of Duke of Norfolk.
Boxgrove (St Mary and St Blaise)
Relic of Benedictine priory. Fine 13th-century choir with 16th-
century painted decoration on vaulting. 16th-century chantry; Late
Gothic and Renaissance, richly decorated, carved and coloured.
Chichester Cathedral
Norman on modest scale. Finest part is retrochoir built in 1186 in
Transitional style between Norman and earliest Gothic. Very fine
pair of large Romanesque relief sculptures in south choir aisle.
Hardham (St Botolph)
11th century with series of 12th-century wall paintings.
New Shoreham (St Mary de Haura)
Only tower transepts, long chancel and aisles remain. 12th–13th
century. Rich details in carving and capitals of north arcade;
clustered columns on south triforium. Lancet clerestory, stone vaults.
Sompting (St Mary)
11th-century Saxon tower with unique 'Rhenish helm' spire. Rest of
church 12th century. North transept has 2 east chapels, stone vaulted;
south transept, the Templars' chapel, originally separate from church.

Steyning (St Andrew)
12th-century lofty chancel arch; imposing arcades with chevron mouldings. Tile-capped tower, c. 1600. Queen Anne Royal Arms.
Trotton (St George)
c. 1300. Table tomb with 15th-century canopied brasses. Wall paintings; 17th-century altar, rails and font cover. Georgian Royal Arms.
Upmarden (St Michael)
13th century, unrestored. Plastered walls, brick floors, box pews.
Warminghurst (Holy Sepulchre)
13th century, remodelled in 1770. Complete 18th-century deal furnishings. Royal Arms. Hatchments; wrought-iron crane for font-canopy; 2 13th-century monuments; brass to Shelley.
West Chiltington (St Mary)
Chevroned north doorway; Transitional south arcade; wall paintings. Kingpost roof, 1602.
Worth (St Nicholas)
Late 10th century with chancel arch forming largest Saxon arch in England and massive arches to transepts. German carved pulpit, 1511; altar rails probably of same date and origin. West gallery, 1610.

GARDENS
Borde Hill Garden, *Haywards Heath*
Rare trees and shrubs, views, borders, woodland walks.
Heaselands, *Haywards Heath* (Ernest Kleinwort, Esq)
Flowering shrubs and trees, water gardens, woodland, aviary and small collection of waterfowl.
Highdown, Nr *Ferring*
Laid out in chalk pit with rock plants, flowering shrubs, and daffodils.
Leonardslee, *Horsham* (Sir Giles Loder, Bt, VMH)
Spring flowering shrub garden, camellias, rhododendrons, lakes.
Nymans Gardens, *Handcross* (National Trust)
Partly enclosed by walls, rare trees, shrubs and plants, herbaceous borders, bulbs.
South Lodge, *Lower Beeding* (Miss E. Godman)
Flowering trees, shrubs, rhododendrons, and rock garden.
Wakehurst Place Garden, Nr *Ardingly* (National Trust, administered by Royal Botanic Gardens, Kew)
Exotic plant species including many fine specimens of trees and shrubs. Watercourse linking several ponds and lakes.

HISTORIC MONUMENTS
Bramber Castle, *Bramber*
Ruined Norman stronghold.
Cowdray Ruins, *Midhurst*
Ruined 16th-century mansion.

Roman Palace, *Fishbourne*
Largest Roman residence found in Britain. Thought to be palace of King Tiberius Claudius Cogidubnus.
Roman Villa, *Bignor*
Occupied 2nd–4th century.

MUSEUMS AND GALLERIES
Bignor Roman Villa Collection, *Bignor*
4th-century mosaics, Samian and other pottery, jewellery, plaster, hypocaust, etc.
Chichester District Museum, 29 Little London, *Chichester*
Local history and archaeology, collections of Royal Sussex Regiment, special exhibitions.
Guildhall Museum, Priory Park, *Chichester*
Archaeology of Chichester and surrounding area.
Horsham Museum, Causeway House, *Horsham*
Housed in 16th-century gabled building. Local history, costumes, toys, early bicycles, domestic and rural life, crafts and industries of Sussex.
House of Pipes, *Bramber*
Exhibits from 150 countries covering 1,500 years.
Littlehampton Museum, 12A River Road, *Littlehampton* (Arun District Council)
Collections of sailing and marine material and objects of local interest including paintings.
Marlipins Museum, High Street, *Shoreham* (Sussex Archaeological Trust)
Building dating from the 12th century, housing collections of ship models, paintings and photographs of locality, geological specimens, old maps, household articles and coins.
Parsonage Row Cottages, High Street, *West Tarring*
Group of three late 15th-century close-timbered houses. Small folk museum of bygones.
Potters Museum of Curiosity, 6 High Street, *Arundel* (James Cartland, Esq)
Life and works of Victorian naturalist and taxidermist, Walter Potter, and other curiosities.
Priest House, *West Hoathly* (Sussex Archaeological Society)
15th-century monks' hall converted into dwellinghouse containing old furniture, bygones, dolls and embroideries.
*Richard Cobden Collection, Dunford, *Midhurst* (National Council of YMCAs)
Portraits and library of Richard Cobden and family.
Weald and Downland Open-air Museum, Singleton, *Chichester*
35-acre site used for re-erecting historic buildings from south-east England. Museum is also country park.

Worthing Museum and Art Gallery, Chapel Road, *Worthing* (Worthing Borough Council)
Archaeology, geology, costume, Sussex bygones and pottery, works of art including early English watercolours, dolls and jewellery.

WEST YORKSHIRE
CASTLES AND HISTORIC HOUSES
*Ackworth School, *Pontefract* (Co-educational Boarding School, Society of Friends)
Georgian building (1750). Only remaining building of London Foundling Hospital.
Bolling Hall, *Bradford* (Bradford Metropolitan Council)
Domestic architecture dating from 15th to late 18th century.
Bramham Park, *Wetherby* (Mr and Mrs George Lane Fox)
Queen Anne mansion. Fine furniture, pictures and porcelain. Grounds landscaped in style of Le Nôtre.
East Riddlesden Hall, *Keighley* (National Trust)
17th-century manor house. Tithe barn. Small formal garden.
Harewood House and Bird Gardens, Nr *Leeds* (Earl of Harewood)
18th-century house with decoration and furniture by Robert Adam and Thomas Chippendale. Fine pictures. Park and garden by Capability Brown.
Heath Hall, Nr *Wakefield* (Mr and Mrs Muir M. Oddie)
18th-century house by Carr of York. Fine carved woodwork and plasterwork by York stuccodors.
Lotherton Hall, *Abeford* (Leeds Metropolitan District Council)
Edwardian house with attractive gardens. Gascoigne collection of pictures and furniture.
Manor House, *Ilkley* (Bradford Metropolitan Council)
Small Tudor manor built on the site of Roman fort. Exposed Roman wall in grounds.
Nostell Priory, *Wakefield* (National Trust)
Built for Sir Rowland Winn by Paine; wing added in 1766 by Robert Adam. State rooms contain pictures and Chippendale furniture. Motor cycle museum.
Oakwell Hall, *Batley* (Kirklees Metropolitan Council)
16th-century period house. Brontë associations. Wall earth closet or 'secret passage'. Period furniture. Park and rural museum.
Redhouse, *Cleckheaton* (Kirklees Metropolitan Council)
Built in 1660 of red brick. Associations with Charlotte Brontë.
Shibden Hall, *Halifax* (Corporation of Calderdale)
15th-century timber-framed house with 17th-century furniture; 17th-century barn; early agricultural implements; coaches and harnesses.

Temple Newsam, *Leeds* (Leeds Metropolitan District Council)
Tudor–Jacobean house, birthplace of Lord Darnley, pictures and
furniture.

CATHEDRALS AND CHURCHES

Adel (St John the Baptist)
Norman nave and chancel. Sumptuous south portal with carvings in
gable. Norman closing ring. Rich chancel arch with interesting
capitals. 3 paintings by Vanderbank; stained glass by Henry Gyles,
1681 and 1706.

Halifax (St John the Baptist)
Perpendicular with 12th- and 13th-century work. Grand west tower.
Heraldic ceilings to nave and chancel, 1636; 15th-century font cover,
Jacobean pews in nave and altar rails of 1693; life-size figure known
as Tristram, 1701: 2 fine carved Royal Arms; 18th-century monu-
ments; Cromwellian glass.

Hemingborough (St Mary)
Formerly Collegiate; 13th- and 15th-century misericords. 16th-
century bench-ends in nave; early English pulpit; hatchment to
Dame Lennox Pilkington.

Leeds (St John the Evangelist)
1632–4. Twin naved plan in perpendicular survival; arabesque
plasterwork on ceiling; Jacobean screen, pulpit, bobbin-ended and
crested pews. Fine restoration by R. N. Shaw, 1868.

Leeds (St Peter)
Consecrated 1841, perpendicular style. Exterior with fine towers.
Black Gothic galleries; brasses and 10th-century cross from old
church; continental glass in east window; armorial glass in west
window.

Sprotbrough (St Mary)
Much altered 13th-century church. Decorated tower with perpendicular belfry. Rood screen with return stalls; decorated wall niche with
13th-century effigy; brass pulpit with traceried panels; 16th-century
bench-ends; Jacobean altar rails; early 19th-century organ. Chancel
and chapel furnishings by Comper.

Thornhill (St Michael)
Fine perpendicular west tower. Savile chapel, 1447, with much
original glass and monuments; Saxon fragments; alabaster and oak
effigies.

Tickhill (St Mary)
Splendid 15th-century tower on 13th-century base, remainder is late
15th century. 15th-century font under ciborium by G. G. Pace, 1959;
medieval panelling in pulpit; 15th- and 16th-century monuments;
coeval figure sculpture on tower.

375

GARDENS

Harlow Car Gardens, *Harrogate* (The Northern Horticultural Society)
Ornamental gardens and woodlands.

Parcevall Hall, *Wharfedale* (Walsingham College Trust)
Terraces with views. Natural rock and water gardens, herbaceous borders.

HISTORIC MONUMENTS

Pontefract Castle, *Pontefract*
Ruined stronghold including Norman clover-leaf keep, apsidal chapel, ovens and dungeons.

MUSEUMS AND GALLERIES

Abbey House Museum, Kirkstall, *Leeds* (City of Leeds)
Folk museum illustrating life and work of people of Yorkshire over the last 300 years. Houses 3 full-sized 19th-century streets of houses, shops and workplaces.

Art Gallery, Market Place, *Batley* (Kirklees Metropolitan Borough Council)
Paintings and drawings, etc. Loan exhibitions.

Art Gallery and Museum, Cartwright Hall, *Bradford* (Bradford Metropolitan Council)
Paintings, watercolours, drawings and prints from 17th century onwards. Antique and modern ceramics and sculpture.

Bagshaw Museum, Wilton Park, *Batley* (Kirklees Metropolitan Borough Council)
Local history, archaeology, geology, ethnography and oriental arts, natural history and bygones.

Bankfield Museum and Art Gallery, Akroyd Park, Halifax, *Calderdale* (Calderdale Borough Council)
Textile machinery, textiles, costume, archaeology, local history and natural history of area. Duke of Wellington's Regimental Museum and the 4th/7th Royal Dragoon Guards Regimental Museum.

Brighouse Art Gallery, *Brighouse*
Works mainly by 19th-century English artists. Temporary exhibitions.

Brontë Parsonage Museum, *Haworth*
Bronteana and Bonnell collection of manuscripts, etc.

Cartwright Hall, Lister Park, *Bradford*
European and British paintings, sculpture, drawings, modern prints, ceramics. Temporary exhibitions of natural history, geology and archaeology.

City Art Gallery, *Leeds* (City of Leeds)
Old masters, English watercolours; 19th- and 20th-century British and French paintings; representative modern painting and sculpture. Leeds and Staffordshire pottery. English silver. Study collections and public picture lending scheme.

City Art Gallery, Wendworth Terrace, *Wakefield* (Wakefield Metropolitan District Council)
Paintings, sculpture, drawings and prints; old masters; 18th-century English watercolours and drawings. Emphasis on modern school.

City Museum, Municipal Buildings, *Leeds* (City of Leeds)
Natural history, ethnography and archaeology.

City Museum, Wood Street, *Wakefield* (Wakefield Metropolitan District Council)
British 20th-century art and 17th- and 18th-century British and Continental paintings and watercolours.

Cliffe Castle Art Gallery and Museum, *Keighley*
Fine and applied art, natural history, archaeology and folk-life material, including reconstructed craft workshops. Frequent temporary exhibitions.

Clitheroe Castle Museum, *Clitheroe*
Carboniferous fossils and items of local interest.

Colne Valley Museum, Cliffe Ash, Golcar, *Huddersfield* (Colne Valley Museum Trust)
Local history, weaving workshop in weaver's cottage with living-room of about 1860. Clog-maker's shop lit by gas. Folk-life and industrial history.

Dewsbury Museum and Art Gallery, Crow Nest Park, *Dewsbury*
History of Dewsbury. British natural history. Travelling art exhibitions and local art.

Fulneck Moravian Museum, *Pudsey*
Moravian exhibits and Victoriana.

Heptonstall Old Grammar School Museum, Hebden Bridge, *Calderdale* (Hepton Rural District Council)
17th-century stone.

Huddersfield Art Gallery, Princess Alexandra Walk, Huddersfield (Kirklees Metropolitan Borough Council)
Oil paintings, watercolours, drawing, prints, sculpture, dating from the mid-19th century.

Industrial Museum, Moorside Mills, Moorside Road, Eccleshill, *Bradford* (Bradford Metropolitan Council)

Library and Museum, Carlton Street, *Castleford* (Wakefield Metropolitan District)
Roman objects and artefacts found in Castleford and Castleford pottery and glass.

Library of the Thoresby Society, 23 Clarendon Road, *Leeds*
Books, manuscripts, pictures, medals, coins, maps and relics of old Leeds.

Museum of Hand Tools, Banney Royd Teacher's Centre, Halifax Road, *Huddersfield*
Hand tools only.

377

Piece Hall, Halifax, *Calderdale* (Calderdale Borough Council)
Smith Art Gallery, Halifax Road, Brighouse, *Calderdale* (Calderdale Borough Council)
Oil paintings and watercolours, mainly 19th century.
Tolson Memorial Museum, Wakefield Road, *Huddersfield* (Kirklees Metropolitan Borough Council)
Geology, natural history, archaeology, folk-life, toys, development of cloth industry, horse-drawn vehicles.
Tong Hall, *Bradford* (Bradford Metropolitan Council)
18th-century brick hall.

NATIONAL PARKS
Peak District (part)

WILTSHIRE
AREAS OF OUTSTANDING NATURAL BEAUTY
Cotswolds (part)
North Wessex Downs (part)

CASTLES AND HISTORIC HOUSES
Chalcot House, *Westbury* (Mr and Mrs A. Rudd)
Small 17th-century Palladian manor.
Church House, Crane Street, *Salisbury*
15th-century house, once home of cloth merchant.
Corsham Court, *Chippenham* (Lord Methuen, ARICS)
Elizabethan (1582) and Georgian (1760–70) house, fine 18th-century furniture. British, Italian and Flemish old masters. Park and gardens by Capability Brown and Humphrey Repton.
Great Chalfield Manor, *Melksham* (National Trust)
15th-century moated manor house.
Lacock Abbey, Nr *Chippenham* (National Trust)
13th-century abbey converted into house in 1540 with 18th-century 'Gothick' alterations. Medieval cloisters, brewery and house open to public. Fine trees.
Littlecote, Nr *Hungerford* (D. S. Wills, Esq)
Tudor manor c. 1490–1520. Moulded plaster ceilings, panelled rooms. Great hall with Cromwellian armoury.
Longleat House, *Warminster* (Marquess of Bath)
Early Renaissance house built 1566–80 with later alterations early 1800s. Decorated in Italian Renaissance fashion during 19th century. Fine state rooms, furnishings, paintings and books. Restored Victorian kitchens. Game reserve.
Luckington Court, *Luckington* (Hon. Mrs Tevor Horn)
Mainly Queen Anne with magnificent group of ancient buildings. Mainly formal garden with collection of ornamental trees and shrubs.

Lydiard Mansion, *Purton* (Borough of Thamesdown)
Dating from medieval times, reconstructed 1743–9. Outstanding mid-Georgian decoration.

Malmesbury House, *Salisbury* (John H. Cordle)
Queen Anne house dating in part from 14th century. Baroque and Rococo plasterwork.

Mompesson House, *Salisbury* (National Trust)
Fine Queen Anne town house in Salisbury Close. Georgian plasterwork.

Newhouse, *Redlynch* (Mr and Mrs G. Jeffreys)
Brick Jacobean 'Trinity' house, c. 1619, with 2 Georgian wings, 1742 and 1760. Family portraits.

Phillips House, *Dinton* (National Trust)
Classical house built in 1816 by Sir Jeffry Wyatville for Wyndham family.

Pythouse, *Tisbury* (Mutual Households Association Ltd)
Palladian style Georgian mansion.

Sheldon Manor, *Chippenham* (Mrs E. Gibbs)
Plantagenet manor. 13th-century porch and 15th-century chapel. Terraced gardens with yew trees, roses, water, trees and shrubs.

Stourhead, *Stourton* (National Trust)
Celebrated mid-18th-century landscape gardens; fine trees. Palladian house designed in 1722 by Colen Campbell. Thomas Chippendale the Younger furniture.

Wardour Castle, *Tisbury* (Governors of Cranborne Chase School)
Magnificent house designed in the Palladian manner by James Paine in 1768. Fine rooms.

Westwood Manor, *Bradford-on-Avon* (National Trust)
15th-century manor house altered in the 16th and 17th centuries.

Wilton House, *Salisbury* (Earl of Pembroke)
Work of Inigo Jones (c. 1650) and later James Wyatt (1810). Notable 'Double Cube' room. Fine paintings. Kent and Chippendale furniture. Spacious lawns, fine cedar trees. Palladian bridge. Exhibition of model soldiers.

CATHEDRALS AND CHURCHES

Amesbury (St Mary and St Melor)
13th century refashioned in 15th century and restored in 19th century. Fine timber roofs; stone-vaulted chapel of north transept; Norman font; 15th-century screen; remains of medieval painted glass.

Bishops Cannings (St Mary the Virgin)
13th and 15th century. Note early windows at west end of north aisle; fine arcading for recessed altars in transept; Chapel of Our Lady of the Bower with monuments and Jacobean holy table; rich porch doorway; 17th-century alms-box.

Bishopstone (St John the Baptist)
Remodelled in 14th century. Decorated windows to chancel and transept. Vaulted chancel and south transept; north transept and nave have timber roofs with plaster panels; coeval sacristy on north side. Note sedilia; canopied niches; founder's tomb; doorway of south side of chancel.

Bradford-on-Avon (St Lawrence)
Most notable Saxon church in England. Fine architectural details and sculpture.

Cricklade (St Sampson)
Great Tudor central tower. 12th–16th-century detail. Tower vault; late 15th-century south chapel; 18th-century chandelier.

Dauntsey (St James)
Mainly 14th–15th century with Norman north and south doorways. 14th- and 17th-century screen; painted tympanum; 16th-century painted glass; Jacobean seating; Danver monuments.

Dilton (St Mary)
Late medieval. 18th-century furnishings. Plastered tympanum.

Durnford (St Andrew)
Fine 13th-century tower. Remains of wall paintings and glass; 17th-century pulpit, lectern, communion rails.

Edington (Blessed Virgin Mary, St Katherine and All Saints)
14th-century Collegiate church. Rich moulding in quire; fine pulpit; 15th-century oak screen and pulpitum; 12 consecration crosses; 17th-century panelling and plaster ceiling in nave; 17th-century altar and tester, font cover, altar piece and communion rails; 14th-century glass; monuments.

Inglesham (St John the Baptist)
Medieval wall paintings; some old glass; remains of painted screens; high pews; old floors; clear glass; well-carved Georgian tombstones in churchyard.

Lacock (St Cyriac)
Mainly 14th–15th century. Very fine north chapel with pendant stone vault. Note window over chancel arch; nave roof; early 16th-century brass; medieval covered cup; fragments of old painted glass; mid-16th-century Sharington monument.

Lydiard Tregoze (St Mary the Virgin)
15th century. Extensive remains of murals; painted Jacobean screen; old glass; wrought-iron work; Renaissance monuments, finest in county.

Malmesbury (St Mary)
Norman, refashioned in 14th century. Fine Romanesque sculpture on south porch; 12th-century arcades; 14th-century clerestory; 15th-century stone pulpitum; 15th-century table tomb.

Mere (St Michael)
Rebuilt in 14th century. Fine tower, c. 1450. 7 old screens; vaulted

north porch; nave roof; 14th–15th-century brasses; 15th-century painted glass, monuments and stalls; 17th-century seating.

Mildenhall (St John the Baptist)
Fine 'Gothick' interior. Box pews, 2 pulpits, panelling reredos, communion rails and font.

Potterne (St Mary)
Mostly 13th century with 14th-century central tower and 15th-century parapet. Fine 13th-century work. Note inscribed Norman tub font and 15th-century wooden pulpit.

Purton (St Mary the Virgin)
13th–15th-century west tower and central spire. Niches and corbels; wall decoration; painted glass.

Salisbury Cathedral
1220–1380. Stone spire above fine decorated tower. Rest of exterior mostly early English. Interior with dark Purbeck marble contrasting with light Chilmark limestone. Front of original stone pulpitum preserved. Fine large early decorated cloisters.

Salisbury (St Thomas of Canterbury)
Rebuilt in 15th century. 'Doom' painting over chancel; mural paintings in south chapel; fine roofs in nave and south chapel; late 12th-century font; 14th–15th-century glass; embroidered funeral pall; 17th-century monuments.

Steeple Ashton (St Mary the Virgin)
15th century. Fine vaulting; notable roof to nave; monuments; remains of painted glass; brass chandeliers.

Tisbury (St John the Baptist)
Mainly 14th and 15th century. Fine 2-storied porch and chancel. 15th–17th-century roofs to nave and aisles. 17th-century seating.

Urchfont (St Michael)
Mainly 14th century with 15th-century additions. Notable chancel with gables, buttress and stone vaulting with carved bosses. Note 14th-century details in south aisle; round columns of nave arcades; 17th-century roof; 14th-century painted glass; 13th-century monuments.

Winterbourne Bassett (St Katharine and St Peter)
Fine decorated work. Note window and recessed tomb in transept with 13th-century tomb slab. Late Norman font and 17th-century cover. 17th-century furnishings; monuments; hatchments.

GARDENS
Bowood Gardens, *Calne* (Earl of Shelbourne)
100-acre garden containing many exotic trees, 40-acre lake, waterfalls, caves, and Doric temple. Arboretum. Pinetum, rose garden and Italian garden. 60 acres of rhododendrons separate to gardens.

Broadleas, *Devizes* (Lady Anne Cowdray)
Rare and interesting plants.

The Courts, *Holt* (National Trust)
Topiary garden with lily pond and arboretum.
Milton Manor, *Milton Lilbourne* (Mrs R. Gentle)
Gardens only open.

HISTORIC MONUMENTS
Avebury
Remains of gigantic circular gathering place, dating from between 2700–1700 BC.
Bratton Camp and White Horse, *Bratton*
Large hill fort above white horse.
Ludgershall Castle, *Ludgershall*
Norman motte and bailey castle, retaining earthworks and flint walling of later royal castle.
Old Sarum, Nr *Salisbury*
Probably first Iron Age camp, later Roman 'Sorviodunum', finally site of Norman castle and cathedral town.
Old Wardour Castle, *Wardour*
Ruins dating from 14th century.
Silbury Hill, Nr *Avebury*
Conical mound built perhaps as memorial, c. 3000–2000 BC.
Stonehenge, Nr *Amesbury*
Prehistoric monument. Encircling ditch, bank and Aubrey holes are Neolithic. Stone circles probably Early Bronze Age.
West Kenet Long Barrow, Nr *Avebury*
Communal burial place used between c. 4000–2500 BC.
Windmill Hill, Nr *Avebury*
'Causewayed-camp' occupied between c. 3000–2300 BC.

MUSEUMS AND GALLERIES
Alexander Keiller Museum, *Avebury* (Department of Environment)
Pottery and other objects of Neolithic and Bronze Ages and later dates from excavations of Avebury and Windmill Hill.
Athelstan Museum, Cross Hayes, *Malmesbury*
Articles concerned with town: coins, household articles and an old fire engine.
Bedwyn Stone Museum, *Great Bedwyn*
Open-air museum in village where Stonehenge was carved.
Borough of Thamesdown Museums and Art Gallery, *Swindon*
  Great Western Railway Museum, Faringdon Road
  Historic GWR locomotives, wide range of nameplates, models, illustrations, posters, tickets, etc.
  Lydiard Park, *Lydiard Tregoze*
  Fine Georgian mansion in park, together with adjoining parish church of St Mary, which contains memorials to the St John family. Permanent and travelling exhibitions.

Museum and Art Gallery, Bath Road
Archaeology, natural history and geology of Wiltshire; local by-
gones, coins and tokens; Manners collection of pot lids and ware.
20th-century British art collection and travelling exhibitions.
Richard Jefferies Museum, Coate
Personal items, manuscripts, first editions, etc, relating to Richard
Jefferies and Alfred Williams.
Devizes Museum, 41 Long Street, *Devizes* (Wiltshire Archaeological
and Natural History Society)
Unique archaeological and geological collections, concerned with
Wiltshire, including Sir Richard Colt-Hoare's Stourhead collection
of prehistoric material.
Lackham College of Agriculture, *Lacock*
Agricultural implements and tools.
Phillips Countryside Museum and Woodland Park, *Brokerswood*
Forestry exhibition. 88 acres of national woodland.
Salisbury and South Wiltshire Museum, St Ann Street, *Salisbury*
Natural and social history of Salisbury and South Wiltshire in all
periods. Models of Stonehenge and Old Sarum. Local guild and
craft relics, pottery and costumes.

SCOTLAND

There are no national parks or officially designated areas of outstanding national beauty in Scotland, though many areas, including almost
the whole of the Highlands, are regarded as such.

BORDER REGION
CASTLES AND HISTORIC HOUSES
Abbotsford House, *Melrose* (Mrs P. Maxwell-Scott)
Home of Sir Walter Scott, containing many historical relics collected
by him.
Bowhill House, Nr *Selkirk* (His Grace the Duke of Buccleuch)
House contains an outstanding collection of pictures, porcelain and
furniture.
Floors Castle, *Kelso* (Duke of Roxburghe)
Built in 1721 by William Adam, added to by Playfair. Tapestries,
French furniture, Chinese porcelain, paintings.
Mellerstain, *Gordon* (Lord Binning)
Scotland's famous Adam mansion. Beautifully decorated and fur-
nished interiors. Italian gardens and lake.
Traquair House, *Innerleithen* (P. Maxwell Stuart, Esq)
Historic mansion. Oldest inhabited house in Scotland. Rich in
associations with Mary, Queen of Scots and the Jacobite risings.

CATHEDRALS AND CHURCHES
Dryburgh Abbey
Romantic ruins, with tombs of Sir Walter Scott, Lord Haig and James II of Scotland.

GARDENS
Dawyck House Gardens, *Stobo* (Lt-Col A. N. Balfour of Dawyck)
Woodland garden with rare trees and shrubs by river Tweed. Narcissus in season, arboretum.
Kailzie Gardens, Nr *Peebles* (Mrs J. M. Richard)
Snowdrops, daffodils, mature timber and new shrubs. Herbaceous border and floral beds in walled garden. Wild garden and burnside walk.

HISTORIC MONUMENTS
Dryburgh Abbey, *Dryburgh*
Remains of monastery founded by David I.
Hermitage Castle, Nr *Stobo*
14th-century castle, wall restored.
Jedburgh Abbey, *Jedburgh*
Mostly Norman and Transitional remains of Church. Small museum.
Neipath Castle, *Peebles*
Dates from 14th century.

MUSEUMS AND GALLERIES
Hawick Museum and Art Gallery, Wilton Lodge Park, *Hawick*
Geological sections, natural history, coins, medals and church tokens. Local history and hosiery machinery section.
Chambers Institution, High Street, *Peebles*
Flora, fauna, geological specimens and exhibits connected with local history.
Coldstream Museum, *Coldstream*
House where General Monk raised Coldstream Guards, 1650. Uniforms, medals, old silver, horse brasses, stone and Bronze-Age flints.
Mary, Queen of Scots' House, Queen Street, *Jedburgh* (Roxburgh District Council)
Articles dealing with life of Mary, Queen of Scots; paintings and engravings.
Melrose Abbey Museum, *Melrose* (Secretary of State for Scotland)
Commendator's house fitted up to form attractive museum containing architectural and sculptural detail and other items associated with abbey.

CENTRAL REGION
CASTLES AND HISTORIC HOUSES
The House of the Binns, By *Linlithgow* (National Trust for Scotland (1944) and Mrs Dalyell of the Binns)
Fine plaster ceilings. Interesting pictures. Panoramic viewpoint.

Doune Castle, *Doune* (Earl of Moray)
Built 14th century and used as royal palace. Restored in 1883 and is now one of best preserved medieval castles in Scotland.
Linlithgow Palace, *Linlithgow* (Secretary of State for Scotland)
Birthplace of Mary, Queen of Scots.
Menstrie Castle, *Menstrie* (Clackmannan District Council (Central) and the National Trust for Scotland)
Birthplace of Sir William Alexander who became James VI's lieutenant for Plantation of Nova Scotia. Commemoration rooms only open.

GARDENS
Doune Park Gardens, *Doune* (Earl of Moray)
Garden originally laid out early 19th century by Earl of Moray. Walled garden, herbaceous borders, rose garden, flowering shrubs, rhododendrons, azaleas and rare exotic conifers. Woodland walks.

HISTORIC MONUMENTS
Cambuskenneth Abbey, Nr *Stirling*
Ruins of abbey founded in 1147. Scene of Bruce's 1326 parliament. Burial place of James III.

MUSEUMS AND GALLERIES
Falkirk Museum, 15 Orchard Street, *Falkirk*
Local and natural history
Kinnell House and Museum, *Bo'ness*
Wall paintings, temporary exhibitions. Industrial heritage of Bo'ness.
Grangemouth Museum, *Grangemouth*
Local canals.
Smith Art Gallery and Museum, Albert Place, *Stirling*

DUMFRIES AND GALLOWAY REGION
CASTLES AND HISTORIC HOUSES
Carlyle's Birthplace, *Ecclefechan* (National Trust for Scotland)
Thomas Carlyle was born here in 1795. Mementoes and manuscripts.
Drumlanrig Castle, Nr *Thornhill* (Buccleuch Estates)
Late 17th-century Scottish architecture in local pink sandstone set in parkland. Louis XIV furniture and fine paintings.
Maxwelton House, Nr *Moniaive* (Maxwelton House Trust)
Stronghold of Earls of Glencairn in 14th–15th century. House, garden and museum of agriculture and early domestic life.
Rammerscales, *Lockerbie* (A. M. Bell Macdonald)
Georgian manor house dated 1760. Fine views over Annandale.

GARDENS
Arbigland Gardens, *Kirbean* (Capt. J. B. Blackett)

Corsock House, *Corsock* (F. Ingall, Esq)
Gardens with fine rhododendrons, woodland walks, water garden, classical temple and bridge.
Kinmount Gardens, Kinmount, *Annan* (Hoddom and Kinmount Estates)
Rock garden and woodland walks. Signed walks.
Threave Gardens, *Dumfries* and *Galloway* (National Trust for Scotland)
Trust's school of practical gardening.

MUSEUMS AND GALLERIES
Annan Museum, Moat House, *Annan* (Burgh of Annan)
Natural history, archaeological, historical. Local shipping section. Thomas Carlyle and Dr Arnott material. Original Bruce Motte of 1124 in the garden.
Burns House, *Dumfries*
Memorials and personal relics of Robert Burns.
Castle Douglas Art Gallery, *Castle Douglas*
Paintings by Ethel S. G. Paterson. Temporary exhibitions.
Dumfries Museum, The Observatory, Corberry Hill, *Dumfries*
Natural history, archaeological and folk collections. Branch: Old Bridge House Museum, Old Bridge Street. 17th-century house with 6 period and historic rooms.
Ellisland Farm, Nr *Dumfries*
Material associated with Robert Burns.
Wigtown County Museum, The County Library, London Road, *Stranraer*
Collection of local interest.
Whithorn Priory Museum, Whithorn Priory, *Whithorn* (Secretary of State for Scotland)
Early Christian monuments including Latinus stone, dating from 5th century, and St Peter stone, showing a late form of the Christogram or Chi-Rho monogram.

FIFE REGION
CASTLES AND HISTORIC HOUSES
Culross Palace, *Fife* (Secretary of State for Scotland)
Built between 1597 and 1611. Very fine series of paintings on wooden walls and ceilings.
Falkland Palace, *Fife* (Her Majesty the Queen, Hereditary Constable, Capt. and Keeper; Major M. Crichton Stuart, MC, JP, DL, Deputy Keeper; National Trust for Scotland)
Attractive 16th-century royal pleasaunce, gardens now laid out to the original royal plans.

386

Hill of Tarvit, *Fife* (National Trust for Scotland)
Mansion house built 1696, remodelled 1906. Collection of furniture, tapestries, porcelain and paintings. Part let as convalescent home.
Kellie Castle, *Fife* (National Trust for Scotland)
Fine example of 16th- to 17th-century domestic architecture of lowland counties of Scotland.
Town House, *Culross* (National Trust for Scotland)
Scottish 17th-century burgh architecture, carefully restored.

CATHEDRALS AND CHURCHES
Dunfermline
Beautiful abbey church. Mainly Norman, with modern east end and central tower in midst of ruins and abbey buildings.
Durisdeer
17th century, with mausoleum of dukes of Queensbury.
St Monance
Church of rock above sea dating from 14th century. Choir, transepts, central tower with small tower.

HISTORIC MONUMENTS
Aberdour Castle, *Aberdour*
14th–17th-century stronghold still partially roofed.
Inchcolm Abbey, Nr *Dunfermline*
Remains of Augustinian foundation. Fine 13th-century chapter house.
St Andrew's Castle, *St Andrew's*
Ruined 14th-century castle where Cardinal Beaton murdered, 1546.

MUSEUMS AND GALLERIES
Andrew Carnegie Birthplace, Junction of Moodie Street and Priory Lane, *Dunfermline*
The weaver's cottage where the great philanthropist was born, and memorial hall with new displays covering the life of Andrew Carnegie and work of trusts he established.
Broughton House, *Kirkcudbright* (Trustees of the late E. A. Hornel)
Large reference library with valuable Burns collection. Pictures by Hornel and other artists. Furniture and other works of art. Garden.
Dunfermline Museum, Viewfield, *Dunfermline*
Local history and natural history of region: occasional art and travelling exhibitions.
Dunimarle Museum, *Culross*
Napoleonic furniture, oil paintings, library, ceramics, glass, silver and *objets d'art.*
Industrial and Social History Museum, Forth House, *Kirkcaldy*
Display relative to Fife industries, including linoleum, coal. Collection of horse-drawn vehicles.

387

Museum and Art Gallery, War Memorial Grounds, *Kirkcaldy*
Archaeological, historical, maritime, earth and natural sciences, and decorative art collections. 19th- and 20th-century Scottish and English paintings.
Pittencrieff House, Pittencrieff Park, *Dunfermline*
Costume collection, c. 1800 to present day; travelling and temporary art exhibitions etc.
St Andrews Cathedral Museum, St Andrews Cathedral and Priory, *St Andrews* (Secretary of State for Scotland)
Collection of early Christian and medieval monuments, also pottery, glass work and other relics discovered on the site.
The Scottish Fisheries Museum, *St Ayles,* Harbourhead, Anstruther (Scottish Fisheries Museum Trust Limited)
Architectural Heritage Year Award winner housing marine aquarium, fishing and ships' gear, model fishing boats, period fisher-home interiors, reference library.
The Stewartry Museum, *Kirkcudbright*
Regional museum depicting history and culture of Galloway.

GRAMPIAN REGION
CASTLES AND HISTORIC HOUSES
Braemar Castle, *Braemar* (Captain A. A. Farquharson of Invercauld)
17th-century castle, originally of Earls of Mar, of architectural and historical interest.
Castle of Drum, Nr *Aberdeen* (National Trust for Scotland)
Dates from 13th century. Mansion added in 1619.
Castle Fraser, *Sauchen* (National Trust for Scotland)
Spectacular Z-plan castle, begun 1575, completed 1636.
Craigievar Castle, *Lumphanan* (National Trust for Scotland)
Tower house, structurally unchanged since its completion in 1626.
Crathes Castle, *Banchory* (National Trust for Scotland)
16th-century baronial castle. Early painted ceilings. Beautiful gardens.
Druminnor Castle, *Rhynie* (Miss Joan Wright)
15th-century castle and museum. Stronghold of Clan Forbes. Built 1440, restored in 1966.
Haddo House, Nr *Methlick* (Marchioness of Aberdeen)
Georgian house built in 1732 by William Adam. Home of Gordons of Haddo for over 500 years. Terraced gardens.
Leith Hall, *Kennethmont* (National Trust for Scotland)
Home of Leith family since 1650. Jacobite relics. Charming gardens.
Muchalls Castle, *Stonehaven* (Mr and Mrs Maurice A. Simpson)
Early 17th century. Elaborate plasterwork ceilings and fireplaces. Built by Burnetts of Leys, 1619.

Provost Ross's House, *Aberdeen* (National Trust for Scotland)
One of oldest surviving houses in Aberdeen.
Towie Barclay Castle, Nr *Auchterless* (Marc Ellington, Esq)
Recently restored, rib and grain vaulted great hall and gallery
provide finest example in Scotland.

CATHEDRALS AND CHURCHES
Aberdeen Cathedral
Originally Norman but rebuilt from 13th century onwards. Relatively
small, 2 squat towers. Choir demolished during 20th century in
preparation for rebuilding which has never taken place.
Elgin
Cathedral, now in ruins following dissolution of see in 1560. Im-
posing monuments, etc.

GARDENS
Balmoral Castle, Nr *Ballater* (Her Majesty the Queen)
Grounds only open.
Cruickshank Botanic Gardens, *Aberdeen* (University of Aberdeen)
Developed at end of 19th century. Rock and water gardens, heather
garden, spring bulbs, gentians and alpine plants and succulent
plants. Trees and shrubs.
Kildrummy Castle Garden, *Donside* (Kildrummy Castle Garden
Trust)
10-acre garden with shrubs, heaths, gentians, rhododendrons, lilies,
etc. Alpine and water garden dominated by ruins of 13th-century
castle.
Pitmedden, *Udny* (National Trust for Scotland 1952)
Reconstructed 17th-century garden. Fountains.

HISTORIC MONUMENTS
Balvenie Castle, *Dufftton*
Ruins of 15th–16th-century castle, preserving iron 'yelt'.
Deer Abbey, *Old Deer*
13th-century ruins.
Duffus Castle, *Duffus*
Motte and bailey castle. Rebuilt 15th-century hall and 14th-century
tower.
Elgin Cathedral, *Elgin*
13th-century ruins.
Glenelb Brochs, *Glenbuchat*
Remains of two Iron-Age brochs.
Huntly Castle, *Huntly*
Derelict 15th-century castle.

Tolquhon Castle, *Taves*
16th-century roofless mansion enclosing 15th-century tower. Fine gatehouse and courtyard.

MUSEUMS AND GALLERIES

Aberdeen Art Gallery and Museum, Schoolhill, *Aberdeen* (Aberdeen District Council)
Oil paintings, watercolours, drawings, prints and sculpture. Collection of applied arts. Special exhibitions. Museum of north-east of Scotland (Maritime).

Arbuthnot Museum, St Peter Street, *Peterhead* (Peterhead Town Council)
Local history; whaling and Arctic section; coins.

Aberdeen University Anthropological Museum, *Aberdeen*
General archaeological and ethnographical museum with classical, Oriental, Egyptian, American and Pacific collections. Local antiquities and skeletal remains of Short Stone Cist (Beaker) people.

Aberdeen University, Natural History Museum, Tillydrone Avenue, *Aberdeen*
Zoology Department – teaching and study collections of natural history.

Brander Museum, *Huntly* (North-East of Scotland Library Service– Museum Service)
Local bygones. Travelling exhibitions.

Buckie Museum and Peter Anson Gallery, *Buckie*
Maritine museum relating to fishing industry of Moray Firth. Peter Anson collection of pictures of fishing vessels.

Falconer Museum, *Forres*
Exhibits relating to Culbin Sands.

Inverurie Museum, Public Library Building, *Inverurie*
Prehistoric material from locality. Small geological and natural history collections. Bygones.

James Dun's House, 61 Schoolhill, *Aberdeen* (Aberdeen District Council)
18th-century house renovated for use as children's museum with permanent display and changing exhibitions.

Provost Skene's House, Guestrow, City Centre, *Aberdeen* (Aberdeen District Council)
17th-century house, restored as museum of local history and domestic life.

Schools Museum Service Centre, *Banff* (Banff–Buchan District Council)
Antiquities, local and natural history. James Ferguson relics.

Tolbooth Museum, *Stonehaven* (North-East of Scotland Library Service–Museum Service)
Items associated with fishing and local bygones.

HIGHLAND REGION
CASTLES AND HISTORIC HOUSES
Cawdor Castle, *Nairn* (Earl of Cawdor)
14th-century keep with later additions. Gardens, nature trail.
Dunrobin Castle, *Golspie* (Countess of Sutherland)
Furniture, paintings, plate and other exhibits. Museum: exhibits of local and general interest. Trophies of chase. Gardens by Barry.
Dunvegan Castle, *Isle of Skye* (John MacLeod of MacLeod)
Dating from 13th century and continuously inhabited by Chiefs of MacLeod. Fairy flag.
Eilean Donan Castle, *Wester Ross* (J. D. H. MacRae, Esq)
13th-century castle. Jacobite relics, mostly with Clan connections.
Hugh Miller's Cottage, *Cromarty* (National Trust for Scotland)
Birthplace (1802) of Hugh Miller, stonemason, who became eminent geologist, editor and writer. Thatched cottage dates from 1650, contains small museum.

GARDENS
Castle of Mey, Nr *Gills* (H.M. Queen Elizabeth, the Queen Mother)
Gardens only shown.
Dundonnell House, *Dundonnell* (Alan, Neil and Alastair Roger)
Rare plants and shrubs.
Highland Wildlife Park, *Kincraig*
Native animals of Scotland past and present.
Inverewe, Poolewe, *Wester Ross* (National Trust for Scotland)
Garden created by the late Osgood Mackenzie. Rare and sub-tropical plants.
Langwell, *Berriedale* (Duke of Portland)
Fine gardens showing plant growth in exposed areas.
Rovie Lodge, *Rogart* (Mrs G. Rawstrone)
Herbaceous heath borders and lawns with shrubs and plants.
Trust Visitor Centre, *Torridon*
Walks, live animals, audio-visual material.
Visitor Centre, *Balmacara*
Self-guided and guided walks. Ranger–naturalist service.

HISTORIC MONUMENTS
Beauly Priory, *Beauly*
Ruins of church of house of Valliscaulian order, founded 1230.

MUSEUMS AND GALLERIES
Carnegie Library and Museum, *Wick*
Local antiquities and natural history specimens.
Clan Macpherson House and Museum, *Newtonmore* (Clan Macpherson Association)
Clan relics and memorials.

Elgin Museum, 1 High Street, *Elgin* (The Elgin Society)
Varied collection including unique fossils, Pictish stones, local bygones.

Fort George and Queen's Own Highlanders Museum, *Fortrose*
Museum of Queen's Own Highlanders in 18th-century fort.

Great Glen Exhibition, *Fort Augustus*
History and traditions of people of the Great Glen.

Highland Folk Museum, *Kingussie*
Old Highland things including examples of craft work and tools, household plenishings, tartan, etc. In the grounds there is a furnished cottage with mill and farming shed.

Inverness Museum and Art Gallery, Castle Wynd, *Inverness*
Highland and Jacobite collection.

Landmark, *Carrbridge*
Exhibition of history of Strathspey.

Thurso Museum, The Library, *Thurso*
Zoological, geological and botanical collections. Dick collection of plants and mosses.

The West Highland Museum, Cameron Square, *Fort William*
Historical, natural history and folk exhibits. Local relics and large Jacobite and tartan section. Processing of aluminium. Exhibition: 'Prince Charles Edward and the '45 Rising'.

LOTHIAN REGION
CASTLES AND HISTORIC HOUSES

Achescon House, *Edinburgh* (Scottish Craft Centre)
Fine 17th-century mansion.

No 7 Charlotte Square, *Edinburgh* (National Trust for Scotland)
Robert Adam's masterpiece of urban architecture. Main floors of No 7 are open as typical Georgian house and centre for cultural and conservation activities.

Craigmillar Castle, *Edinburgh*
14th-century stronghold. 16th–17th-century apartments.

Dirleton Castle and Garden, *Dirleton* (Secretary of State for Scotland)
13th-century castle, attractive gardens.

Edinburgh Castle, *Edinburgh* (Crown Property)
Ancient fortress of great importance. St Margaret's Chapel has Norman features.

Gladstone's Land, *Edinburgh* (National Trust for Scotland)
Built 1620, later occupied by Thomas Gladstone. Remarkable painted wooden ceilings.

***Hamilton House,** *Prestonpans* (National Trust for Scotland)
Built in 1628 by John Hamilton, prosperous Edinburgh burgess.

Hopetoun House, *South Queensferry* (The Marquess of Linlithgow)
Fine example of 18th-century Adam architecture. Magnificent
reception rooms, pictures. Deer parks. Grounds laid out on lines of
Versailles.
John Knox's House, *Edinburgh*
15th century with old wooden galleries.
Lamb's House, *Leith* (National Trust for Scotland)
Residence and warehouse of prosperous merchant of late 16th or
early 17th century. Renovated 18th century. Now old people's day
centre.
Lauriston Castle, *Edinburgh* (City of Edinburgh District Council)
Associated with John Law (1671–1729) founder of the first bank in
France.
*****Luffness Castle,** *Aberlady* (Col and Mrs Hope of Luffness)
16th-century castle with 13th-century keep. Dry moat and old
fortifications. Built on the site of a Norse raiders' camp.
Palace of Holyrood House, *Edinburgh* (Royal Palace)
Official residence of Her Majesty the Queen when in Scotland.
Largely reconstructed by Charles II. Relics of Mary, Queen of Scots.
Winton House, *Pencaitland* (Sir David Ogilvy, Bt)
Rebuilt 1620. Twisted stone chimneys and plaster ceilings in honour
of Charles I's visit. Enlarged 1800. Fine pictures and furniture.
Terraced gardens.

CATHEDRALS AND CHURCHES
Dalmeny
Good example of Scottish Romanesque, 2nd half of 12th century.
Apse, chancel and south doorway with impressive carvings.
Edinburgh (Church of the Holy Rood)
15th-century church in which Mary Queen of Scots was crowned.
Divided into east and west churches mid-17th century, reunited 1938.
Haddington
Splendid large cruciform church dating from 14th century. Nave
consistently in use, but tower and rest of building subject of magnifi-
cent rescue scheme.
Linlithgow (St Michael)
Large 15th-century church with west tower and 3-sided apse; fine
carvings.
Roslin
15th-century mausoleum chapel of proposed collegiate church.
Splendid carvings including Prentice pillar. Ruined cathedral
(founded 12th century) abandoned after Reformation.
Torpichen
Church on site of hospital of Knights of Jerusalem. Tower was once
part of domestic buildings.

GARDENS
Dalkeith Park, Nr *Edinburgh* (Buccleuch Estates)
Woodland walks beside river in grounds of Dalkeith Palace. Tunnel
walk, 18th-century bridge and orangery. Nature trail.
Inveresk Lodge, *Inveresk* (National Trust for Scotland)
New garden, with large selection of plants.
Malleny Garden, *Balerno* (National Trust for Scotland)
Good collection of shrub roses.
Royal Botanic Gardens, *Edinburgh* (Department of Agriculture and
Fisheries for Scotland)
Founded 17th century. Beautiful rock garden. Exhibition plant
houses.
Tyninghame Gardens, Nr *Whitekirk*
Old-fashioned roses, climbing clematis, miniature arboretum.

HISTORIC MONUMENTS
Rosslyn Castle, *Rosslyn*
Ruin of 14th–17th-century castle.

MUSEUMS AND GALLERIES
Art Centre, Regent Road, *Edinburgh* (City of Edinburgh)
Historic building by Thomas Hamilton houses City's permanent
collection of Scottish painting and sculpture. Frequent temporary
exhibitions.
Burgh Museum, Burgh Chambers, High Street, *South Queensferry*
(Town Council)
Manuscripts, prints, photographs, exhibits illustrative of local social
history.
Canongate Tolbooth, Canongate, *Edinburgh* (City of Edinburgh)
Was burgh courthouse and prison for more than 300 years. Collec-
tion of Highland dress and tartan, with occasional exhibitions.
Fruit Market Gallery, 29 Market Street, *Edinburgh*
Changing programme of exhibitions of contemporary artists.
Huntly House, 142 Canongate, *Edinburgh* (City of Edinburgh)
Local history and topography; important collection of Edinburgh
silver, glass and Scottish pottery. Reconstruction of old Scots kitchen.
Original copy of 'National Covenant' of 1638. Also personal collec-
tion of Field Marshal Earl Haig.
Lady Stair's House, Lady Stair's Close, Lawnmarket, *Edinburgh*
(City of Edinburgh)
Reconstructed town house, dating from 1622. Relics connected with
Robert Burns, Sir Walter Scott and R. L. Stevenson.
Lauriston Castle, Cramond Road South, *Edinburgh* (City of
Edinburgh)
16th-century with 19th-century additions. Period furniture, tapestries,
Blue-John Wool Mosaics.

Museum of Childhood, 38 High Street, *Edinburgh* (City of Edinburgh)
Covers all aspects of childhood: games, toys, books, costume, health and education.

National Gallery of Scotland, The Mound, *Edinburgh*
European paintings, sculpture, drawings and prints from the 14th to the 19th century and Scottish art up to 1900.

National Museum of Antiquities of Scotland, Queen Street, *Edinburgh*
Collections cover whole of Scotland from Stone Age to recent times; notably those of prehistoric and Roman objects, sculptured stones, relics of Celtic Church, Scottish coins and medals, Stuart relics, Highland weapons, domestic life; also reference library.

North Berwick Museum, School Road, *North Berwick*
Archaeology, history and natural history.

Queensferry Museum, *Edinburgh* (City of Edinburgh)
Council Chambers of former Royal Burgh of Queensferry. Local history.

Register House, *Edinburgh* (Scottish Record Office)
Exhibition: Scotland and America in house designed by Robert Adam.

Royal Scottish Museum, Chambers Street, *Edinburgh* (National Institution administered by the Scottish Education Department)
National collections of decorative arts of world, archaeology, ethnography, natural history, geology, technology and science. Temporary exhibitions.

Russell Collection of Harpsichords and Clavichords, St Cecilia's Hall, Niddry Street, Cowgate, *Edinburgh* (University of Edinburgh)
Keyboard instruments, including harpsichords, clavichords, forte-pianos, regals, spinets, virginals and chamber organs. Pictures. Tapestries and textiles.

Scottish Arts Council, 19 Charlotte Square, *Edinburgh*
Changing programme of exhibitions.

Scottish National Gallery of Modern Art, Royal Botanic Gardens, *Edinburgh*
20th-century collection of national galleries of Scotland.

Scottish National Portrait Gallery, Queen Street, *Edinburgh*
Portraits of famous Scottish men and women from the 16th century to modern times; a reference section of engraved portraits and a large collection of photographs of Scottish portraits.

Scottish United Services Museum, Crown Square, Edinburgh Castle, *Edinburgh* (Secretary of State for Scotland)
Illustrates by display of uniforms, head-dress, arms and equipment, medals, portraits and models, history of armed forces of Scotland. Extensive library and collection of prints and uniforms.

West Register House, *Edinburgh* (Scottish Record Office)
Museum of Scottish Record Office in former church designed by Robert Reid.

ORKNEY
CATHEDRALS AND CHURCHES
Kirkwall (St Magnus)
Cathedral dating mainly from 12th century. Magnificent nave and fine memorials.

STRATHCLYDE REGION
CASTLES AND HISTORIC HOUSES
*__*Bachelors' Club,__ Tarbolton_ (National Trust for Scotland)
17th-century thatched house where Burns and his friends formed their club in 1780. Period furnishings.
Brodick Castle, *Isle of Arran* (National Trust for Scotland)
Historic home of Dukes of Hamilton. Castle dates in part from 14th century, furniture, *objets d'art.*
Burns Cottage, *Alloway* (Trustees of Burns Monument)
Thatched cottage in which Robert Burns was born, 1759. Museum with Burns's relics.
Cameron House, *Alexandria* (Patrick Telfer Smollett)
Includes family literary museum devoted to the celebrated 18th-century novelist and historian, Tobias Smollett. Also has fine furniture, porcelain, glass and unique 'Whisky Galore' room. Victorian nursery, etc. Extensive gardens landscaped by Lanning Roper.
Culzean Castle, *Maybole* (National Trust for Scotland)
One of finest Adam houses in Scotland. Spacious policies and gardens.
Hunterston Castle and Gardens, *Hunterston* (Charles Hunter of Hunterston, Younger)
Restored castle, mainly 16th–17th century. Armour and artifacts. Vintage motor cycle museum. Walled garden.
Inverary Castle, *Inverary* (His Grace the Duke of Argyll)
Since 15th century headquarters of Clan Campbell. Present castle built 18th century by Robert Morris and Robert Mylne.
Pollok House and Park, *Glasgow* (City of Glasgow and District Council)
Designed by William Adam, built 1747–52. Contains Stirling Maxwell collection of Spanish and other paintings and displays of European decorative arts especially Spanish glass. Park includes rhododendron walk and Royal National Rose Society trial garden. Extensive woodland and walks.
Provan Hall, *Glasgow* (National Trust for Scotland)
Fine 15th-century mansion.
Provand's Lordship, *Glasgow* (Provand's Lordship Society)
Oldest house in Glasgow, built 1471.

Rossdhu, *Luss* (Sir Ivar Colquhoun of Luss, Bt, DL, JP)
Historic home of Chiefs of Clan Colquhoun, built in the 18th century
near site of original 15th-century castle on banks of Loch Lomond.
Souter Johnnie's Cottage, *Kirkoswald* (National Trust for Scotland)
Thatched home of original Souter in Burns's 'Tam o' Shanter'.
Burns relics.
Weaver's Cottage, *Kilbarchan* (National Trust for Scotland)
Typical cottage of 18th-century handloom weaver; looms, weaving
equipment, domestic utensils.

CATHEDRALS AND CHURCHES
Glasgow (Caledonia Road Church)
Fine Grecian style church built by Alexander 'Greek' Thompson.
Tall tower and fine Ionic portico.
Glasgow (St Mungo)
Cathedral built between 12th and 15th centuries. Cruciform in plan
with low central spire and tower; crypt; interior mostly 19th century.
Glasgow (St Vincent)
Alexander 'Greek' Thompson (1859). Elaborate tower is landmark.
Now used by spiritualists. Magnificent Ionic porticos; spacious
interior with galleries.

GARDENS
Achamore, *Isle of Gigha* (D. W. N. Landale, Esq)
Extensive gardens. Roses, hydrangeas, rhododendrons, azaleas,
camellias and other shrubs.
Ardanaiseg, *Kilchrenan*
Rare shrubs, trees, azaleas and rhododendrons.
Arduaine Gardens, Nr *Kimelford*
Shrub garden.
Bargany Gardens, *Dailly*
Woodland walks, snowdrops, daffodils, rhododendrons, azaleas,
hyacinths.
Bellahouston Park, *Glasgow* (City of Glasgow District Council)
175 acres. Sunk, wall and rock gardens. Wildlife. Dry ski-slope.
Athletic and indoor sports centre.
Benmore, *Glasgow* (Younger Botanic Garden) (Secretary of State for
Scotland)
Woodland garden on grand scale.
Botanic Gardens, *Glasgow* (City of Glasgow District Council)
43 acres. Plants of unusual species.
Culzean Country Park, *Maybole* ·
Exhibition centre. Eisenhower exposition. Ranger–naturalist service.
Finlaystone Estate, *Port Glasgow*
Garden centre, woodland walks.

Glenapp Castle Gardens, *Ballantrae* (Rt Hon. the Earl and Countess of Inchcape)
Daffodils, rhododendrons, azaleas, flowering shrubs, terraces, lily ponds, herbaceous borders. Woodland walks.

Glencoe Visitors' Centre, *Glencoe*
Ranger–naturalist service.

Greenbank, *Glasgow* (National Trust for Scotland)
Trust's garden advice centre.

Kilmun Arboretum and Forest Plots, *Kilmun*
Conifers and broad leaf specimens.

Linn Park, *Glasgow* (City of Glasgow District Council)
212 acres pine and deciduous woodlands with riverside walks. Nature centre.

Loch Lomond Park, *Loch Lomond* (Dumbarton District Council)
200 acres situated beside Loch Lomond containing many conifers, azaleas and other shrubs. Walled garden. Fairy Glen. Castle, site of old castle and moat. Wildlife. Nature trail.

Ross Hall Park, *Glasgow* (City of Glasgow District Council)
33 acres. Majestic trees by Rivert Cart. Extensive heather and rock gardens, with water features; nature trails.

Rouken Glen Park, *Glasgow* (City of Glasgow District Council)
156 acres. Magnificent trees. Waterfall. Walled garden, alpines and boating pond.

Strone House, *Cairndow* (Rt Hon. the Lord Glenkinglas, PC)
Rhododendrons, azaleas, daffodils, conifers.

Victoria Park, *Glasgow* (City of Glasgow District Council)
Fossilized tree stumps 300 million years old. 58 acres. Extensive carpet bedding depicting centennial events.

HISTORIC MONUMENTS

Bothwell Castle, *Bothwell*
Ruined 13th–15th-century stronghold.

Castle Sween, *Kilmory*
12th-century ruin.

Crookston Castle, *Crookston*
13th-century castle associated with Mary Queen of Scots.

Crossraguel Abbey, Nr *Maybole*
Remains of 13th-century abbey.

Dunstaffnage Castle, Nr *Oban*
Ruined 13th-century Campbell stronghold.

Newark Castle, *Port Glasgow*
16th–17th-century castle with fine turrets.

Rothesay Castle, *Rothesay*
13th-century moated castle.

MUSEUMS AND GALLERIES

Airdrie Public Museum, Wellwynd, *Airdrie* (Burgh of Airdrie)
Local historical material; regular programme of exhibitions.

Ayr Museum and Art Gallery, 12 Main Street, *Ayr* (Kyle and Carrick District Council)
Local history. Art Gallery exhibitions changed monthly.

Burns's Monument and Museum, Kay Park, *Kilmarnock* (Kilmarnock Corporation)
Holograph manuscripts dealing with Robert Burns. Burns original first edition, McKie Burnsiana.

Buteshire Natural History Society Museum, Stuart Street, *Rothesay*
Natural history, archaeology, geology and history of County of Bute.

Campbeltown Museum, *Campbeltown* (Burgh of Campbeltown)
Archaeological, geological and natural history of Kintyre.

Colzium House, *Kilsyth*
Partly museum, walled garden, and associations with Montrose's victory over Covenanters in 1645.

Dean Castle, *Kilmarnock*
Medieval arms and armour, musical instruments, tapestries.

Dick Institute Museum, Elmbank Avenue, *Kilmarnock*
Geological, ornithological, archaeological and ethnological collections. Walker collection of Scottish basket-hilted swords; Cater collection of small arms; documents of the Boyd family; Incunabula, early Bibles and bibliographical works of Elizabethan period: Children's Museum. Paintings.

Gladstone Court, *Biggar*
Small indoor street of ten shops and workshops, a bank, telephone exchange, school room, and library. Bed used by Cargill the Covenanter in 1861.

Glasgow Art Gallery and Museum, *Glasgow*
Old master paintings, armour, archaeology, history, natural history, ethnology, technology, Bunell collection of tapestries, furniture, porcelain, glass, silver, and other *objets d'art*.

Glencoe and North Lorn Folk Museum, *Glencoe*
Thatched restored 'Cruck' cottage. Exhibits include domestic bygones, costume, weapons, Jacobite relics and photographs of local wild flowers.

Haggs Castle, *Glasgow*
Museum for children in castle built 1585.

Hunterian Museum, *Glasgow* (Glasgow University)
Geological, archaeological, ethnographical, numismatic and historical collections.

John Hastie Museum, *Strathaven*
Local history.

Maclaurin Gallery, *Ayr* (Kyle and Carrick District Council)
Range of exhibitions.
McLean Museum, 9 Union Street, West End, *Greenock*
Picture gallery and comprehensive natural history, geology and shipping exhibits. Relics of James Watt.
Museum of Costume, Aikenhead House, *Glasgow*
New developing museum.
North Ayrshire Museum, Kirkgate, *Saltcoats*
History, industry and life in North Ayrshire.
Old Glasgow Museum, *Glasgow*
History and life of Glasgow.
Open-Air Museum, *Auchindrain*
Life of early communities in district.
Paisley Museum and Art Galleries, High Street, *Paisley* (Paisley Corporation)
Paisley shawls; Renfrewshire history, geology and natural history. Arbuthnot manuscripts. Gallery of Scottish painters; ceramics.
People's Palace, *Glasgow*
Visual record of rise and development of Glasgow.
Robertson Museum and The Aquarium, Marine Station, *Millport*
Marine life found in Clyde Sea area.
Scottish National Memorial to David Livingstone, *Blantyre*
Personal relics, tableaux and working models in house where missionary explorer was born.
Transport Museum, *Glasgow*
Life-size presentation of land transport.

TAYSIDE REGION
CASTLES AND HISTORIC HOUSES
Barrie's Birthplace, *Kirriemuir* (National Trust for Scotland (1937))
Mementoes of Sir James Barrie.
Blair Castle, *Blair Atholl* (His Grace the Duke of Atholl)
Comyn's Tower built c. 1269. Mansion in Scottish baronial style. Jacobite relics in Atholl museum.
Edzell Castle and Gardens, *Edzell* (Secretary of State for Scotland)
16th-century castle. Unique Renaissance garden.
Glamis Castle, *Glamis* (Earl of Strathmore and Kinghorne)
Owes present aspect to 3rd Earl (1630–95) with portions much older. Celebrated for legend of secret chamber. Grounds laid out by Capability Brown.
Kellie Castle, *Arbroath* (A. Kerr Boyle, Esq)
Built 1170 by William de Mowbray. Restored 1679. Built from pink sandstone quarried within 60-acre estate.
Kinross House, *Kinross*
17th-century house designed by Sir William Bruce.

Scone Palace, *Perth* (Rt Hon. the Earl of Mansfield)
Largely rebuilt in 1803 for 3rd Earl incorporating parts of old 1580
palace. French furniture, china, ivories and Vernis Martin vases and
objets d'art.
Trust Visitor Centre, *Dunkeld* (National Trust for Scotland)
'Little houses' dating from 1689.

CATHEDRALS AND CHURCHES
Angus
Fine steeple, including famous Big Peter bell which tolls curfew every
night. Splendid chandelier and chalices. Church originally part of
ancient abbey, restored 19th century.
Arbroath
Mortuary chapel (1875–84) designed as mausoleum for Alan-Frazer
family. Elaborate carvings.
Fowlis
Mid-15th-century church with painted panels of former rood screen;
tabernacle with sculpture of annunciation.

GARDENS
Abercairny, *Glimerton* (W. Drummond Moray, Esq)
Large shrub garden.
Branklyn Garden, *Perth* (National Trust for Scotland)
One of the finest gardens of its size in Britain (2 acres).
Drummond Castle Gardens, *Drummond* (Earl of Ancaster)
Gardens only are open.
Falkally Wayside Centre, Nr *Moulin*
Nature trail.
Loch of Lowes Wildlife Reserve, Nr *Blairgowrie*
Variety of wildlife.
Mountain Visitors' Centre, *Ben Lawers*
Noted for variety of alpine flowers and species of birds. Self-guided
and guided trails.

HISTORIC MONUMENTS
Burleigh Castle, Nr *Milnathort*
16th-century tower house. Courtyard enclosure. Roofed angle tower.
Loch Leven Castle, Nr *Kinross*
Ruined 15th-century stronghold associated with Mary, Queen of
Scots.

MUSEUMS AND GALLERIES
The Angus Folk Museum, Kirkwynd Cottages, *Glamis* (National
Trust for Scotland)
Early furnishings, clothing, domestic utensils and agricultural
implements from former County of Angus.

Arbroath Abbey Museum, *Arbroath* (Secretary of State for Scotland)
Small collection of architectural and other exhibits primarily connected with Abbey.

Arbroath Art Gallery, Public Library, Hill Terrace, *Arbroath* (Arbroath Town Council)
General art collection, emphasis on local artists. Collection of pastels and watercolours by J. W. Herald.

Barrack Street Museum, Ward Road, *Dundee*
Museum of Dundee shipping and industries.

Black Watch Museum, Balhousie House, *Perth*
Headquarters and museum of Black Watch (Royal Highland Regiment) in tower house restored in 17th century and added to in 1862.

Broughty Castle Museum, Broughty Ferry, *Dundee*
Relics of local and military history. Natural history of the Tay. Whaling gallery.

Camperdown House Museum, Camperdown Park, *Dundee*

Donnachaidh Museum, *Struan*
Items associated with Clan Donnachaidh.

Dunblane Cathedral Museum, The Cross, *Dunblane* (Society of Friends of Dunblane Cathedral)
Pictures of cathedral before restoration. Communion tokens. Reproductions of bishops' seals. Leightoniana, medieval carving, library, archives room, local history.

Dundee Museum and Art Galleries, Albert Square, *Dundee*
Regional collection of archaeological, historical, natural history, botanical and geological material. Flemish, Dutch, French and British paintings particularly Scottish schools.

Glenesk Museum, The Retreat, *Glenesk*
Local scene with emphasis on immediate past. General display with available historical records; examples of farming and trades, domestic interiors, costumes, music and children's interests. Sound recently installed.

Meffan Institute Museum, *Forfar*
Collections of archaeological, historical, geological and natural history material.

Meigle Museum, *Meigle* (Secretary of State for Scotland)
25 sculptured monuments of the Celtic Christian period. Outstanding collection of Dark-Age sculpture.

Michael Bruce Cottage and Museum, *Kinnesswood*
Birthplace of poet, Michael Bruce. Relics.

Montrose Museum, Panmure Place, *Montrose* (Montrose Natural History and Antiquarian Society)
Regional collection of archaeological, historical, natural history and geological exhibits, including sculptured stones and collection of Scottish coins and medals. Reference library.

Museum of Scottish Tartans, *Comrie*
Dress, books, maps, pictures, early photographs and specimens.
Orchar Art Gallery, Broughty Ferry, *Dundee*
Oil paintings and watercolours, mostly by Scottish artists of 19th
century. Etchings, including 36 by Whistler.
Perth Art Gallery and Museum, George Street, *Perth* (Perth and
Kinross District Council)
Art collection mainly of Scottish School. Fine regional natural
history museum. Ethnographical, geological and antiquarian
exhibits; tropical aquaria.
St Mary's Tower, Nethergait, *Dundee*
Tower of St Mary's Church, site museum.
St Vigeans Museum, *Arbroath* (Secretary of State for Scotland)
Sculptured monuments of the Celtic Christian period, including the
Drosten stone.
Signal Tower Museum, Ladyloan, *Arbroath* (Angus District Council)
Once shore base of Bell Rock lighthouse, Signal Tower contains
history and development of Arbroath and its district, including
building of famous lighthouse.
Trust Visitors' Centre, *Killiecrankie*
Battle museum close to site of 1689 battle where Jacobite army
victorious.

WALES

CLWYD
CASTLES AND HISTORIC HOUSES
Bodrhyddan Hall, Nr *Rhyl* (Col the Lord Langford)
17th-century manor house. Famous portraits, armour, furniture;
garden.
Chirk Castle, Nr *Wrexham* (Lt-Col Ririd and Lady Margaret
Myddleton)
Built 1310. Exterior is a unique unaltered example of a border castle
of Edward II's time. Interesting portraits, tapestries, etc. Gardens.
Erddig, Nr *Wrexham* (National Trust)
Late 17th-century house with 18th-century additions. Much original
furniture. 18th-century formal garden.

CATHEDRALS AND CHURCHES
Holywell (St Winifred)
A well chapel and chamber (late 15th century), well forming base-
ment of chapel. One of best examples of its kind.
Llangollen (St Gollen)
Roof with elaborate carvings reputed to have come from Valle
Crucis Abbey.

Llanrhydd (St Meugan)
15th-century roof and screen; 17th-century pulpit and monuments.
Llanrwst (St Grwst)
Church damaged in 15th century and rebuilt in 17th. Good rood
screen with original gallery; 17th-century mausoleum.
Mold (St Mary)
Spacious perpendicular with west tower rebuilt in 1773. Fine carving
on capitals; good memorials.
Ruabon (St Mary)
Monuments, including work by Nollekens and Rysbrack.
Ruthin (St Peter)
Basically 14th-century church, part demolished after Dissolution.
Much restored during 18th and 19th centuries. Aisle roofs with carved
bases are original 15th-century work; brasses and monuments.
St Asaph Cathedral (St Asaph and St Cyndeyrn)
Smallest cathedral church in England and Wales, much smaller than
many parish churches. Cruciform with central tower. Mainly dating
from late 13th century. Restored by Scott in 19th century; good
15th-century stalls and 19th-century glass.

HISTORIC MONUMENTS
Basingwerk Abbey, Nr *Holywell*
Fragments of abbey founded in 1131.
Denbigh Castle, *Denbigh*
Ruined 13th–14th-century castle. Also remains of town walls which
include ruined church.
Ewloe Castle, *Ewloe*
Ruins of minute castle of Welsh Prince.
Flint Castle, *Flint*
Remains of 13th-century garrison castle.
Hawarden Old Castle, *Hawarden*
Remains of 14th-century castle.
Rhuddlan Castle, *Rhuddlan*
13th-century castle built to diamond plan.
Valle Crucis Abbey, *Llangollen*
Much of church of small 13th-century Cistercian abbey survives.
Whiteford Cross, Nr *Holywell*
Tall cross of AD 1000.

MUSEUMS AND GALLERIES
Plas Newydd Museum, *Llangollen* (Llangollen Urban District
Council)
Black and white house and home from 1780–1831 of the 'Ladies of
Llangollen', eccentric blue-stockings.
Wrexham Exhibition Hall, Public Library, *Wrexham*
Various exhibitions normally changed monthly.

DYFED

CASTLES AND HISTORIC HOUSES

Picton Castle, *Haverfordwest* (The Hon Hanning and Lady Marion Philips)
Home of the Philips family since the 12th century. Shrub and walled gardens.

Tudor Merchant's House, *Tenby* (National Trust)
Merchant's house of 15th century and National Trust information centre.

CATHEDRALS AND CHURCHES

Bosherston (St Govans)
Cliff-top chapel on rugged coastline.

St Davids (St David)
Cathedral (12th–14th century) to patron saint of Wales. Splendid oak nave roof and fine tower.

GARDENS

Bwich Nant-yr-Arian Forest Visitors' Centre, Nr *Capel Bangor* (Forestry Commission)
Interprets the forest as part of landscape, form of land use, part of local community.

Cymerau, *Glandyfl* (Major-General Lewis Pugh)
Gardens in superb country with fine panoramic views, rhododendrons, azaleas, unusual shrubs, herbaceous borders.

The Hall, *Angle* (Major and Mrs J. N. Allen-Mirehouse)
On banks of Milford Haven: woodland, shrubs, roses, walled garden, greenhouses.

Manor House Leisure Park, *St Florence*
Wooded grounds and gardens. Wildlife.

HISTORIC MONUMENTS

Aberystwyth Castle, *Aberystwyth*
Remains of 12th–13th-century castle.

Bishop's Palace, *St David's*
Ruined fragment of principal residence of bishops of St Davids. Dates from 13th century.

Careg Cennen Castle, Nr *Llandeilo*
Hillside ruin, originally native Welsh stronghold, rebuilt in late 13th century.

Carew Castle, *Carew*
Ruins of 13th-century castle, enlarged during 15th century.

Carew Cross, *Carew*
Fine early 11th-century stone cross.

Cilgerran Castle, Nr *Cardigan*
13th-century ruin.

Dryslwyn Castle, *Dryslwyn*
Ruined 13th-century native Welsh stronghold.
Haverfordwest Castle, *Haverfordwest*
Ruined 12th-century stronghold. Museum.
Kidwelly Castle, *Kidwelly*
12th-century castle with later additions.
Lamphey Palace, *Lamphey*
Ruined 13th-century palace of archbishops of St David.
Llanstephan Castle, *Llanstephan*
Remains of 11th–13th-century-stronghold.
Llawhaden Castle, *Llawhaden*
Ruined 13th-century fortified residence of bishops of St David.
Manorbier Castle, *Manorbier*
Ruined 12th–13th-century castle. Inner court remains intact.
Pembroke Castle, *Pembroke*
12th–13th-century fortress.
Pentre Ifan Burial Chamber, Nr *Nevern*
Part of vanished long barrow.
St Dogmael's Abbey, *St Dogmael's*
12th-century ruins on site of Celtic monastery.
St Non's Chapel, *St David's*
Foundations of chapel dating from Celtic period.
Strata Florida Abbey, Nr *Pontrhydfendigaid*
Remains of church and cloister of Cistercian abbey, founded in 1164.
Talley Abbey, Nr *Llandeilo*
Ruins of 12th-century abbey founded for Premonstratensian canons.
Tenby Castle, *Tenby*
13th-century ruins of keep and walls.

MUSEUMS AND GALLERIES
Castle Museum and Art Gallery, *Haverfordwest* (Pembrokeshire Museums)
Regional museum with collections of archaeology, folk-life, local industry and works of art. Changing displays and frequent temporary exhibitions.
County Museum, *Carmarthen* (Carmarthenshire County Council)
Stone-Age relics, Romano–British and Ogham inscribed stones. Collection of Roman gold, jewellery and other antiquities.
Museum of the Woollen Textile Industry, *Dre Fachfelindre*
Collection of textile machinery dating back to 18th century.
National Library of Wales, *Aberystwyth*
Books, manuscripts and records relating to Wales and the Celtic counties, topographical prints, maps, drawings, etc, of historical interest. Copyright library.
Parc Howard Museum and Art Gallery, *Llanelli* (Llanelli Corporation)
Llanelli pottery. Exhibits of Welsh artists. Items of local interest.

Penrhos, *Haverfordwest* (Pembrokeshire Museums)
Traditional Welsh cottage, furnished. Branch museum and information centre near Preseli Hills.
Scolton Manor Country Park Museum, *Scolton,* Nr Haverfordwest (Pembrokeshire Museums)
Regional museum and nature trail, study centre, etc.
Tenby Museum, Castle Hill, *Tenby*
Local geology, archaeology, history and natural history, maps, pictures and bygones.
University College of Wales Gallery, *Aberystwyth*
Visiting exhibitions of painting and sculpture. Small display of museum art objects, pottery, etc, in gallery.

NATIONAL PARKS
Brecon Beacons (part)
Pembrokeshire Coast

MID GLAMORGAN
HISTORIC MONUMENTS
Caerphilly Castle, *Caerphilly*
Late 13th-century fortress.
Coity Castle, *Coity*
12th–16th-century stronghold with hall, chapel and 3-storied round tower.
Ewenny Priory, *Ewenny*
Ruins of priory founded c. 1120.
Newcastle, *Bridgend*
12th-century ruin. Richly carved Norman gateway.
Ogmore Castle, *Ogmore*
12th-century 3-storied stone keep.

MUSEUMS AND GALLERIES
Art Gallery and Museum, Cyfarthfa Castle, *Merthyr Tydfil*
Paintings, ceramics, coins and medals, silver and other art objects, natural history and local history. Small Welsh kitchen.

NATIONAL PARKS
Brecon Beacons (part)

GWENT
AREAS OF OUTSTANDING NATURAL BEAUTY
Wye Valley (part)

CASTLES AND HISTORIC HOUSES
Llanvihangel Court, *Abergavenny* (Col and Mrs Somerset Hopkinson)
16th-century manor house. Front rebuilt 1559, internally remodelled 1660.

Tredegar House, *Newport* (Newport Borough Council)
Former home of Lords of Tredegar. Fine Restoration house.
Portraits, extensive grounds.

CATHEDRALS AND CHURCHES
Abergavenny (St Mary)
Church of Benedictine priory founded in 12th century. Cruciform
with central tower; mainly 14th century – canopied choir stalls,
monuments, large wooden figure of Jesse.
Caerlon (St Cadog)
Norman church largely rebuilt at the end of 15th century. Extensive
19th-century restoration; 19th-century glass commemorative win-
dows.
Gwent (St Woolos)
Cathedral. Magnificent Norman work with Gothic additions. Much
restored in 19th century.
Monmouth (St Mary)
Norman church pulled down in 18th century. Rebuilt in Classical
style by Smith of Warwick, 14th-century tower retained. Gothicized
by Street, 1880; good monuments and 19th-century glass.

GARDENS
Scenic Forest Drive, *Cwmcarn* (Forestry Commission)
7-mile drive through mountain scenery.

HISTORIC MONUMENTS
Abergavenny Castle, *Abergavenny*
Remains of 12th-century stronghold. Walls, towers and gateway.
Amphitheatre, *Caerleon*
Roman amphitheatre dated AD 80–100.
Caerwent Roman Town, *Caerwent*
Remains of Roman town of Venta Silurum, founded c. AD 75.
Caldicot Castle, *Caldicot*
Remains of Norman castle.
Chepstow Castle, *Chepstow*
Norman castle, altered in 16th century.
Grosmont Castle, *Grosmont*
Ruined Marches stronghold, rebuilt in 13th century.
Hen Gwrt, *Llantilio Crossenny*
Rectangular enclosure of medieval house with wet moat.
Llanthony Priory, *Llanthony*
Ruins of 12th-century Augustinian foundation.
Monmouth Castle, *Monmouth*
12th-century castle keep.
Newport Castle, *Newport*
Only 14th–15th-century façade survives.

408

Raglan Castle, *Raglan*
Mainly 15th-century ruin.
Runston Chapel, Nr *Caerwent*
Roofless Norman chapel surrounded by earthworks of deserted medieval village.
Skenfrith Castle, Nr *Monmouth*
13th-century castle on site of earlier Norman earthwork castle.
Tintern Abbey, *Tintern*
Extensive remains of fine 13th-century church.
White Castle, Nr *Llantilio Crossenny*
12th–13th-century Marches stronghold.

MUSEUMS AND GALLERIES
Abergavenny and District Museum, Castle House, Abergavenny (Monmouth District Council)
Antiquities of town and district.
Caldicot Castle Museum, *Caldicot*
Local history.
Legionary Museum, Caerleon
Branch archaeological gallery of National Museum of Wales. Displays of objects found on the site of Roman legionary fortress of Isca.
The Museum, Bridge Street, *Chepstow*
Chepstow Society collection of local antiquities, prints and photographs.
Nelson Museum, The Market Hall, Priory Street, *Monmouth*
Relics of Admiral Lord Nelson, his contemporaries and Lady Hamilton. Local history centre, archives, exhibits, maps, etc.
Newport Museum and Art Gallery, John Frost Square, *Newport* (Newport Corporation)
Natural history; art, specializing in early English watercolours; Roman remains from Venta Silurum (Caerwent); folk-life including Pontypool Japan ware. Temporary art exhibitions.
Rural Crafts Museum, *Llanvapley*
Old agricultural tools, items from farmhouse kitchen and implements used in country crafts.

NATIONAL PARKS
Brecon Beacons (part)

GWYNEDD
AREAS OF OUTSTANDING NATURAL BEAUTY
Anglesey Lleyn

HISTORIC HOUSES AND CASTLES
Bishop Morgan's Cottage, *Ty Mawr* (National Trust)
Birthplace of Bishop William Morgan (c. 1541–1604). First translator of Bible into Welsh.

Bodysgallen Hall, *Llandudno* (Mr and Mrs T. Andersen)
Elizabethan house incorporating medieval tower. Open as private
hotel and restaurant.

Bryn Bras Castle, *Llanrug* (Mrs M. Gray-Parry and R. D. Gray-
Williams, Esq)
Lawns, woodland walks, stream, waterfalls and pools, mountain
walk. Castle built in 1830s around earlier structure built before 1750.

Gwydir Castle, Nr *Llanrwst* (Richard Clegg, Esq)
Historic royal residence, magnificently furnished Tudor period,
beautiful grounds. Peacocks and many tropical birds.

Penrhyn Castle, *Bangor* (National Trust)
19th-century castle is unique and outstanding example of neo-
Norman architecture. Garden and grounds have exotic and rare
trees and shrubs. Industrial railway museum; exhibition of dolls,
and natural history display. Extensive grounds; Victorian formal
garden.

Plas Newydd, *Isle of Anglesey* (National Trust)
18th-century house by James Wyatt. Rex Whistler's largest wall
painting. Fine spring garden. Military museum.

Plas-yn-Rhiw Estate, *Plas-yn-Rhiw* (National Trust)
Small manor house, part medieval with Tudor and Georgian
additions; ornamental gardens. Open permanently: Porth Ysgo,
Rhiw, sheltered cove: Mynydd-y-graig, Rhiw, rising 800 ft from the
sea with hill fort; Cilan, a renowned view point; the Porth Orion
cliffs at Aberdavon; Foel Fawr Mynytho, old windmill on hill.

CATHEDRALS AND CHURCHES

Capel Newydd
Oldest surviving non-conformist chapel in North Wales (licensed
October 1769), carefully restored in 1956–8. Barn-like structure,
original earth floor.

Gwydir Uchaf
Small private chapel built by Sir Richard Wynn in 1673. Painted
ceiling; excellent example of vernacular style.

Llandegai (St Pegai)
Small medieval parish church.

Llandwrog (St Twrog)
Mid-19th century, with good 19th-century monuments.

Llanegryn (St Mary and St Egryn)
Splendid rood screen and gallery. Norman font.

Llanengan (St Engan)
Large church en route to Bardsey Island for pilgrims. Much dates
from late Middle Ages. 3 aisles; fine tower (1534); original roof with
rood screen and loft; medieval stalls and 17th-century communion
rails.

GARDENS
Bodnant Garden, *Tal-y-Cafa* (National Trust)
Laid out in 1875 by Henry Pochin.
Gilfach, *Roewen* (Miss I. Gee)
Small garden specializing in shrubs.
Portmeirion, Gwyllt Gardens, *Cardigan Bay* (Sir Clough Williams-Ellis)
Wild gardens and woodlands, famous for rhododendrons, azaleas and sub-tropical flora.
Ty'n-y-Coed, *Argoth* (Dowager Viscountess Chetwynd)
Woodland grounds. Waterfall. Shrubs.

HISTORIC MONUMENTS
Beaumaris Castle, *Beaumaris*
14th–18th-century moated castle.
Bryn Celli Dou, Nr *Llanedwen*
Prehistoric circular cairn covering passage with polygonal chamber.
Burial Chamber, *Capel Garmon*
Prehistoric long barrow.
Caer Gybi, *Holyhead*
Small Roman fort.
Capel Garmon, *Llanrwst*
Long barrow with three chambers.
Capel Lligwy, Nr *Penmon*
Shell of 12th-century chapel.
Castell-y-Bere, Nr *Tal-y-Llyn*
Slight remains of 13th-century castle.
Conway Castle, *Conway*
Triangular 13th-century fortress built by Edward I and extensive town walls.
Criccieth Castle, *Criccieth*
Remains of 13th-century keep.
Cymmer Abbey, Nr *Dolgellau*
Remains of church of small early 13th-century Cistercian monastery.
Din Lligwy Ancient Village, Nr *Marianglas*
Remains of 4th-century village.
Dolbadarn Castle, *Llanberis*
Native Welsh stronghold with 13th-century round tower.
Dolwyddelan Castle, *Dolwyddelan*
12th-century keep with 13th-century curtain walls.
Dyffryn Long Barrow, *Dyffryn*
Badly ruined long barrow with 2 chambers.
Harlech Castle, *Harlech*
13th-century fortress built by Edward I.
Penarth Fawr, Nr *Chwilog*
Part of early 15th-century house preserving hall, butlery and screen.

411

St Cybi's Well Chambers, *Llangybi*
Well chamber attributed to St Cybi.
St Seiriol's Sacred Well, *Penmon*
Partly 14th-century and partly 17th-century well.
Segontium Roman Fort, *Caernarfon*
Remains of Roman fort.

MUSEUMS AND GALLERIES
Bangor Art Gallery and Museum of Welsh Antiquities, *Bangor*
(University College of North Wales)
Art Gallery: monthly exhibitions of contemporary paintings and sculpture. Museum: history of North Wales. Collections of Welsh prehistoric and Roman antiquities, furniture, domestic objects, textiles and clothing.
Ffestiniog Railway Museum, Harbour Station, *Porthmadog* (Ffestiniog Railway Company)
Past history and present activity of Ffestiniog Railway.
Lloyd George Museum, *Llanystumdwy*
Relics and mementoes.
Museum of Childhood, Water Street, *Menai Bridge*
Dolls and educational toys, paintings and needlework, money boxes (savos), wind-up toys, pottery and glass depicting children and commemoratives and audio and visual pastimes.
Narrow Gauge Railway Museum, *Tywyn* (The Narrow Gauge Railway Museum Trust)
Locomotives, rolling stock, and exhibitions illustrating narrow gauge railways of British Isles.
North Wales Quarrying Museum, *Llanberis* (National Museum of Wales in conjunction with the Department of the Environment)
Machinery and equipment associated with local quarrying industry.
Plas Mawr, *Conway*
Finest example of an Elizabethan town mansion in Wales (1550–80). Headquarters of the Royal Cambrian Academy of Art. Exhibitions of art.
Rapallo House Museum and Art Gallery, Fferm Bach Craig-Y-Don, *Llandudno*
Prints, watercolour drawings, pastels and oil-paintings; porcelain, sculpture and bronzes; armour and weapons, Roman relics and Welsh kitchen. Ornamental and secluded garden.
Segontium Roman Fort Museum, *Caernarvon* (National Museum of Wales in conjunction with the Department of the Environment)
The museum is on site of fort and mostly contains material excavated there.

NATIONAL PARKS
Snowdonia

POWYS

CASTLES AND HISTORIC HOUSES

Powis Castle, *Welshpool* (National Trust)
13th–14th-century castle, reconstructed in early 17th century. Fine plasterwork, murals, furniture, paintings and tapestry. Terraced garden; herbaceous borders, rare trees and shrubs.

CATHEDRALS AND CHURCHES

Esyronen
Chapel dating from 1679. Internal arrangements mainly original. Adjacent chapel house earlier.

Llananno (St Anno)
Small church with extravagant rood screen with carved foliage decoration.

Llandegley (St Tegla)
Early Quaker meeting house dating from 1745. Simple rectangular building divided by screen into schoolroom and meeting-room. Much original seating. Thatched roof.

HISTORIC MONUMENTS

Brecon Gaer, Nr *Brecon*
Ruins of Roman fort.

Bronllys Castle, *Bronllys*
13th-century tower on Norman motte.

Dolforwyn Castle, *Dolforwyn*
Ruined 13th-century Welsh castle.

Montgomery Castle, *Montgomery*
Ruined 13th-century castle built by Henry II.

Tretower Castle and Court, *Tretower*
Remains of 13th-century Norman castle and 14th–15th-century Welsh fortified manor house.

MUSEUMS AND GALLERIES

Brecknock Museum, *Brecon* (Powys County Council)
Local and natural history of Brecknock. Archaeology, agriculture, domestic material, pottery, porcelain and lovespoons. Assize Court reconstruction, library and archive collection.

Llandrindod Museum, Temple Street, *Llandrindod Wells*
Archaeological material mainly from Castell Collen excavations (Roman). Paterson Doll Collection.

Museum of Local History and Industry, Market Hall, *Llanidloes* (Powys County Council)
Articles of local interest and industry.

Powysland Museum, *Welshpool* (Powys County Council)
Material of folk-life, archaeology and historical interest relating to the area.

Robert Owen Memorial Museum, Broad Street, *Newtown*
Books, documents, relics, etc, relating to Robert Owen.
24th Regimental Museum, *Brecon*
Museum of South Wales Borderers.

NATIONAL PARKS
Brecon Beacons (part)

SOUTH GLAMORGAN
CASTLES AND HISTORIC HOUSES
Cardiff Castle, *Cardiff* (Cardiff City Council)
Begun 1090 on site of Roman Castrum. Rich interior decorations.
Location for Cardiff Searchlight Tattoo.
Castell Coch, *Whitchurch* (Department of the Environment)
13th-century castle, restored on original lines for the Marquess of
Bute in 19th century and made habitable.
St Fagans Castle, *Cardiff* (Welsh Folk Museum)
16th-century house built within curtain wall of 13th-century castle.
Extensive folk museum.

CATHEDRALS AND CHURCHES
Llandaff Cathedral (St Peter and St Paul)
First church built in 6th century but present building founded in
12th century. Early English decorated. Building lost roofs at
Reformation and south-west tower collapsed. Much restored in
19th century, new tower and spire. Bombed during Second World
War, now repaired. Latest and most noticeable feature is the great
concrete arch in nave with figure of Christ by Epstein.

GARDENS
Dyffryn Gardens, *St Nicholas*
Rare trees and shrubs.

HISTORIC MONUMENTS
St Lythan's Burial Chamber, *St Nicholas*
Prehistoric burial chamber dating from c. 2000 BC.
Tinkinswood Burial Chamber, *St Nicholas*
Long cairn with forecourt leading to large rectangular chamber.

MUSEUMS AND GALLERIES
National Museum of Wales (Amgueddfa Genedlaethol Cymru),
Cardiff
Archaeology, art, botany, geology, industry and zoology.
Turner House, *Penarth* (National Museum of Wales)
A branch art gallery of National Museum of Wales.
Welsh Folk Museum, St Fagans Castle, *Cardiff*
Extensive folk museum in 16th-century house built within curtain
walls of 13th-century castle.

WEST GLAMORGAN
AREAS OF OUTSTANDING NATURAL BEAUTY
Gower

CATHEDRALS AND CHURCHES
Amargam (St Mary the Virgin)
Abbey Church in midst of abbey ruins.

HISTORIC MONUMENTS
Loughor Castle, *Loughor*
Slight remains of castle, originally Norman.
Neath Abbey, *Neath*
Ruins of Cistercian abbey, founded 1130.
Oystermouth Castle, *Mumbles*
Ruined gatehouse, chapel and great hall, 13th–14th-century.
Oxwich Castle, *Oxwich*
Remains of mid-16th-century building, used partly as farm.
Park le Breos Burial Chamber, Nr *Bishopston*
Remains of Neolithic burial tomb.
Penrice Castle, *Penrice*
Ruined 11th-century stronghold.
Swansea Castle, *Swansea*
Remains of 15th-century keep undergoing restoration.
Weobley Castle, *Llanrhidian*
Very complete 12th–14th-century fortified manor house.

MUSEUMS AND GALLERIES
Glynn Vivian Art Gallery and Museum, Alexandra Road, *Swansea*
(Swansea City Council)
British paintings, drawings and sculpture, old and contemporary
ceramics including Welsh pottery and porcelain; glass. Loan
exhibitions.
Industrial Museum of South Wales, Victoria Road, *Swansea*
Industrial relics and displays of local industries covering steel,
copper, aluminium, oil, light industries and transport.
**Royal Institution of South Wales and University College of Swansea
Museum,** Victoria Road, *Swansea*
Collections of antiquarian interest; archaeology; ceramics. Welsh
folk culture, ornithology, botany, zoology, geology, art, industry.
Library.
Stones Museum, *Margam*
Prehistoric carved stones and crosses.

A Select List of
Conservation and
Amenity Societies

This list does not claim to be exhaustive but merely seeks to give the more important national societies.

ADVISORY BOARD FOR REDUNDANT CHURCHES Fielden House, Little College Street, Westminster, London SW1P 3SH (01-930 1603/4)

ANCIENT MONUMENTS SOCIETY 33 Ladbroke Square, London, W11 3NB (01-221 6178)

ARBORICULTURAL ASSOCIATION 59 Blythwood Gardens, Stanstead, Essex CM24 8HH (027-971 3160)

ASSOCIATION FOR INDUSTRIAL ARCHAEOLOGY 3 The Wharfage, Iron-bridge, Telford, Salop TF8 7RE (095-245 3522)

ASSOCIATION FOR THE PROTECTION OF RURAL SCOTLAND 20 Falkland Avenue, Newton Mearns, Renfrewshire G77 5DR (041-639 2069)

BRITISH ASSOCIATION FOR THE CONTROL OF AIRCRAFT NOISE 30 Fleet Street, London EC4 (Horley 4200)

BRITISH CYCLING BUREAU Greater London House, Hampstead Road, London NW1 7QX (01-387 6868)

BRITISH ECOLOGICAL SOCIETY Hon. Council Secretary: Dr E. A. G. Duffey, Monks Wood Experimental Station, Abbots Ripton, Huntingdon PE17 2LS (Abbots Ripton 381)
Hon. Meetings Secretary: Dr J. A. Lee, Department of Botany, The University, Manchester M13 9PL (061-273.3333)

BRITISH TOURIST AUTHORITY 64 St James's Street, London SW1A 1NF (01-629 9191)

BRITISH TRUST FOR CONSERVATION VOLUNTEERS Zoological Gardens, Regent's Park, London NW1 4RY (01-722 7112)

CENTRAL COMMITTEE FOR THE ARCHITECTURAL ADVISORY PANELS
4 Hobart Place, London SW1W 0HY (01-235 4771)
CENTRAL COUNCIL FOR RIVERS PROTECTION Fishmongers' Hall,
London EC4R 9EL (01-626 3531)
CENTRAL RIGHTS OF WAY COMMITTEE Suite 4, 166 Shaftesbury
Avenue, London WC2H 8JH (01-836 7220)
CIVIC TRUST 17 Carlton House Terrace, London SW1Y 5AW
(01-930 0914)
CIVIC TRUST FOR THE NORTH EAST 34–5 Saddler Street, Durham
(0385 61182)
CIVIC TRUST FOR THE NORTH WEST 56 Oxford Street, Manchester
M1 6EU (061-236 7467)
CIVIC TRUST FOR WALES/TREFTADAETH CYMRU c/o Wales Tourist
Board, Welcome House, Llandaff, Cardiff CF5 2YZ (0222 567701)
CLEAN AIR COUNCIL Department of the Environment, Queen Anne's
Chambers, 28 Broadway SW1H 9JU (01-930 4300 Ext 396)
CLEAN AIR COUNCIL FOR SCOTLAND Scottish Development Depart-
ment, Government Buildings, Pentland House, 47 Robb Lane,
Edinburgh (031-443 8661)
COMMISSION FOR THE NEW TOWNS Glen House, Stag Place, London
SW1E 5AJ (01-834 8034)
COMMITTEE FOR ENVIRONMENTAL CONSERVATION (COENCO) 29–31
Greville, London EC1N 8AX (01-242 9647)
COMMONS, OPEN SPACES AND FOOTPATHS PRESERVATION SOCIETY
Suite 4, 166 Shaftesbury Avenue, London WC2H 8JH (01-836 7220)
CONFERENCE ON TRAINING ARCHITECTS IN CONSERVATION (COTAC)
Hon Secretary: 19 West Eaton Place, London SW1X 8LT (01-245
9888)
CONSERVATION SOCIETY 34 Bridge Street, Walton-on-Thames,
Surrey KT12 1AJ (Walton-on-Thames 41793)
COUNCIL FOR BRITISH ARCHAEOLOGY 8 St Andrew's Place, Regent's
Park, London NW1 4LB (01-486 1527)
COUNCIL FOR NATURE Zoological Gardens, Regent's Park, London
NW1 4RY (01-722 7111)
COUNCIL FOR PLACES OF WORSHIP 83 London Wall, London EC2M
5NA (01-638 0971)
COUNCIL FOR SMALL INDUSTRIES IN RURAL AREAS Advisory Services
Division, 35 Camp Road, Wimbledon Common, London SW19 4UP
(01-946 5101)
COUNCIL FOR THE PROTECTION OF RURAL ENGLAND 4 Hobart Place,
London SW1W 0HY (01-235 4771)
COUNCIL FOR THE PROTECTION OF RURAL WALES/CYMDEITHAS DOIGELU
HARDDWYCH CYMRU Meifod, Powys SY22 6DA (Meifod 383)
COUNTRY LANDOWNERS' ASSOCIATION 16 Belgrave Square, London
SW1X 8PQ (235 0511)

COUNTRYSIDE COMMISSION 1 Cambridge Gate, Regent's Park, London NW1 4JY (01-935 5533)
COUNTRYSIDE COMMISSION FOR SCOTLAND Battleby, Redgorton, Perth PH1 3EW (0738 27921)
CROFTERS COMMISSION 4–6 Castle Wynd, Inverness IV2 3EQ (0463 37231)

DUKE OF EDINBURGH'S AWARD SCHEME 2 Old Queen Street, London SW1H 9HR (01-930 7681)

ENGLISH TOURIST BOARD 4 Grosvenor Gardens, London SW1W 0DU (01-730 3400)
ENTERPRISE YOUTH 49 Melville Street, Edinburgh EH3 7HL (031-226 3192/6412)

FARM BUILDINGS ASSOCIATION Roseleigh, Deddington, Oxford OX5 4SP (Deddington 234)
FARMERS' UNION OF WALES Llys Amaeth, Queen's Square, Aberystwyth SY2 3EA (0970 2755)
FEDERATION AGAINST AIRCRAFT NUISANCE 60 Beckenham Place Park, Beckenham, Kent
FORESTRY COMMISSION 22 Savile Row, London W1X 2AY (01-734 0221)
FRIENDS OF FRIENDLESS CHURCHES 12 Edwardes Square, London W8 6HG (01-602 6267)
FRIENDS OF THE EARTH LTD 9 Poland Street, London W1V 3DG (01-437 6121)

GEORGIAN GROUP 2 Chester Street, London SW1X 7BB (01-235 3081)
GREEN BELT COUNCIL FOR GREATER LONDON 1–4 Crawford Mews, London W1H 1PT (01-262 1477)

HIGHLANDS AND ISLANDS DEVELOPMENT BOARD Bridge House, Bank Street, Inverness IV1 1QR (0463 34171)
HISTORIC BUILDINGS BUREAU Department of the Environment, 25 Savile Row, London W1X 2BT (01-734 6010)
HISTORIC BUILDINGS COUNCIL FOR ENGLAND 25 Savile Row, London W1X 2BT (01-734 6010)
HISTORIC BUILDINGS COUNCIL FOR SCOTLAND Argyle House, Lady Lawson Street, Edinburgh EH3 9SF (031-229 9191 Ext 402)
HISTORIC BUILDINGS COUNCIL FOR WALES St David's House, Wood Street, Cardiff CF1 1PQ (0222 397083)
HISTORIC CHURCHES PRESERVATION TRUST Fulham Palace, London SW6 6EA (01-736 3054)

418

INLAND WATERWAYS AMENITY ADVISORY COUNCIL 122 Cleveland Street, London W1P 5DN (01-387 7973)

INLAND WATERWAYS ASSOCIATION 114 Regent's Park Road, London NW1 8UQ (01-586 2510/2556)

INSTITUTE OF FORESTERS OF GREAT BRITAIN Newton House, Newton of Falkland, Freuchie, Fife KY7 7RZ (Falkland 291)

INSTITUTE OF LANDSCAPE ARCHITECTS 12 Carlton House Terrace, London SW1Y 5AH (01-839 4044)

INSTITUTE OF PARK AND RECREATIONAL ADMINISTRATION Lower Basildon, Reading, Berkshire RG8 9NE (Goring-on-Thames 3558)

KEEP BRITAIN TIDY GROUP First Floor, Circus House, New England Road, Brighton BN1 4GW (0273 691217)

LANDSCAPE RESEARCH GROUP Longmoor, 8 Cunningham Road, Banstead, Surrey (Burgh Heath 55932)

LIGHT RAILWAY TRANSPORT LEAGUE 64 Grove Avenue, London W7 3ES

LOCAL AUTHORITIES AIRCRAFT NOISE COUNCIL Bristol and West House, 173 Friar Street, Reading RG1 1JB (0734 55911 Ext 302)

MEN OF THE STONES The Rutlands, Tinwell, Stamford, Lincolnshire PE9 3UD (0780 3372)

MEN OF THE TREES Crawley Down, Crawley, Sussex

METROPOLITAN PUBLIC GARDENS ASSOCIATION 4 Carlos Place, London W1Y 5AE (01-493 6617)

MUSEUMS ASSOCIATION 87 Charlotte Street, London W1P 2BX (01-636 4600)

NATIONAL ASSOCIATION OF PROPERTY OWNERS 14–16 Bressenden Place, London SW1E 5DG (01-828 0852)

NATIONAL CARAVAN COUNCIL Sackville House, 40 Piccadilly, London W1V 0ND (01-734 3681)

NATIONAL COUNCIL ON ISLAND TRANSPORT Woodside House, High Road, London N22

NATIONAL FARMERS' UNION Agricultural House, Knightsbridge, London SW1X 7NJ (01-235 5077)

NATIONAL FEDERATION OF HOUSING SOCIETIES 86 Strand, London WC2R 0EG (01-836 2741)

NATIONAL FEDERATION OF WOMEN'S INSTITUTES 39 Eccleston Street, London SW1W 9NT (01-730 7212)

NATIONAL HERITAGE 202 Great Suffolk Street, London SE1 1PR (01-407 7411)

NATIONAL MONUMENTS RECORD (ENGLAND) Fortress House, 23 Savile Row, London W1X 1AB (01-734 6010)

419

NATIONAL MONUMENTS RECORD (SCOTLAND) 52–4 Melville Street, Edinburgh EH3 7HF (031-225 5994)

NATIONAL MONUMENTS RECORD (WALES) Edleston House, Queen's Road, Aberystwyth, Dyfed SY23 2HP (0970 4381/2)

NATIONAL PLAYING FIELDS ASSOCIATION 57b Catherine Place, London SW1E 6EY (01-834 9274/5 and 01-828 8151)

NATIONAL SOCIETY FOR CLEAN AIR 136 North Street, Brighton, Sussex BN1 1RG (Brighton 26313)

NATIONAL TRUST 42 Queen Anne's Gate, London SW1H 9AS (01-930 0211)

NATIONAL TRUST FOR SCOTLAND 5 Charlotte Square, Edinburgh EH2 4DU (031-226 5922)

NATIONAL WATER COUNCIL 1 Queen Anne's Gate, London SW1 (01-930 3100)

NATURAL ENVIRONMENT RESEARCH COUNCIL Alhambra House, 27–33 Charing Cross Road, London WC2H 0AX (01-930 9232)

NATURE CONSERVANCY COUNCIL 19–20 Belgrave Square, London SW1X 8PY (01-235 3241)

NEW TOWNS ASSOCIATION Glen House, Stag Place, London SW1E 5AJ (01-828 1103)

NOISE ABATEMENT SOCIETY 6–8 Old Bond Street, London W1 (01-493 5877)

NOISE ADVISORY COUNCIL Secretariat: Queen Anne's Chambers, 28 Broadway, London SW1H 9JU (01-930 4300)

PILGRIM TRUST Fielden House, Little College Street, London SW1P 3SH (01-839 4727)

RAMBLERS' ASSOCIATION 1–4 Crawford Mews, London W1H 1PT (01-262 1477)

REDUNDANT CHURCHES FUND St Andrew-by-the-Wardrobe, Queen Victoria Street, London EC4V 5DE (01-248 3420)

RESCUE: A Trust for British Archaeology 15a Ball Plain, Herts ATR TSD

ROYAL COMMISSION ON ANCIENT AND HISTORICAL MONUMENTS IN WALES Edleston House, Queen's Road, Aberystwyth, Dyfed SY23 2HP (0970 4381/2)

ROYAL COMMISSION ON ENVIRONMENTAL POLLUTION Church House, Great Smith Street, London SW1P 3BL (01-222 6991)

ROYAL COMMISSION ON HISTORICAL MONUMENTS (ENGLAND) Fortress House, 23 Savile Row, London W1X 1AB (01-734 6010)

ROYAL COMMISSION ON THE ANCIENT AND HISTORICAL MONUMENTS OF SCOTLAND 52–4 Melville Street, Edinburgh EH3 7HF (031-225 5994)

ROYAL FINE ART COMMISSION 2 Carlton Gardens, London SW1Y 5AA (01-930 3935)
ROYAL FINE ART COMMISSION FOR SCOTLAND 22 Melville Street, Edinburgh EH3 7NS (031-225 5434)
ROYAL FORESTRY SOCIETY OF ENGLAND, WALES AND NORTHERN IRELAND 102 High Street, Tring, Hertfordshire HP23 4AH (0442 82 2028)
ROYAL INSTITUTE OF BRITISH ARCHITECTS 66 Portland Place, London W1N 4AD (01-580 5533)
ROYAL SOCIETY FOR THE PROTECTION OF BIRDS The Lodge, Sandy, Bedfordshire SG19 2DL (0767 80551)
ROYAL SOCIETY OF ARTS John Adam Street, Adelphi, London WC2N 6EZ (01-839 2366)

SALTIRE SOCIETY Gladstone's Lane, 483 Lawnmarket, Edinburgh EH1 2NT (031-225 7780)
'SAVE THE VILLAGE POND' CAMPAIGN 111–13 Lambeth Road, London SE1 (01-582 0185)
SCOTTISH CIVIC TRUST 24 George Square, Glasgow G2 1EF (041-221 1466)
SCOTTISH COUNTRYSIDE ACTIVITIES COUNCIL 15 Main Street, Dundonald, Kilmarnock, Ayrshire KA2 9HF (056-385 406)
SCOTTISH GEORGIAN SOCIETY 39 Castle Street, Edinburgh EH2 3BH (031-225 8391)
SCOTTISH RIGHTS OF WAY SOCIETY 32 Rutland Square, Edinburgh EH1 2BZ
SCOTTISH TOURIST BOARD Administration Offices: 23 Ravelston Terrace, Edinburgh EH4 3EU (031-332 2433)
Information Centre: 2 Rutland Place, Edinburgh EH1 2YU (031-332 2433)
SMALL INDUSTRIES COUNCIL FOR RURAL AREAS OF SCOTLAND 27 Walker Street, Edinburgh EH3 7HZ (031-225 2846)
SOCIETY FOR ENVIRONMENTAL EDUCATION 33 Mallory Crescent, Fareham, Hants (Fareham 6469)
SOCIETY FOR THE PROMOTION OF NATURE RESERVES The Green, Nettleham, Lincoln LN2 2NR (0522 52326)
SOCIETY FOR THE PROTECTION OF ANCIENT BUILDINGS 55 Great Ormond Street, London WC1N 3JA (01-405 2646)
SOCIETY OF ARCHITECTURAL HISTORIANS OF GREAT BRITAIN 8 Belmount Avenue, Melton Park, Newcastle upon Tyne NE3 5QD (Wideopen 2524)
SOCIETY OF INDUSTRIAL ARTISTS AND DESIGNERS 12 Carlton House Terrace, London SW1Y 5AH (01-930 1911)
SOIL ASSOCIATION Walnut Tree Manor, Haughley, Stowmarket, Suffolk IP14 3RS (044-970 235)
SOLICITORS' ECOLOGY GROUP c/o The Law Society's Hall, 113 Chancery Lane, London WC2A 1PL (01-242 1222)

421

SPORTS COUNCIL 70 Brompton Road, London SW3 1EX (01-589 3411)

TOWN AND COUNTRY PLANNING ASSOCIATION 17 Carlton House Terrace, London SW1Y 5AS (01-930 8903)
TRAFFIC TRUST 5 New Bridge Street, London EC4V 6HL (01-353 3112)
TRANSPORT AND THE ENVIRONMENT GROUP Rosenmullion, Holmesdale Road, South Nutfield, Surrey (Nutfield Ridge 2351)
TREE COUNCIL Secretary: Room C10/06, 2 Marsham Street, London SW1 (01-212 3876)
TREES FOR PEOPLE 38 High Street, Watford, Herts WD1 2BS

ULSTER ARCHITECTURAL HERITAGE SOCIETY 30 College Gardens, Belfast BT9 6BT (0232 660809)
ULSTER SOCIETY FOR THE PRESERVATION OF THE COUNTRYSIDE West Winds, Carney Hill, Holywood, Co Down BT18 0JR (Holywood 2300)

THE VICTORIAN SOCIETY 1 Priory Gardens, London W4 (01-994 1019)

WATER RESEARCH CENTRE Ferry Lane, Medmenham, Marlow, Bucks SL7 2HD (049-166 282)
WORLD WILDLIFE FUND Panda House, 29 Greville Street, London EC1N 8AX (01-404 5691)

Bibliography

I hesitate to dignify this booklist with the title of 'Bibliography', as it is, of necessity, so selective. Anyone interested in the heritage will find a subscription to *Country Life* a necessity. The articles, especially by Marcus Binney, John Cornforth, are essential reading and notable at once for their content and for their authors' felicity of style. *Built Environment* is another journal which repays regular study, as does *Apollo*, *The Connoisseur*, and the *Burlington Magazine*. Of the national press, the *Guardian*, *The Times* and *Daily Telegraph*, the *Sunday Times* and the *Observer*, together with the *Evening Standard* act as splendid watchdogs on behalf of those for whom the heritage and its defence are matters of prime concern. Among the books which I have found most useful are the following:

Aldous, T., *Battle for the Environment* (Fontana, 1972)

Amery, C. and Cruickshank, D., *The Rape of Britain* (Elek, 1975)

Barker, Sir Ernest, *The Character of England* (Oxford University Press, 1947)

Barr, J., *Derelict Britain* (Penguin, 1975)

Beazley, E., *The Countryside on View* (Constable, 1971)

Binney, Marcus and Burman, Peter, *Change and Decay: The Survival of Our Churches* (Studio Vista, 1977)

——, *Who Cares – Chapels and Churches* (Country Life and B.T.A., 1977)

Booker, C. and Lycett-Green, C., *Goodbye London* (Fontana, 1973)

Braun, Hugh, *Parish Churches: Their Architectural Development in England* (Faber, 1970)

Buglar, Jeremy, *Polluting Britain* (Pelican, 1972)

Cantucazino, ed, *Architectural Conservation in Europe* (Architectural Press, 1975)

Christian, Garth, *Tomorrow's Countryside* (Murray, 1966)

——, *A Place for Animals* (Lutterworth, 1958)

Civic Trust, The, *Heritage Year Awards* (Civic Trust, 1975)

Condy, William, *Woodlands* (Collins, 1974)

Cooper, ed, *Great Private Collections* (Weidenfeld & Nicolson, 1963)

Cornforth, John, *Country Houses in Britain: Can They Survive?* (Country Life, 1974)

Cullen, G., *Concise Townscape* (Architectural Press, 1971)

Cullingworth, J. B., *Problems of an Urban Society*, Vol 3 (George Allen and Unwin, 1973)

——, *Town and Country Planning in Britain* (George Allen and Unwin, 1972)

Dutton, R., *The English Country House* (Batsford, 1935)

Edinburgh University Press, *The Conservation of Georgian Edinburgh; the Proceedings and Outcomes of a Conference* (1972)

Fedden, Robin, *The National Trust; Past and Present* (Cape, 1970)

Fergusson, Adam, *The Sack of Bath* (Compton Russell, 1973)

Gregory, R., *The Price of Amenity* (Macmillan, 1971)

Gresswell, Peter, *Environment; an Alphabetical Handbook* (Murray, 1971)

Harrod, Lady, ed, *Norfolk County Churches and the Future* (Norfolk Society, 1972)

Harvey, J., *The Conservation of Buildings* (J. Baker, 1972)

——, *The Medieval Craftsman* (Batsford, 1975)

Hayward, J. and Watson, M., *Planning, Politics, and Public Policy* (Cambridge, 1975)

HMSO, the following Countryside Commission Publications; *The Planning of the Coastline* (1970); *The Coastal Heritage* (1970); *New Agricultural Landscapes* (1974)

Four Studies in Conservation published in 1968 – *York*, *Bath*, *Chester* and *Chichester*.

The Report and Proceedings of the Select Committee on the Wealth Tax, 1975.

Hoskins, W. G., *The Making of the English Landscape*, Vol 1 (Hodder and Stoughton, 1955)

Insall, Donald, *The Care of Old Buildings Today* (Architectural Press 1972)

Kennet, Wayland, *Preservation* (Temple Smith, 1972)

MacEwan, M., *Crisis in Architecture* (RIBA, 1974)

Nicolson, Nigel, *Great Houses of Britain* (Weidenfeld & Nicolson, 1965)

Nuttgens, P., *York* (Studio Vista, 1971)

Page, Robin, *The Decline of an English Village* (Davis-Poynter, 1974),

Patmore, J. Alan, *Land and Leisure* (Pelican, 1970)

Peel, J. H. B., *An Englishman's Home* (Cassell, 1972)

Richards, Raymond, *Old Cheshire Churches* (Moreton, 1974)

Robertson, C., *Bath: An Architectural Guide* (Faber, 1975)

Smith, D. L., *Amenity and Urban Planning* (Crosby, Lockwood, Staples, 1974)

Strong, Binney and Harris, *The Destruction of the Country House* (Thames & Hudson, 1974)

Taylor, Alec Clifton, *The Pattern of English Building* (Faber, 1972)

——, *English Parish Churches as Works of Art* (Batsford, 1974)

Taylor, R., ed, *Britain's Planning Heritage* (Croom Helm, 1975)

Wallwork, K. L., *Derelict Land* (David and Charles, 1974)

West, Trudy, *The Timber Frame House in England* (David and Charles, 1971)

Williams-Ellis, C., *Britain and the Beast* (Dent, 1937)

UNESCO, *The Conservation of Cities* (Croom Helm, 1975)

Finally, no one anxious to explore our heritage should be without those indispensible annual publications *Historic Houses, Castles and Gardens* and *Museums and Galleries* (ABC Publications). They give full details of opening times of the majority of houses etc. listed in the Gazetteer. I am most grateful to their editor for permission to draw extensively on the 1977 editions.

Index

British Parliamentary Acts will be found grouped together under 'Acts of Parliament'

Aachen, 150
Aarhus, 179
Abbey Dore, 122
Abercrombie, Patrick, 32
Aberdeen, 93
Abervan, 113
Acts of Parliament:
Civic Amenities Act (1962), 23–4, 96, 102
Community Land Act (1975), 45
Country Amenities Act (1974), 18–24
Countryside Act (1968), 33
Finance Act (1975), 61, 77
Local Authorities (Historic Buildings) Act (1962), 22, 186
Local Government Act (1972), 33
London Building Act (1888), 82
amendment, 189
Town and Country Planning Act (1971–2), 18–19, 32
Adelphi Terrace, 82
Africa, 150
Airport, third London, 31
Aitkin, Alexander, 158
Aldeburgh, 198
All Saints, Martock, 125–6
All Saints, Warham, 127
America, 136, 159, 173–4, 179, 192
Amsterdam, 83, 168–70, 198

Armstrong, Lord, 142
Arnhem, 175
Arundel Castle, 76
Ashmolean Museum, 154, 194
Assisi, 166–7
Aston Eyre, Shropshire, 123, 125
Aston Hall, 63
Augsburg, 144
Auvergne, province of, 69
Avebury, Lord, 17–18
Avebury Stone Circle, 18
Aylesbury, 92

Bacon, Francis, 136
Banqueting Hall, Whitehall, 165
Barbican district, Plymouth, 96
Bateman's Mill, 195
Bath, 22, 88, 93–6
Bavaria, 172
Bay of Naples, 175
Bedfordshire, 28, 153
Belgium, 171–2, 178
Belgravia, 85
Belton House, 55, 156
Benen, 150
Bentinck, Cavendish, 17
Bergslagen, 176–7
Berkeley Square, 82
Berkhamsted, 93
Berwick-upon-Tweed, 98–100, 102
Berlin, 172

Betjeman, John, 93–4, 97, 106, 122, 126–7
Binney, Marcus, 90
Birk, Baroness, 73, 76
Birmingham, 63, 87, 155–6, 194
Bishop's Castle, 106
Blakeney, 126
Blenheim, 52
Blickling, 70
Bloomsbury, 83
Bologna, 167–8
Booker, Christopher, 84
Boston, parish church, 121–2, 126
Boughton, 69
Braemore House, 55–6
Bramham Park, 55
Branford, 132
Brecon Beacons, 32
Bremen, 172
Brewood, 117
Bridgnorth, 106, 108
Bristol, 95, 154, 194
British Library, 158
British Museum, 155, 161, 193
Brown, Capability, 56–7, 185, 189, 196
Bruges, 171
Brympton D'Evercy, 66
Buchanan, Professor, 97
    conservation study, 94
Buckingham, 93
Buckinghamshire, 69
Buildwas Abbey, 32
Burgundy, Dukes of, 150
Burghley, 56
Burton Constable, 65–6
Butler, Reg, 136

Calder, Lord Ritchie, 174
Cambridge, 101, 121, 125, 154, 194
Cambridge Circus, 84
Camoys, Lord, 70–1, 76
Campion, Edmund, 70
Canaletto, 82, 156
Cannock Chase, 35
Canterbury, 52, 140–1
    Cathedral, 119, 121, 140–6, 183
Capital Gains Tax, 43–4, 46, 49, 57, 59, 77–8, 115, 158–61, 178, 186

Cardiff, 155
Carlisle, 93
Carlton Towers, 69.
Castle Howard, 156
Cawston, 126
Central America, 179
Central Electricity Generating
    Board, 31–2
Centre Point, 84, 90
Chandos, Duke of, 125
Channon, Paul, 22–3
Charing Cross Road, 84
Charles I, 150
Charlotte Square, Edinburgh, 97
Chartres, Cathedral, 120, 140, 171
Chatsworth, 52–3, 65, 193
Cheshire, 50, 76
Chester, 22, 88
Chesterfield, Earl of, 151
Cheviots, the, 27
Chicheley, 69
Chichester, 22, 88
Chillington, 57, 60–2, 189
China, 150
Chipping Camden, 107, 161
Chipping Norton, 107
Churchill, Winston, 22
Church of the Saviour, Bolton, 92
Cirencester, 56, 96, 107
    Cathedral, 121
City of London, 86
Clare, 126
Clark, Lord Kenneth, 142
Cley-next-the-Sea, 126
Clubs, London, 90
Clun, 106
Clyro, 199
Clytha Castle, 198
Cologne, 150
Constable, John Chichester, 65, 157
Copenhagen, 89, 179
Corby New Town, 45, 54
Cornforth, John, 52, 77
    report, 78
Cornwall, 69
Cotswolds, 35
Cotton, Charles, 141
Courtauld, Samuel, 158
    Gallery, 153

Cousteau, Jacques, 174
Covent Garden, 83–4
Cripps, Sir Stafford, 22, 51, 78
Crystal Palace, 72
Cublington, 31
Curzon, Lord, 20

Dalmeny, 72
Dalton, Dr, 187–8
Dartmoor, 27, 32
Davis, Misses, 152, 158
Death duties, 66
Dedham Vale, 35
Delft, 179
Denmark, 178
Derbyshire, 56
Development Land Tax, 45
Devizes, 108
Devon, 66
Devonshire House, 82
Dobry, Sir George, 189
Documentation Centre on Dutch
   Architecture in Amsterdam, 169
Donatello, 161, 192
Dorchester, 108
Dorchester House, 82
Dorset, 56
   Downs, 41
Douglas, James, 43–4
Downland, 41
Drouais, 161
Drumlanrig, 69
Dumfriesshire, 69
Duncan-Sandys, Lord, 22–3, 26,
   88, 95–6
Durham Cathedral, 120–1, 165

Eaton Square, 85
Edinburgh, 96–100, 155
Education Heritage Year, 196
Egmere, 132
Egypt, 149
Eliot, T S, 28
Elsworth, 125
Ely Cathedral, 120
Enfield/Edmonton, 77
Englesberg, 176–7
Englishman, William the, 141
Enterprise Neptune, 36, 185
Erasmus, 141

Erdigg, 69
Erpingham, 126
Essex, 104
Estate Duty, 50
   office, 72, 159
Este, 150
European Architectural Heritage
   Year (1975), 26, 49, 69, 88,
   90–2, 95–6, 165–6, 177, 180, 196
European Economic Community,
   165
Euston Arch, 90
Euston Station, 83
Exeter Cathedral, 120
Exmoor, 32–3

Fareham, Hampshire, 103–4
Farming, 36–48
Ferens Art Gallery, 154
Fielden, Bernard, 139–40, 179–80
Fife, 110
Fishguard, 113
Fitzroy Road, 84
Fitzwilliam Museum,
   Cambridge, 154, 194
Flatford Mill, 35
Florence, 166
Fordingbridge, 55
Forth Bridge, 140
Fort William, 32
France, 67–8, 100, 150–2, 170–1,
   178–9, 188, 190
Frenzel, Dr, 144
Friarmere, Pennines, 132
Fuller, Peter, 163–4

George Square, Edinburgh, 96
Germany, Federal Republic of,
   172, 178
Gervase, Fr, 141
Ghent, 171
Gifford, Peter, 60–2
Gladstone Pottery Museum, 176
Glasgow, 87, 90, 194
Gloucester, 95, 101, 125
   Cathedral, 120
Golden Valley, Herefordshire, 122
Gonzaga, 150
Goodman, Lord, 93, 191
Goodwood House, 63–5, 156

Gore, Frederick, 136
Gospel Oak, 84
Gowers, Sir Ernest, 22
  committee, 51, 78
  report (1950), 170, 186
Graham, Ted, 77
Grand Beguinage, Louvain, 172
Grantham, 55
Grants, government, 22, 24–5, 57
Great Lakes, USA, 174
Great Snoring, 126
Great Walsingham, 126
Greece, 149–50
Gresswell, Don, 197
Grimsby, 95
Grosvenor Estates, 82, 85
Grosvenor House, 82
Grosvenor Square, 82
Green Belt, 27–8, 30

Haarlem, 168
Haddington, 111–12
Haddon, 56
Hailsham, Lord, 142
Halford, Lord, 97
Ham, 72
Hamburg, 172
Hamilton, Duchess of, 110, 112
Hampshire, 55, 103–4
Hampstead, 85
Harewood House, 157
Harlow Old Town, 104
Harrod, Lady, 127–9, 131–3
Hatch Court, 69
Haverfordwest, 113
Heidelberg, 172
Hess, Myra, 182
Hendon Church, Yorkshire, 125
Hereford Cathedral, 120
Herefordshire, 122
Hervey, Lord Francis, 17
Hever, Lord Astor of, 142
Hevingham Hall, 76, 78
Hill, Octavia, 19
Historic Monuments Law (1913)
  France, 170
Hitchens, Ivor, 136
Hodges, Desmond, 97
Holbein, 161–2

Holker, Sir John,
  Attorney-General, 17
Holkham, 56
Holland, 168–70, 177
Holt, 127
Holy Trinity, Bishop's Bridge
  Road, 83
Holy Trinity, Elsworth, 125
Holy Trinity, Hull, 121, 123
Houghton, 69
Houseman, 105
Hull, 93, 121, 123, 154
Hulse, Sir Westrow, 56
Humber River, 125
Hunter, Sir Robert, 19
Huntingdon, 41
Huntingdon, Countess, 130
Hylands House, Chelmsford, 93

Ife, 150
Income Tax, personal, 178–9
Ireland, Republic of, 163, 178
Iron Bridge, 175–6
Iron Bridge Gorge Museum, 176
Iron Bridge power station, 32
Italy, 150, 152, 166–8, 178

Jackson, Senator Henry, 174
Jamestown, 173
Japan, 150
Jenkins, Mr Hugh, 163
Johnson, Dr Samuel, 151

Lamp of Lothian, 111
Land Use Bill, USA, 174
Lane, Sir Hugh, 152, 158
Lanfranc, 140–1
Langton, Bennet, 115
Langton-by-Spilsby, 115
Lake District, 19, 32
Lavenham, 126
Lea, the, 39
Leeds, 132, 154, 194
Leeds Castle, 69
Leggatt, Mr Hugh, 157
Leicester, 194
Leningrad, 82, 173
Lennoxlove, 111, 156
Lincoln, 52, 95, 103
Lincoln Cathedral, 120–1

Lincoln College, Oxford, 132
Lincolnshire, 55, 106, 115, 121, 123, 126, 153
Linstrum, Derek, 179–80
Liverpool, 87, 153, 194
Longleat, 52, 67
Long Melford, 126
Los Angeles, 174
Lothian, 111
Lothian, Marquess of, 50
Louth, 106–7
  Church, 121, 123
Louvain, 172, 179
Lower Saxony, 172
Lubbock, Sir John, 17–20
Lubeck, 172
Ludlow, 105–6
Lutheran Church, round, Amsterdam, 170
Lyons, 171

Madrid, 179
Mahon, Denis, 152, 160
Malraux Law (1962) France, 170–1
Manchester, 87, 89–90, 108, 154–5, 194
Marais district, Paris, 171
Mantua, Dukes of, 150
Maplin, 31
March, Earl of, 63–5
Marsh, Peter, 142–7
Marston Hall, 55
Martin, Sir Leslie, 83
Medici, 150
Mediterranean, 174–5
Melbourn Hall, 56
Mentmore, 72–6, 162, 187–8
Merthyr Tydfil, 93, 113
Middleburg, 169
Milton Keynes, 31
Monmouthshire, 113
Mompesson House, 69
Monuments Act of 1961, Netherlands, 169
Moore, Henry, 136
Morris, William, 18
Much Wenlock, 106
Munich, 172

Naples, 166–7, 179

National Army Museum, 155
National Coal Board, 31, 102
National Gallery, 154–7, 159, 161, 193
National Gallery of Scotland, 155
National Museum of Wales, 155
National Portrait Gallery, 155, 157, 161, 193
National Westminster, 83
Netherlands, 168–70, 175, 178, 198
Newcastle, 87, 89–90
Newport, 113
Newport Arch, Lincoln, 103
New Scotland Yard, 198–9
Nicholson, Ben, 136
Nile Street, Birmingham, 92
Norfolk, 26, 41, 127–9
  Broads, 42, 69, 76, 118, 126
Norfolk, Duke of, 76
Norfolk House, 82
Northamptonshire, 45, 53–4, 69, 115
Northumberland, 26, 33
North Wales, 69
North Yorkshire Moors, 33
Norway, 178
Norwich, 95, 129, 131, 194
Norwich Cathedral, 120, 139
Nottinghamshire, 31
Nuremberg, 145, 172

Oakham, 107
Old White Hart, Newark, 102
Olney, 107
Osterly, 72
Oxford, 56, 89, 101, 121, 131, 154, 194

Paris, 83
Park Lane, 82
Parliament Square, 199
Pasmore, Victor, 136
Paxton, Sir Joseph, 72
Peak district, 32
Pembroke, 113
Pembrokeshire, 113
  coast, 32
Pencarrow, 69
Pennine Way, 34
Perth, Lord, 74

Peterborough Cathedral, 120
Petworth (House), 57, 185, 189
Piccadilly Circus, 84
Piper, John, 136
Pisa, 166
Plas Newydd, 69
Poland, 172–3
Poldrate Mill, 111
Poulson, Mr, 87
Primrose Hill environmental area, 84
Pulteney Bridge, 93

Queen's Hotel, Micklegate, York, 92

Radnor, 159
Radnorshire, 113
RAF Museum, 155
Rathous, Bonn, 172
Rawnsley, Canon, 19
Regensburg, 172
Regent Street, 82
Rembrandt, 161
Reynolds, 161–2
Rhône River, 175
Ripon, 107, 120
Rippon, Geoffrey, 189
Rockingham, 115
Rockingham Castle, 45, 53–6, 65
Rodgers, Sir John, 24
Rodwell, Dennis, 166
Rome, 83, 149–50, 166, 179
Rosebery, Earl of, 72–5
Rothenburg, 172
Rothschild, Baron Mayer de, 72
Rousham House, 56
Royal Academy, 155, 157, 193
Royal Hospital Conservation Area, 84
Ruskin, John, 18, 20
Russia, 173
Rye, 107

St Andrew's, 108, 115
St Benet's, Cambridge, 125
St Clement's, Sheepscar, 132
St David, 113
St Enoch's Station, Glasgow, 92
St Florence, Whitchurch, 125

St George, Isle of Portland, 132
St John's, Smith Square, 131
St Mary's, Kempley, 125
St Mary Magdalene, 127
St Paul's Cathedral, 86–7, 139
St Peter's, Wolverhampton, 121, 123
St Stephen's, Rosslyn Hill, 83
St Thomas a' Becket, 140–1
Salisbury, 96
    Cathedral, 119, 121
Salle, 126
Scorer, Dr R, 39
Segovia, 179
Sens, William of, 141, 143
Severn Gorge, 175–6
Severn River, 106
Sforza, Count, 97
Shaw, Norman, 198
Sheffield, 194
Shepherdess Walk, Hoxton, 85
Sheringham, 126
Shersby, Michael, 24
Shirley, John, 141
Shotely, Northumberland, 132
Shrewsbury, 106
Shropshire, 26, 63, 105–6, 123, 125, 153
Shugborough, 50
Siena, 167
Sites Law (1930), France, 170
Skidbrooke, Lincolnshire, 132
Smail, Jim, 100
Smedmore, 56
Smith, John, 197
Smith, Paul, 105
Smith, Mr T Dan, 87
Snettisham, 126
Snowdonia National Park, 32, 34
Soane, Sir John, 60
Solzhenitsyn, 117
Somersby, 106
Somerset, 26, 69, 125
Somerset House, 155
South America, 179
South Street, 108–9
Southwell, 107
Spear, Ruskin, 136
Staffordshire, 31, 45, 50, 57, 60, 63, 104, 117, 129, 189, 198

Stanstead, 31
Stockholm, 176, 179
Stoke-on-Trent, 176
Stonehenge, 19
Stonor Park, 70–2, 75–6, 188
Stow, 196, 198
Stow Church, 121–2
Stratfield Saye, 56
Strong, Dr Roy, 72–3, 193
Stroud, 92
Suffolk, 126, 153
Surrey Commons, 19
Sussex, 57, 63, 69
   Downs, 34–5
Sutherland, Duke of, 155
Sutton Coldfield, 93
Sweden, 176–8
Swindon, 92

Tapestry Factory, Streatham
   Street, 92
Tate Gallery, 154–7, 161, 193
Tatton Park, 50, 76
Taxes, see Income tax
   Wealth tax
Taylor, Lord, 48
Tedworth Square, 84
Telford, 106, 108
Teme River, 105
Tenby, 113
Tennyson, 106
Tewkesbury, 107
   Abbey, 18
Thames, the, 39
Thorold Family, 55
Titian, 157, 159
Topolski, Feliks, 136
Trafalgar House, 74
Truro, 93
Turner, 155
Tutankhamen, 149

Ullswater, 32
UNESCO, 179
Upton Cresset, Shropshire, 132
Urbino, 167
USA, see America
Utrecht, 168

Vale of Belvoir, 31

Value Added Tax, 60, 107, 126,
   137, 187, 191–2, 195
Velazquez, 159
Venice, 97, 166–7
Victoria and Albert Museum, 50,
   62, 72, 129–30, 132, 161, 166, 192
Victoria Street, 86

Wales, Prince of, 142, 146
Walker Art Gallery, 153
Walker, Peter, 189
Wallace Collection, 153
Walpole St Peter's, 126
Warham St Mary Magdalene, 127
Warsaw, 82, 172
Washington DC, 173
Watson, Michael, 45, 53–4, 65
Wealth Tax, 43–4, 49, 57, 59–62,
   65, 77–9, 107, 115, 136, 153,
   156–9, 161, 163, 178, 186
Wear River, 165
Wellington, 106
Wellington House, Westminster, 92
Wells Cathedral, 120
Westminster Cathedral, 86
Westminster Palace Hotel, 92
Weston Park, 63, 156
Wetherby, 55
Wheathampstead, 24
Whitehall, 165
Wigan Pier, 93
Williamsberg, 173
Wilton House, 183
Wiltshire, 69
Winchester, Chalk Downs, 41
   Cathedral, 119, 196
Woburn, 52, 65, 67, 69–70, 156
Wolverhampton, 61, 121, 153
Woodstock, 107
Worcester, 95, 101, 130
   Cathedral, 120
Wotton-under-Edge, 92
Wren, Sir Christopher, 55
Wright Report, 159

York, 22, 88–9, 131
York Glaziers Trust, 140
York Minster, 120–1, 139, 146
Yorkshire, 55, 60, 65, 69, 76, 125
   Dales, 33